The Frank Sinatra Reader

★ ★ ★ *The* ★ ★ ★
Frank Sinatra
Reader

EDITED BY

STEVEN PETKOV   LEONARD MUSTAZZA

OXFORD UNIVERSITY PRESS
New York   Oxford

Oxford University Press

Oxford   New York
Athens   Auckland   Bangkok   Bogota   Bombay
Buenos Aries   Calcutta   Cape Town   Dar es Salaam
Delhi   Florence   Hong Kong   Istanbul   Karachi
Kuala Lumpur   Madras   Madrid   Melbourne
Mexico City   Nairobi   Paris   Singapore
Taipei   Tokyo   Toronto

and associated companies in
Berlin   Ibadan

Copyright © 1995 by Oxford University Press, Inc.

First published by Oxford University Press, Inc., 1995

First issued as an Oxford University Press paperback, 1997

Oxford is a registered trademark of Oxford University Press

Library of Congress Cataloging-in-Publication Data
The Frank Sinatra reader / edited by Steven Petkov and Leonard Mustazza.
p.   cm.   Discography: p.   Filmography: p.
Includes bibliographical references and index.
ISBN 0–19–509531–6
ISBN 0–19–511389–6 (Pbk.)
1. Sinatra, Frank, 1915– . 2. Popular music—United States—History and criticism.
I. Petkov, Steven, 1940– . II. Mustazza, Leonard, 1952– .
ML420.S565F74   1995
782.42164'092–dc20   95–197

Since this page cannot accommodate all the copyright notices,
the following pages constitute an extention of the copyright page.

1 3 5 7 9 10 8 6 4 2

Printed in the United States of America
on acid-free paper

ACKNOWLEDGMENTS

Excerpt from *The Great American Popular Singers*, by Henry Pleasants. Copyright © 1974 by Henry Pleasants. Reprinted by permission of Simon and Schuster, Inc., and Collier Associates.

"Sinatrauma: The Proclamation of a New Era." From *Sinatra: Twentieth-Century Romantic*, by Arnold Shaw. Copyright © 1968 by Arnold Shaw. Reprinted by permission of the author and the author's agents, Scott Meredith Literary Agency, L.P., 845 Third Avenue, New York, New York 10022.

"The Voice and the Kids," by Bruce Bliven. From *The New Republic*, 6 November 1944, pp. 592–93.

"Phenomenon: The Fave, the Fans, and the Fiends." Reprinted by permission: © 1946, 1974 E. J. Kahn, Jr. Originally in *The New Yorker*. All rights reserved.

"The Bobby Sox Have Wilted, but the Memory Remains Fresh," by Martha Weinman Lear. From *The New York Times*, 13 October 1974, sec. 2, pp.1, 12. Copyright © Martha Weinman Lear; reprinted from *The New York Times* by permission of the author.

"I Remember Frankee," by Neil McCaffrey. From *National Review*, 26 September 1975, pp. 1060–61. Reprinted by permission.

Excerpt from *Frank Sinatra: A Celebration*, by Derek Jewell. Copyright © 1985 by Derek Jewell. Reprinted by permission of Pavilion Books.

"Back on Top." From *Time*, 10 May 1954, pp. 72–74. Copyright © 1954 Time, Inc. Reprinted by permission.

"Paramount Piper." From *The New Yorker*, 25 August 1956, pp. 23–24. Reprinted by permission: © 1956, 1984 The New Yorker Magazine, Inc. All rights reserved.

"Guide to Middle Age," by Stephen Holden. From *The Atlantic*, January 1984, pp. 84–87. Reprinted by permission of the author.

Excerpt from *Sinatra: An American Classic*, by John Rockwell. Copyright © 1984 by Rolling Stone Press. Reprinted by permission of Random House, Inc. World rights courtesy of Straight Arrow Publishers, Inc. 1984. All rights reserved. Reprinted by permission.

"Sinatra: Where the Action Is." From *Newsweek*, 6 September 1965, pp. 39–42. Copyright © 1965, Newsweek, Inc. All rights reserved. Reprinted by permission.

"Frank Sinatra Has a Cold." From *Fame and Obscurity* by Gay Talese. Copyright © 1966 by Gay Talese. Originally published in *Esquire*. Reprinted by permission of the author.

"Sinatra Power," by Roy Newquist. From *McCall's*, July 1968, pp. 79, 120–22.

"The Performance and the Pain," by Gene Lees. From *High Fidelity*, May 1967, p. 95. Reprinted with the permission of Hachette Filipacchi Magazines, Inc.

"Frank Sinatra: Confessions and Contradictions," by Gene Lees. From *High Fidelity*, March 1969, p. 120. Reprinted with the permission of Hachette Filipacchi Magazines, Inc.

"Frank Sinatra's Swan Song," by Thomas Thompson. From *Life*, 25 June 1971, pp. 70A–74. Copyright © Time Warner. Reprinted with permission.

"Sinatra: An American Classic," by Rosalind Russell. Copyright © 1973, Meredith Corporation. All rights reserved. Reprinted from *Ladies' Home Journal.*

"He's Still—Well, Sinatra," by Morgan Ames. From *High Fidelity*, February 1975, p. 114. Used with the permission of Hachette Filipacchi Magazines, Inc.

"TV: The Expert Pacing and Polish of the Sinatra Show," by John P'Connor. From *The New York Times*, 15 October 1974, p. 79. Copyright © 1974 by The New York Times Company. Reprinted by permission.

"Sinatra at the Garden Is Superb TV as Well," by John Rockwell. From *The New York Times*, 14 October 1974, p. 42. Copyright © 1974 by the New York Times Company. Reprinted by permission.

"'Trilogy'—The Voice in Command," by Leonard Feather. From *The Los Angeles Times*, 20 April 1980, Calendar Section, p. 3. Copyright © 1980, Los Angeles Times. Reprinted by permission.

"Pop's Patriarch Makes Music Along with His Heirs," by Stephen Holden. From *The New York Times*, 31 October 1993, sec. 2, p. 79. Copyright © 1993 by The New York Times Company. Reprinted by permission.

"Sinatra: The Lion in Winter," by Murray Kempton. From *New York Newsday*, 17 June 1993, pp. 7, 112. Copyright © 1993 Newsday. Reprinted by permission of the Los Angeles Times Syndicate International.

"Sinatra and Martin, Rock Stars," by Robert Palmer. From *The New York Times*, 19 May 1977, sec. 3, p. 22. Copyright © 1977 by The New York Times Company. Reprinted by permission.

"The Majestic Artistry of Frank Sinatra," by Mikal Gilmore. From *Rolling Stone*, September 18, 1980. By Straight Arrow Publishers, Inc. 1980. All rights reserved. Reprinted by permission.

"King Again." From *Goodbyes and Other Messages: A Journal of Jazz, 1981–1990* by Whitney Balliett. Copyright © 1991 by Whitney Balliett. Reprinted by permission of Oxford University Press and Harold Ober Associates Incorporated. First published in *The New Yorker*. Copyright © 1982 by Whitney Balliett.

"Concert: Frank Sinatra," by Stephen Holden. From *The New York Times*, 11 December 1983, sec. A, p. 116. Copyright © 1983 by The New York Times Company. Reprinted by permission.

"Concert: Frank Sinatra Begins Carnegie Series," by Stephen Holden. From *The New York Times*, 12 September 1987, sec. 1, p. 15. Copyright © 1987 by The New York Times Company. Reprinted by permission.

"Frank Sinatra Opens and Then Cancels," by Stephen Holden. From *The New York Times*, 17 May 1990, sec. C, p. 21. Copyright © 1990 by the New York Times Company. Reprinted by permission.

"Twilight Time," by Wayne Robins. From *New York Newsday*, 12 June 1993, sec. 2, p. 21. Copyright © 1993 Newsday. Reprinted by permission of the Los Angeles Times Syndicate International.

"Ol' Blue Eyes Still Has the Magic," by Ray Kerrison. From *New York Post*, 25 August 1993, p. 14. Copyright © 1993 *New York Post.*

"The Selling of Sinatra," by Mike Mallowe. This article originally appeared in *Philadelphia* magazine, September 1983, pp. 114–18 +. Reprinted by permission.

"Singing and Swinging by the Sea: Welcome Home, Francis Albert Sinatra," by Don Brennan. From *The News Gleaner*, 17 October, 1990, pp. 3–4. Reprinted by permission.

"Frankly Magic, but It's a Quarter to Three," by Pete Hamill. From The New York *Daily News*, 21 November 1993, pp. 3, 21. Reprinted by permission of International Creative Management, Inc. Copyright © 1993 by Pete Hamill.

"Displaying Frank Admiration: In South Philadelphia, Sinatra is Everywhere," by Laurie Hollman. From *The Philadelphia Inquirer*, 10 November 1991, sec. B, pp. 1–2. Reprinted with permission from *The Philadelphia Inquirer.*

"Please, Mister, Please; Play Fifty-Two-Oh-Nine," by Clark DeLeon. From *The Philadelphia Inquirer*, 24 October 1993, sec. B, p. 2. Reprinted with permission from *The Philadelphia Inquirer*.

"Frank: Then & Now," by Ralph J. Gleason. From *Rolling Stone*, June 6, 1974. By Straight Arrow Publishers, Inc. 1974. All rights reserved. Reprinted by permission.

"Sinatra: The Legend Lives," by Pete Hamill. From *New York* magazine, 28 April 1980, pp. 30–35. Reprinted by permission of International Creative Management, Inc. Copyright © 1980 by Pete Hamill.

"Me and My One-Nighters with Sinatra." Reprinted by permission of The Putman Publishing Group from *Me and Bogie*, by Armand Deutsch. Copyright © 1991 by Armand Deutsch. World rights courtesy of Ed Victor, Ltd.

"Sinatra: In the Wee Small Hours," by Jonathan Schwartz. From *GQ* magazine, June 1989, pp. 228–31 +. Reprinted by permission of International Creative Management, Inc. Copyright © 1989 by Jonathan Schwartz.

"A Perfect Singer Ever Since He Began the Beguine," by Harry Connick, Jr. From *The New York Times*, 9 December 1990, sec. H, p. 26. Copyright © 1990 by The New York Times Company. Reprinted by permission.

"Frank Sinatra: Pluperfect Music." From *Riding the Yellow Trolley Car* by William Kennedy. Copyright © 1990 by WJK, Inc. Used by permission of Viking Penguin, a division of Penguin Books USA, Inc.

"The Wonder of Sinatra," by Mikal Gilmore. From *Rolling Stone*, January 24, 1991. By Straight Arrow Publishers, Inc. 1991. All rights reserved. Reprinted by permission.

"*Sinatra* Portrays a Singer and a Survivor," by Jonathan Storm. From *The Philadelphia Inquirer*, 8 November 1992, sec. N, pp. 1, 10. Reprinted with permission from *The Philadelphia Inquirer*.

"Carnegie Tribute." Copyright © 1995 by Will Friedwald. Reprinted by permission.

For Janet and Kate
S.P.

For two Sinatra fans named Joe,
My father and my son
L.M.

PREFACE

Although we work at Penn State University and have known each other for over a decade now, it was not professional or collegial interests that made us friends. It was Frank Sinatra.

After learning from others of our mutual interest in the singer, we began comparing notes and experiences, often finding occasion to talk about Sinatra recordings or concert appearances or films or news items or spaghetti sauce. Above all else, though, we were interested in the music. That talk eventually led to this book. In 1990, when Sinatra turned seventy-five, Capitol and Reprise Records each issued retrospective packages of Sinatra recordings. We bought these collections and talked about them for weeks afterward until finally we hit on an idea that, in many ways, we regarded as a complement to those recordings. We reasoned that if people were interested in these musical anthologies—and from what we had heard about the sales figures, they were—why not a Sinatra reader, a collection of pieces published since the start of Sinatra's career in 1939.

The main problem with the project, we soon discovered, was deciding what to include from among the literally thousands of articles, book chapters, and books about him. After a good deal of investigation and discussion and hand-wringing over what to leave out, we chose the pieces included here. Taken together, these selections represent, we believe, some of the very best assessments of Sinatra's long and remarkable career in music, which, to the delight of millions, is still going strong as he approaches his eightieth year.

Even though it is arranged chronologically, this book is not a biography of Sinatra, nor does it offer comprehensive discussions of all the aspects of his long and distinguished career. For instance, his work in films is not extensively surveyed, although it is noted in the filmography at the end of the book, and his television work is considered only in passing. Most of all, while we try, particularly in the final section, to consider Sinatra the man—notably through the eyes of people with whom he has been associated—we are not interest in the details of his personal life, much less in the lurid accounts of his associations and behaviors that the media have enjoyed "exposing" lo these many years. Rather, we are concerned mostly with his remarkable music and the effect it has had on popular culture since the late 1930s, and that is why most of the articles in this reader are primarily focused on Sinatra's work as a musician.

There are many people to whom we owe debts of gratitude: our colleagues at Penn State University's Ogontz Campus for their advice, support, and encouragement, especially Jim Smith, Ellen Knodt, and Bill Mistichelli; the tireless, cheerful, and wonderfully competent library staff here—Nancy Evans, Marge Hindley, Carol Julg, Linda Kinter, Binh Le, and Jeanette Ullrich; Alice Parsha, our former computer-center specialist, and her successor, Jeff Payne, for patiently and eagerly helping us to understand the intricacies of various pieces of computer equipment; the support staff for their expert work and caring encouragement, particularly Margaret Bodkin, Dinah Geiger, Phyllis Martin, and Patricia Smith; Jack Royer, Karen Sandler, and Tony Fusaro for their generous financial support; Jerome Klinkowitz for his sound advice; the superb editorial staff at Oxford University Press, especially Soo Mee Kwon and Irene Pavitt; Anne Ricco and John Pizzarelli for sharing with us their experiences with and enthusiasm for Ol' Blue Eyes; Rita Taylor for her expert typing of parts of the manuscript; the many writers who have agreed to allow us to reprint their work in this volume, notably John Rockwell and Stephen Holden of the *New York Times* for responding to our inquiries and talking with us about their own work on Sinatra; and our families for their patience and unyielding confidence in us. Especially noteworthy are Zena Petkov for teaching her son about the wonders of music, Teresa Mustazza for her love and encouragement, Anna Mustazza for inspiring her husband with true love and loyalty, and Christopher Mustazza, who, beginning at the tender age of one, shared his dad's love of The Voice. In addition to these good people, our prime sources of inspiration are recorded in the dedication.

Abington, Penn.   S. P.
January 1995   L. M.

CONTENTS

BIOGRAPHICAL CHRONOLOGY

The following list includes some of the major events in Frank Sinatra's long and distinguished life. It would not be practicable to include here all of his professional accomplishments and the many formal recognitions of his work and of his humanitarian efforts through the years. Nor does this listing include the release dates of his albums and films (see Filmography and Discography at the end of the book). For a comprehensive listing of Frank Sinatra's accomplishments, the reader is referred to Nancy Sinatra's book, *Frank Sinatra: My Father* (1985; reprint, New York: Pocket Books, 1986). For extensive information on Sinatra's recording career, the reader should consult Albert I. Lonstein and Vito R. Marino, *The Revised Compleat Sinatra*, 3rd ed. (New York: Musicprint, 1981), or Ed O'Brien and Scott P. Sayers, *Sinatra: The Man and His Music: The Recording Artistry of Francis Albert Sinatra, 1939–1992* (Austin: TSD Press, 1992).

1915	December 12	Birth of Francis Albert to Martin Sinatra and Natalie Catherine "Dolly" Garavente in Hoboken, New Jersey
1935	September	With Hoboken Four, wins *Major Bowes Original Amateur Hour*
1937		Takes a job as a singing waiter at the Rustic Cabin in Englewood, New Jersey
1939	February 4	Marries Nancy Barbato at Our Lady of Sorrows Church in Jersey City, New Jersey
	June	Joins the Harry James Band, first appearing at the Hippodrome Theatre in Baltimore
	July	First recordings with the James band: "From the Bottom of My Heart" and "Melancholy Mood"
		Harry James releases Sinatra from contractual obligations so that the singer can join the Tommy Dorsey Band
1940	January	Joins the Tommy Dorsey Band, appearing first in Rockford, Illinois

	February	First recording with the Dorsey Band: "The Sky Fell Down" and "Too Romantic"
	June 8	Birth of first child, Nancy Sandra
1941		First film appearance: *Las Vegas Nights* Voted outstanding Male Vocalist by *Billboard* and *Downbeat* magazines (first of many such music publication awards)
1942	January	First solo recordings with Axel Stordahl on RCA's subsidiary label, Bluebird, including "Night and Day"
	September	Last appearance with the Dorsey Band
	December 30	First solo appearance at the Paramount Theatre as the "extra added attraction" to Benny Goodman's band
1943	February	Joins the radio program *Your Hit Parade* First solo nightclub appearances at Riobamba Club and the Waldorf's Wedgwood Room
	June	First Columbia recording session includes "Close to You," backed by a vocal chorus owing to the musicians' union recording ban
1944	January 10	Birth of second child, Franklin Wayne Emanuel
	October 12	Columbus Day riot at the Paramount Moves his family to California
1945		Signs with MGM
	December	Conducts orchestra for recording of Alec Wilder's music
1946		Wins a special Oscar for his role in the film *The House I Live In*
1948	June 20	Birth of third child, Christina
1950	May	Television debut on *The Star-Spangled Review*
	October	First television series, *The Frank Sinatra Show*
1951		Divorces Nancy Barbato
	November 7	Marries Ava Gardner in Philadelphia
1952	September	Final recording session at Columbia Records: "Why Try to Change Me Now"
1953	April	Signs with Capitol Records. First recordings: "I'm Walking Behind You" and "Lean Baby"
1954	March 25	Wins Oscar as Best Supporting Actor in *From Here to Eternity* Divorces Ava Gardner
1955	September	Plays role of Stage Manager in NBC television production of Thornton Wilder's *Our Town*, which produced hit song "Love and Marriage," the first popular song to garner an Emmy

1957	October	Second television series, *The Frank Sinatra Show*
1959		Wins Grammy awards for Album of the Year (*Come Dance with Me*) and Best Solo Vocal Performance
1960		Forms Reprise Records Produces John F. Kennedy's inaugural
1961		First album with Reprise: *Ring-a-Ding-Ding*
1963	December 8 December 12	Kidnapping of Frank Sinatra, Jr. Released on singer's birthday
1965	November November	Emmy and Peabody Award–winning special, *Sinatra: A Man and His Music* CBS News television special *Sinatra: An American Original*, hosted by Walter Cronkite Wins Grammy awards for Best Album of the Year (September of My Years) and Best Solo Vocal Performance ("It Was a Very Good Year")
1966	July 19	Marries Mia Farrow Wins Grammy awards for Album of the Year (*Sinatra: A Man and His Music*) and Record of the Year ("Strangers in the Night")
1968		Divorces Mia Farrow
1969	January 24	Death of Martin Sinatra
1971	April 15 March June 13	Wins special Oscar, the Jean Hersholt Humanitarian Award Announces his retirement from show business Final performance at Los Angeles Music Center
1973	November	Ends retirement with television show and album, *Ol' Blue Eyes Is Back* Receives Entertainer of the Century Award by the Songwriters of America
1974	May 22 October 14	Birth of first granddaughter, Angela Jennifer Lambert "The Main Event" tour (televised)
1976	March 17 July 11	Birth of second graddaughter, Amanda Katherine Lambert Marries Barbara Marx
1977	January 6	Death of Dolly Sinatra
1983		Receives Kennedy Center Honors Award for Lifetime Achievement
1985	 May 23	Produces Ronald Reagan inaugural Receives Honorary Doctor of Engineering degree from Stevens Institute of Technology, Hoboken, New Jersey

	May 23	Awarded Medal of Freedom
1988		Goes on "The Ultimate Event" world tour with Sammy Davis, Jr., and Dean Martin (later replaced by Liza Minnelli)
1990		Goes on "The Diamond Jubilee World Tour" to commemorate his seventy-fifth birthday
1992	November 8	Airing of TV biography, *Sinatra: The Music Was Just the Beginning*
1993	November 16	Receives Capitol Records' first Tower of Achievement Award
	November 17	Inaugurates the Fox Theatre at the Foxwoods Casino-Resort, Ledyard, Connecticut
1994	March 1	Receives Grammy Legend Award

The Frank Sinatra Reader

INTRODUCTION

Sinatra's Enduring Appeal: Art and Heart

LEONARD MUSTAZZA

EOPLE mill about outside the boardwalk entrance to Merv Griffins's
Resorts Hotel and Casino as they do before no other hotel in Atlantic
City. It's not that his particular gateway is especially opulent or
impressive. In fact, there's much more to gawk at up the road at Donald
Trump's Taj Mahal. Rather, what those people are doing there is paying
homage at a kind of shrine, a shrine to celebrity. Along the pavement and
on walls, numerous concrete flagstones bear the hand-prints, greetings,
and autographs of celebrities who have appeared in the hotel's Superstar
Theatre—performers like Tom Jones, Joan Rivers, Johnny Mathis, and
even Luciano Pavarotti.

The literal and symbolic centerpiece of the collection is on the wall
between the two main doors. What is most remarkable about this particular slab, even apart from its studied placement, is its conception. As in all
the others, hand-prints (curiously small ones) appear frozen in concrete,
but that is where the similarity ends. In place of an autograph, there is a
gilt-edged plaque bearing the legendary performer's name, and in place of
the funny or pithy or syrupy greetings that one finds on the others, someone (perhaps the performer himself) has drawn . . . a bow tie. A bow tie!
At first glance, one is bound to be disappointed. It's not often that you get
to see an honest-to-goodness autograph of a legend, especially one as
private as Frank Sinatra.

And yet, whoever conceived of substituting bow tie for autograph was
far wiser than one might at first imagine, for that drawing is nothing less
than an icon, a fitting symbol for a man who, after more than fifty active
years in show business, has assumed iconic proportions himself. It was in
a bow tie that he began his extraordinary career, and it soon became his
hallmark, clearly visible in almost all the photographs, drawings, and cari-
catures that appeared in popular magazines and newspapers in the early
1940s. In a 1943 *Life* article, the rising young star is quoted as saying, "I
wear bow ties, sports jackets and sweaters, and kids like 'em. . . . I'm

their type."* And "their type" he would remain for the next half-century, although the venues at which he would come to sing demanded a change from casual to formal wear, from sports jackets to tuxedos. And still, the bow tie remained—remains—his peculiar icon, the distinctive mark of the singer as live performer. "There's no Sinatra better than the Sinatra in tuxedo," reads a sentence in the liner notes to his album *The Main Event*. It's true, and that sentiment is recorded in concrete in Atlantic City.

By the same token, however, sentiments and icons do not by themselves sell concert tickets, particularly when those tickets can cost $200 for fair-to-middlin' seats, particularly when it is never altogether clear whether the unpredicatable singer will be in good voice or muff the words to your favorite song or even show up on a given night; and particularly when the singer is fast approaching his eighth decade on earth, a time when most opera singers have long since sung their last notes. Nevertheless, he continues to play to full houses all over the world, often performing in cavernous sports arenas to accommodate the huge crowds he draws. A good question is, why? Why does he still draw the kinds of crowds that seem to be reserved these days only for rock-and-roll royalty, the Paul McCartneys and Billy Joels? (Incidentally, Billy Joel has correctly called Sinatra a singer whom many musicians respect and *"the* pop star," even before the rock revolution. Sinatra's image has always been an important part of the singer's appeal, although it's not what impressed Joel most: "The voice is what got to me."†)

There are a couple of easy answers to the question of Sinatra's long-term popularity, neither of them quite adequate, but both incontestably true. The first one says that Sinatra *is* show-business royalty—"a full-blown American legend," in Pete Hamill's words.‡ In this age of mass media, legendary status is conferred as much by publicity as by accomplishment, and Sinatra's near-mythic status is indeed a product of both his prodigious talent and the press he has received, favorable as well as critical. Perhaps more than any other celebrity in the twentieth century, Sinatra has been and remains newsworthy, not only for his records, concerts, and movies, but for just about everything he does or says—his famed marriages and affairs, his fabulous generosity, his retirement and return, his friendships and enmities. Even things that happen *to* him seem to be newsworthy. During the first week of March 1994, for instance, Sinatra was cut off during his rambling acceptance speech as he received the Grammy Legend Award, and a few days later, he collapsed from heat exhaustion while performing in Richmond, Virginia. Each event made headline news that week, each raised, respectively, the ire and concern of

---

*George Frazier, "Frank Sinatra," *Life*, 3 May 1943, p. 59.
†Billy Joel, "Frank Sinatra," *Esquire*, June 1986, p. 300.
‡Pete Hamill, "An American Legend: Sinatra at 69," *50 Plus*, April 1985, p. 26.

his many fans, and each served to magnify his legend even more. Indeed, for a half-century, we have seen his image, heard his voice, and read about his life so often that he has become every bit a "legend."

The other reason we hear more and more these days has to do with nostalgia. Calling him a "spokesman for his generation," John Rockwell, author of *Sinatra: An American Classic,* said in a *People* magazine interview that Sinatra's style "has reflected—epitomized, really—the concerns of someone the same age as his audience. . . . He has never burned out, and the fact he has kept going is, to his audience, a reaffirmation of themselves."* In other words, what Elvis was and the remaining Beatles are to the aging baby boomers, Sinatra is to those who came of age in the 1940s.

These reasons are certainly valid enough, and yet there is more, much more, to the Sinatra *phenomenon,* a term that E. J. Kahn used to describe the singer near the beginning of his remarkable career and that rings even truer today. Equally important factors in maintaining, undiluted, his enormous stature as a performer are what I would like to call Sinatra's *art* and *heart.* His art—the unmatched phrasing and breath control; the emotional readings of American popular song; the work with the finest arrangers, conductors, and musicians in the country; the untiring musical perfectionism—are too well known and accepted by fans and musicians alike to require elaboration. Besides, there are the recordings, about 1,800 of them by one estimate, the vast majority absolute gems. But now that he records so very little, what of Sinatra the concert performer? At nearly eighty, he still packs sporting arenas, famed concert halls, and casino shows, even when he doesn't have a record to promote.

In a curious way, Sinatra's longevity and fame have inextricably wedded the recorded and live performances of his songs. He *is* the music, the embodiment of the popular American songs that he has made famous. So what if he isn't always perfect in the execution these days? You can hear the record in your head as soon as the music pipes up, and somehow the live performance, even when it is flawed, meshes with the perfect rendition you know so well. In some ways, the live concert is even better than the recording—more spontaneous, more casual, certainly more charismatic, and always thrilling to behold. When he is in top form, he has no equal; when he is in less than perfect voice, you still get your money's worth, for what he lacks in vocal control he makes up for in dramatic intensity.

Indeed, such drama is and always has been a major part of his art. "No pop singer before him sought or achieved so complete an identification, both personal and emotional, with his material," Arnold Shaw aptly notes. "Through him, involvement and intensity became the touchstone of popu-

---

*Ralph Novak, "Looking Back on 50 Years of Popular Music, a Critic Has Two Words for Sinatra: 'The Best,'" *People,* 28 January 1985, p. 82.

lar singing, as they always were of folk and blues singing."* This dramatic intensity is clearly evident in his live performances; in fact, it's even more palpable than it is on record. With the help of an awed and worshipping audience, it begins even before he opens his mouth to sing. In his article "The Selling of Sinatra," Mike Mallowe complains that there was no introduction to the singer when he saw Sinatra in Atlantic City, but rather "abruptly, with disappointingly swift dispatch and economy of movement, Frank Sinatra stands before us, rendered other-worldly by the hot lights."† On the contrary, most fans who have experienced the same thing feel an electrical jolt of excitement when Sinatra walks out unannounced, and Sinatra knows the effect it will have. Everyone expects a big intro, particularly those who know the openings of the three live albums that Sinatra has recorded: *Sinatra and Sextet: Live in Paris* (1962, released 1994), *Sinatra at the Sands* (1966), and *The Main Event* (1974). What they get, instead, is a man in a tuxedo strolling out to familiar music, but he's not just any man, and if he seems "other-worldly," it has less to do with the hot lights than with image and personal magnetism and expectation. The drama of this entrance is akin to the dramatic renderings of the songs he will sing for the next hour. In other words, part of the art of performance is predicated on the performer's awareness of his audience's expectations and his manipulation of those expectations, through either direct satisfaction or studied reversal.

Interestingly, Sinatra himself provided a view from the other end of the footlights in an interview with Larry King a few years ago. Emphasizing his sincerity by swearing on the soul of his beloved mother, he said that every single time he walks onto the stage his hands are trembling. In some sense, Mike Mallowe's refrain near the beginning of his article, "Will he love us?" is ironically echoed in this admission. The singer wonders whether the audience will love him, whether he looks all right, whether, when he opens his mouth to sing, the voice will be there, controlled, strong, and clear. That fear would be unnecessary if Sinatra were truly an arrogant man, a performer who knows that the audience is there for him, that they consider him a "legend" (a term he scoffed at in his interview with King), that it doesn't matter whether or not he is up to performing since, after all, it's his show, not theirs. But he does worry about such things, and that worry, although it is not noticeable to the audience, is translated into a quality the audience notices immediately, instinctively. That quality is called *honesty*.

In a 1963 interview in *Playboy*, Sinatra himself spoke of this quality. "Whatever else has been said about me personally is unimportant," he asserted. "When I sing, I believe, I'm honest. If you want to get an audi-

---

*Arnold Shaw, *Sinatra: Twentieth-Century Romantic* (1968; New York: Holt, Rinehart and Winston, 1968), p. 2.

†Mike Mallowe, "The Selling of Sinatra," *Philadelphia*, September 1983, p. 115.

ence with you, there's only one way. You have to reach out to them with total honesty and humility.'"* Although one would hardly call Frank Sinatra a *humble* man, that term describes his attitude toward performing as well as any other. When he does a good job onstage, he accepts the audience's applause with grace and modesty; when he fails, the disappointment is written all over his face, a tacit rejection of the applause that is proferred regardless of the quality of performance. In a recent performance at the Westbury Music Fair in Westbury, New York, Sinatra even apologized to his audience for "a throat that sounds like I ate a piece of broken glass" and admitted that this particular performance had been "tougher . . . than fighting four rounds."†

Taking credit for one's successes is easy, but what does it cost the ego—especially one not accustomed to failing or losing—to make such public admissions? Never mind that admiring audiences will applaud no matter what he does on stage. Never mind that Sinatra "owns" virtually all the songs he does in a performance, whether or not he was the first to record them. Never mind that for years he was voted the favorite singer of jazz musicians, even though he never considered himself a jazz singer. Never mind that a professional songwriter like Gene Lees has said that many Sinatra performances are "so definitive that a singer—male, anyway—has to think twice about taking any of them on."‡ Jonathan Schwartz offers similar praise. After Sinatra takes material and runs it "through the prism of his instinct," Schwartz writes, what one hears on record or on stage is "something so candid . . . that it is not really possible to consider any other performer of the music in the same thought."§ All of this is true, but never mind. When Sinatra walks out there, as he has on thousands of other nights, he feels he has to prove himself again, if only to his worst critic—himself. The audience feels this humility coming from a man who is not accustomed to being humble, this honesty from a man who can understandably rest on past glories, and they love him for it.

And that love of man and music brings us to the other quality that I think is responsible for Sinatra's enduring appeal—heart, a term that, when applied to him, means many things. On the most obvious level, it refers to sentimental human emotion, and the musical rendering of that emotion begins and ends with Sinatra. "If the song is a lament at the loss of love," he has said, "I get an ache in my gut, I feel the loss myself and I cry out the loneliness, the hurt and the pain that I feel. . . . I know what the cat who wrote the song is trying to say. I've been there—and back. I guess

---

*"Frank Sinatra" (1963), in *Playboy Interviews* (Chicago: Playboy Press, 1967), pp. 4–5.

†Wayne Robins, "Twilight Time," *New York Newsday*, 12 June 1993, sec. 2, p. 21.

‡Gene Lees, "The Sinatra Effect," in *Singers and the Song* (New York: Oxford University Press, 1987), pp. 112–13.

§Jonathan Schwartz, "Sinatra: In the Wee Small Hours," *GQ*, June 1989, p. 282.

the audience feels it along with me."* Indeed they do. Even now, at a time in his life when Sinatra can no longer count on the perfect control over his voice that he enjoyed through his fifties, he and his audience can count on his heart. In a review of a Sinatra concert in New York about a decade ago, Whitney Balliett wrote that "the early Sinatra sang with veiled emotion; the present one was clearly moved by much of what he did the other night at Carnegie Hall, and his transports were passed on to the audience."† Such "transports" are a given in any Sinatra performance, and no matter that he grows older, that he requires a TelePrompTer to remember the lyrics, that he devises ways to compensate for the loss of total vocal control—the dramatic range of the actor remains. No one is any better at wringing emotion from song—not only sadness and loneliness, but also happiness, love, joie de vivre and nostalgia—and folks keep coming back for more.

Heart also refers to Sinatra's courage. The audience's sense of this quality in the singer goes beyond his ability to evoke emotion at a concert. Rather, it is something more visceral and vicarious, having much to do with his public persona and his audience's own wishful thinking. Let's face it, one reason that Sinatra's personal life continues to make news is that there are probably far more intense Sinatra lovers and Sinatra bashers than there are neutral parties, and I think he wouldn't have it any other way. He is the kind of person who seems to believe that the measure of a person's character is sometimes best judged by the quality of his or her enemies. Those who hate him love the basher biographies and lurid press accounts; those who love him think all the better of him because of the bad press he gets. Interestingly, his fans often cite his great kindnesses to friends and strangers, as evidence of his essential goodness, but they do not necessarily dismiss as untrue the accounts of his head-on collisions with various individuals (such as gossip columnists) and institutions (such as the United States Congress). Instead, they admire him for doing things they can only daydream about in their carefully self-controlled and deco- rous Apollonian lives. To these Sinatra lovers, the man on stage also em- bodies their own Dionysian yearnings to, say, tell off the boss, give a dressing down to a rude store clerk, or take a poke at some malicious jerk who enjoys giving grief.

As many commentators have suggested, Sinatra's bad press has never been a problem for him. "If he lost his temper and let go with a fist or a million-dollar lawsuit," Arnold Shaw has said, "the admiration he drew from a timid world more than compensated for the beating he sometimes took in the public prints."‡ John Rockwell calls Sinatra "crazy like a fox. All

*"Frank Sinatra," p. 4.
†Whitney Balliett, "King Again," *New Yorker*, 4 October 1982, p. 143.
‡Shaw, *Sinatra*, p. 3.

that stuff bolsters his image as a feisty guy who won't take crap from anybody. Every time he gets into a fight and he gets his name in the papers, it just reinforces his image."* Two articles have appeared that play on this image—one in *Esquire* and the other in the *Philadelphia Inquirer*. Both half-jokingly pose the question, What would Frank do? and then proceed to set up scenarios familiar to all of us—rude salespeople or waiters who blame the customer for their own errors, people who bump into us without apologies, and the like. What the real Frank would do no one can know, but the public persona's instantaneous and viscerally satisfying response is clear to anyone who has read his press.

Most satisfied perhaps are the many Italian Americans in his audience, notably those who are close to his own age. Not only have they grown up with the first Italian-American superstar, but, more important, those who have felt the weight of prejudice owing to their names or accents or complexion feel "empowered" by one who, without shame or apology, has kept his ethnic identity. Long before people with Italian names sat on the United States Supreme Court, in various governors' mansions, at the National Institutes of Health, and along other corridors of power, there was Sinatra, and a great part of his audiences' loyalty is based on their gratitude for his helping to break down a few of the walls that separate us. The Sinatra who strolls out onto the stage carries with him the baggage of this public image, and audiences that have paid good money to watch him sing a song like "My Way" know, admire, and wish they could emulate what they imagine "his way" is.

It is probably safe to say that no other performer in American show business has had a more controversial public life than Frank Sinatra. Nor has any other performer prompted writers to use unabashedly cosmic epithets to describe him, as Tony Sciacca did in calling Sinatra "a man of Olympian proportions."† Pete Hamill, one of America's best-known syndicated columnists and novelists, is even more emphatic: "Sinatra is loved, he is hated, but it is hard to imagine America over the past five decades without Frank Sinatra as part of its basic fabric. When the long career is finally over, it's possible that he will be remembered best for his ability to endure, to survive, to triumph over time itself."‡ The articles in this book account for that ability to endure. Whether favorably disposed toward him or not, they are, collectively, an effective testament to a man whose art and heart have made him a legend.

---

*Novak, "Looking Back on 50 Years of Popular Music," pp. 81–82.
†Tony Sciacca, *Sinatra* (New York: Pinnacle, 1976), p. 245.
‡Hamill, "American Legend," p. 65.

I

Phenomenon

★ ★ ★

1 9 3 9 – 1 9 4 8

"To HELL with the calendar. The day Frank Sinatra dies the twentieth century is over."* Just what kind of phenomenon is Frank Sinatra that he can draw such extravagant praise from David Hajdu and Roy Hemming, two seasoned music critics? Their assertion is based on a view that is shared by countless Americans and most of the entertainment industry—that Sinatra is "the most enduring figure of the World War II generation."

Many Americans, particularly his contemporaries, are familiar with the basic events and personalities that make up the Sinatra story: the kid from Hoboken, New Jersey, who appeared as part of a foursome on the Major Bowes talent show; the solo appearance at the Rustic Cabin and the subsequent signing by Harry James; James graciously agreeing to release Sinatra so that he could advance to become the boy singer with the Tommy Dorsey Band; the tempestuous two-and-a-half-year tenure with the trombonist and the murky dealings that led to Sinatra's release from a lifetime percentage indenture to Dorsey; the Paramount Theater, the bobby-soxers, and Sinatra's acclaim as the Phenomenon; *Your Hit Parade* and the contract with Columbia Records; the decline due to divorce, throat problems, temperament, and *l'affaire* Gardner; artistic differences with Columbia A&R man Mitch Miller and the singer's release from Columbia; his award-winning role as Maggio in *From Here to Eternity*; his signing on with Capitol Records and the amazing discography he compiled with the company; the forays into politics, first from the left and later from the right; the alleged mob ties and the brawls (verbal and physical) with the press in several nations; the establishment of his own record company; the nicknames over the years— The Voice, The Chairman of the Board, Ol' Blue Eyes, retirement and yet another comeback; and the endurance of the performing artist well past his seventy-fifth birthday. Many of these events have been recounted by

*David Hajdu and Roy Hemming, *Discovering Great Singers of Classic Pop* (New York: Newmarket Press, 1991), p. 117.

13

Sinatra biographers, and his life was dramatized in a television miniseries. By the same token, however, most of these events are really extraneous to the most fundamental role that Sinatra has played in his seven-decade run of celebrity—his life in music.

After signing on with Harry James, Sinatra began his recording career on July 13, 1939, when Brunswick recorded the James band doing "From the Bottom of My Heart" and "Melancholy Mood." Although these records did not sell especially well, Sinatra did receive important notice when George T. Simon, in a September 1939 *Metronome* review, mentioned the "very pleasing vocals of Frank Sinatra, whose easy phrasing is especially commendable."* After a half year with James, Sinatra requested and received his release in order to join Tommy Dorsey's band. James's graciousness in this matter was never forgotten by the singer.

During his time with Dorsey (January 1940–fall 1942), Sinatra became the hottest singer in the country—second only to Bing Crosby—performing the vocals on a dozen top-ten hits. In all, he made over eighty recordings, but, of course, these were Dorsey records featuring his boy singer and not Sinatra records as such. Nevertheless, the singer's reputation kept growing, as reflected by *Downbeat* and *Billboard* voting him best male vocalist. He also recorded without Dorsey while still under contract to the bandleader. In January 1942, Sinatra recorded four songs with Axel Stordahl as arranger and conductor: "The Song Is You," "Night and Day," "The Lamplighter's Serenade," and "The Night We Called It a Day." These recordings laid the groundwork for the great Sinatra solo work that was to follow. From the beginning, his professionalism was evident. Even these four songs are not merely the work of the boy band singer trying to fly alone, but the masterful work of a singer who is about to carve his initials deep in your heart. Something else was also going on when Sinatra made these first solo records—something potently symbolic. Without knowing it, he was playing a major role in ending the Big Band Era and ushering in the age of the solo performer as popular idol—as the phenomenon.

---

*Quoted in Frank Sinatra, Foreword to George T. Simon, *The Big Bands,* 4th ed. (New York: Schirmer, 1981).

Many have attributed the Sinatra phenomenon to all kinds of deep-seated needs in his audience; others, particularly musicians, were able to see, from the beginning, the making of a musical genius. In the following excerpt from his book *The Great American Popular Singers,* Henry Pleasants, classical music critic for the *Philadelphia Evening Bulletin* (1930–1942), the *New York Times* (1945–1955), and the *International Herald Tribune* (1967–), recounts some initial observations on the young singer's confidence and charisma. He also analyzes the unique vocal style that made Sinatra such an instant success.

from The Great American Popular Singers
Henry Pleasants ★ 1974

The one man who, from the very beginning, sensed his true worth and potential was—Frank Sinatra. Harry James, back in 1939, years before anything happened, told a *Down Beat* staffer: "He considers himself the greatest vocalist in the business. Get that! No one ever heard of him. He's never had a hit record. He looks like a wet rag. But he says he's the greatest!"

E. J. Kahn, in a *New Yorker* Profile in 1946, noted:

> He regards his voice as an instrument without equal, and although he tries scrupulously to be polite about the possessors of other renowned voices, he is apt—if the name of a competitor comes up abruptly in conversation—to remark: "I can sing that son of a bitch off the stage any day in the week!"

Harry Meyerson, the RCA A&R man who supervised the two sessions in 1942 when Frank recorded "Night and Day," "The Night We Called It a Day," "The Song Is You" and "The Lamplighter's Serenade" with the Dorsey band, recalls:

> Frank was not like a band vocalist at all. He came in self-assured, slugging. He knew exactly what he wanted. Most singers tend to begin with the humble bit. At first they're licking your hand. Then, the moment they catch a big one, you can't get them on the phone. Popularity didn't really change Sinatra. On that first date he stood his ground and displayed no humility, phoney or real.

Musicians were quicker than others to sense the musical genius behind the charisma. Jo Stafford, for instance, who was with Dorsey as lead singer of the Pied Pipers (little knowing that her new colleague would shortly be the greatest pied piper of them all), remembers his first appearance with the band: "As Frank came up to the mike, I just thought, Hmmm—kinda thin. But by the end of eight bars I was thinking, this is the greatest sound I've ever heard. But he had more. Call it talent. You knew he couldn't do a number badly."

John Garvey, now on the faculty of the University of Illinois, and director of the university's famous jazz band, was playing violin with the Jan Savitt orchestra in Pittsburgh in 1943 when Sinatra did some dates with them.

> The musicians were skeptical [he recalls] until one day, at rehearsal, Sinatra and the orchestra were handed a new song. Sinatra just stood there with the lead sheet in one hand, the other hand cupping his ear, following along silently while the orchestra read through the Stordahl chart. A second time through he sang in half voice. The third time through he took over. We all knew then that we had an extraordinary intuitive musician on our hands.

What stumped the less perceptive, and encouraged them to dismiss Sinatra as a singer, was, paradoxically, just those characteristics in his singing that brought him closer to the art of the classical singer than any other popular vocalist had ever come. What unsophisticated listeners, brought up on Rudy Vallee and Bing Crosby, heard as "mooing" was, in fact, the long line, the seamless legato, of *bel canto*. Frank knew it.

> When I started singing in the mid-1930's [he wrote in an article, "Me and My Music" for *Life* in 1965] everybody was trying to copy the Crosby style—the casual kind of raspy sound in the throat. Bing was on top, and a bunch of us—Dick Todd, Bob Eberly, Perry Como and Dean Martin—were trying to break in. It occurred to me that maybe the world didn't need another Crosby. I decided to experiment a little and come up with something different. What I finally hit on was more the *bel canto* Italian school of singing, without making a point of it. That meant I had to stay in better shape because I had to sing more. It was more difficult than Crosby's style, much more difficult.

Frank was actually working closer to *bel canto* than he knew, or than has been generally acknowledged by others to this day. Consider the following:

> Let him take care that the higher the notes, the more necessary it is to touch them with softness, to avoid screaming.
>
> Let him learn the manner to glide with the vowels, and to drag the voice gently from the high to the lower notes.
>
> Let him take care that the words are uttered in such a manner that they be distinctly understood, and no one syllable lost.
>
> In repeating the air, he that does not vary it for the better is no great master.

> Whoever does not know how to steal the time in singing [tempo rubato] is destitute of the best taste and knowledge. The stealing of time in the pathetic is an honorable theft in one that sings better than others, provided he makes a restitution with ingenuity.
>
> Oh! How great a master is the heart!

If Frank Sinatra were ever to conduct master classes for aspiring vocalists, he might well address his students in just such a fashion. Not in those words, to be sure. The language is far from his. But the advice to singers, and the admonitions, recouched in his own. North Jersey American, might stand as a tidy summation of the fundamental principles, the distinguishing characteristics, and even the specific devices of his own vocal art.

It is the more remarkable, therefore, and certainly the more significant, that the counsel set forth above, so pertinent to and so admirably exampled in the art of this utterly twentieth-century and utterly American man, should have been offered by Pier Francesco Tosi, of the Philharmonic Society of Bologna, in *Observations on the Florid Song*, first published in Bologna in 1723.

Nor does Tosi's counsel cover everything in Sinatra's singing that looked back to *bel canto*. Frank was a master of *appoggiatura*, knowing not only when and how to use it, but also when not to use it. He employed the slur and *portamento* (sometimes referred to as *glissando* in critical assessments of his singing) with exemplary propriety. His melodic deviations were rarely extravagant, but they were always tasteful. And he was extraordinarily inventive in devising codas (tails) for his songs—"One for My Baby" and "How About You?" for example.

Frank was not the first popular singer to be guided unwittingly by the objectives and criteria of *bel canto* as codified by Tosi. Others before him had worked intuitively toward a kind of singing closer to the rhetorical objectives of early Italian opera, and Frank could profit by their example. His accomplishment was to unite the rhetorical with the melodic, much as Italian singers of the seventeenth century had done as they progressed from the *recitativo*, *parlando* and *ariosos* procedures of Caccini and Monteverdi to the more sustained, mellifluous manner of singing represented by the term *bel canto*.

On December 30, 1942, Sinatra was booked as an added attraction to the King of Swing, Benny Goodman, at New York's Paramount Theater. By the end of that show, the "added attraction" had become a national sensation. Indeed, the audience's hysterical response to the singer was to change the course of American popular music—and even the way that teenagers would from then on respond to their singing idols. (Elvis Presley, the Beatles, and Michael Jackson may owe Frank one in this regard.) The wild reception Sinatra received at this and subsequent performances was the subject of much speculation: Why were the young flocking to the singer's shows? What caused, in the words of Gene Lees, "this mass self-debasement of women"?* Was Sinatra a father-figure, a vulnerable son to be mothered, a sign of cultural degeneration, a substitute for the boys overseas, a passing fad, a musical genius?

The following articles present several explanations for the Sinatra phenomenon. The first is from Arnold Shaw's biography, *Sinatra: Twentieth-Century Romantic*. Shaw, who was director of the Popular Music Research Center at the University of Nevada, Las Vagas, and is the winner of three ASCAP–Deems Taylor Awards, describes the beginnings of Sinatra's solo career (1942–1944) and the ways in which the singer affected his early fans. The second piece, a commentary by Bruce Bliven, currently of the *New Yorker*, was published in the *New Republic* in 1944. Bliven attempts to account for the near-religious ecstasies The Voice inspired, concluding that this response was the product of a shallow, hero-starved society. A third view, offered by E. J. Kahn, Jr., suggests that the emotional response of Sinatra's teenage fans may simply have been "the desperate chemistry of adolescence." The piece originally appeared in the *New Yorker* in 1946 as the second in a series of articles on the Sinatra phenomenon. Kahn, who published twenty-seven books and worked as a staff writer at the *New Yorker* for fifty-seven years, subsequently published these articles, along with additional material, in his book *The Voice: The Story of an American Phenomenon*.

Sinatrauma: The Proclamation of a New Era
Arnold Shaw ★ 1965

When Bob Weitman, a weary-looking, wire-haired man, then managing director of the New York Paramount Theatre, drove out to Newark one evening in November, 1942, he little anticipated that he would bring before the entertainment world what the *New Yorker* dubbed "an American phenomenon." In making the trip to the Mosque Theatre, Weitman was merely catching another act, an act that was not entirely unknown to him since the thin, young singer had appeared with the Dorsey band at his theater. Accompanying him was Harry Romm, Sinatra's handler at GAC,

*Gene Lees, "The Sinatra Effect," in *Singers and the Song* (New York: Oxford University Press, 1987), p. 102.

who had been pressuring him for weeks to hear Sinatra, now that he was on his own.

Although Romm was waxing as enthusiastic as an agent should, the truth is that neither Romm nor GAC was too pleased with the young baritone's progress. While only two months had elapsed since his leaving Dorsey, Frank was not as easy to sell as they had hoped. After his exit from the band, he had gone to the Coast to sing "Night and Day" in a Columbia picture *Reveille with Beverly*, (It was an unbilled three-minute spot, but after his success, his name appeared on theater marquees as if he were the star.) While in Hollywood, he had made a pitch for the job of staff singer at NBC, a post then held by Johnny Johnstone. He was unsuccessful, but the gambit marked the beginning of still-warm musical friendships with Skitch Henderson, NBC's Hollywood staff pianist, and Gordon Jenkins, the station's musical director. Returning east, he appeared on a twice-weekly CBS sustainer, secured for him by Manie Sachs, A&R head at Columbia Records, and the man who had brought him to GAC executive Mike Nidorf. He was riding a new Tommy Dorsey record, "There Are Such Things," which eventually sold a million. But as with "I'll Never Smile Again," it was listed as a Dorsey hit. His most severe setback was, of course, the strike of recording musicians, initiated on August 1, which prevented him from making new disks.

When Weitman and Romm entered the Mosque Theatre, the cavernous hall was more than half empty. They sat through several acts, Romm uneasy and Weitman bored. "But then," Weitman recalls, "this skinny kid walks out on the stage. He was not much older than the kids in the seats. He looked like he still had milk on his chin. As soon as they saw him, the kids went crazy. And when he started to sing, they stood up and yelled and moaned and carried on until I thought, you should excuse the expression, his pants had fallen down."

Aware that Sinatra came from Hoboken, Weitman figured that that might explain the audience's excitement. But he was impressed, so impressed that the following day he phoned Benny Goodman, who was the star attraction of the Paramount's New Year's show. Despite Sinatra's years with Dorsey, Goodman's reaction to Weitman's mention of Sinatra was: "Who's he?"

He became an "Extra Added Attraction" on the show that opened Wednesday, December 30, 1942. Featured with the King of Swing, who received top billing, were Peggy Lee, Jess Stacy (piano), and the BG Sextet. Goodman made no attempt to build up the Extra Added Attraction. His introduction was a laconic, "And now, Frank Sinatra." But the response from the bobbysox audience was another matter. As Frank has described it: "The sound that greeted me was absolutely deafening. It was a tremendous roar. . . . I was scared stiff. . . . I couldn't move a muscle. Benny froze too. . . . He turned around, looked at the audience and asked, 'What the hell is that?' I burst out laughing and gave out with 'For Me and My Gal.'"

Almost immediately the Paramount management sensed that something unusual was happening. Business after New Year's, which generally dipped, continued on a festive holiday level. Weitman began to wonder: Was the strong box office due to BG, still the King of Swing, or to the thin singer? After Goodman was gone, Sinatra remained for four additional weeks on bills that included the lesser-known bands of Sonny Dunham and Johnny Long. Instead of diminishing, audience excitement continued to mount, and larger and more hysterical crowds of bobbysoxers flocked to the Paramount. Although actual rioting did not occur at the theater until the following year, this was the earliest, large-scale manifestation of what movie director Billy Wilder has described as something in Sinatra that is "beyond talent—it's like some sort of magnetism that goes in higher revolutions." To historians of popular music, this was, in *Life's* phrase, "the proclamation of a new era."

In effect, Sinatra's first Paramount panic marks the onset of the decline of the big bands. By the end of World War II, the swing era was no more. Popular music was then in a sing era, and dominated by the big baritones and the big ballads.

It is doubtless easier to analyze the elements of an entertainment triumph than to determine why it occurs at a given moment. Several American record companies unsuccessfully released recordings by the Beatles more than a year before their raucous acceptance in 1964. The beautiful Rodgers and Hart ballad "Bewitched, Bothered and Bewildered" did not register during the original run of *Pal Joey*, but became a smash ten years later as the result of a piano record by a minor artist. Whatever the elusive explanation, for Francis Albert Sinatra of Hoboken, the moment of impact was January of the year that saw *Oklahoma!* open for a run of 2,248 performances after a hard fight for backers.

The recent Beatlemania and, before that, the hysterical furor over Elvis Presley, have often been compared to Sinatra's reception by the bobbysoxers. And yet in retrospect, it seems easier to explain the more recent teen-age crazes than the Sinatra syndrome. Presley was a provocative performer with his choked-up voice, holy-roller eyes, knocking knees, and gyrating pelvis. The mop-haired youngsters from Britain were odd-balls from the tips of their pointed, high-heel boots to the bushy tops of their buster-browns.

By contrast young Sinatra was quite tame. The oddest parts of his getup were his oversized bow ties, and a curl straggling across or calculatingly disarranged on his forehead. He did not gesture, swing his hips, stamp his feet, or leap in the air. He just stood at a microphone, clutching it as if he were too frail to remain standing without it. But the mike mannerism, the limp curl, the caved-in cheeks, the lean, hungry look, "the frightened smile," as one reporter put it—all emphasized a *boyishness* that belied a wife and child and brought him as close as the boy next door. The scenes at the Paramount, and later at broadcasting studios, were the nearest thing to mass hypnosis the country had seen until then, with girls moaning ecstatically. shrieking uncontrollably, waving personal underthings at him, and just crying his name in sheer rapture.

During his first appearance at the Paramount, as the fever spread among the bobbysoxers, extra guards had to be retained to maintain order. Girls remained in their seats from early morning through Frank's last show at night. Some fainted from hunger, others from excitement. Fearful of losing their precious seats, many would sit through several shows without taking time out for the ladies' room. As his engagement lengthened, the windows of his dressing room had to be blacked out, since the mere sight of him from the street below resulted in traffic jams. Getting him in and out of the theater, his hotel, a restaurant, developed into an elaborate ritual in which his handlers schemed, and not always successfully, to outwit the fans. When they failed, he did not come away with all of his clothes and belongings. On one occasion, two girls caught hold of the loose ends of his bow tie and, in the pulling match for the memento, almost strangled him to death.

To theater attendants, Sinatra's impact was evident in one simple fact known to everyone associated with the Paramount, but not previously reported. As one usher put it: "That Sinatra hit those kids right in the kidneys! At the end of the day, there was more urine on the seats and carpets than in the toilets." *Time* magazine said it more delicately: "Not since the days of Rudolph Valentino has American womanhood made such unabashed public love to an entertainer."

Sinatra remained at the Paramount for eight roaring weeks, a record exceeded only by Bing Crosby when crooning first caught the public's fancy, and equaled only by Rudy Vallee at the peak of his popularity. But audience reactions, as Frank rocketed to fame, far exceeded anything Vallee or Crosby had elicited, or the world had witnessed. The King of Swing's annoyance about the notice being showered on the Extra Added Attraction was apparent long before the engagement was over. Benny Goodman's displeasure manifested itself in mid-January when the results of *Down Beat's* 1942 poll were announced. BG and his Sextet came in first in the small combo division, while Frank stood at the top of the country's male vocalists. To celebrate the occasion, Bob Weitman arranged for Madeleine Carroll to present the winning plaques on the Paramount stage. But Goodman insisted on receiving his award separately.

Before the end of the month, the top vocal plum in radio fell into Frank's lap. He was signed by George Washington Hill, ardent proponent of the hard sell on radio (LSMFT), to succeed Barry Wood on the all-important, coast-to-coast show *Your Hit Parade*. And before he made his first broadcast on February 6, 1943, he had an RKO picture contract in his pocket. In less than four months, from the position of an aspiring band vocalist, and in less than four years, from a lowly fifteen-dollar-a-week job as a roadhouse singer, he had risen to become "the biggest name of the moment in the business." This was *Down Beat*'s mid-April estimate.

There were many, however, who regarded the first of the Paramount panics skeptically. Among these was Arthur Jarwood, who was struggling to keep his Riobamba Club solvent during the wartime scarcity of customers. When the club's press agents, Gertrude Bayne and Irving Zussman, suggested that he book Sinatra, the most Jarwood would offer was $750 a week—good money compared to Rustic Cabin standards but less than Jarwood had paid Jane Froman and Benny Fields. As in the case of the Paramount, Sinatra was billed as "Extra Added Attraction"; the advertised stars of the show were Walter O'Keefe veteran comic and m.c., and comedienne Sheila Barrett.

Opening night, Frank suffered from a bad case of jitters. Show business was skeptical, and he was uncertain that he could make it with the older, moneyed crowd of the Riobamba. On his closing night four weeks later, Walter O'Keefe told a jampacked audience: "When I came into this place, I was the star and a kid named Sinatra, one of the acts. Then suddenly a streamroller came along and knocked me flat. Ladies and gentlemen, I give you the rightful star—Frank Sinatra!"

By then, the "Voice that Thrills Millions" had been raised to one thousand dollars a week and resigned for an additional three weeks. Frank's stay was extended another three weeks, making ten in all, and his pay rose to fifteen hundred dollars a week. Not only did he save a club on the verge of bankruptcy, but he demonstrated, according to *Variety*, that "what he has to offer is as stirring for Park Avenue as it is among the Tenth Avenue coin-machine set." To one of Sinatra's ringsiders, his boyish self-assurance and sensational acceptance were overwhelming rather than stirring; Dean Martin, then an aspiring baritone, left the club feeling that, perhaps, singing was not the career for him.

From the Riobamba, Sinatra went to Frank Dailey's Meadowbrook in Cedar Grove, New Jersey, where the name bands played when he was marking time at the Rustic Cabin. Then in mid-May he returned to the

Paramount, the scene of his initial triumph. By this time, a *Down Beat* reviewer suggested that "his spell is not as artless as it looks. He knows his feminine audience and fires romance—moonlight moods—at them with deadly aim." On his second Paramount appearance, Frank's weekly take rose from twenty-one hundred to thirty-one hundred dollars.

When he was booked into the Waldorf's Wedgwood Room, he felt that he had climbed to the top. On opening night, October 1, the audience was heavy not only with the Park Avenue social set but with luminaries from every phase of show business. Frank was so excited that, stepping out of his shower, he slipped, struck his head against the tub, and twisted an ankle. Despite the discomfort, he went on to face the smug, opulent audience. Some nights later, one of the patrons who became irritated with his wife's ecstatic cooing, rose in the middle of a song and exclaimed loudly: "You stink!" Frank stopped the band, walked quickly to the table and, as the startled audience strained to see the heckler, did what any outraged Hoboken kid would do—invited his commentator outside for a bit of air. The heckler stared arrogantly through inebriated eyes at Sinatra, but after a moment, plumped down in his chair. Back at the mike, Frank said with a show of self-possession that concealed his vulnerability: "Ladies and gentleman, I like to sing. I'm paid to sing. Those who don't like my voice are not compelled to come and surely are under no obligation to stay." The well-heeled audience applauded. And *Down Beat* approved in a story headlined, even though there were no fisticuffs: "Don't Say Sinatra Stinks Unless You Can Punch!"

To Earl Wilson, Frank admitted that the engagement kept him on edge. Of opening night, he said: "If I hadn't been nervous, I'd be a self satisfied guy and that would stink." Wilson felt that this was a feigned lack of self-confidence. But Sinatra's entourage, then known as the Varsity, knew that he was really bothered by Park Avenue hauteur. "No matter how important they are," Wilson commented. "Frank whittled them down to sighs." In appreciation of both the confidence and the space, the columnist soon was toting a gold watch inscribed: "Oil, youse a poil, Frankie."

But there were still doubters who needed the Paramount booking of October 1944, the following year, to be persuaded. Coming in the Columbus Day period, this appearance brought on the mightiest demonstration of female hysteria that any entertainment star had until then been accorded. When Frank arrived the first day for a 6:00 A.M. rehearsal, almost one thousand girls were on line. Police estimated that the queue had begun forming at 3:00 A.M., despite Mayor LaGuardia's 9:00 P.M. curfew of juveniles. The very first in line had been there since 4:30 P.M. of the preceding day. As Frank rehearsed sleepy-eyed in the empty theater, going over songs without singing while the Raymond Paige orchestra ran over the arrangements for tempi and dynamics, the line outside continued to grow.

By 7:00 A.M. it stretched halfway down the block to Eighth Avenue. When the thirty-six-hundred-seat theater opened its doors at 8:30 A.M., enough youngsters were admitted to fill it to capacity. The picture preceding the stage show, *Our Hearts Were Young and Gay*, was utterly ignored. The bobbysoxers chattered, joked, exchanged Sinatra stories, and intermittently set up cries of: "We want Frankie! We want Frankie!" And after he was on stage, excitement reached such proportions that he had to plead for quiet and threaten to leave if the audience did not settle down.

The following day, a school holiday, was the haymaker. News reports spoke of "The Columbus Day Riot at the Paramount." It was hardly less than that. Over ten thousand youngsters queued up in a line, six abreast, that ran west on Forty-third Street, snaked along Eighth Avenue, and east on Forty-fourth Street. An additional twenty thousand, according to police estimates, clogged Times Square, making it impassable to pedestrians and automobiles. Prowl cars were summoned by radio from outlying precincts, while almost two hundred policemen were called from guard duty at the Columbus Day parade on Fifth Avenue. According to news reports, the final police complement included: 421 police reserves, twenty radio cars, two emergency trucks, four lieutenants, six sergeants, two captains, two assistant chief inspectors, two inspectors, seventy patrolmen, fifty traffic cops, twelve mounted police, twenty policewomen, and two hundred detectives.

The additional forces, including fifty extra ushers in the theater, could not cope with the frantic crowds. The ticket booth was destroyed in the crush. Shop windows were smashed. Passersby were trampled and girls fainted. When the first show finished, only 250 came out of the thirty-six-hundred-seat house. The average youngster remained glued to her seat for two or three Sinatra appearances. A woman on line with her daughter told a reporter that the girl had threatened to kill herself unless she saw the show.

"Several outside swooned on schedule," the *Daily News* reported. "One sixteen-year-old from Lynbrook rallied sufficiently to insist upon being allowed inside to look at the Voice. Her success prompted a succession of fake faints thereafter, but none was successful."

On the third day, a small riot broke out inside the theater when a stocky eighteen-year-old youth threw an egg at Sinatra. Frank was in the final bars of "I Don't Know Why I Love You Like I Do" when he was struck. Startled, he glanced down at the light gray jacket he wore, then walked offstage. Pandemonium broke loose. Girls began screaming. Others broke into tears. Still others made a dash for the egg-thrower. Ushers and police raced down the aisles, pursued by an angry pack of girls. By the time they reached the egger, he was cowering in abject fear, the center of a wild screaming mass of bobbysoxers. As the ushers peeled off girl after girl, the orchestra struck up "The Star-Spangled Banner." It was a desperate attempt to quiet the turbulent audience, which did not simmer down until the marksman, surrounded by a dozen ushers and police, was led off to the manager's office. After questioning, the cowed egg-thrower was released without having any charge placed against him. One report had it that a newsman had paid him to do the egging. Later that day, Frank showed reporters the stain on his jacket. "I don't think it was an egg," he said, displaying a surprising degree of ruffled pride. "It was small and moist enough to have been a grape." The following day's tabloids printed pictures, taken in the wee hours of the morning, of sailors hurling overripe tomatoes at cutouts of Frank atop the Paramount marquee.

The unrestrained displays of the bobbysox brigade were not limited to New York. In Boston Frank was greeted by three thousand kids. In Chicago the windows of his train were shattered and a priest was knocked down and trampled. In Pittsburgh school authorities were so outraged by absenteeism that they threatened to expel anyone who missed school during Sinatra's engagement.

The slavish antics of his fans were beyond belief. Frank could not discard a cigarette butt without having girls make a scramble for it. A girl whom he accidentally touched in a crowd, covered the spot with a Band-Aid, which she did not remove for weeks. Girls hid in his dressing rooms, in hotel rooms, in the trunk of his car. Cleaning maids were bribed for an opportunity to lie between his bedsheets before they were changed. After the girls discovered where he lived in New Jersey, they camped outside his house day and night, making human ladders to get a glimpse of him inside. When it snowed, girls fought over his footprints, which some took home and stored in refrigerators. Older women were not immune to the orgiastic hysteria. In the Waldorf one evening, a smartly dressed woman approached him as he waited for an elevator, opened the top of her dress, and begged him to autograph her bra.

The idolatry was not limited to females. Baritone Alan Dale, who later subbed for an ailing Sinatra at the Paramount, tells of being "among the first" in line for Frank's first date at the theater. "We brought our lunch," Dale writes in his autobiography, "and stayed to see him for three shows. . . . We had our hair cut the way he wore it. . . . We waited at the stage door of the CBS studio for a glimpse as he entered or exited. . . . We idolized him. . . . We envied him. . . ." and Sammy Davis, Jr., then an aspiring flash dancer, waited eagerly outside a Hollywood broadcasting studio in a melee of five hundred swooning girls. "God, he looked like a star," Davis recalls. "He had the aura of a king as he sat signing autographs with a solid gold pen."

Before long, interviewers were asking Sinatra how he could stand his fans. To a reporter who had to fight his way to his dressing room, he replied: "Now, wouldn't it be awful for me if there weren't people around that stage door?" He added: "I can't tell you much about how I handle them. It all depends on the individual case. Some of them follow me to restaurants in taxis. I don't mind that because it doesn't go too deep.

"There's one girl, though, who's always in the audience. When I look accidentally in her direction, she lets out an awful yell. And sometimes she gets hysterical. The other morning she got that way and they told her they'd let her come up and see me. When I saw her, she was still crying. After a while she promised she'd be a good girl if I'd just give her my bow tie—you know how girls have started to wear bow ties. So I did and she promised to be quiet. The next day. I got out on the stage and there she was yelling worse than before."

Some observers tried to dismiss the unprecedented bobbysox hysteria as a hoax and fabrication. But radio audiences were responding just like theater audiences, and girls in Hollywood reacted just as hysterically as girls in New York. Reporters and critics were by turns amazed, baffled, incredulous, or just cynical about Sinatra's appeal. Writing in *Life*, George Frazier snidely referred to Frank's bulging shirt-front, characterized his dinner coat as one that "would horrify Lucius Beebe," noted that his talk was filled with "youthful awe"—Harry James was *so* sensational, Dorsey *so* terrific, etc.—and described him as a chap whose neck was scarred, eyes sunken, cheeks hollow, hair a mop, and ears too big. Frazier's verbal caricature was a reflection of a question being widely asked by querulous males: "What's he got?" *Newsweek* echoed Frazier's bewilderment: "As a visible male object of adulation, Sinatra is baffling. He is undersized and looks underfed—but the slightest suggestion of his smile brings squeals of agonized rapture from his adolescent adorers."

Paul Bowles, novelist and then a music reviewer on the New York *Herald Tribune*, admitted that he was both upset and bewildered by the reactions of Sinatra's fans. "The hysteria which accompanies Sinatra's presence in public," he wrote, "is in no way an artistic manifestation. It is a slightly disturbing spectacle to witness the almost synchronized screams that come from his audience as he closes his eyes or moves his body slightly sideways, because the spontaneous reaction corresponds to no common understanding relating to tradition or technique of performance, nor yet to the meaning of the sung text."

Variety editor Abel Green, seeking to explain "Why the Whole World's in a Sinatrance," concluded that Frankie possessed the ability to make the kids feel that he was *one of them* and that he was *genuinely* interested in their problems. (His press agents kept telling of his insatiable appetite for banana splits.) "He's made us feel like we're something," one youngster announced. Another wrote to *Down Beat:* "Frankie has that certain something that makes every girl think he's singing just for her." And she added less dispassionately that while she would forsake her beau for a jam session with Tommy Dorsey, Harry James, or Benny Goodman, she would give her right arm "for a smile from Frankie."

But many editors and writers felt that his ability to identify with the youngsters was a rather superficial explanation for the idolatry that enveloped him. Noting that the response to Sinatra was a *generation* response rather than the reaction of scattered individuals, they turned to the psychiatrists and psychoanalysis for an explanation.

"Purely mass psychology built up by his press agent," a Brooklyn psychiatrist stated. "They all *work* on each other. It's an emotional situation no different than the Holy Rollers."

"Wartime degeneracy," another analyst suggested. The absence of millions of young men from their communities deprived girls of dancing and courting partners. As a result, they made Frankie an image of their innermost desires, a person to whom they could address their pent-up drives.

Still another psychologist argued that Frankie's appeal was a product of the maternal urge "to feed the hungry." In the yearning, beseeching quality of his voice, "almost like the plaintive cry of a hungry child," the doctor found an amazing auditory equivalent of Sinatra's famished appearance. This particular analyst felt that any noticeable increase of weight could destroy Sinatra's magical appeal. There is a story that Frankie once emerged from an overseas plane, his trench coat bulging with souvenirs; George Evans, his press agent who had come to meet him, took one look and exclaimed: "My God, look at Frankie! He's put on so much weight, we're ruined!"

An English critic, Harold Hobson of the London *Sunday Times,* argued that it was not the Voice but the "Smile" that worked the magic. "The shy deprecating smile," he wrote, "with the quiver at the corner of the mouth makes the young ladies in the gallery swoon in ecstasy and the maturer patrons in the dress circle gurgle with delight."

While there was some ribbing, some needling, and some raillery in the attempts to explain the Sinatra charisma, there was also a great deal of concern. The unbuttoned display of feeling troubled the older generation. There was a sense of shocked embarrassment, as if mother or father had unintentionally come upon daughter in a moment of intimacy. The guardians of our heritage of Puritan restraint saw something unwholesome in the Sinatra hysteria.

In a long, intellectual article in the *New Republic.* Bruce Bliven argued that the bobbysox reaction, while it may have begun as a publicity stunt, was "a genuine mass phenomenon . . . a phenomenon of mass hysteria. Such hysteria, he explained, occurred only two or three times in a century. The Sinatra euphoria was comparable to the Children's Crusade in the

Middle Ages, or the dance madness that overwhelmed the young in certain medieval German Villages. He reviewed different explanations for the battling "Dionysian ceremonial," including wartime female frustration, faddism, Sinatra as a father image or success symbol, as well as "just plain sex." To Bliven, the most significant consideration was that Sinatra aligned himself, not only with the younger generation, but *against* the adult world. He was thereby rejecting the things that teen-agers allegedly hated in the crassly commercial cosmos of their elders and allowing them to express an unfulfilled hunger" for heroes and idealism.

Although there was something nonesthetic in the reactions provoked by Sinatra, it is still strange that most commentators paid so little attention to his actual singing ability. "There was this fantastic rage," a historian was to write, "for a nice, clean, skinny, practically voiceless [*sic!*] kid with jug-handle ears and golf-ball Adam's apple, who moved into a microphone and caused teenagers . . . to go into spasmodic imitations of sex convulsions. . . ." Considering the hold which "the voiceless kid" has maintained on the public's ears for more than two decades, there must have been something special about his singing and his showmanship.

"Elsa, what is there about that boy," Loretta Young once asked Miss Maxwell, "that makes you feel he is singing to you—and you, alone?" From the moment he trod upon the Paramount stage, women of all ages have had this feeling. There have been many explanations. At least one has never appeared in print before. It has to do with his eyes.

For me, their strange role and power were forcefully established at a Capitol recording session several years ago. Most singers prefer to work in an isolation booth or "gobo" (spun glass enclosure), which provide contact with the conductor and control booth, eliminate all studio distractions, and permit total concentration on the all-mighty microphone. By contrast, Sinatra demands an audience and likes to work close to the musicians. He makes a studied effort to reach both, singing not to the mike but to the people around him. Now, at this particular session, I was in the control booth. It was crowded, not only with the normal complement of technicians, but with a very large entourage. The studio itself was mobbed. A large orchestra conducted by Nelson Riddle, a bubbling bevy of school-age youngsters, and in the area in front of the control booth, a group that included daughter Nancy, her fiancé Tommy Sands, orchestra leader Dick Stabile, and actress Dorothy Provine, whom Frank had brought to the session.

Sinatra worked out in the open at the music stand, snap-brim on his head. He was about twenty feet from the double glass windows of the booth and at least fifty feet from me, with both the people in the booth and those outside between us. Yet every time he turned his head toward the booth, I had the feeling that he was addressing himself specifically to me. It was purely a matter of his eyes, which even now, after thirty tough years in the limelight, are still as piercingly a peacock blue and as clear in their outlines as if he were a young boy. If one can speak of hypnotic eyes, Sinatra has them. The "you-and-me" feeling, communicated by the eyes, is projected in their absence by a style whose keynote is intense intimacy.

Apart from a unique and identifiable sound that no one can miss recognizing as Sinatra's, his singing represents communication of a rare order. It is so potent because it has been for him a vent for his own feelings. Like the blues singers of old, he sang to give expression to deeply felt needs and experiences. And in his early days, he was emotionally close enough to his youthful yearnings for affection and affirmation that the kids sensed a kinship for their own unfulfilled longings.

Surprisingly, a facet of his early singing style that drew both humorous and scornful barbs was never properly evaluated for its contribution to the mass hysteria. I refer to the slow, the extremely slow tempo—*marche à la funebra* was one critic's derisive characterization—at which Sinatra sang romantic ballads like "Fools Rush In," "I'll Be Seeing You," "Try a Little Tenderness," "Dream," and "You'll Never Know." Listening to early recordings of those songs, one can sense the tremendous tension, the mounting emotional anticipation, the demand for release that the delayed fondling of words and notes engendered. It required only a twist of the head, a glimmer of a smile to provoke a young audience, tried beyond endurance by the suspenseful sound.

Because of early references to Sinatra as the Crooner, his initial style has generally been called crooning. This is a misnomer. Since crooning is midway between humming and projecting with full voice, it is clear that Sinatra never really was a crooner. Not too long ago, he himself characterized his early style as *bel canto*, a mode of singing he allegedly developed in opposition to Crosby's casual, crooning delivery. Historically, *bel canto* is a vocal operatic style in which the emphasis is on beauty of tone rather than emotional expressiveness, on the inventive employment of ornament, and the smooth use of sustained tone rather than a declamatory or dramatic delivery. While Frank was less of a crooner and more a sustained singer than his early appreciators realized, he never subordinated feeling to form, thought to technique, or stress to style. His singing was never merely an entertainment but an experience to which audiences were compelled to respond, not only with applause, but with their hearts. From the start of his solo career, he was an *involved* singer who forced involvement upon his listeners.

This was a quality he shared with the great Negro songstress whose style deeply dyed his own, and whose influence, transmitted through Sinatra, made intensity of feeling a touchstone of pop singing. "It is Billie

Holiday," Frank has said, "whom I first heard in 52nd Street clubs in the early thirties, who was and still remains the greatest single musical influence on me." And what was that influence? Depth of emotion was just one phase of it. There were others, like the use of contrasting textures, the feeling of intimacy, the intense personalization of lyrics—and the glow of sheer sex.

The fact is that the pop singers before Sinatra, including Crosby, were sexless. Just as songwriting was then circumscribed by the euphemisms of Victorian nature imagery—the movies panned to the sea or sky to suggest intimacy—so most singers affected poses of nonchalance, ebullience, or gaiety to suggest, but also to shield audiences from, the realities of epidermis. Without thinking about it, Billie Holiday exuded sex both as a woman and as a singer. So did Francis Albert Sinatra. More than one fan succumbed to the spell of the flesh as well as the art of the voice.

The Voice and the Kids
Bruce Bliven ★ 1944

At nine o'clock in the morning, the Paramount Theatre is full and already the line outside, waiting to buy tickets, goes around the corner. But today is nothing; you should have been here Thursday, which happened to be a legal holiday in New York. On Thursday there were 10,000 trying to get in, and 150 extra policemen totally failed to keep order. Shop windows were smashed; people were hurt and carried off in ambulances. Because the average fan stayed for two or three performances, the trouble outside went on all day. Out of 3,500 who were in their seats when the first show began, only 250 came out when the second show started. Some people were in line before midnight of the previous day. One man said he had tried to buy an early place in line for his daughter for $8, but had been refused. A woman, in line with her daughter long before the doors opened, said the girl threatened to kill herself if kept home.

This, as you have guessed, is the magic spell of The Voice, a phenomenon of mass hysteria that is seen only two or three times in a century. You need to go back not merely to Lindbergh and Valentino and Admiral Dewey, to understand it, but to the dance madness that overtook some medieval German villages, or to the children's crusade. The Voice wields a not inconsiderable power. He can break up a demonstration for someone, as important as Governor Dewey, merely by appearing on the sidelines. He needs a hollow square of policemen to protect him anywhere he goes; his telephone calls swamp any switchboard; his mail runs into the thousands per day. So does his income; he averages more than $20,000 a week the year around, and in some busy weeks earns as much as $30,000, which is about $4,300 per day. His admirers send him all sorts of presents, and when he advises them to put their money into war bonds, they try to give the war bonds to him, or one of his children. One girl wore a bandage for three weeks on her arm at the spot where "Frankie touched me." Another went to fifty-six consecutive performances in a theatre where he was playing (this means five or six performances a day). Merely to see him cross the sidewalk from an automobile to a broadcasting station, young idolators lined up five hours in advance.

Two girls picked up by police in Pittsburgh had spent their whole savings and run away from their home in Brooklyn because The Voice was appearing in the Pennsylvania city. A soldier who happens to have the same name gets burning love letters by the dozen. When he appeared in public (he resembles The Voice) he was mobbed by feminine admirers who tore off most of this clothes. The Voice's home is invaded nearly every day by young girls who make a pretext of asking for a drink of water, or to use the bathroom. Trained nurses have to be on the premises in any theatre where he appears, to soothe the hysterical. (Some of those who faint have gone ten or twelve hours without food, to see successive performances.) It is something to think about.

At 9:10 A.M., inside the theatre, the over-ornate red and gold decorations, somebody's idea of the last word in luxury, are almost submerged under a sea of youthful femininity. The house is already packed, but the watchful ushers will not let them stand in the aisles, and therefore the many hundreds who are waiting are shepherded behind glass in the lobby. Four-fifths of those present are of the feminine sex and of these, at least four-fifths belong to the bobby-socks brigade, age perhaps twelve to sixteen. Hundreds of them are wearing the polka-dotted blue bow tie popularized by their idol. Although his appearance is still an hour away, they are in a mood to squeal, and squeal they do. The movie which grinds its way across the screen is a routine affair, but the bobby-socksers take it big, with wild bursts of applause in unexpected places.

The electric contagion of excitement steadily mounts as the film ends and the stage show begins. Everything gets twice the reception it deserves. Then, at a familiar bar of music, the crowd goes completely crazy. It is the entrance cue for The Voice, which was instantly recognized by the devout. The shrieks rise to a crashing crescendo such as one hears but rarely in a lifetime. Through the portieres at the side of the stage comes a pleasant-appearing young man in an expensive brown tweed coat and brown doe-skin trousers. With gawky long steps he moves awkwardly to the center of the stage, while the shrieking continues. The bobby-socksers are on their feet now, applauding frantically. A few of them slump into their seats, either fainting or convincing themselves that they are doing so. Some of them rush down the aisle to get as close as possible to their hero. (When he leaves the theatre, a double line of police has to fight back the adorers who yearn to touch him, as, in the Middle Ages, victims of disease sought the healing touch of the king.)

Standing at the microphone, he looks, under the spotlight, like a young Walter Huston. He has a head of tousled black curls and holds it awkwardly to one side as he gestures clumsily and bashfully with his long arms, trying to keep the crowd quiet enough for him to sing "Embraceable You." Contrary to expectation, he appears in excellent health, with a face that seems tanned, not made up. A girl sitting by me says, "Look, he has broad shoulders," and her boy friend replies scornfully, "Aw, nuts! Pads!" Obviously he is right.

Now, having with difficulty created a partial state of order, The Voice performs. Diffidently, almost bashfully, yet with sure showmanship and magnificent timing, he sings five or six songs, with intervals of patter between them. His voice, to this auditor, seems a pleasant, untrained light baritone—a weak one, were it not boosted in power by the microphone. His talk is inconsequential chatter, which I assume was written for him by someone in the entourage that naturally goes with an income of $1,100,000 a year. He complains a little about highbrow psychologists who write articles about him; carries on a routine artificial "feud" with Bing Crosby (who of course is not present). One or two of his songs were evidently chosen to elicit a frantic response from the audience. When he sings sadly "I'll walk alone," the child sitting next to me shouts in seemingly genuine anguish, "I'll walk wid ya, Frankie," and so, in various words, do several hundred others. When the song says that nobody loves him, a faithful protagonist on my right groans, "Are you kiddin', Frankie?" Then the whole audience falls into an antiphony with him, Frankie shouting "No!" and the audience "Yes!" five or six times, the point in debate being whether he is popular or not.

Presently he is singing a song—"Everything Happens to Me"—which seems to be a running diary of his recent life. He brings in the fact, skillfully and without offense, that he recently had tea with the president. Frankie is a Roosevelt fan, he and his wife have given $7,500 to the NCPAC and, if his adorers were old enough to vote, he could win the election single-handed. He breaks all rules for romantic heroes by talking about his wife and two children and mentions the fact that another child is on the way. Far from being repelled by this evidence of domestic bliss, his audience seems enraptured. They shriek, even during his songs, until he is forced to take steps. "Shut UP!" he cries, with mock ferocity. The kids see through him; they understand perfectly that he doesn't mean it.

Another song, and he has vanished, amid a continuing hailstorm of those astonishing high-pitched shrieks. Instantly the orchestra swings into

"The Star-Spangled Banner," and twin spotlights center on American flags whipping in the breeze created by electric fans—obviously the only way to avoid a riot.

What is the cause of it all? It is reasonable to suppose that it began as a publicity stunt, with the first swooners and screamers hired by a press agent. (The young man who threw eggs at Frankie the other day admitted he had been paid $10 to do so, by "a reporter.") But today, it is a genuine mass phenomenon, far beyond the power of any press agent to control. Thousands of girls profess to be spellbound just from hearing The Voice over the radio, never having seen him in the flesh. Undoubtedly, just plain sex has a great deal to do with the whole matter. If the bobby-socksers were a little older, much of it might be explained, at least partly, in terms of wartime frustration, with 11 million young men away in uniform. Doubtless the phenomenon has several sources. Partly, it has become a fad now, with girls of a certain age, to join in the hysterics. You go expecting to be overpowered, and if you weren't, you'd feel you hadn't had your money's worth. But it runs deeper than that. Although I am told that devotion to The Voice is found in all classes of society, nearly all of the bobby-socksers whom I saw at the Paramount gave every appearance of being children of the poor. Oddly enough, this fragile young singer has, among other qualities, a sense of strength and power: there is a solidity and sureness about him that are out of all proportion to his physical frailness. I would guess that these children find in him, for all his youthfulness, something of a father image. And beyond that, he represents a dream of what they themselves might conceivably do or become. He earns a million a year, and yet he talks their language; he is just a kid from Hoboken who got the breaks. In everything he says and does, he aligns himself with the youngsters and against the adult world. It is always "we" and never "you."

But my strongest impression was, not that Frankie means so much to the bobby-socksers, as that everything else means so little. Our civilization no doubt seems wonderful to the children of half-starved, dictator-ridden Europe; our multiplicity of gadgets is the envy of the world. And yet, if I read the bobby-socksers aright, we have left them with a hunger still unfulfilled: a hunger for heroes, for ideal things that do not appear, or at least not in adequate quantities, in a civilization that is so busy making things and selling things as ours. Whatever else you may say of the adoration of The Voice, it is a strictly non-commercial enterprise, a selfless idolatry which pays its 75 cents at the box-office and asks in return only the privilege of being allowed to ruin its vocal cords. Perhaps Frankie is more important as a symbol than most of us are aware.

The Fave, the Fans, and the Fiends
E. J. Kahn, Jr. ★ 1946

Frank Sinatra is a professional singer with an extremely pleasant voice, but often, when he uses it, his most ardent admirers, or fans, are so overcome by the sight of him that they drown out the sound of him by emitting ecstatic little yelps of their own. According to George Evans, his press agent, who likes to say that his association with Sinatra has brought him, Evans, more publicity than most other singers' press agents get for their clients, there are 40 million Sinatra fans in the United States. Evans estimates that there are two thousand fan clubs, with an average membership of two hundred, and he has further estimated (by means of logarithms and a press agent's intuition) that only one per cent of the Sinatra fans have yet bothered to join a club. These calculations may be imprecise, but there are unquestionably millions of Sinatra fans, mostly young women in their middle teens. The adulation they have been pouring, like syrup, on their idol since early in 1943 is not without precedent. When Franz Liszt played the piano, every now and then some woman listening to him would keel over. Women kissed the seams of Johann Strauss's coat and wept with emotion at the sight of Paderewski's red hair. In 1843, when the Norwegian violinist Ole Bull, who had long, golden hair and a striking build, gave some recitals over here, his feminine followers unhorsed his carriage and pulled it around town themselves. Then there was Rudolph Valentino's funeral. The astonishing affection lavished by some women on men to whom they have never even been introduced is, as a rule, not entirely platonic. Few of Sinatra's fans, however, seem to have designs on him. Of the five thousand letters they send him every week, not many are as amorous as one from a young lady who wrote, on stationery smeared with lipstick, "I love you so bad it hurts. Do you think I should see a doctor?" Most of the fans were honestly distressed by his recent separation from his wife, and were jubilant at the news that the Sinatras had patched things up.

The fans have always considered it one of Sinatra's lovable assets that he married his childhood sweetheart, Nancy Barbato. They have been married seven years, and they have a daughter of six, Nancy-Sandra, and a son of two, Franklin Wayne. Mrs. Sinatra and the children have, among them, received as many as two thousand fan letters in a week, and some Sinatra admirers have professed to be nearly as fond of them as they are of the man of the house. A few people have found this attitude incredible. Some months ago, the San Francisco *Chronicle* published an article beginning, "Believe it or not, there is a Mrs. Sinatra. On the whole, the Ameri-

can public is unaware of it and swooning bobby-soxers care not at all."
(Sinatra's female fans are generally described by a reference to their socks,
or sox, even though many of them actually wear nylons or leg paint.) The
girls seem to regard Mrs. Sinatra as a cross between a godmother and an
older sister. Whenever one of the Sinatra children has a birthday, enough
presents pour in to equip an orphanage. Last year, some friends of Sinatra
composed a song about his daugher, entitled "Nancy with the Laughing
Face." Sinatra had it published by the music company of which he is part
owner and recorded it himself. Though practically no other ranking vocalist plugged the song, over a million copies of the record have been sold—a
tribute less to its musical merits than to the esteem in which all close
relatives of Sinatra are held. "I think you are the most average family in the
United States, and therein lies your greatness," one girl has written to him.
Most of his fans are plain, lonely girls from lower-middle-class homes.
They are dazzled by the life Sinatra leads and wish that they could share in
it. They insist that they love him, but they do not use the verb in its
ordinary sense. As they apply it to him, it is synonymous with "worship"
or "idealize." They rarely think of him as a potential mate, and even when
they do, they are generous about it. "I wish Frank were twins," a fan once
wrote in a fan-club bulletin, "one for me and one for big Nancy."

Because it was in 1943 that Sinatra caught on, his popularity has often been
called a by-product of the war, the theory being that young women turned
to him as compensation for the absence of their young men. Some of his ill-
wishers have even blamed him for the wartime increase in juvenile delin-
quency. A great many psychologists, psychiatrists, psychopathologists,
and other experts on the psyche have tried to define the relationship
between Sinatra and young womanhood. "A simple and familiar combination of escapism and substitution, to be expected in times of high
emotional stress," said one. "Mass frustrated love, without direction,"
declared another. "Mass hysteria," said a third; "mass hypnotism," said a
fourth; "increased emotional sensitivity due to mammary hyperesthesia,"
said a ninety-seventh. One of the editors of the *New Republic,* a journal of
opinion, went on a safari to the Paramount while Sinatra was in season
there and reported that in his opinion many members of the audience had
seemed to find in the man on the stage a "father image," and added,
"Perhaps Frankie is more important as a symbol than most of us are
aware." A romantic psychologist attributed Sinatra's eminence to " a sort
of melodic strip tease in which he lays bare his soul. His voice," he continued, "haunts me because it is so reminiscent of the sound of the loon I hear
in the summer at a New Hampshire lake, a loon who lost his mate several
years ago and still is calling hopefully for her return." Sinatra's appeal to
his fans, whether they think of him as a father, a hypnotist, or a widowed

loon, can probably be ascribed simply to the desperate chemistry of adolescence. Some of his more rabid admirers have conceded guiltily that they may cast off a tiny bit of the love they bear for him when they get married, and it is perhaps significant that when the president of a Sinatra fan club in New Zealand became engaged, she resigned her office, and that when she broke her engagement, she applied for reinstatement. In Detroit, early this summer, a radio station conducted a "Why I Like Frank Sinatra" contest. Among the fifteen hundred essays submitted was one that read, "I think he is one of the greatest things that ever happened to Teen Age America. We were the kids that never got much attention, but he's made us feel like we're something. He has given us understanding. Something we need. Most adults think we don't need any consideration. We're really human and Frank realizes that. He gives us sincerity in return for our faithfulness."

Sinatra has male fans, too, including twenty members of the crew of a Navy vessel, who, just before their departure for the atom-bomb tests at Bikini, asked him for a photograph to pin up on a bulkhead. For a while, there was a Sinatra fan club whose membership requirements were nearly as exacting as the Union League's; you not only had to be male and to admire Sinatra, but you also had to be named Frank yourself. His fans are, however, overwhelmingly young women. Their versions of the effect he has on them are, on the whole, more daintily phrased than the callous judgments of the psychologists. "I shiver all the way up and down my spine when you sing," a girl wrote Sinatra, "just like I did when I had scarlet fever." "After the fourth time I fell out of a chair and bumped my head," said another, "I decided to sit on the floor in the beginning when I listen to you." And when a local radio station held an essay contest to find out "Why I Swoon at Sinatra," the prize-winning answer, which could readily serve as the basis of a song lyric, was "If lonesome, he reminds you of the guy away from your arms. If waiting for a dream prince, his thrilling voice sings for you alone."

Sinatra is skilled at giving each of his listeners the impression that she is the particular inspiration of, and target for, the sentiments he is proclaiming. While singing to an audience, he rarely gazes abstractedly into space. Instead, he stares with shattering intensity into the eyes of one trembling disciple after another. Though his fans usually greet his appearance with loud acclaim, occasionally they are as hushed as if they were in church, and in some fan-club publications all pronouns of which he is the antecedent are reverently capitalized. Sinatra handles his kids, as he calls them, with artful skill. "I never saw anything like the way he milks 'em and kicks 'em around," one Broadway theatrical agent said as he emerged, in a daze, from a Sinatra show at the Paramount. Experienced comedians appearing as guests on Sinatra's weekly radio program have been so perplexed by the antics of his studio audiences that they have lost all sense of timing and gone up in their lines. Sinatra, on the other hand, is unperturbed when his chaotic fans are screaming, shivering, and falling off chairs. Never was a man more attuned to the discord of his accompaniment. His fans seemingly will do almost anything he tells them to, and it is fortunate for the rest of the population that he does not have a hankering for, say, arson. Their obedience falters only when he asks them to keep quiet, as he usually does just before a broadcast. "It's like trying to tell the tide not to come in," the producer of his program has said. Sinatra fans have a party line, like Communists. Lately they have been preaching self-control. It was once policy to make as much noise as possible, but the older hands among them now profess to disapprove of squealing unless Frankie does something so wonderful that you can't help yourself. They are reduced to helplessness by, for one thing, Sinatra's celebrated use of glissandos; whenever he slides gently from one note to another, their admiration is exceedingly open-mouthed. They insist that they do not really scream but merely murmur "Ooh" or "Aah," but to the unaccustomed ear the bleat of many lambs can sound as harsh as a lion's roar. The girls are currently puzzled by a throbbing dilemma. They fear that if they don't continue to react boisterously to their idol, other citizens, by now conditioned to hearing him only over the strident obbligato of their affection, will conclude, an intolerable idea, that he is losing his grip. "What can a poor fan do?" one of them asked recently.

Sinatra fans express their devotion to him in odd ways. They sign letters "Frankly yours" or "Sinatrally yours," and they begin postscripts not with "P.S." but with "F.S." They try, as nearly as is feasible for young women, to dress as he does. Once, after he had absentmindedly appeared in public with the sleeves of his suit coat rolled up, thousands of other coat sleeves were tortured out of shape. The fans pin club buttons not only over their hearts but also on their socks, and they inscribe his name on sweaters and coats. One of them painstakingly inked the titles of two hundred Sinatra songs on the back of a beer jacket. Another braided her hair and tied up one braid with a ribbon labelled "Frankie" and the other with one labelled "Sinatra." A girl whose arm he had accidentally brushed while trying to escape from a pack of fans wore a bandage over the spot for two weeks, to prevent anybody else from brushing it. Another became the envy of her gang when, after Sinatra had checked out of a hotel room, she got into it before the maids did and escaped with a cigarette butt and a half-used packet of matches, both of which she assumed he had touched. After he had left a restaurant, an equally lucky girl got to his table ahead of the bus boy and managed to polish off a bowl of cornflakes he had unquestionably touched. Girls have plucked hairs from his head and, at somewhat less trouble to him, have collected clippings of his hair from the floors of barbershops. One Sinatra fan carried around in a locket what she insists is a Sinatra hangnail. Souvenir-hunting young ladies broke into his Hasbrouck Heights, New Jersey, house after he had moved out of it in 1944 and incestuously made off with a discarded bundle of old fan mail, some of which they had doubtless written themselves. So that some girls could get his autograph, others have momentarily immobilized him by throwing themselves sacrificially beneath the wheels of his car.

No entertainer's audience is more resolute than Sinatra's. Five New York girls borrowed their parents' savings of two thousand dollars and went to Montreal to hear him sing at a theatre there. The expedition was a failure. For one thing, he had left Montreal two weeks before, and for another, they had to flee from a rooming house so precipitately, to escape some police who were tracking them down, that they abandoned forty precious photographs of Sinatra they had brought along as luggage. One stay-at-home fan has listed in a notebook every song he has sung over the air in the past three years, and another takes down his broadcasts in shorthand and transcribes them, so that she will have something to read at night. Among his other fans are a girl who saw one of his movies so often that she memorized the dialogue, which she then wrote out and mailed to Sinatra; a girl who made a hundred and twenty-one pilgrimages to a movie in which he appeared only in one brief scene; and a girl who announced, after her fifty-ninth viewing of another Sinatra movie, that he spoke fourteen hundred and seventy-six words in it, not counting the lyrics of songs.

Sinatra's evolution, in the past two years, into a crusader for civil liberties and a political orator has delighted his fans. They are impressed by the knowledge that they are pledged to an entertainer of such versatility, and they look down upon the more limited idols of other fans. "Van Johnson," one Sinatra fan said in disparagement of an actor who has quite a few fans of his own, "hasn't done a darn thing for anybody except sit around and look cute." While Sinatra was stumping for Roosevelt in 1944, his fans dutifully put on buttons saying, "Frankie's for F.D.R. and so are we," and took to nagging at their parents to vote a straight Sinatra ticket. The Sinatra-fan-club papers run editorials condemning intolerance and urging their readers to cut down on ice-cream sodas so that they can contribute—in Sinatra's name, of course—to humanitarian causes. Last winter, the National Foundation for Infantile Paralysis collected money for its March of Dimes by conducting a popularity contest at a stand in Times Square. Passersby were invited to drop change into any one of forty-eight bottles, each labelled with the name of an entertainer. As soon as the local Sinatra clubs heard of the competition, they mobilized for action, and when the coins were finally counted, it was discovered that Sinatra's bottle contained nearly twice as much money as that of the runner-up, Bing Crosby.

Sinatra has undoubtedly made his fans tolerance-conscious and persuaded them to champion the rights of minority groups, but on the whole they have not learned to be tolerant of critics of Sinatra. When Ben Gross, the radio editor of the *Daily News,* remarked that he did not consider Sinatra the greatest singer in the world, one Sinatra fan wrote him that she "would love to take you to Africa, tie you to the ground, pour honey on you, and let the ants come and bite you to pieces," and another that "you should burn in oil, pegs should be driven into your body, and you should be hung by your thumbs." For unwavering loyalty to the man of their choice and antipathy for his detractors, Sinatra fans have no peers. He likes the color blue; so do they. He likes chocolate and pistachio ice cream; so do they. It was once reported that he had switched from purple to brown fountain-pen ink; many of them changed theirs, too, and one girl, who had just bought a large supply of purple and couldn't afford not to use it up, decided to write letters three times as long to expedite the exhaustion of her supply. Before the Joe Louis–Billy Conn fight this summer, Sinatra's New York fans learned that Sinatra's pal Toots Shor was rooting for Conn. The fans, assuming that no true friend of the singer would differ with him on an important matter and that therefore Sinatra must be for Conn, too, began rooting for the challenger. Just before the fight, Sinatra came to New York, and the fans learned that he not only was favoring Louis but had bet fairly heavily on him. Impassively switching their party line, the fans were solidly behind the champion from there on in.

Sinatra's fans can be demure enough young ladies when they are by themselves, and even en masse they are not always disorderly, but they have nevertheless compiled an impressive rcord of shenanigans from coast to coast. In 1943, when Sinatra was on his way to Hollywood, to fulfill a movie contract with Radio-Keith-Orpheum, the studio anticipated, and may just possibly have inspired, trouble at the railway station when it requested an escort of twenty-five policemen to protect Sinatra on his arrival. R.K.O. then decided to have him disembark secretly at Pasadena instead of publicly at Los Angeles. This secret was whispered over the radio. R.K.O. sent a collection of bit players to Pasadena to welcome Sinatra, in case his fans had missed hearing the whisper. They hadn't. Five thousand of them met the train, and in the ensuing turmoil at least one girl bit at least one reporter in the arm. In Boston, Sinatra was once welcomed at a station by three thousand young women. One of them, clutching wildly at him, missed and gashed a detective with her fingernails, and another, perhaps enraged by a local newspaper's report that the singer was contributing all his fan mail to a wastepaper drive, made a flying tackle at him from a divan in a hotel lobby. She missed, too. Some months later, when Sinatra was to appear in a Boston armory, the management had the seats bolted to the floor. In Chicago, Sinatra fans broke a few windows of a train on which he had just arrived, and another time there an enthusiastic young miss, trying to hand him a bouquet of flowers, knocked down a bishop who happened to be in her way. In San Francisco, fifty-six girls lined up at four in the morning outside a theatre in which he was singing, to wait for the box office to open, and were arrested for violating a local wartime curfew. Sinatra protested to the police, in their defense, that they had not stayed up late but had merely arisen early. A plane in which he was travelling landed at the Detroit airport just before the arrival of a car bearing Secretary of War Patterson, for whom a police escort had been provided. The secretary took a quick look at the crowd closing in on Sinatra and told the escort to take care of him instead. In Pittsburgh, a candy store next to a theatre into which Sinatra had been booked prudently boarded up its windows ahead of time, and the schools prepared for his arrival in decreeing expulsion as the penalty for inexplicable absenteeism. . . . As a rule, any public appearance by Sinatra is a guarantee of at least a modest riot, and some of his old, experienced friends are no longer willing to accompany him to a rendezvous with his impulsive public. "You can enjoy that sort of thing for five minutes," one of them remarked, "but six minutes is too goddam much."

Nowhere are Sinatra's fans more exuberant than in New York, and nowhere in New York is their exuberance more spirited than at the Paramount, where in the past four years the singer has made four appearances, covering eighteen weeks in all. The Paramount is the shrine of their disorder. "No holds are barred there," a Sinatra fan said cheerfully a few weeks ago. "That's the home of swoon." Sinatra has broken the house records almost everywhere he has appeared, but not at the Paramount, for when he is there many of his fans literally consider the theatre their home and spend the day in it, occupying a seat through half a dozen shows for the price of one ticket. A girl who sat through fifty-five stage and screen shows in the three weeks of Sinatra's last tour of duty at the Paramount quivers with remorse when she recalls that during his first engagement there she left after one performance. She points out that she was only twelve then, but she says, "I die every time I think of it." The management of the theatre, trying desperately to increase the turnover, has resorted to various devices in an attempt to clear the house. It has, for instance, required young patrons who bring box lunches to check them in the lobby. This rule is difficult to enforce. Many fans hide sandwiches, candy bars, and other emergency refreshment in their purses and under their clothes. Furthermore, those who comply with the rule paralyze the operation of the cloakroom by milling around it when they finally depart and complaining bitterly that they deposited a peanut butter on white instead of the pressed ham on rye the attendant is trying to palm off on them. The theatre tries to book as inferior a movie as possible to complement Sinatra, hoping that recurrent flashes of mediocrity on the screen will discourage fans from waiting around for the next stage show, but the fans either take naps or turn their backs to the screen and chat with one another during the picture.

Before Sinatra opens at the Paramount, the management summons its ushers to a lecture on a social kind of tolerance and warns its staff to watch out for patrons' attempts to reach the performer's dressing room by sneaking underneath the stage. Sinatra's recent appearances there have been big parties in which the audience has participated almost as fully as the paid hands. At the final performance of an engagement in the fall of 1945, Sinatra and the spectators joined in singing "Auld Lang Syne." A year before, while Sinatra was on the Paramount stage, an eighteen-year-old boy sitting in the orchestra threw three eggs at him. One hit its mark. The orchestra swung into "The Star-Spangled Banner," but a lively fracas developed anyway. In the course of it, the assistant manager of the theatre suffered a sprained finger while helping to save the assailant from being mauled to death. A fifteen-year-old young lady who had been sitting next to the egg thrower said afterward, "I grabbed him right after the third egg. I got in a couple with my handbag. My friend hit him with her binoculars." (Sinatra fans, even when seated in the second or third row, often use binoculars.) Sinatra, unwounded, forgave his foe, and the audience took up a collection and later interrupted the show again to present the singer with four large bouquets of flowers. Even during shows not featured by assault, the fans usually present him with at least one large bouquet. At the Paramount, he has received innumerable other gifts, including a loving cup, a heart-shaped arrangement of carnations, a golden key (the card explained that he already possessed the hearts it would unlock), two Teddy bears, and a portable bar.

Ever since the Sinatra tide began to swell, it has been alleged that his popularity, though perhaps not altogether undeserved, is not altogether uninspired, either. Some people have even come right out and blamed the whole business on press-agentry. George Evans, who has been Sinatra's press man for nearly four years, was once quoted by a newspaper reporter as having said that he had urged girls to moan and suffer unaccountable dizzy spells at the Paramount. He has frequently offered to donate a thousand dollars to the favorite charity of anyone who could prove that "a kid was given a ticket, a pass, a gift, or a gratuity of any kind in any shape or manner at all to go in and screech." Recently, perhaps because of the inflationary nature of the times, Evans has raised the stakes to five thousand. He does not maintain, though, that Sinatra's acclaim has always been entirely spontaneous. "Certain things were done," he says mysteriously. "It would be as wrong for me to divulge them as if would be for a doctor to discuss his work."

The word "swoon," now inseparably attached to Sinatra, was firmly tied to him in an imaginative item that two press agents for the Riobamba, a New York night club in which he toiled in the spring of 1943, persuaded a gossip columnist to publish. Its import was that women were swooning and otherwise acting up all over the joint. One of the few actual cases of coma induced by Sinatra's singing turned out to be simply the result of malnutrition; a young lady had been waiting in line outside a theatre nearly all night and then had sat through seven shows without nourishment. Many other girls, however, have obligingly lost consciousness for a moment to accommodate photographers.

To many unenlightened visitors to Evans' office, at 1775 Broadway, the place looks pretty much like any other press agent's headquarters, but to Sinatra fans it is mecca. Though Sinatra is scarcely ever there, it is the nerve center for the vast activities of his fans, whom Evans undeniably eggs on. "It's almost like a public service," he explains in extenuation. "If the kids weren't doing this, they'd be doing something less elevating." He maintains liaison with most of the Sinatra fans through a middle-aged widow named Marjorie Diven, who sits in a cluttered cubicle stacked to the ceiling with scrapbooks, photographs, card files, and unanswered fan mail. Many Sinatra fans would consider it a treat to be permitted to help Mrs. Diven paste up clippings and slit envelopes, but ordinarily only fan-club presidents enjoy the privilege. This system serves the double purpose of giving club members aspiring to office an extra incentive and of providing Evans with a certain amount of superior unpaid clerical assistance. Sinatra's fans have huge respect for Mrs. Diven, and she has been elected to honorary membership in hundreds of their clubs. "Marj is just about the busiest person I have ever seen," one of the girls has said. Sinatra fans, like Sinatra, hardly ever use last names. "Calling Frank Mr. would be as silly as calling my mother Mrs.," said one recently. They call Evans, who has a married son, George. They are, though, rather afraid of him and try hard not to annoy him, for fear of getting in bad with Frank.

Marj has been handling Frank's fans for George since the spring of 1944. Hers is so much a labor of love that she keeps at it nights and weekends. "People think it's strange that I take this business so seriously," she says, "but I've seen many things it does that go beyond the eye. There was a sixteen-year-old girl in Alsace-Lorraine who, maybe because of some war experience, was suspicious of all men but Frank. Why, she wouldn't even trade stamps. After she wrote in, I got in touch with a forty-five-year-old male fan in Iceland—the serious, responsible type—and had him write her a couple of letters. Five months later, she wrote Frank and asked if it would be all right if she wrote back to the man in Iceland, and I said yes. Now she's happy; she sleeps with his letters under her pillow. We in New York cured that girl in Alsace-Lorraine with the help of a man in Iceland."

Mrs. Diven has organized Sinatra cells in many foreign places, including Ceylon, Nigeria, and the Isles of Wight and of Man. His fans in Argentina, she says, are the most excitable and those in England the most reserved. "Turkey is becoming very Sinatra-conscious," she announced matter-of-factly one day. She tries to get domestic fans to correspond with ones abroad, and has organized the Adopt a Foreign Fan Association. "I wrote for your picture three months ago and haven't got it yet," a fan reported to Sinatra, "but I got a wonderful friend in Canada." Mrs. Diven, who is without doubt the world's greatest expert on the Sinatra fan, has a clear image of what she thinks is the typical one. "She's a fourteen-year-old girl living in a small town," she says. "She never gets to see anybody except her family, who haven't much money, and her schoolmates. She's lonely. On the way home from school, she stops at a drugstore for an ice-cream soda and picks up a movie magazine. She reads about Frank's life and it sounds wonderful: a pretty wife, two children—a boy and a girl—plenty of money, a home in Hollywood near the other movie stars. She writes him a letter. She imagines he gets about six or seven letters a day, and she visualized him at his breakfast table, with her letter propped against the toaster. She calculates how long it will take for his answer to her to come back. When the time arrives and she hears the postman coming, she runs down the lane to her mailbox, one of those wobbly rural boxes. She keeps this up for three weeks, while her family makes fun of her. It's the thought of that fourteen-year-old girl running down that lane to that wobbly mailbox that makes me sympathetic to the fans."

Of the five thousand fan letters Sinatra receives a week, few ever feel the comforting warmth of his toaster. Nearly all, no matter how they are addressed, eventually end up in Evans' office. New York fans who have visited the place and made this discovery are sometimes disillusioned. "Why the devil do I write him every Wednesday night?" cried one girl, up to the top of her bobby sox in other fans' mail. Most of the letters are either requests for photographs, renditions of certain songs, or buttons off his suits, or else are run-of-the-mill expressions of admiration. (There are also many postcards, which Mrs. Diven simply puts aside until her office gets unbearably cramped. Then she throws them out, as many as fifty thousand at a time.) There are, in addition, a few crackpot notes and a quantity of appeals for information, advice, or comfort. A surprisingly large number of young people think Sinatra is omniscient and thus qualified to answer such questions as "What does a girl do whose world seems to have come to an end?" or, as a fourteen-year-old boy put his problem, "Do you think you should talk to your best girl about sex?" Some of the most ticklish queries are tackled by Evans himself, perhaps the only press agent on Broadway who spends an hour or so a day telling young women how to get over being wallflowers at dances. "Not every girl can be popular," he writes, and suggests that they take up the piano. Mrs. Diven, a prodigious correspondent, answers all other letters that seem to require a reply, signing herself as Sinatra's secretary. "I wonder what he *really* thinks about the kids," she once remarked, when no kids were present. On the whole, Sinatra thinks well of them, since they have helped to make him what he is. He is usually patient with them, but now and then he admits that their aggressiveness exasperates him, and an article, entitled "If My Daughter Were Seventeen," that appeared a while ago under his signature in *Photoplay*, contained the statement "Personally, I've always admired girls who have a certain amount of reserve."

Most prominent entertainers who appeal to young people have one or two fan clubs; Sinatra has two thousand, among them the Subjects of the Sultan of Swoon, the Bow-tie-dolizers. Frankie's United Swooners, the Hotra Sinatra Club, the Our Swoon Prince Frankie Fan Club, the Bobbie Sox Swoonerettes, and the Frank Sinatra Fan and Mah-Jongg Club. Some fans belong to several dozen clubs. Dues generally run around a dollar a year, and business meetings amount to little more than convening around a phonograph or radio and listening to The Voice. Some of the clubs have elaborate constitutions; the preamble to that of the Society for Swooning Souls of the Sensational Sinatra, a Pittsburgh organization, says that "We will never believe anything awful about Frank unless we hear him verify it." A few dozen of the clubs are affiliated with the Modern Screen Fan Club Association, run by *Modern Screen* as a circulation device. This magazine also conducts an annual contest to find out what movie actor is most popular with its readers. Sinatra won the contest in 1944, Van Johnson in 1945, and Sinatra again this year. His eminence is at least in part a result of the feverish letter writing of his fans. They are as diligent a bunch of correspondents as any older pressure group, and, at the instigation of their leaders, they keep bombarding people in the radio, movie, and recording business with demands for more of Frankie.

Most of Sinatra's fans are insatiable for information about him and find that the sustenance provided by movie magazines is, like chop suey, filling enough but of little nutritive value. Their fan-club publications, mostly mimeographed affairs, which deal exclusively, and often lengthily, with Sinatra, provide more nourishment. Nearly every issue contains sentimental poems and an account of a dream in which the author met the singer. (Any club member who does meet or even see him can be counted on for two thousand words about the experience.) The club papers carry no advertisements, but many of them ask their subscribers to buy products with whose manufacturers Sinatra is or has been professionally associated. The text is usually laced with the slang Sinatra uses. Two recurrent words are "fave" and "natch," for, respectively, "favorite" and "naturally." The fans' fave adjectives are "cute," "sweet," and "smooth," most frequently employed in modification of Sinatra. (Often, to tease his fans, Sinatra sticks his tongue out at them, and one fan-club correspondent who got a closeup view of this spectacle disclosed to her circulation that his tongue was smooth, too.) The fave utility word is "hey," which Sinatra occasionally uses, as if it were a period, to end his sentences. "If you're old enough to smoke, try an Old Gold hey," the fans tell each other, or "Now please send in your dues hey." There are social notes ("Our president is a very fortunate girl. Her brother-in-law met a soldier who knew Frank"), political notes ("Frankie for President in 1956"), contests ("An 8 × 10 glossy action pose of Frankie for completing the sentence 'Frank is an average American because . . .' in less than fifty words"), and fashion notes ("He was wearing dark gray trousers, white shirt, black sleeveless sweater, a floppy black and white polkadot bow tie, light gray jacket, and a white carnation. Sharp, natch!!").

A conscientious Sinatra fan carries at least half a dozen snapshots of him in her purse wherever she goes and is always ready to trade with other Sinatra fans. No one can say how many pictures of Sinatra repose in how many homes, but one girl is known to have four hundred and twenty-four in hers; this was discovered when she wrote to Mrs. Diven requesting a four-hundred-and-twenty-fifth. Fans who can afford cameras take shots of Sinatra whenever he comes within range. (He carries a camera, too—a miniature the size of a cigarette lighter—but he never photographs fans.) Often, in their eagerness, they make the mistake of photographing someone who looks like him, but they usually manage to trade the resulting pictues off, in a dim light. The fans are so anxious to get any new pictures of Sinatra that when the Columbia Recording Corporation distributed to its dealers a handsome, almost life-size likeness of him, several unscrupulous retailers made a nice profit by selling them to well-heeled fans at ten dollars apiece. The fans also buy plain, normal-size photographs of Sinatra. Kier's Book House, a cramped bazaar on the Avenue of the Americas, is one of their favorite shops. Kier's publishes a catalogue which lists the more than three hundred entertainers for whose likenesses there is a more or less steady demand. Sinatra's name is the only one followed by any remark; after it appears the notation "35 Poses."

When performing, Sinatra often makes himself the butt of all jokes, possibly because he knows that his fans regard it as a duty to express shrill resentment of any slur, no matter how slight, on his person or personality. He cannot, in their presence, sing beyond the title words of "I Got Plenty o' Nuttin'" without hearing cries of "Oh, no, Frankie, you got everyt'in." When he made a guest apperance on a broadcast from New York this summer, he requested the audience, before the program started, to keep quiet, but though the girls in it tried hard to obey, the script imposed fearful temptations on them. They uttered smothered groans when their hero was called a skinny runt. They bit their lips when, immediately after he had expressed amazement at the notion that he should be expected to knock down a door, a slip of a woman, in collaboration with a sound-effects man, knocked it down. Sinatra often impishly improvises tortures for his fans, and while the door smashing was going on he hummed snatches of the easily recognizable theme song of Bing Crosby, whom Sinatra fans profess to consider a second-rate singer. Their other official villain is Van Johnson. The house organ of an Illinois outfit ambitiously called the National Association of Frank Sinatra Fans always refers to the movie actor as van johnson. Early this year, Sinatra invited Johnson to appear as a guest on his radio show, put on that week in San Francisco, where Sinatra was also playing at a theatre. Johnson wandered over to the theatre while Sinatra was onstage and watched him from the wings. The producer of the radio program, who was hanging around, too, noticed Johnson and suggested that he walk out on the stage and add some unexpected zest to Sinatra's act. "Van was overawed by Frank," the producer said afterward. "He said, 'Oh, I couldn't do that. I don't know Frank well enough.' I couldn't get anywhere with him, so finally, when Frankie was finished and another act was working, I beckoned him to the wings for a moment and he agreed that it would be a wonderful idea for Van to break up his act. 'When'll I do it?' Van asked Frank. 'When the fellow here tells you,' Frank said, pointing to me. Well, a couple of minutes later, right in the middle of a speech Frank was making, I gave Van the nudge. 'I'll wait till he's finished talking,' Van said. I could see he wasn't getting the idea at all, so I pushed him out on the stage. There was the damnedest clamor you ever saw. The kids screamed, and waved at Van to get the hell out of there. Van looked worried. The kids yelled louder. Van looked scared. Then Frank ran over and put his arm around Van. That calmed the kids. They can take anything if it's all right with Frank. Sinatra fans are very loyal to Sinatra."

The most loyal of his fans are those who follow him doggedly about whatever city he happens to be in. They usually run in packs of about ten. Lots of these girls, who have been fans of his for two or three years, are now sixteen or seventeen. They consider it poor taste to pester him with requests for autographs, and they rarely try to converse with him, being content merely to stare at him. They insist that there are two kinds of Sinatra admirers—themselves, who are the true fans, and a younger, noisier element, who do not trouble to pursue him but simply gather outside stage doors or restaurant entrances and howl for his autograph. The "fans" refer to this rowdy faction as "fiends." A man who was confused by this distinction once asked Sinatra if he understood the difference between a fan and a fiend. "Certainly," he said. "The kids who hang around stage doors and ask for an occasional autograph—they're fans. But the ones who follow me all over the place—they're fiends." Whatever they are, the roving admirers work extraordinarily hard at their singular hobby. "You know," one of them reflected a few minutes after she had bruised her knee and lost a silver-plated barrette in a scuffle involving many fiend-ish fans, "you have to like someone an awful lot to go through what we go through."

Even decades later, Sinatra maintains his appeal to the fans who first heard him at the Paramount and at similar venues throughout the country. The following articles offer backward looks by two writers who were youngsters during the Sinatra phe-nomenon. On the eve of Sinatra's televised concert, *The Main Event,* in October 1974, Martha Weinman Lear recalls her days as a swooning bobby-soxer in Boston thirty years earlier. In the second piece, publishing executive Neil McCaffrey recalls, from a male perspective, an early Sinatra appearance at the Paramount and sug-gests that the greater effect that Sinatra-mania had on the music scene was to herald the end of the Big Band Era.

The Bobby Sox Have Wilted, but the Memory Remains Fresh
Martha Weinman Lear ★ 1974

Ah, Frankie everlovin', here we are at the Garden dancing cheek to cheek and the lights are low and it's oh so sweet. We haven't been this close since the old days when I played hookey from school to come see you in the RKO-Boston. You remember me, don't you? I was the one in the bobby sox.

Lord, what that man meant to me. If you didn't go through it, you wouldn't believe it. Look at him now, what do you see? A paunch, a jowl, a toupee. What could have driven me so crazy—the cuff links? But no, in the beginning he was no sartorial splendor. Suits hung oddly on him. Suits with impossible shoulders jutting like angle irons from that frail frame. He used to make jokes about hanging on the microphone for support, Bob Hope–type jokes, badly delivered, which we found adorable. He had cab-bage ears and the biggest damned Adam's apple you ever saw. It wobbled like a crow's when he sang. The voice was delicious, the phrasing superb.

But listen, what did I know about phrasing? Those cabbage ears could have been pure tin and it wouldn't have made any difference, not to me. So what drove me so crazy?

Sinatra at Madison Square Garden, last night and tonight, and I am a thirteen-year-old again, packing my peanut-butter sandwiches off to the RKO-Boston to shriek and swoon through four shows live, along with several thousand other demented teen-agers, while he crooned to some princess who wasn't even in the house. "Frankie!" we screamed from the balcony, because you couldn't get an orchestra seat unless you were standing on line at dawn, and how could you explain to Mom leaving for school before dawn? "Frankie, I *love you!*" And that glorious shouldered spaghetti strand way down there in the spotlight would croon on serenely, giving us a quick little flick of a smile or, as a special bonus, a sidelong tremor of the lower lip. I used to bring binoculars just to watch that lower lip. And then, the other thing: The voice had that *trick*, you know, that funny little sliding, skimming slur that it would do coming off the end of a note. It drove us bonkers. My friend Harold Schonberg, the *Times*'s music critic, says that it must have been what is called *portamento*, although he can't swear to it, he says, because he's never heard Sinatra sing. Elitist. Anyway, whatever it's called, it was an invitation to hysteria. He'd give us that little slur— "All . . . or nothing at *aallll* . . ."—and we'd start swooning all over the place, in the aisles, on each other's shoulders, in the arms of cops, poor bewildered men in blue. It was like pressing a button. It *was* pressing a button.

We loved to swoon. Back from the RKO-Boston, we would gather behind locked bedroom doors, in rooms where rosebud wallpaper was plastered over with pictures of The Voice, to practice swooning. We would take off our saddle shoes, put on his records and stand around groaning for a while. Then the song would end and we would all fall down on the floor. We would do that for an hour or so, and then, before going home for supper, we would forge the notes from our parents: "Please excuse Martha's absence from school yesterday as she was sick . . ."

We were sick, all right. Crazy. The sociologists were out there in force in those mid-forties, speculating about the dynamics of mass hysteria, blathering on about how his yearning vulnerability appealed to our mother instincts. What yo-yo's. Whatever he stirred beneath our barely budding breasts, it wasn't motherly. And the boys knew that and that was why none of them liked him, none except the phrasing aficionados. In school they mocked us, collapsing into each others' arms and shrieking in falsetto: "Oh-h-h, Frankie, I'm fainting I'm *fainting*." The hell with them. Croon, swoon, moon, spoon, June, Nancy with the Smiling Face, all those sweeteners notwithstanding, the thing we had going with Frankie was *sexy*. It was exciting. It was terrific.

I don't remember exactly when it stopped being terrific, but by the end of the decade he was bombing. His voice went bad. He sang terrible songs—he sang "Mairsy Doats," and on one record he barked like a dog, and I wept for the glory of the empire—and in movies he was developing into the loser incarnate, a bumpkin sailor boy who got to say dumb lines and kept losing Kathryn Grayson to somebody else. I mean, it was *over*. And so was his marriage to Nancy, and he was chasing around after Ava Gardner, whom he later (briefly) married, and in news photos there they were, Gardner gorgeous and Sinatra with a silly little mustache on his face; Beauty and the Schlep.

The comeback that began with his winning of an Oscar for *From Here to Eternity*, in 1953, must still stand as the most fantastic comeback in show-business history, because he really *had* been reduced to total schlephood, not only professionally, which we can forgive, but in the personal image, which we usually cannot. And to come back from that kind of rock-bottom takes—what? an extraordinary self-discipline. I suppose. What clicked in that head, what lights went on? All of a sudden the little loser was coming on like a bigger winner than we or he had ever dreamed, the voice sounding great and the man coming on cool, arrogant, exuberant, extravagant, *powerful*—the Swinger, *Il Padrone*, Chairman of the Board, all that business, with his pinkie rings flashing and his cuffs splendidly shot and his women and his starched $100 bills at the gambling tables in Las Vegas, with his own Rat Pack and his own Clan, his own court jesters, all those Dinos and Sammys and Joeys, his own myth in his own time. And even if only a fraction of it were true, what a myth!

And we were all grown up and our swoons were memories, but I tell you, the gravity was as powerful as ever. I remember, and still blush to remember, going to an opening night party that the film producer Norman Lear (a relative of mine by marriage), gave when *Come Blow Your Horn* opened here in New York City in the early sixties. I was standing around talking to some people, all adult and cool, right? when my husband came over and said, "Sinatra's just come in." *Wham!* A child again, beguiled again, zooming backward through time and space and I stood there shaking like a thirteen-year-old, hands clasped *tight* behind my back and wailing, "No, I *can't*." (And didn't.) *"What would I say to him?"* Oh, well. He probably wouldn't have remembered me, anyway.

A few years later, it started getting . . . seamy. Tacky. With the henchmen and the talk of mob connections, the mean-mouthed confrontations with the press, the public degrading of women, the spectacle of baggey-eyed, boozed-up, middle-aged men trying to make it New Year's Eve forever: We're gonna have fun if it *kills* us. The Kennedy White House, into whose Camelot he had drifted for a time, dropped him. The Clan faded, maybe of age. His third marriage, to nymphet Mia Farrow, broke up. A lifelong Democrat, he got chummy with Reagan and then, good grief, with Agnew. Not that it was hard to understand: two boys who had made it from nowhere, and possibly each longed for the other's brand of power. The gossip columns told us that his Palm Springs house was filled now with the good burghers of the Beverly Hills Establishment, with the Brissons, the Goetzes, people like that; just plain suburban folk.

But listen: The punch was still there. I can't explain it, but it was still there. It was just two years ago that the prominent portrait painter Aaron Shickler got a business call from Sinatra's office. His wife, Pete, answered the phone. Wait a minute, a voice at the other end said, we have Mr. Sinatra on the line. And, as Mrs. Shickler tells it, she damn near died. Her hand was unsteady, her breath came heavy. And then he said, "Hello," and here was this woman, mature, poised, veteran of a thousand cocktail-party ripostes—but she was one of us, you see, she had swooned at the Paramount when I was swooning at the RKO-Boston, and that is something you never quite get over—and what she said, her lips fluttering like wings around the mouthpiece, was this: "Oh, my goodness," she said, "It sounds *just like you.*"

What I mean is, it's Ol' Blue Eyes, now, at fifty-nine, with the paunch and the jowl and the wig, and the hell with them. The blue eyes still burn, the cuffs are still incomparably shot, the style, the *style*, is still all there, and what's left of the voice still gets to me like no other voice, and it always will. Hey, out there in Boston. Hey, Rudi Litman, Therese O'Reilly, Nettie Holzman, Lillie Lefkovitz, and all the rest of that old RKO-Boston gang of mine: Are you listening? Could you swoon?

I Remember Frankeee
Neil McCaffrey ★ 1975

Sinatra?

I remember Frankeee. Before he was Frankeee, Harry James hired an unknown vocalist for his swinging 1939 band, his first male singer. Frank was a slim little guy with a thin little voice. Everybody yawned. I'd like to be able to say that I saw the greatness that was to come, but the fact is that I yawned too.

Meanwhile, back at Tommy Dorsey's, the Sentimental Gentleman wasn't getting along with star vocalist Jack Leonard. After four years with the band and hits like "Marie," Jack in 1939 was the most popular male band vocalist around. Bob Eberly, with brother Jimmy Dorsey, was a year away from stardom. Brother Ray Eberle (he kept the family spelling of the name) was just emerging with Glenn Miller. Kenny Sargent, popular through most of the thirties with Glen Gray, was nevertheless no longer a serious rival to Leonard. When Jack quit Tommy that November, everyone wondered how TD would ever replace him.

Tommy first tried a journeyman singer named Allan DeWitt, who lasted only a couple of months (but soon caught on with another good band: Jan Savitt and His Top Hatters). Dorsey had better luck with his second choice. Frank joined early in 1940 and stayed two and a half years. Maintaining my record as a prophet without peer, I assured my friends that Tommy's band would never be the same with this skinny kid trying to step into Jack's shoes.

Though Frank became one of the top band singers with Tommy, nobody guessed what was going to happen when he quit in September 1942 to try it as a single. Anyway, I didn't.

It is now December 30, 1942. The Paramount, brightest jewel on Times Square when Times Square was Times Square, is about to usher in the New Year with a show that is, even by the Paramount's standards, fairly sensational. The picture is *Star Spangled Rhythm*, one of those wartime musicals with a hundred and umpteen big names. The band is Benny Goodman—no longer Number One, but among us aficionados still the King. Oh yes—second billing goes to that former Dorsey vocalist.

The day is raw with sleet. My hip friends and I arrive early, about 9:30 A.M. The crowd is already winding around toward Eighth Avenue. We finally get in and sit through the movie. Then, the great moment. The band climbs onto the stage (which is down in the pit during the movie. The stage moves up like an elevator for the in-person show). Benny gives the downbeat. The Paramount swells with the swinging sound of the Goodman theme, "Let's Dance." The stage rises. The lights go up. Three thousand voices become one roar. Here's Benny!

I quickly scanned the sections and noticed a host of changes. There were four trumpets, not three—among them stars Yank Lawson and Lee Castle. There were three trombones, not two—and they included the legendary Miff Mole, a giant two decades before with the Original Memphis Five and later with Red Nichols. Pianist Jess Stacy was back, now that the war had scattered Bob Crosby's Bobcats. Young Lou Bellson was on drums, reminding you of Krupa. Dave Barbour, later Mr. Peggy Lee, strummed his guitar.

Benny opened with "Bugle Call Rag," a galvanizing arrangement based on the old one, but half new. He followed with a rollicking version of a novelty of the day, "Rosie the Riveter"—which Benny himself sang! Benny was in good spirits, and the band sounded brilliant. (Did any hall ever show off a band's sound like the Paramount?)

Then a collective gasp from the three thousand oglers. Peggy Lee! Trim and young and blonde, beauteous in something white, Peggy had just made her breakthrough with two BG hits, "Why Don't You Do Right?" and "Somebody Else Is Taking My Place." She sang these along with something torchy, which I forget. Then Benny came on with the Quintet for "Lady Be Good," followed by a dance act.

Then Frankeee.

With my habit of underestimating Frank and his fans, I was dumbstruck at the ovation that welcomed him. But I should have expected something. There were more girls than usual in the audience. Indeed, they surrounded us. "Is that bad?" you may ask. In this case, yes. The girls chattered while Benny was playing. Clearly, they were there for something else—and now, here he is.

Frank sang four songs, all in the bedroom style he favored at the time. Songs like "There Are Such Things" and "She's Funny That Way." Of course there was an encore. There were *four* encores—as far as I know, unprecedented at the Paramount.

Benny looked less than ecstatic. We felt the same. In fact, we got even with the girls, making irreverent remarks to interrupt their transports. I've since learned to enjoy a good ballad. But in those days, swing was mostly for guys. Ballads were for girls.

Something happened that morning, but I was too dim to see it. There was none of the squealing or phony swooning over Frankeee. That came later, around fall 1943, as I recall. But that morning at the Paramount heralded the beginning of the end for the Big Band Era. The singers were about to take over.

Sinatra's early influence was felt not only at home, but abroad, notably in war-torn England. In the following excerpt from his book *Frank Sinatra: A Celebration*, Derek Jewell, Ellington biographer and jazz and popular music critic for the *Sunday Times* of London, reflects on his earliest encounters with Sinatra's recordings. He describes his personal identification with the songs and his sense, also shared by others, that Sinatra was "singing just to me." Few have better captured the singer's ability to be a mentor, tutor, or adviser to the romantically inclined listener.

from Frank Sinatra: A Celebration
Derek Jewell ★ 1985

Certainly it was the voice (and its effect) which mattered to me. When I first fell under Sinatra's spell, at around seventeen, in 1945, towards the end of the Second World War, as I waited to go to Oxford University, I was neither a girl nor a homosexual. So the swooning and scratching of the American teenage bobbysoxers of that time was irrelevant to me, if not virtually unknown. I'd read a bit or two about crowd scenes in America, but little news of that kind made the four-page British newspapers then. So it must have been the voice, heard on the blessed American Forces Network of those years, which got to me. Come to think of it, Mr. Kahn wasn't the only one to use those two words as if they were identification enough. Chief among Sinatra's nicknames at the time was, in fact, *The Voice*. They painted it on the nose fuselages of some American bombers around then. The planes were flown by men too. The point is a serious one. From the beginning, Sinatra's fans included a substantial number of males—a fact central to his evolution into a world idol, as we shall discover—and they undoubtedly included me.

The reasons were simple. I liked his sound. Even then, he was better than any of his rivals, more open, lighter and less mannered of tone, giving a personal stamp to a song like no one else I'd ever heard, making you feel he was singing only to you even if you weren't female. Very soon, too, up at Oxford, he was to become my ally, in the unparalleled way that he has been an ally all my life in musical terms—and the ally of all those other millions of men who share some at least of my feelings about him. The first Sinatra record I bought was a 78 on which "The Charm of You" was coupled with "I Fall in Love Too Easily." I swiftly discovered that this was a surefire aid to breaking the ice in the affairs of late adolescence. The words, like many others in popular song, were pretty mushy. *The Charm of You is comparable to a Christmas tree with toys, to little girls and boys when first they see the tree. . . .* Never mind. They seemed to do the trick every time and, in Sinatra's mouth, they really did have the ring of the finest poetry. What was more, he sounded, incredibly, as if he actually *believed* them. How true this was became apparent when the words on the other side of the 78 helped as well. *I fall in love too easily, I fall in love too fast, I fall in love too terribly hard for ever love to last . . .* and this appeared to say we should both (the girl and I) get on with things (although the relative innocence of the time debarred us from many actions which would simply be shrugged at today) without worrying too much if the whole affair came to an end in a week or two. That proposition seemed to suit quite a number of the men and women around Oxford at the time.

I retain my affection for those early Sinatra songs still (others included "Nancy," "I Couldn't Sleep a Wink Last Night," "This Is a Lovely Way to Spend an Evening") even though my critical faculties compel me to admit that the over-rich orchestrations of Axel Stordahl, all weeping strings and sweeping harps, were later to be improved upon by the bitter-sweet arrangements of Nelson Riddle and Don Costa. And these examples of Sinatra's hold upon me, seeing him as musical friend, supporter and sympathiser, were only the beginning of his spell. By the time I was out of undergraduate and National Service days, and into the arms of both career and bride, a new Sinatra had arisen. He was more mature, more dangerous, more scarred and infinitely more swinging and more affecting. So now his songs were the accompaniment to the blissful early and then middle years of marriage.

If we felt happy or wanted to be happier, we would play "Come Fly with Me" in the arrangement of Billy May, or "Our Love Is Here to Stay," "South of the Border" and "Witchcraft" as conceived by Nelson Riddle; if our mood was more mellow, we might turn to "Little Girl Blue" or "The One That Got Away" (again, Riddle's arrangements) or the Gordon Jenkins version of "Autumn Leaves"; and if we were really downcast—or if we felt we wanted to empathise with Sinatra's suffering, since we were well aware by now of the hell of his affair with Ava Gardner and the mixture of pain and pleasure he seemed compulsively to cook up for himself—we'd go to that darkest of songs, "I'm a Fool to Want You," perhaps the greatest arrangement Axel Stordahl ever did, or later to classics like Riddle's peerless chart-topper, "One for My Baby," or the 1959 Gordon Jenkins gloss on "I'll Never Smile Again," the touching song which had done so much to set the young singer on his way back in 1940.

The point need scarcely be laboured. Sinatra had given me the songs of youth. As we both grew older, even though I trailed him by well over a decade, he offered the songs of experience. Many were songs for the present, a few looked forward, far more looked backward, and still more could not be dated in this fashion at all. They were never-ending songs, frozen in time. Happy or sad, triumphant or humiliated, extrovert or darkly inturned—these were songs for all seasons of my life, throughout my life, somehow never seeming old-fashioned and certainly not just a cause for nostalgia, even though nostalgia was a part of the charm as one's children grew up and sought their independent pleasures. My experience of identification with what Sinatra has sung down the years is, of course, shared by multitudes of other people, both famous and unknown. One terrifying version of the death of Marilyn Monroe (accident . . . suicide . . . even murder?) has her, on the last night of her life, offended by a call from Bobby Kennedy and Peter Lawford inviting her to a party "with a couple of hookers," and trying to sleep *while a stack of Sinatra records played*. In fact, she scarcely awoke, making just one further telephone call—in a voice furred with the bucketing syncopation of sleeping-pill stupor—before being found many hours later dead, in the nude. How many other souls, in the depths of depression as well as when elated, will not similarly have sought communion with the voice they knew so well? This intense sense of identification between audience and artist is one of the roots of Sinatra's greatness.

Even before he had begun seriously to suffer for his art (which he did first in the late 1940s and early 1950s), when his voice and his way of using it were most of what he had to offer, he could reach out to the most unexpected corners of the world. At my Oxford college, Wadham, I met in 1946 a Russian under-graduate called Alexander (Shura) Shiwarg, born of a businessman father in Harbin, Manchuria, who became one of our set although I lost touch with him after university. He was a remarkable and mysterious fellow, who had been studying medicine in Hong Kong when the Japanese overran it in 1941. Although the holder of a Russian passport, he joined the British army (rare if not unique) and his fighting career on the streets of Hong Kong lasted just eighteen days before he was thrown into a prison camp until 1945. I again met, and had dinner with, Shiwarg in the spring of 1985 after a hiatus of forty years and when he heard I was writing about Sinatra he exploded with laughter:

> Amazing. That takes me back all the way to 1945. When I got out of prison camp, I was desperate for news. We'd heard nothing reliable for years, only rumours of victories and defeats, and hearing names like Roosevelt and Churchill spat out by Japanese guards, and then there was talk about some terrifying explosion—that was Hiroshima, of course. So I wandered down to the waterfront looking for people who could speak English and I found a British submarine mother ship and I asked the sailors, "What's been happening? What's been happening?" And they said, "Frankie Sinatra, that's what." And I thought it must be some damn Pacific atoll I'd missed the name of, like Iwojima, but they soon put me right. "He's an American singer, a kid just like us, and girls swoon and go crazy when he sings, and sometimes he doesn't even have to sing."
>
> I couldn't believe it. I was shattered. Just as I thought the brave new world was congealing like scabs on the wounds of war, all these people could talk about was Frankie Sinatra. Anyway, they put some records on an old windup gramophone and I heard him, and Bing Crosby too doing "Don't Fence Me In," and that became the theme song of my liberation. I still get goosepimples today if I hear it—but can you beat that damned Sinatra? More important to these kids than the war, and they were English too!

II

Back on Top:
The Capitol Years

★ ★ ★

1 9 5 3 – 1 9 6 1

SINATRA went on to become pop music's biggest star. He performed regularly on the radio program *Your Hit Parade* and became Columbia Records' biggest-selling artist. Sinatra's first recordings with Columbia were performed a cappella, backed up by only a vocal chorus, owing to a musicians' union recording ban. In the early days, Sinatra enjoyed much control over his Columbia recordings, and he fought for improvements on *Your Hit Parade.* In fact, on recorded rehearsals Sinatra can be heard taking on the producers or stalking from the studio because the mood wasn't right. As the decade progressed, however, personal and professional problems began to plague him. His family life unraveled, and his personal turmoil became headline news. Disenchantment with the pop hits of the day and changes in the management style of Columbia Records also took their toll, and his association with the record label ended in 1952. Even his voice—The Voice—began to fail him.

Now that the bobby-soxers were gone and his life had taken a wicked turn, the real test for Sinatra the artist began in earnest. After his fame as the Phenomenon had ended, how did he reinvent himself to become an enduring classic? The next stages in Frank Sinatra's musical life provide a fascinating lesson on the reversals of fortune. Sinatra began the 1950s with no recording contract, no film career, and a passionate but dying personal romance. By the end of the decade, he was at the top of *two* professions— as a musician and a screen actor—and had a series of great recordings, two Oscar nominations, and one Oscar award under his belt.

The 1950s were Sinatra's glory years as a singer. After signing with Capitol Records in 1953, he began recording a series of albums that would come to be known as "the fabulous sixteen"—sixteen albums that, to this day, are considered by many to be the definitive performances of some of the greatest American songs. It was at Capitol, too, that Sinatra rejoined his best arranger during his Columbia years, Axel Stordahl, and that he met such greats as Nelson Riddle, Billy May, and Gordon Jenkins. All these fine arrangers would help to produce the thematically unified albums that were to become Sinatra trademarks.

The alliance with Nelson Riddle warrants further remark. Riddle was a trombonist–arranger who had recorded with Nat Cole (for whom he arranged "Mona Lisa"), Les Baxter, and others. His first work with Sinatra involved some Billy May sound-alikes, such as "South of the Border," but also included arrangements that were uniquely his, such as "I've Got the World on a String" and "Don't Worry 'Bout Me." Riddle's ability to build a song to a peak meshed with Sinatra's passion for lyrics, and both found their format in the newly developed long-playing record, which permitted extended storytelling. Riddle noted, "In working out an arrangement, I look for the peak of a song and build to it. We're telling a story. It has to have a beginning, a middle, a climax, and an ending."*

As a result of Riddle's musical conceptions, Sinatra's music really began to swing during this period, and this can best be appreciated on the recordings appropriately labeled the "swinging ballads." These Riddle arrangements include strings traditionally associated with ballads, plus the patented Riddle "burping bones" and other brass figures. On albums such as *Songs for Swingin' Lovers* are performances that do not fit the jump-tune mold, nor do they match the emotional intensity of Sinatra's classic ballad recordings, such as on *Only the Lonely* and *No One Cares*. Is the Sinatra–Riddle rendering of "Love Is Here to Stay" a ballad or a swing tune? It most certainly is a great romantic ballad, not a swinger. And yet Sinatra's sensual reading and Riddle's pulsating arrangement manage to achieve great romantic tension while swinging all the way—a neat feat.

While Sinatra was busy perfecting his vocal art, he was equally busy in front of movie cameras. During the Capitol years, he made such films as *From Here to Eternity*, *Suddenly*, *Young at Heart*, *The Tender Trap*, *Guys and Dolls*, *The Man with the Golden Arm*, *Johnny Concho*, *High Society*, *The Joker Is Wild*, *Pal Joey*, *Some Came Running*, *A Hole in the Head*, *The Manchurian Candidate*, and *Come Blow Your Horn*. His performances ranged from dreadful to outstanding (his best may be *Suddenly* and *The Manchurian Candidate*), and he became a major film box-office attraction.

Although he emerged in the 1950s as a major movie star, it was his singing at this time that elevated both his own stature and that of the American popular song. He may have been a phenomenon in the 1940s, but he was now a very serious singer who carefully chose his material. He revolutionized his art by taking the American song and laying it out before the world in a way that exposed the melody, the lyrics, and the feelings associated with each song. No one before or since has so happily wedded musical material in this way.

---

*Quoted in Arnold Shaw, *Sinatra: Twentieth-Century Romantic* (New York: Holt, Rinehart and Winston 1968), pp. 173–74.

The three articles that follow assess, from different perspectives, Sinatra's work during the Capitol period, a time when his high-quality musical and dramatic work put him at the top of the entertainment industry. In the first piece, *Time* magazine reports on Sinatra's 1950s recording comeback. His concern for the music and satisfaction in finally gaining artistic control over his recordings are reflected in his comments on his enforced servitude to shoddy material during his association with Columbia. More than a decade after he launched his career at the Paramount, Sinatra returned to perform there in 1956. By then, another teen sensation, Elvis Presley, had taken over the national scene. The *New Yorker* article describes the scene and the singer, both far different from their earlier manifestations. It provides a period retrospective on the teen phenomenon turned mature performer. In the third article, published in the *Atlantic* in the mid-1980s, Stephen Holden, music critic for the *New York Times,* uses the release of *Sinatra,* a sixteen-disk collection of the singer's Capitol recordings, as an occasion to assess Sinatra's singing during that period and to compare the original teen phenomenon with those who came later— Elvis and the Beatles.

Back on Top
1954

> I've got the world on a string
> Sittin' on a rainbow
> Got the string around my finger . . .

Not long ago, Francis Albert Sinatra seemed at the other end of his string. The crooner and his career dangled hopelessly as one competitor after another zipped up the popularity and bestselling list, and Frankie's public and private relations (i.e., with his second wife, Cinemactress Ava Gardner) grew progressively worse. Over their coffee and cheesecake at Lindy's, the Broadway arbiters of show business pronounced their verdict: Frankie was about washed up.

By last week, the verdict had been reversed. *Billboard* had listed Sinatra's record, "Young at Heart," as a bestseller for eleven straight weeks. Three others ("Don't Worry About Me," "From Here to Eternity," "I've Got the World on a String") were selling fast, and jukeboxes across the land again reverberated with the voice that once launched a million swoons. Having won an Academy Award for acting in *From Here to Eternity,* Frankie was sifting a stack of movie offers. The world was his yo-yo.

THE AGE OF MILLERISM

Sinatra, now thirty-six and still a skinny 135 lbs., thinks he knows just what happened since the early '40s when bobby-soxers were curling their toes at his boyish glissando. Says he: "I was weaned on the best popular music ever written. When I was bumming around with Tommy Dorsey and Harry James it was all good. Guys like Mercer and Berlin and Hammerstein were writing their best. In those days a singer was just another guy, and the one-nighters, listening to the band by the hour—this is the experience a singer needs. You learned what it was to be hungry, but you also learned about music."

As his popularity grew, Frankie decided to go out on his own. Somehow, with the decline of big-name bands, Sinatra's type of tune seemed to drop out too. In 1942 Sinatra signed with Columbia Records, whose artist and repertory chief is bearded Mitch Miller. Says Frankie: "Came the age of Millerism. Mind you, I'll admit he's a great musician, but I can't go along with him. Instead of a real interest in the lyrics or the melody, all Miller cared about was gimmicks. One day he said to me: 'Frank, we're going to make a record with a washboard.' I looked at him and said, 'Mitch, you're kidding.' But he wasn't. I refused to do it. I guess I did a lot of refusing between 1949 and 1952."

BARK WORSE THAN BITE

Sinatra rejected so many tunes, in fact, that his worried business managers began hounding him to accept one. "Finally I told them: 'The next song Mitch suggests, I do.' You know what it was? 'Mama Will Bark'—and I sang it with Dagmar. I growled and I barked on the record, and I guess it sold, but the only good it did me was with the dogs."

Frankie finally switched to a different firm (Capitol). Sales of his records began to pick up. His movie success helped. Audiences decided that he was not just a mannered crooner, but a mature pro.

Today, his style remains pretty much the same, but he has escaped gimmicks ("Sure there's a fast buck in the echo chamber, but, it can't last"). His only trick lies in changing the pace of the songs he records (e.g., jump tunes, ballads, well-written novelty songs): "Music is getting better," Frankie says, and so is he. "Everything's ahead of me, Man. I'm on top of the world. I'm buoyant."

Paramount Piper
1956

Frank Sinatra moved into the Paramount Theatre for a one-week stand the other day, and we went over to Times Square to see how he was doing on his old stamping ground. We arrived in the neighborhood of the theatre at about half past eight in the evening, and although the singer wasn't due to perform until an hour later, crowds were lined up all around the place, and quite a throng of adolescents, mostly female, were clustered outside the Paramount stage door, on Forty-fourth Street. They were much more subdued than they used to be when the very thought of seeing Frankie plain sent them into caterwauling ecstasies. In passing, we heard a policeman chatting about them with a colleague. "It's a funny thing, but all they do is just stand and look at that door," he said. "In the old days, they were always jumping up and down and screaming and hollering, but this mob isn't hard to handle at all." While the waiters at the stage door were uniformly young, there were a good many older types among those lined up before the box office. It made us feel a trifle melancholy to realize that perhaps some of the quiet matrons in the queue were the phrenetic bobby-soxers of yesteryear. When a drunken sailor staggered by, shouting, "Down with Sinatra, up with Elvis!" he was booed good-naturedly, whereas in the dear dead days he would have been dismembered on the spot.

When we got inside the theatre, we found ourself [sic] viewing the tail end of a Western movie called *Johnny Concho,* which was produced by Mr. Sinatra and in which he plays the leading character. The spectators seemed endlessly amused at the sight of Frankie riding a horse on the lone prairie, and when, at the climax of the film, he faced a couple of badmen, although armed with nothing but the conviction that right must prevail in the cow country, they cheered him along enthusiastically. Presently, the Dorsey brothers' band was elevated from the pit to the Paramount stage, and after the boys had run through several fine old pieces and a comedian had completed a monologue, the audience sat back happily in the assurance that Sinatra would soon be there. However, at this point Walter Winchell appeared onstage wearing a blue suit and a panama hat and trailing a small blond girl, aged about six and clad in a bikini. He announced that while he had hoped to bring Miss Universe of 1956 to Sinatra's opening night, he couldn't do it, because she was flying out to Toledo with some Runyon Fund checks. As a substitute, he introduced the six-year-old as Miss Universe of 1970. He then asked that the house lights be put up so that he could introduce various celebrities. He adjusted a pair of horn-rimmed glasses, took out a piece of paper, and began to read off the names of notables. He hadn't gone very far with this when he interrupted himself to shout, "Put up the house lights!" He kept on for some time, until Tommy Dorsey nudged him and murmured something in his ear. Mr. Winchell forthwith removed his glasses, peered around the Paramount, and said, "Oh, the house lights *are* up. I couldn't see them with these glasses on." He asked several celebrities to rise and take bows, and finally instructed Jackie Gleason, the television comic, to join him on the stage. Mr. Gleason didn't appear, and Mr. Winchell remarked ominously, "This is no time for a stage wait." Mr. Gleason never did show up, and Mr. Winchell decided at last to wind up his part of the doings in a hurry. He said that Frank Sinatra should always remember that a stone flung from the gutter could never hit a star, whereupon Mr. Sinatra came onstage, and the audience let out a yelp of welcome.

After Mr. Winchell went away, Mr. Sinatra sang all kinds of songs, ranging in mood from "Little Girl Blue" to "I've Got You Under My Skin." He did a masterly job, and the audience behaved with reasonable decorum. Occasionally, they clapped rhythmically and called out requests, which Mr. Sinatra had not solicited, but it wasn't until he sang "All of Me" that anything really untoward happened. In the midst of his rendition of the song, a woman of thirty or so piled up on the stage and tried to take all of Mr. Sinatra in her arms. He repelled her, and eventually she gave up.

We had been informed by a beater for *Johnny Concho* that when Mr. Sinatra finished his stint at the Paramount, he would attend a party in his honor at Toots Shor's restaurant, and we decided to go over to the place and have a chat with him. At the party, we were given a large button reading "Vote for Johnny Concho" and were served by bartenders and waiters wearing cowboy hats. A quartet of musicians, also wearing cowboy hats, played selections from *Can-Can*. Mr. Sinatra, when he turned up, seemed a trifle worn, but when we sought him out, he assured us that he had no complaints. "I'm tired all right, but who cares when you've got a good crowd like that?" he said. "I guess the Paramount's a lot quieter than it used to be when the bobby-soxers were really letting go, but there's still plenty of life in the place. It's funny, you know, the kind of people who come up and ask me for autographs. A fellow grabbed hold of me today, a dignified guy, and he told me he'd been a fan of mine when he was just an office boy or something in the dress business. Well, let's face it, I'm forty, and the kids I used to sing for are getting up there, too." He went on to say that he likes straight acting fine but he wants to keep on doing musicals. "The trouble is so much of this stuff in movie musicals is geared for Nelson Eddy," he said. "But anyhow, I'm getting set for *Pal Joey*, which is really something." A buxom blonde interrupted us. "Mr. Sinatra," she said, "you're the only man whose picture ever hung in my bedroom." "My God!" said Mr. Sinatra. "This is like the old days!"

Guide to Middle Age
Stephen Holden ★ 1984

In 1969, the year the drums of the rock counterculture beat their wildest tattoos, Frank Sinatra turned fifty-four. Pop music's "chairman of the board," whose rightward-tending politics and friendship with the youth-baiting Vice President Spiro Agnew made him a symbol of establishment cynicism to the Woodstock generation, enjoyed his last Top-40 hit for the next eleven years that spring, when "My Way," a surly roar of self-satisfaction, reached number 27 in Billboard's Hot 100. In 1980, Sinatra returned to the Top 40 with the equally feisty "Theme from *New York, New York*," from *Trilogy*, his monumental three-disc album.

It was with *Trilogy* that Frank Sinatra began to gain the attention of the previously disdainful rock press. *Rolling Stone* ran a review of a Sinatra concert soon after the release of the album which offered the ultimate in rock-critic flattery, comparing Sinatra's singing to that of John Lydon, the Sex Pistols' screaming punk moralist. Instead of being viewed as an enemy of sixties radical-liberal communalism, Sinatra began to be viewed as a kind of proto-punk rocker, spitting at the world with pugnacious arrogance.

More than three years after *Trilogy*, Sinatra's reputation as a pop artist for all culture—post-counter and post-punk as well as old-guard—has continued to build. In 1982, RCA Records released the complete Tommy Dorsey–Frank Sinatra sessions in three double-album sets. This month, Twyla Tharp will mount a dance piece called *Nine Sinatra Songs* at the Brooklyn Academy of Music. Linda Ronstadt made a hit album of torch songs, *What's New*, with Nelson Riddle, Sinatra's most gifted arranger–conductor. It included three songs that Sinatra and Riddle had recorded together twenty-five years earlier, on the album *Only the Lonely*.

Mobile Fidelity Sound Labs, the southern California company that in 1982 released a fourteen-disc, $325 Beatles collection, with the discs mastered at half-speed and pressed in Japan, followed it up last fall with a $350 boxed set called *Sinatra*. The collection includes sixteen albums that Frank Sinatra recorded for Capitol Records from 1953 to 1962, when he was at the peak of his artistry. Each record comes with the original Capitol artwork and detailed information about musical personnel and recording dates. Cuts that had been deleted when Capitol reissued the records have been restored, and the set's aural quality is excellent. Beautifully clear and balanced monaural sound on the earlier discs gives way to crisp, deep stereo on the later ones, which, like many stereo albums of the fifties, widely separated the orchestral voices.

Sinatra isn't as complete as the advertising for it implies. Left out are Capitol's first two collections of Sinatra's singles—*This Is Sinatra* and *This Is Sinatra, Volume 2*—which contain such crucial hits as "Young-At-Heart," "Learnin' the Blues," and "Hey! Jealous Lover." And the three later collections of singles that are included—*All the Way, Look to Your Heart*, and *Sinatra Sings . . . of Love and Things!*—are cluttered with junky novelties and second-rate movie songs that no singer could redeem. Another omitted album is one of Sinatra's last for Capitol, *Point of No Return*, on which he teamed up again with his regular arranger–conductor from the forties, Axel Stordahl. Also left out are a Christmas album and soundtracks from Sinatra's movies.

The thirteen core albums, however, constitute a body of pop music conceived for the LP record which, in its scope and consistency, has been matched only by the work of the Beatles. Oddly, the music on *Sinatra* is in some ways more pertinent than that of the Beatles—at least at the moment. Sinatra has, after all, outlasted many of the formidable pop phenomena that were supposed to depose him. Elvis Presley is dead, and his biggest posthumous hit, ironically, is an eerily nervous and out-of-breath rendition of "My Way." The Beatles died with John Lennon. Bob Dylan resurfaces periodically, an erratic bohemian voice in the wilderness, out of phase with Reagan-era realities.

Frank Sinatra is in phase—socially, as a Reagan family friend, and artistically, as a hardy individualist. At sixty-eight, he still gives concerts and makes records the old-fashioned way—with a live orchestra, eschewing rock rhythms and fancy overdubs. And his ubiquitous new signature song, "Theme from *New York, New York,*" unabashedly glorifies worldly success. In today's trend-crazed world of pop music, Frank Sinatra is not simply the ultimate survivor but the ultimate victor.

It was in 1953 that Sinatra, who had spent the previous decade at Columbia Records, moved to Capitol. He was thirty-seven, an age at which all but the most enduring rock acts have lost their followings. Sinatra was not a big star when he made the move—in fact, some considered him a washed-up crooner. But in winning an Oscar that year for his portrayal of Maggio in *From Here to Eternity*, Sinatra made one of the most dramatic comebacks in Hollywood history. The following year, his recording career was rejuvenated as well, as the single "Young-At-Heart" became his first top-five hit in eight years.

The aura of cocky self-assurance in Sinatra's Capitol albums suggests someone who has arrived safely at adulthood having just barely survived an irresponsible and foolishly romantic youth. This posture hasn't changed significantly since, even as the voice has coarsened and darkened with age. The mature Sinatra is a lapsed romantic. While capable of great tenderness, compassion, and joy, beneath the surface he is always reflecting on his loss of faith in the quasi-religious romantic ethos that engulfed movies and pop music in the forties and early fifties. In that ethos, ineffable sexual ecstasy inside marriage was supposed to be everybody's reward for sexual postponement; "true love" was the happy ending everyone was coaxed into anticipating. And, despite a great deal of evidence to the contrary, it was supposed to last "forever."

Sinatra's voice had embodied this dream in the forties with a fervent intensity that no other singer has matched. With his rounded baritone, suggestive of the trombone at its most purringly lyrical, he conjured a fantasy world of tender rapture, at once virile and delicate. Sinatra's *bel canto* phrasing turned the most flowery lyrics into plainspoken, believable outpourings of emotion. Faith in romantic love as a possible and permanent salvation seemed built into his voice, which lent a compelling spiritual conviction to the love songs that he recorded in the forties—"The Girl That I Marry," "How Deep Is the Ocean," and "I Concentrate on You," for example. If Bing Crosby, Sinatra's great forerunner, projected a comforting hominess, in which eroticism had its cherished but modest place, Sinatra exalted the erotic with a dedication that made it a world unto itself. Axel Stordahl exquisitely orchestrated Sinatra's best Columbia singles like aural valentines, trimmed with lacy violins and tinkling bells.

It wasn't until the Beatles' psychedelia, exemplified by "All You Need Is Love," that a vision of love was again so thoroughly and successfully captured in pop music. But the love the Beatles conjured was a communal and polymorphously exploratory utopia of peace, cuddly sex, and eternal youth. Sinatra's love had been a yearning daydream. Both visions were rooted in carefully distilled concepts of musical beauty that had been established in late-Romantic European music.

But beauty has a way of evaporating, and Frank Sinatra arrived at Capitol at just the moment when his voice had begun to lose its spellbinding loveliness. The lapsed romantic had to rebuild his world from inside himself instead of trusting to magic and looking to heaven. In defining his adult self, Sinatra made the first real "concept" albums, in the rock sense. One after another, Sinatra's records explored different styles of adult love and alternatives to love, as the singer tried out different roles: flippant roué (*Swing Easy*), warmly reflective companion (*In the Wee Small Hours*), optimistic, fun-loving hedonist (*Songs for Swingin' Lovers*), happy globe-trotter (*Come Fly with Me*), mysterious loner (*Where Are You?*), jaded sensation-seeker (*Come Swing with Me*).

While at Capitol, Sinatra favored three arranger–conductors: Nelson Riddle (nine albums), Billy May (three albums), and Gordon Jenkins (two albums). With Gordon Jenkins, who used heavy strings and French horns arranged into a tortured Wagnerian chromaticism, Sinatra made the introspective albums *Where Are You?* (his first stereo release) and *No One Cares*. In *Where Are You?* the singer summons the ghosts of old flames with a formal, almost operatic intensity enhanced by a bleating twenty-two-piece string section. In *No One Cares*, made two years later with the same orchestration, Sinatra's voice is frayed and his phrasing hesitant; he "acts" songs like "Stormy Weather" and "I Can't Get Started" as a dark night of the soul.

With May, Sinatra made his toughest, hardest-swinging records. Their third collaboration, *Come Swing with Me*, is a musical fistfight in which two enlarged brass sections throw punches at each other while Sinatra socks out angry, anti-romantic remakes of ballads he recorded in the forties, like "Day by Day" and "That Old Black Magic." This swing has to it almost a rock harshness. Billy May also arranged and conducted one of Sinatra's more mellow albums, *Come Fly with Me*, a spirited travelogue that blends ballads with the swinging numbers.

It was with Nelson Riddle that Sinatra struck his most consistent balance between toughness and angst. *Songs for Young Lovers* (1954), *Close to You* (recorded in 1956, with a string quartet), and especially *In the Wee Small Hours*, which may contain Sinatra's warmest ballad performances, sustain a mood of quiet intimacy and reminiscence. In *Songs for Swingin' Lovers* (1956), the quintessential Sinatra–Riddle medium-tempo album, Riddle expanded the orchestra to thirty-five pieces to achieve the optimum hybrid of swing band and Hollywood studio orchestra. "I've Got You Under My Skin," which Sinatra and Riddle jauntily syncopated against a light, finger-snapping beat, becomes not the sophisticated yet abject confession of love that Cole Porter's lyrics imply but the fond tribute of one sensualist to another. In the song's climax, Sinatra admits that for the moment he's a smitten fool, and this exhilarating expression of a perfect balance between intoxication and wry knowingness may be the apex of all his "swinging" music. As Fred Astaire's graceful courtliness transformed Cole Porter's musical sophistication into a dancing style that seems to be the purest kind of pleasure, Sinatra's artfully casual readings of Porter embody a comparably enviable ideal of grown-up fun.

Sinatra and Riddle achieved another peak in *Only the Lonely* (1958), a reflective album that avoids the sepulchral gloom of the Gordon Jenkins records by putting Sinatra musically in the world instead of in a room by himself at 3 A.M.; the cautious bounce of jazz-inflected rhythms and the impressionistic foliage of brass and woodwind choirs in Riddle's forty-six-piece ensemble prompted performances from Sinatra less solemn than those with Jenkins's ghostly strings and horns. For *Nice 'n' Easy* (1960), their last great collaboration, Riddle pared the orchestra back to thirty pieces. All but one of the twelve songs are standards that Sinatra had recorded between 1940 and 1950. Riddle's smoothest arrangements for Sinatra enhance his cool mastery of ballad phrasing. Sinatra stopped acting songs; the album is above all a demonstration of technique.

Sinatra's Capitol years ended when Warner Bros., then a nascent corporate giant, offered Sinatra his own label, Reprise, in 1961. Unwilling and probably unable to come to terms with rock's technology, he continued to sort through his past, as he had on *Nice 'n' Easy*. While Sinatra's Reprise catalogue is rich, it's spottier than his Capitol output, and the explorations of mature aspirations are frozen into patterns. Sinatra the symbol rose above Sinatra the interpreter.

In the sixties, when the rock-and-roll culture wrested the airwaves from pop traditionalists and made the rock LP album the musical art form of a generation, Sinatra seemed to have no place in the revolution, which in the end turned out to be more technological than cultural. Today, as we look back, very little of the billions of dollars' worth of corporate merchandise marketed as artistically worthy rock seems to have any enduring value.

In 1969, the turmoils and victories of people reaching middle age were of no concern to a generation so contemptuous of its elders that it cherished Pete Townshend's sneer "Hope I die before I get old." But to those of us who are still alive, the "chairman of the board" no longer looms as a disapproving surrogate parent; he has become an adult role model for how to make it to the top and stay there.

If "true love"—epitomized by Sinatra crooning "All or Nothing at All" or "Nancy" or "Dream"—was a false salvation for the parents of the Woodstock generation, the sexual revolution has proven just as false an ideal. The rock generation may have won the opportunity to prolong adolescent pleasure-seeking for as long as it liked, but it didn't anticipate the complexity of middle-age desires.

What, then, is there to pursue? The albums explore every avenue of possibility except religion: knowledge, reflection, friendship, travel, "swinging" in most of its manifestations, and, finally, accomplishment and power.

One wouldn't ordinarily expect a singer to communicate so much lived experience. But Sinatra's greatness is his ability to lay bare the emotional facts. These albums are about continuing, and not only continuing but trying to get better in spite of the realities of aging. They are heroic feats of self-generation, of finding more with less and gaining in the struggle a reason for going on.

Sinatra is a master technician with a song, and expert musicians and critics alike are often impressed with his techniques. In the following articles, two writers offer technical analyses of Sinatra's singing. Critic John Rockwell, in an excerpt from his excellent book *Sinatra: An American Classic*, comments on the 1959 Grammy Award–winning album *Only the Lonely* and provides a detailed musical analysis of Sinatra's rendition of the Harold Arlen–Johnny Mercer song "One for My Baby." Steven Petkov follows with a commentary on the evolution of the conventions of American popular singing and Sinatra's mastery and further development of these conventions in his 1950s recordings.

from Sinatra: An American Classic
John Rockwell ★ 1985

Individual tastes vary, of course, but there is a surprising consensus among Sinatra enthusiasts that the best of his albums from the fifties, one from the uptempo side of the fence and one made up entirely of ballads, were *Songs for Swingin' Lovers* and *Only the Lonely*. Both, not uncoincidentally, were arranged by Riddle and recorded in Hollywood; the former was produced by Gilmore, the latter by Cavanaugh, his first full album for Sinatra.

Songs for Swingin' Lovers was recorded in October 1955 and January 1956. It may be a "swinging" collection, but it epitomizes Riddle's ability to soften the brassiness of such arrangements; most of the punchy brass interjections, for instance, are literally muted. Even the occasional ballad, such as "We'll Be Together Again" (a BMI song by Frankie Laine and Carl Fischer), get a jazzish rhythmic underpinning.

Sinatra's singing on this album has a verve and conviction that make his records from the forties sound bland. He has learned to tease and twist a vocal line without violating its integrity. By now, he knows how to kick forward a song's rhythmic impetus by the percussive articulation of key one-syllable words—the *such* at the outset of the first song, for instance, the very title of which, "You Make Me Feel So Young," suggests the association in Sinatra's mind between youthful energy and his swinging idiom. The album as a whole breathes with a delightful blend of Riddle's naughty sweetness and Sinatra's witty bravado—as in the counterbelting conclusion to the last song, Porter's "Anything Goes," where instead of reaching up for a Manilow-like top note, he plummets giddily down to a low E.

Only the Lonely, recorded in May and June 1958, is Sinatra's greatest album—the quintessential combination of deeply emotional songs, telling arrangements, youthful vocal resources and interpretive maturity. That is not just my opinion, but his: Asked at a New York party in the mid-seventies if he had a favorite among all his recordings, he unhesitatingly chose this one. The album's excellence does not encompass its visual design, even if it did win a Grammy in 1959 for best album cover. The jacket comes adorned with a clown portrait of Sinatra's face, a maudlin touch reflecting his own predilection for clowns when he himself paints. On the back of the LP is another of Sinatra's recurrent visual motifs, a lamppost.

Sinatra's song selection on this album is nearly flawless: a sequence of brokenhearted torch songs that are never gratuitously depressing or unvariegated in their gloom. There are wonderful songs by fine songwriters, either older masters of American popular music or younger men linked directly with Sinatra's circle ("Spring Is Here" by Rodgers and Hart, the title tune by Cahn and Van Heusen, "What's New" by Bobby Haggart and Johnny Burke, "Goodbye" by Jenkins, "Blues in the Night" by Harold Arlen and Johnny Mercer, and "Guess I'll Hang My Tears Out to Dry" by Cahn and Styne). Some critics have groused that Robert Maxwell and Carl Sigman's "Ebb Tide," with its atmospheric sentimentality, constitutes an intrusion into the otherwise consistent mood of adult resignation. But it seems appropriate enough to me.

Riddle's arrangements are the quintessence of his ballad style, applying pastel daubs of instrumental color only but always when necessary. The album is shot through with piano (Miller) and strings, but when other instruments solo, you remember them: the trombone in "What's New," the woodwinds in "Goodbye." One strong but characteristically subtle touch is a rising, then falling, contrapuntal wind line to a single phrase— "No desire, no ambition leads me"—in "Spring Is Here" (the song was deleted when the album was rereleased in stereo, along with "It's a Lonesome Old Town"). The winds intertwine with a chamber delicacy that Mahler wouldn't be ashamed of.

As ever, though, it is Sinatra's singing that makes this album great. For those interested in such details, he "covers" one high note with an operatic artificiality, an F in "Ebb Tide." But elsewhere, this is Sinatra singing at his intimate, vulnerable, conversational best, the voice suffused with an almost unbearable, tremulous fragility. If the "swinging" records symbolize youth, then these ballad collections herald the onset of age: *Songs for Swingin' Lovers* led off with "You Make Me Feel So Young"; here, in "Angel Eyes," by Matt Dennis and Earl Brent, Sinatra refers sadly to "my old heart."

"Angel Eyes" is a drinking song, and another such song, perhaps the greatest of all of Sinatra's torchy lamentations and as intense and true a performance as any he has committed to disc, ends *Only the Lonely*. The song is "One for My Baby (And One More for the Road)," composed by Mercer (lyrics) and Arlen (music) for a 1943 film, *The Sky's the Limit*, where it was sung by Fred Astaire; Ida Lupino also had a memorable version in a 1948 film, *Road House*. Sinatra recorded it three times. His first version, with Stordahl in 1947, is innocently balladic; it sounds sweet but almost astonishingly callow next to this 1958 performance. The last version, from the *Sinatra at the Sands* live album, dates from 1966; although the album is a collaboration with Count Basie and his orchestra, arranged and conducted by Quincy Jones, "One for My Baby" is done as a piano solo with Bill Miller, an honorable but coarser reworking of the version from 1958. The 1958 performance, incidentally, forms the centerpiece of Twyla Tharp's Sinatra ballets.

In the song the protagonist is addressing a bartender, Joe, who remains silent throughout, sympathetic or indifferent, in the time-honored manner of his profession—part psychiatrist, part confessor and part God. The singer has love troubles, bad ones, but he never overdramatizes himself or tries to get us to wallow with him; his reticence suggests the pent-up intensity of his passions. He never even tells just exactly what has happened; by alluding to the plot without actually revealing it, his story becomes everyone's story. The mood is forlorn and alone, yet it rises to an emotionality in the final chorus that is all the more painful for its very muted helplessness.

Structurally, "One for My Baby" is a sophisticated song. It is built in the standard AABA chorus form, meaning a section repeated, a contrasting passage (the *release* in Tin Pan Alley terminology, the *bridge* in rock) and a final return to the first section. This form is central to Western art music of the past two hundred years, most clearly in the "sonata form" that provides the organizational principle for the first movements of most symphonies. It is not simply arbitrary; the idea of statement, repetition with variation, contrast or development and recapitulation evolved naturally to reflect the basic human emotional need for variety and reaffirmation.

In the first two or three decades of this century, Tin Pan Alley songs of this type were preceded by introductory verses. But by the fifties verses were usually omitted in performance, recording and even, as here, composition. "One for My Baby" hardly eschews the conversational directness verses were meant to provide, however; the entire song is suffused with such naturalness. The very structure of its choruses incorporates miniature verses and refrains within each A section, offering eleven verselike bars before each mini-"chorus," which consists of the three-bar statement of the title and subtitle. What makes this less schematic than it sounds is the subtly conversational nature of the melodic line itself, the way it mirrors speech like an operatic recitative, rarely breaking into a real "tune" except in the "chorus" refrain.

This subtlety is echoed by the song's melodic and harmonic language. The vocal line is bluesily chromatic, adding and dropping sharps and flats at will and suggesting thereby the protagonist's unstable, disturbed state of mind. The first section in the sheet music is in E flat major, rising in tension and pitch to the key of G for the final ABA sections. The impression is of "through-composed" form—a seemingly uninterrupted meandering of narration, hesitant and heartbroken. The narrator's late-evening disorientation and despair are conveyed by choppy phrases, unsteady alternations between major and minor (those flatted blues thirds) and the refusal to return to the key in which the song began. A conventional song, based on normal practice in tonal classical music, will return by the end to the original key for symmetry's sake. To do otherwise carries with it dramatic connotations, in this case intimating the singer's inconclusiveness and confusion.

Narrative songs, amounting to miniature operatic vignettes, had been common in American popular music around the turn of the century (hence the greater popularity of verses then). But the narrative style, updated in language and musical idiom, suited Sinatra's dramatic instincts as well as his musical ones. This 1958 recording—singing, arrangement, production—is his greatest because it most completely calls upon his skills as both singer and actor.

The performance begins with a bluesy piano solo by Miller, who is placed at a distance—an effect heard best in stereo, and proof that even this early in stereo's development, when most pop producers contented themselves with vulgar Ping-Pong gimmicks, Cavanaugh was using the medium for dramatic purposes. Sinatra, by contrast, is front and center, as if he is hearing the piano from afar and we are right next to him, eavesdropping. His singing is full of the subtlest touches—recurrent appoggiaturas, or delicate little slurs from above the main note, and a near-classic use of rubato. *Tempo rubato* means "robbed time" in Italian. A soloist (or conductor, with the orchestra as his instrument) varies the flow of the music for expressive purposes, the variations set against the more regular metrical backdrop established in the listener's ear. Here, Riddle's arrangement creates a pulse, and then Sinatra prolongs phrases or bunches short notes together for purposes that are at once musical and dramatic: the lingering pauses of "another nickel . . . in the machine," for instance, or in the refrain "one more . . . for the road."

He also changes words and occasionally notes from the sheet-music version, all to make the lyrics and the vocal line more personal and natural for his own linguistic idiom: replacing *easy* for *dreamy*—it was *pretty* in 1947—and sensuously stretching out the *ea* . . . . His most consistent interpretive touch is a delicious downward glissando, or slide, on the first syllable of *baby*, from the flatted third to the tonic.

Popular singers are expected to transpose songs into the keys most comfortable for their voices but to retain the harmonic relationships within a given song. Thus, "One for My Baby" can begin in any key but must move up a major third after the first chorus. In 1947, Sinatra had sung the song in B flat, ascending to D; in 1958 and 1966, even though his voice had darkened, he raised it up a whole tone, to C and E. The transposition heightens the fragility of the singing even further by shifting the center of the song's range into his slightly unsure transitional area just above middle C; his voice catches affectingly, for instance, at the end of the first chorus on its downward slide from E flat to C on the word *baby*.

Just before the end of that first chorus, Riddle brings up soft strings under the voice, and for the final chorus he inserts a broken saxophone solo. Sinatra's singing rises to a pained, repressed intensity at the climax: "This torch that I've found, must be drowned or it soon might explode . . ." By now, all of his artistry of declamation and phrasing has been forgotten in the face of the sheer, aching vulnerability of his voice—that shake, that quiver creeping in all the way down to his depths.

The song ends with slightly melodramatic coda of Sinatra's invention, extending the composers' "that long, long road" into a musing on *long* and *so long*. The singer drifts off into the aural distance, leaving the silent bartender and his pianist alone by themselves in the bar.

Ol' Blue Eyes and the Golden Age of the American Song: The Capitol Years
Steven Petkov

America has produced a remarkable number of wonderfully talented pop-jazz singers: Bing Crosby, Tony Bennett, Billie Holiday, Peggy Lee, Joe Williams, Mel Tormé, and Ella Fitzgerald, to name just a few. Yet for many musicians, critics, students of American music, and fans, Frank Sinatra is viewed as the greatest of all American popular singers, in a class by himself. He has earned this affection and respect while working in venues that normally would prevent a performer from being taken seriously as a great artist. (Las Vegas and Atlantic City are not the surest routes to artistic respect.) Even Sinatra has labeled himself a saloon singer. Yet he has managed to work the mass, glitzy houses and still be revered by an elite of music lovers. Billie Holiday, who was a master at transmittng the human emotions through popular song, operated in a completely different milieu. An outsider, she was denied the financial success and acclaim that was her due, but was never accused of compromising her art. Yet when serious artists move into the mainstream, they are often accused of selling out their musical integrity. Sinatra, however, continues to receive the adulation of both worlds and has preserved his integrity intact. How has he done this? What separates him from all other American singers? And how has he managed to raise a tired canon of mainly thirty-two-bar popular tunes to the level of serious art?

American popular singing has its own unique performance conventions, which Sinatra, the master of innovation, has brought to mature development. Around the turn of the century, the American popular song consolidated certain unique qualities of melody, lyrics, harmony, and rhythm. Evolved from the work of Stephen Foster and Scott Joplin, a new type of song was born. Totally different from its European predecessors, it found its first true expression in Jerome Kern's compositions. This tradition dominated American music from 1900 to approximately 1950, when rock music began its ascendance. During this fifty-year period, the American song continued to evolve. Characterized by a rhythmically flexible, swinging, even improvisatory approach, it was further influenced by the development of jazz and its traditions.*

Its departure from European musical conventions has made it difficult for some to appreciate the art of American popular song—and by extension, the performers. Referring to someone as a popular singer is bound to have a derogatory connotation for those who dichotomize music, labeling it either serious/classical or popular. I am more inclined to see a distinction between European and African-American musical idioms and to view the American popular singer as someone who works within the latter tradition. We need to rid ourselves of the snobbishness that derogates the specifically American or African-American contributions to twentieth-century culture as compared with the "obviously" superior and vastly more "cultured" European influence. Would so-called cultured Americans have a greater appreciation of such melodists as Kern, Berlin, Gershwin, Porter, Rodgers, and Arlen, and such lyricists as Fields, Hart, Ira Gershwin, Hammerstein, Harburg, and Mercer if these composers had been fortunate enough to be called the composers of twentieth-century lieder?†

It is not merely differences in musical idiom and traditions that separate popular and classical singers. All of us have heard operatic singers such as Robert Merrill and Kiri Te Kanawa venture into the likes of Gershwin's "Summertime." The opera singer who attempts this crossover does not lose his or her status as a classical or European singer. But these crossover attempts do not a popular singer make, nor do they necessarily make for pleasing or even satisfactory renditions. That is because popular singers differ from others in their intentions, goals, and styles. In other words, their performance conventions differ drastically from those who follow the European tradition.

Henry Pleasants, in *The Great American Popular Singers*, has identified several of the main performance conventions adopted by the Americans: (1) using a microphone; (2) clear, textually oriented enunciation of words; (3) taking liberties with the melody and text of a song; (4) phrasing a lyric to

---

*For the most serious, but by no means somber, discussion of the evolution of the thirty-two-bar American popular song, see Alec Wilder's brilliant study *American Popular Song: The Great Innovators, 1900–1950* (New York: Oxford University Press, 1972).

†*Lieder* is the German word for "songs." In the course of time, it has acquired the more specific meaning, art songs.

approximate spoken, conversational English; and (5) flexibility of time.*
Each of these practices requires some explanation.

The advent of radio, with its dependence on the microphone, forever changed the rules of popular singing. The Jolsons of the world had to reach the last row of the balcony via lung power—loudness. Subtlety and vocal intimacies were not available. The radio microphone changed all of that. The slightest whisper could go out to millions of listeners and the romantic, one-to-one communication between singer and listener was born. Properly used or not used, the microphone can reveal the lightest pressure on the vocal cords, hide the taking of a breath, and allow an almost infinite variety of vocal sounds—from breathing to shouting—to reach each listener. It permits the singer to enunciate words in ways that enhance the clarity of the lyric. Released from the need to blast the audience, the singer now had the oportunity to concentrate his or her efforts in other directions. Nuance was possible to a much greater degree than it was in the past.

Some critics view electrical amplification as a technological crutch that allows those with poor voices to project beyond their natural means. In truth, the microphone permits a more natural manner of singing, because the vocal output is more consistent with everyday speech. And rather than aiding weak and flawed voices, it reveals flaws in an almost unforgiving fashion! The microphone is to natural singing what the motion-picture camera is to natural acting. Stage actors are in a fixed position relative to their audience; that is, the physical distance between the actors and their audience cannot be altered. Stage actors must work to project their voices and forgo subtler vocal and physical nuances (the stage whisper is an oxymoron). The screen actor, on the contrary, may speak in more subtle, natural ways and use even slight physical gestures to make a dramatic or comedic point. Thanks to the use of mobile cameras and special lenses, the viewer can be transported as close to the actor or as far away as the director desires. The microphone, likewise, has enabled popular singers to reach deeper into their bag-of-tricks to expand the variety of emotional and textual experiences.

Pleasants asserts that American popular singers take liberties with the melody and text because they have a penchant for viewing the composer's notes and rhythms as being secondary to textual meaning. Thus the singer views his or her performance as a creative improvisational enterprise. But the musical artist who attempts to imprint his or her personality and ideas on the composer's work must always be prepared to accept negative criticism. (Only in the world of jazz do we find a complete acceptance of music as a performer's art.) When classical pianist Glenn Gould was castigated by critics for Bach recordings they considered willfully idiosyncratic, he

*Henry Pleasants, *The Great American Popular Singers* (New York: Simon and Schuster, 1974), pp. 33–48.

countered that if there were a "right" and definitive way to perform a piece, then once it was recorded there would be no need for anyone else to do so.

For the American popular singer, the issue of "taking liberties" is bound up with the goal of achieving a conversational style of phrasing. What does it mean when you hear, "he phrases a lyric well," or, "she gave a great reading of that lyric"? According to Pleasants, the popular singer "wants to talk, to phrase conversationally, easily, and intimately. He wants to tell you what is on his mind or in his heart, not to show you what a great voice he has, or what tremendous things he can do with it."* Anthony Burgess, in offering a description of the lyrics of Lorenz Hart, could well have been describing the goal of the American popular singer. According to Burgess, Hart was "more concerned with heightening the spoken word than with finding a melodic justification for conventional romantic statements in a received pseudo-poetic form."† Thus the popular singer is concerned with singing in a way that is intelligible, casual, and based on conversational phrasing. These goals take precedence over the soaring melodic heights achieved in opera by a Bjorling or DiStefano.

These phrasing intentions may not be easy to achieve. Some singers appear not to have a clue as to how to phrase a lyric. Music lovers often cringe at Vic Damone's phrasing deficiencies while lauding his lovely voice. But what does it serve to have vocal talent if it is not combined with successful lyric interpretation?

Occasionally a popular song is written in such fashion as to prevent *any* singer from giving it a natural reading. For example, Walter Gross's "Tenderly" (1945) has a lovely melody, but it cannot be performed consistent with natural speech. Normally, when we say "tenderly," we stress the first syllable. But the song demands that stress be placed on the last syllable; it cannot be sung otherwise while maintaining the proper melody and rhythm—not even by Sinatra. For many, this turns an otherwise lovely song into an ungainly, awkward piece of music.

A popular singer's performance may also be constrained by a composer who insists on imposing his own artistic directives. (At least Glenn Gould had to deal only with critics; he did not have to fear Bach coming after him.) In his autobiography, *It Wasn't All Velvet*, Mel Tormé discusses his appearance in the musical *Words and Music* (1948), a fictionalized account of the lives of composer Richard Rodgers and lyricist Lorenz Hart. Tormé was assigned "Blue Moon" as his solo number. Rodgers watched as the singing began:

*Ibid., p. 41.
†Anthony Burgess, *This Man and Music* (New York: Avon, 1985), p. 107.

Blue Moon,
You knew just what I was there for.
You heard me saying a prayer . . . [pause]
for someone I really could care for.

Rodgers interrupted, refusing to let Tormé continue until he agreed to sing the phrase as written:

You heard me saying a prayer for [pause]
Someone I really could care for.

A mild battle ensued, and Rodgers stormed off the set. But Tormé performed it his way.* Of course, Tormé's interpretation was closer to the phrasing goals I have been discussing, and he was defending the natural, conversational manner of phrasing a lyric. For the singer, textual clarity was paramount, whereas Rodgers was defending the rhyme. This story has a somewhat amusing coda—Tormé won that battle, but not the war. More than twenty years later, Tormé was invited to appear on a television special celebrating Rodgers's music. But Rodgers, who had final approval, vetoed his appearance, along with those of Frank Sinatra, Peggy Lee, and Ella Fitzgerald. He wanted singers who sang his songs *precisely* the way he had written them.†

American popular singers use time in a more flexible fashion than do other singers to promote the meaning of the lyric; that is, if a lyric phrase is spaced over eight bars of music, popular singers feel free to adjust the amount of time parcelled out to any given note if this will help to clarify the meaning or intention of the lyric. They may choose to hold one note longer than written and another note shorter, "stealing" time from one to give it to another, thereby altering the syncopation of the phrase for the purpose of achieving a lyrical effect. In order to do this well, they must possess a remarkable sense of time and have a solid rhythm section in the background or else snap their fingers. This finger snapping is not done to count or "fix" the time, but to allow the singer to individualize his or her rhythmic flexibility.

Their mastery of these performance conventions enables performers like Billie Holiday and Frank Sinatra to be more successful than Luciano Pavarotti and Placido Domingo at singing Gershwin or Porter. This very success, however, is at the root of the misunderstanding and depreciation of their achievement. The conversational phrasing, the syncopated and jazzy rhythms, the lack of vocal gymnastics for their own sake, the finger snapping, and the seemingly casual manner and appearance seem to contradict our understanding of what "serious art" should be. But here's a

*Mel Tormé, It Wasn't All Velvet (New York: Zebra, 1990), pp. 164–65.
†Ibid., p. 398.

good question: Do you really sound like Sinatra when you are singing in the shower, or have you been deceived by a very sophisticated artist? A singer who successfully puts together the performance conventions of popular song might possess the power to make the listener believe that the "heart might lose its mind." Sinatra's personally crafted musical mutations have the power to forever reshape the song for his listeners. For example, in his *American Popular Song*, Alec Wilder analyzes George Gershwin's "I've Got a Crush on You" and notes that

> in fact, my consciousness of it [the song] is irrevocably influenced by Sinatra's recording. . . .
>
> I am quite certain that five notes were changed by Sinatra in his recording, one in the very attractive verse and four in the chorus. I believe they are better than the original ones. The first occurs in measure twelve of the verse. Sinatra sings an *a* as the last eighth note instead of an *f*. He then sings, in measure seven on the last eighth note, an *e* flat . . . and a *d* on the last eighth of measure eight. . . .
>
> At the last cadence of the song he sings an *f* the second eighth of the thirtieth measure and a *g* the last quarter note of that measure.
>
> So enormously powerful were Sinatra's interpretations of songs that even now, looking at the sheet music, I find it impossible to disassociate the printed notes from the memory of his singing.*

Whether referred to as The Voice, The Chairman of the Board, or Ol' Blue Eyes, Frank Sinatra is surely the greatest singer of American English. He has earned this ranking not only by mastering the performance conventions of American popular singing, but also through innovations that have extended these conventions further than anyone else's. He has given us a body of recordings of unparalled textual and emotional depth. Nowhere is this more evident than in his 1950s recordings—the Capitol years. Each of his stylistic skills is magnificently presented in this body of work.

As previously mentioned, the microphone, with its intimacy, affords the opportunity for the clearest enunciation of consonants, vowels, words, and phrases. The listener should have no difficulty in making out the text unless the singer intentionally blurs it. Sinatra, for example, may drop a word or even a letter of a word in order to make the tune sound "hipper." Some of his pronunciations are unusual enough to have become part of his personal style. "All" is sometimes drawn out, as in "ohlll or nothing at ohll."† Sinatra extends vowel and consonant sounds to emphasize certain lyric meanings or to continue his long-lined phrasings, uninterrupted by the intake of breath. His legendary breath control and its tutorial source in Tommy Dorsey's trombone playing have been noted by Sinatra and music

---

*Wilder, *American Popular Song*, pp. 146–47.

†Gene Lees, "The Sinatra Effect," in *Singers and the Song* (New York: Oxford University Press, 1987), p. 104.

critics. This control has aided his powers of enunciation while simultaneously permitting him to produce lengthy phrases. Also, Sinatra has not committed the sins of enunciation so often associated with improper microphone use. Hard-sounding consonants such as *p* are likely to cause problems known in the trade as "popping one's *p*s." Yet as Gene Lees has noted, "In the entire body of his recorded work, you will not hear Sinatra pop a consonant."[*]

The clarity of his enunciation has been appreciated even outside the world of music. There exists in the mountains of Japan a school established for the purpose of training Japanese corporate executives to speak American English. The curriculum consists of listening to Sinatra records, and for their final examination the trainees do a choral presentation of his songs. During their weeks of preparation, the mountainside is filled, at every hour, with the echoes of these students mimicking his performances.

Sinatra embraces the microphone as his ally. He moves into and away from it for his musical purposes. On his *Swingin' Session* album, he does a relaxed and loosely swinging version of "Blue Moon." After he sings the first chorus, the band begins a slightly rocking second chorus highlighted by a Plas Johnson tenor-sax solo. As the band finishes the repeat of the refrain and approaches the release (the middle part of the song, also known as the channel or bridge), Sinatra can faintly be heard as if he were in the distance or amid the band singing the first word of the release in an extended fashion—*aaa*and. By the time he completes "and," he is loud enough to take center stage and he finishes the line, which is, appropriately, "then there suddenly appeared before me." Thus does technology (the microphone) assist the artist.

The microphone was not the only significant technological development for the art of American popular singing. The long-playing record also opened up new opportunities. Sinatra's attempt to create theatrical moods was limited by the two- or three-minute duration of single recordings. The LP allowed him to expand his set pieces and use a series of songs to create an all-encompassing environment. It is not an accident that most of his greatest recordings are theme albums. While most American popular singers recorded LPs that had a set format—a ballad followed by a swinger followed by a ballad, and so on—Sinatra, especially during the Capitol years, produced entire albums that recorded the fate of *Only the Lonely* or demonstrated that *No One Cares* or showed the listener how to *Swing Easy*. The care Sinatra took to sequence the songs properly is evident in his explanation of the theme of *No One Cares*: "Why did no one care? Because there's a Cottage For Sale, that's why—so it had to be track two. That song's the saddest ever written—it depicts the complete breakup of a home."[†]

[*]Ibid., p. 107.
[†]Derek Jewell, *Frank Sinatra: A Celebration* (Boston: Little, Brown, 1985), p. 83.

Many critics have noted the connection between the theme albums and various stages of Sinatra's personal life. It is not uncommon for artists to transmute the joys and pains of personal experience into their artistic accomplishments. It may be that this ability accounts for the emotional depth of their work. Sinatra's recordings appear to be personal statements, even when they are tempered by the input of the composers, lyricists, arrangers, band members, and recording company personnel with whom he worked. This ability to control the results by impressing his feelings, style, and personality on others is a remarkable achievement. Ironically, in the 1940s one critic chastised Sinatra for sounding as if he actually believed the lyrics he sang. This critic certainly made an acute observation, but his judgment was so flawed that he failed to recognize a significant evolution in American popular singing and the arrival of its greatest artist.

The sixteen concept albums that Sinatra recorded in the 1950s include ones that express joie de vivre and others so sad they could be described as "suicide music." Were these the best twentieth-century song cycles? Had Sinatra, by bringing together and then sequencing certain great American songs, created this century's *Winterreise?**

Robin Douglas-Home describes a Sinatra recording session at which, initially, he could see but not hear the singer:

> I saw complete and utter involvement with the song he was singing—involvement so close that one might feel he was in the throes of composing both tune and lyrics as he went along. . . . He was putting so much into that song, giving off so much of himself that it drained my own energy just to watch him—without hearing a note he was singing; left me so limp that I felt I had actually been living through some serious emotional crisis.†

And Glenn Gould notes that

> a well-ordered career in pop music should be conceived like the dramatis personae of soap-opera—dipping into "The Secret Storm" once every semester should tell you all you really need to know about how things are working out for Amy Ames. And similarly, the title, tempo, and tonal range of a performer's hits should observe a certain bibliographic progression. (You thought Frankie had other reasons for "It's been a very good year"?)‡

The attentive listener increasingly becomes aware that Sinatra will use whatever vocal device available and/or necessary to convey the text and

---

*An art-song cycle composed by Franz Schubert in 1827, the *Winterreise* is based on the poetry of Wilhelm Muller. It represents the explication of a single, basic mood. The twenty-four lieder deal with a young man's love-sick despair.

†Quoted in Jewell, *Frank Sinatra*, p. 83.

‡Glenn Gould, "The Search for Petula Clark," in *The Glenn Gould Reader*, ed. Tim Page (New York: Knopf, 1985), p. 303.

emotional message of the lyric to his audience. He will add, delete, or abbreviate words and interject "hipsterisms"; alter the melody, adjust the cadence, slur from one note to the next (the sexual feeling enhanced by this move may have caused a swoon or two), or extend particular consonants and vowels; rearrange the sections of a tune (Sinatra begins "Angel Eyes" with the release, which immediately allows him to establish the barroom setting of the song); bite off a line, use growls or other guttural sounds, and intentionally strain his voice to convey a specific emotional state (in recent years he has used the decline of his voice as a force or strength for conveying fragility, vulnerability, and tenderness in a lyric); create cadenzas (an improvised or written episode preceding the close of a song); impose a de facto onomatopoeia on a word or an entire phrase; and steal time from one note or phrase and give the stolen time to another note or phrase. Classical musicians use such terms as *glissando, tempo rubato,* and *mordent* to describe many of these practices; they can all be found in Sinatra's singing. But the listener must pay attention because Sinatra makes it seem casual and effortless and never calls attention to the techniques being employed. All he does sounds natural and inevitable, as if it were being composed on the spot. He appears to be artless, and yet his creative ingenuity in finding ways to broaden and transform the emotional impact of what some might consider to be the musically narrow confines of a popular song may well approach genius. As with the best German art-song singers (Dietrich Fischer-Dieskau comes to mind), Sinatra has taken the American song, abandoned its polite presentation, and used it to plumb the very soul of both his and the listener's life experiences.

One interesting technique employed by Sinatra might be referred to as de facto onomatopoeia. Onomatopoeia is a rhetorical device that involves the use of words that derive their meaning from the sound they mimic (such as "boom," "click," "plop," "crunch"). Sinatra employs de facto onomatopoeia by pronouncing words in a certain fashion or by altering melody, rhythm, and words to achieve the aforementioned effect. The simplest use of this device is his one-word exaggerations or emphases. For example, the word "bounce" appears in several songs closely associated with Sinatra. He will exaggerate the word in a very percussive fashion to emphasize its sound–meaning relationship. Listen to his version of "You Make Me Feel So Young" or better yet his "Same Old Song and Dance." The latter tune, to my ears, is the angriest-sounding recording of Sinatra's career. Strangely, it is an up-tempo, swinging tune that still falls into the used-and-rejected lover category of songs. When Sinatra sings "turns out you BOUNCED me like a ball," I can almost feel the rapid vibrations of his head hitting the sidewalk or wall.

In 1959, Ira Gershwin wrote new lyrics for Sinatra's recording of Vernon Duke's melody to "I Can't Get Started" (*No One Cares*). Sinatra turns the release into an onomatopoetic treat:

Oh, tell me why
Am I no kickK to you—
    I,
Who'd always sstick to you,
    Flyyy—
Through thin and tHick to you?

Sinatra's skills are even more evident in his recording of "Stars Fell on Alabama" (*A Swingin' Affair*). On this recording, he employs virtually all the creative devices he has invented and mastered in the interest of enhancing the musical, expressive, and textual clarity of a song. Much of his performance can be described as lilting. The song has a lovely romantic refrain, which he floats over by extending words, bending notes, and slurring from one note to another, but this appears to be part of a setup. He sets you up for an unexpected, percussive approach to one line: "My heart beats like a hammer." This line is sung on two occasions—one very different from the other, but each exemplifying some form of onomatopieia. The first approach to this line maintains a lilting tone until the last word, "hammer." Sinatra bites off the second syllable in such fashion as to call to mind the nail being driven into the hole. The emphasis of the line is on "hammer." The second rendering of this line emphasizes the pounding of the beating heart. Sinatra inserts the word "just," changing the lyric to "my heart beats just like a hammer." He then alters the melody so that the four words "heart beats just like" are sung on the same note. He then alters the cadence by giving each of these four notes (including the inserted "just") the same time value; he does this by stealing time from "hammer" and giving it to the inserted "just" and then going straight from "hammer" to "arms wound around you tight," while dropping the "my" that preceded "arms." The four words are then attacked in a percussive fashion, thereby creating a beating heart cadence throughout the line: "My *heart beats just like* a hammer." Whew! It sounds so easy when he sings it, and it sounds so right.

I have attempted to make a case for Frank Sinatra's mastery of American popular singing and to illustrate how he has used a variety of devices to enhance the textual clarity of American song lyrics. The art of singing, of necessity, raises the question of the relationship of music to language. Most music is performed without the necessity of adjusting or subordinating the music to the words. Yet singing must meet this issue head on. A number of solutions or adjustments are possible. Does the music control the words or vice versa? In the development of European opera, different periods have produced different solutions. The balance between the recitative and the melodic passages (the ones we whistle while leaving the theater) vary among operas. In some instances, singers might be judged by rhetorical (or acting) standards and in other instances by melodic criteria.

(Compare early Italian opera, later Italian opera, and Wagner.) In American popular singing, a similar distinction can be drawn between the jazz-inflected but rhetorical style of Billie Holiday and Frank Sinatra and the instrumental style of jazz singing exemplified by Betty Carter and Sarah Vaughan.

Frank Sinatra is the best rhetorical vocalist to come out of the American popular singing tradition. Earlier, the term "polite" was used to describe a manner of presentation that Sinatra abandoned. I believe that this decision accounts for much of his greatness. Sinatra's immediate predecessor as the Great American Singer was Bing Crosby—a fine singer but exceedingly polite. He was a "crooner." His renditions never intimated danger; they were always tuneful and pleasant. Yet, by the same token, his emotional range was constricted. His public persona matched his music; no one ever saw a dangerous side of Crosby. In some ways, this made him a light weight.

The same cannot be said of Sinatra. His public persona has, for many years, exuded danger. He has been described by many observers as honest, generous, vulnerable, tender, loyal, hostile, surly, and . . . dangerous. And these terms also describe his vocal qualities. The emotional range of his work has the manic quality of someone who can confidently advise you to "sound your A the day you're born" and then sink so low as to give meaning to Nietzsche's dictum that the "thought of suicide gets us through many a bad night." Opera singer Robert Merrill puts it this way:

> Singers want to develop a style. They work at it, strive for it, sometimes they contrive it. Sinatra *instinctively* had a style. I mean, he was born with it. And it grew as he matured. Serious musicians regard him as an artist, a fine artist, a great American interpreter of our music. The beauty of Frank is that he is *word*-conscious and story-conscious and that's why he's so great. He's a storyteller. He's sensitive—so automatically he's sensitive to his words, to the story they tell. What you are comes out in your music.*

This essay will not convert Sinatraphobes into Sinatraphiles. I hope that I make a substantial case in behalf of American popular singing in general and "The Master" in particular. It is difficult to translate into words one's thoughts and feelings concerning music. There are certainly limitations in any such attempt. Therefore the reader and listener would be best served by following this advice: seal yourself in a dark room, kick your shoes off, baby, and listen, dammit, listen!

---

*Quoted in Nancy Sinatra, *Frank Sinatra: My Father* (New York: Pocket Books, 1986), pp. xvi–xvii.

III

Swingin' Toward Retirement

★ ★ ★

1 9 6 1 – 1 9 7 3

FROM THE TIME he left Dorsey, Sinatra became increasingly eager to gain control over his own fortunes. His bad experiences with Columbia Records and its quirky A&R man, Mitch Miller, led to Sinatra's release from the label and eventually to his joining Capitol Records. There would be no more novelty–gag songs like "Mama Will Bark" for Sinatra. If his recordings turned out to be in questionable taste, it would be the result of his own lapses. Capitol allowed him the creative and artistic leeway to succeed, and the product he turned out was, by virtually all accounts, superior.

In 1961, Sinatra decided to extend still further the creative freedom and artistic control he had enjoyed throughout most of the 1950s. Arnold Shaw reports that in December 1960, Sinatra was walking past the Capitol Building in Los Angeles when he turned to a record executive who was accompanying him and said, "I helped build that. Now, let's build one of my own."* By the next year, Reprise Records was in business.

Sinatra's work with his own label, while rarely as successful musically as his work with Capitol, helped him develop yet another singing style and extended further the variety of accompaniments and musical genres that he employed. His first album, *Ring-a-Ding-Ding* (the title is one of the many hipsterisms the singer has coined over the years), arranged by Johnny Mandel, was a jazz-flavored, swinging affair. It made a sensational debut, one critic describing it as "hairy-chested singing." For his following albums, Sinatra sought out some of the giants of the music industry. While he continued using Billy May, Nelson Riddle, and Gordon Jenkins for their tried-and-true arranging and conducting, he also recorded with Don Costa, Neal Hefti, Sy Oliver (a Dorsey arranger who worked on Sinatra's beautiful Dorsey-tribute album), and most notably Quincy Jones, who was soon to become a sensation in the entertainment business. Most of the big-

*Quoted in Arnold Shaw, *Sinatra: Twentieth-Century Romantic* (New York: Holt, Rinehart and Winston, 1968), p. 283.

band arrangements he did at this time were more jazz-oriented than those of the earlier recordings.

Moreover, Sinatra recorded three albums with Count Basie and his band and one with the Duke Ellington Orchestra. He also did a bossa-nova album arranged by Claus Ogerman and accompanied on guitar and voice by composer Antonio Carlos Jobim. It is interesting to note that while all these albums are good, none is viewed as belonging in the pantheon of the singer's best. Why? Was Sinatra intimidated by the company? Not likely. Was there not enough preparation? Did the attempt to bring together such major artists fail to allow each the artistic freedom and control he needed?

Curiously, the best piece of this period is also the most spontaneous (and, therefore, risky): *Sinatra–Basie Live at the Sands*. This live album presents an excellent view of the brash and confident Sinatra of the 1960s. The music and his singing swing harder than ever (as in "Fly Me to the Moon" or "You Make Me Feel So Young"), and the ballad singing is sensitive and intimate (as in "Don't Worry 'Bout Me"). The worst part of the album is the long and boring monologue, but the music is masterful, leaving no doubt about why he was regarded as the best in the business.

In a less muscular vein, Sinatra at age fifty recorded *September of My Years,* a collection of songs arranged by Jenkins about a man looking back on his life. The album, which was introduced via a television special, was tailor-made for a public that had come to regard Sinatra's recordings as a substitute for written autobiography. And the 1969 release of "My Way" brought an even more dramatic public response from an auteur-oriented audience. In live performances, Sinatra has introduced the song as the "national anthem," adding, "but you needn't rise."

In this period, too, Sinatra attempted to stay "relevant" to the changing tides of popular music. His successful album *Strangers in the Night* was subtitled *The Popular Sinatra Sings for Moderns.* He recorded with his daughter, Nancy, who had a 1960s style, and also ventured into country and folk songs. There was nothing earth shaking in any of this—just competent and professional work, and always Sinatra.

Of course, the 1960s was also the period of the "clan," the "rat pack," or, in Nancy Sinatra's words, the "Summit"—a group of show-business pals who clowned, entertained, worked Las Vegas, and made movies together. Along with Sinatra, Dean Martin, Sammy Davis, Jr., Peter Lawford, Joey Bishop, and others made up this rowdy crew. Films such as *Ocean's 11, Sergeants 3, 4 for Texas,* and *Robin and the Seven Hoods* all have the look and feel of the boys having a good workout together. And *Robin and the Seven Hoods* also produced "My Kind of Town," which would become one of Sinatra's concert fixtures. During the early 1960s, this gang was also involved in presidential politics. Sinatra re-recorded "High Hopes," the hit from his 1959 Frank Capra–directed film *A Hole in the Head,* with new lyrics that linked high national hopes to the election of John Kennedy. Sinatra's political attachments—along with his personal life and loves and his high-living, swinging image—dominated the public view in the early part of the decade.

But even while Sinatra reinforced his image as the undisputed champ of the Las Vegas swingers, he still held sway among the singers and jazz artists for whom Las Vegas was anathema. He went on world tours, performing in England, France, Italy, Japan, and Australia. In the United States, his venues ranged from Carnegie Hall, the United Nations, and Madison Square Garden in New York to the Newport Jazz Festival, the 500 Club in Atlantic City, and the University of Southern California. He reigned as America's greatest singer–performer, a summit unto himself.

And then from this lofty peak, Frank Sinatra, at the age of fifty-five, announced his imminent retirement in March 1971 and made good by giving a final benefit performance at the Los Angeles Music Center in June. His formal announcement offered the following explanation:

> For over three decades I have had the great and good fortune to enjoy a rich, rewarding and deeply satisfying career as an entertainer and public figure. It has been a fruitful, busy, uptight, loose, sometimes boisterous, occasionally sad, but always exciting three decades. There has been at the same time little room or opportunity for reflection, reading, self-examination, and that need which every thinking man has for a fallow period, a long pause in which to seek a better understanding of changes occurring in the world. This seems a proper time to take that breather, and I am fortunate enough to be able to do so. I look forward to enjoying more time with my family and my dear friends, to writing a bit—perhaps even to teaching. Thank you.

His final musical words were familiar, but they had a new and poignant meaning. "'Scuse me while I disappear," he sang, and a stunned world watched as he did just that—for a while.

The articles in this section concern the Sinatra of the mid-1960s—at the height of his career, at the height of his form, brash, potent, formidable, and ever so good. The first is a piece that appeared in *Newsweek* in 1965 a few months before his fiftieth birthday. He may have been, as the liner notes to his latest album at the time would have it, in the "September of his years," but his intensive work as a singer, an actor, and a businessman were anything but sedately autumnal. Gay Talese, author of the bestselling *Honor Thy Father* and *Unto the Sons*, attempted to interview Sinatra for *Esquire* in the mid-1960s. Although he never got the interview, he did get to see the Sinatra persona at work. His article offers a more distant, but probably more insightful and incisive, view of the man, his power, and his temperament. Finally, Roy Newquist, onetime literary critic for the *New York Post* and author of two volumes of literary interviews titled *Counterpoint,* finds Sinatra still hard at work and more influential than ever. Working by day on the film *The Lady in Cement* and appearing in concerts nightly at the Fountainebleau Hotel in Miami Beach, Sinatra projected an image of tireless devotion to his work while still having a ball, living the swinging lifestyle well into his fifties—as Newquist chronicles in his 1968 piece for *McCall's.*

Sinatra: Where the Action Is
1965

When, in the fiftieth year of his mortal tumult, Frank Sinatra sings, speaks, jokes, suggests, requests or commands, his adult contemporaries behave like Nipper, the cock-eared dog on the old RCA Victor label. They listen— out of love, fear, devotion or habit—to their master's voice.

The man–boy who serenaded gawky girls, the ardent underdog of another day, has grown up, and up. He is not merely a man today, but The Man, The Leader, The King, The Chairman of the Board. ("I don't know how seriously he takes phrases like that," says a leading disk jockey, "but sometimes I shudder.") On land he fills whole stadiums with admirers. At sea he is surrounded by more vessels and aircraft than the Seventh Fleet's flagship. In the air he moves by private jet, having invited friends to "Come Fly with Me," asked fate to "Fly Me to the Moon," then formed an airline to be sure of reservations. Singer, actor, father, magnate and international playboy, Sinatra goes where the action is. And if perchance it isn't, it is after he gets there.

MUSICAL CIRCUS

A Broadway musical becomes a circus when Sinatra arrives with his lady in tow and the press in pursuit. He helicopters, for "security reasons," to a singing gig at the Newport Jazz Festival. He grosses $224,000 in three nights at the Forest Hills (New York) Music Festival, and has a standing offer from Madison Square Garden: $100,000 for any night he wants to come and sing. Vice President Humphrey asks Sinatra to see him at the Waldorf, CBS television crews get his face on film for a Sinatra documentary to be broadcast in November, NBC lawyers get his signature on paper for a Sinatra spectacular to be televised the same month. He is a man possessed of as much charisma as anyone on public view. He is the senior swinger of the land.

For many, his swings are too violent. The dissenters are repelled by his personal style (American presidents run into this problem too), by the strident sounds surrounding him, by his braggadocio air, by all the brassy trappings of material success and his willingness to outrage convention. In the 1930s, Cole Porter went yachting on the placid Rhine and turned out songs. Sinatra, through whom Porter, Lorenz Hart and many other popular classicists continue to live, goes down to the sea in chaperones, relaxes while the vacation escalates into an escapade marred by a fatal accident, and turns out headlines. Will he? Won't he? Are they already? An anxious public awaits, unavailingly, some sign or proclamation, while the amatory bookies of the land contend, on the strength of no knowledge and less information, that he won't.

His whole life is a spectacular and must be reviewed as such. One day last week, a day as close to normal as any in Sinatra's chockablock calendar, he left his Palm Springs home early in the morning, which begins about noon for him, took Ringo, his ailing Australian sheep dog, to the vet, boarded his six-passenger white and orange Lear Jet and emerged, seventeen minutes older, at Burbank airport. From there he drove his black Dual Ghia to Sinatra Enterprises, a semi-sumptuous bungalow on the Warner Bros. lot, and settled down to work.

There was lunch to be lunched with a visitor. There were songs to be learned and rehearsed with composer Jimmy Van Heusen, a meeting across town at Twentieth Century–Fox and an evening recording session for his Reprise Records at a studio on Sunset Boulevard. And Sinatra was on vacation.

In a sitting room outside his office stands a 1944 bust by the late Jo Davidson, who thought Sinatra looked like young Abe Lincoln and made him look like young Frank Sinatra: thin, tense, intense. The office itself is large but hardly cavernous by Hollywood standards: draperies and cushions of orange, Sinatra's favorite color; orange tablecloth on a table in the middle of the room; beige carpet; a few modish landscapes on the walls; books and non-books in bookshelves; a high-fidelity everything nestling in its recessed cabinet; inscribed photos of the last four Democratic presidents; pictures of his daughter Nancy, of U Thant and of his late friend and agent, Bert Allenberg, and a clown picture overlooking a sub-megalomaniacal desk and black-leather chair in the corner.

NO CHEESECAKE

He came into his office like a runaway locomotive hitting a barricade at the end of the line. There was a telephone call awaiting him from daughter Nancy. She was on her way to the dentist, and her father, gently but urgently, asked her not to drive if the dentist gave her an anesthetic. He riffled through some memoranda on his desk, then sat down to lunch— prosciutto and melon, small veal cutlets, good Chianti and cheesecake, which he passed up—and to an interview with *Newsweek*'s movie editor, Joseph Morgenstern.

Sinatra the movie magnate, in a dark brown suit, brown and black silk tie and white shirt with button-down collar, was unconcerned with playing the hackneyed Hollywood role of the suave, cultivated studio executive. He still has Hoboken on his tongue. He talks fast and thinks faster, with plenty of profanity at times and graceful elaboration at other times. He knows he is an original and exults in it.

"When the load gets a little heavy and I get a quiet moment," he said, "I begin to think that it was fun to be an actor or a singer and just worry about where I'm working tomorrow night and what do I wear. But that's very rare. I'm delighted with all the workings of an organization such as ours, little as it is. It's busy. Everybody's busy and I like it. Work is my hobby, really. I enjoy it."

GUEST SHOT

Among his chores he was considering the feasibility of a quick USO trip to Vietnam. "I gotta do the Hollywood Palace on the morning of the ninth, then I do Sammy's guest appearance with him on the evening of the ninth. Now I could be back here the next morning, the tenth, and get out of here the afternoon of the tenth. How long's it take to get there? Twenty-four hours?" In addition to his performing chores, his business interests include:

- Artanis (Sinatra spelled the Serutan way) Productions, the "little organization" in which Warner Bros. has the minority holding, Sinatra the majority. Artanis produced *None but the Brave*, which Sinatra directed ("I'd love to direct again") and *Marriage on the Rocks*, with a new production in preparation.
- Park Lake Enterprises, a production company outside Warner's bailiwick that has made *4 for Texas, Robin and the Seven Hoods* and the phenomenally successful *Von Ryan's Express*.
- Cal Jet Airway, a small charter outfit with one Lear, one five-place Alouette helicopter, one three-place Morane-Sanbrier and another $600,000 Lear on order. Some recent customers: United Artists, Mirisch Brothers and Paramount.

- Reprise Records, a firm in which Sinatra has a one-third interest and Warner's two-thirds.
- Titanium Metal Forming Co., a firm that makes metal parts for aircraft and missile builders.

He also has extensive acreage in Arizona and California's Marin County, and still owns, but does not operate, Cal-Neva Lodge at Lake Tahoe, an establishment assessed at $4 million. Sinatra's license to operate a gambling casino in Nevada was lifted in 1963 after he had allowed Sam Giancana, a convicted criminal, on the premises, but Sinatra is allowed to retain and lease the hotel. He may, in the future, reapply for a license to operate it. Sources close to the Nevada Gaming Commission say the Giancana incident provided the technical excuse to lift the license, but that Sinatra's profanity during a telephone call with Edward A. Olsen, chairman of the State Gaming Control Board, had a lot to do with the decision to lift it.

One minor but proud Sinatra holding: an acre of ground in Tennessee, gift of the Jack Daniels distillery in return for Sinatra's espousal of the sourmash cause.

Sinatra, therefore, is not only a busy man but a wealthy one. Educated estimates put his annual gross income at $3 million or $4 million. He still gets some $60,000 a year in royalties from Columbia Records, though he hasn't recorded for them in more than a decade. Between 1953 and 1962 he recorded at least $25 million worth (in gross receipts) for Capitol, and his Reprise releases, begun in 1961, have already sold $14.4 million in albums and $1.5 million in singles. If all his records were put in a pile and Sinatra stood on top, he would be right where he is today. His contract for *Von Ryan's Express* called for $250,000 and 15 percent of the gross—quite a leap from his $8,000 salary in 1953 for *From Here to Eternity* and the $150 advance against royalties he got from Capitol in the same year.

PARKING-METER CHANGE

Estimates of Sinatra's personal fortune are less impressive. They come to around $6 million or $7 million, with $13 million or $14 million as the total worth of Sinatra Enterprises. This assures him parking-meter change, but it is a modest bank account compared with those of Texans who dig holes in the ground. Why is this? "He lives like royalty," says a friend, producer William Goetz.

For openers, he has three homes: a rented five-room apartment on Manhattan's East River Drive; a ten-room house in Beverly Hills rented from Buddy Adler's widow, Anita Louise; and a home of his very own, contemporary, beige, in Wonder Palms Road, Palm Springs. This caravansary boasts a salt-water swimming pool, moved eighty feet early this summer when extensions of the house threatened to engulf it. While the main house was built for a bachelor and has only three bedrooms—and, among other conveniences, a $100,000 kitchen—the Wonder Palms digs also include, behind sheltering oleanders, a pair of round five-room guest houses. When Sinatra visits Las Vegas to sing, play, drink, shoot the breeze and blow off steam with the boys and girls—his fugues there are less frequent and frenzied than they used to be—he inhabits the Sands Hotel's Presidential Suite.

FEMININE ASSOCIATIONS

Only rarely is Sinatra alone. He seems to get on with girls. He has been married twice, to the former Nancy Barbato, and to Ava Gardner. He has also been seen with, among others, Lana Turner, Marilyn Maxwell, Gloria Vanderbilt, Kim Novak, Lauren Bacall, Shirley MacLaine, Lady Adelle Beatty, Juliet Prowse, Dorothy Provine, Jill St. John and his current companion, nineteen-year-old Mia Farrow. Sinatra guards the privacy of his feminine associations ferociously, and any intimate reports on them come from liars, fools or astigmatic Peeping Toms.

Apart from the women in his life, he travels with a sizable retinue of friends, employees, hangers-on and hangers on the hangers-on. Sinatra's friends have been categorized by the newspapers into packs, clans and sub-clans, but they categorize themselves by the simple fact of knowing him. To a man, and indeed to a woman, they speak publicly in almost identical terms of his loyalty and generosity. "If he were Jewish," theorized an Atlantic City nightclub operator, "he'd be Moses."

For men like publican Jilly Rizzo, "crowd disperser" Ed Pucci, major domo Henri Giné and 380-pound car salesman Frankie Shore, knowing Sinatra is a full-time career. These Falstaffs and Fixits, some of whom are far more intelligent than their roughhewn exteriors would indicate, some of whom are not, are used by Sinatra, but they are paid generously for their charms and services. Undoubtedly their leader is sometimes a prisoner of his own loyalty, since the retinue is expensive and the tenure long.

Even for his show-biz friends, though, Sinatra remains deep within himself. They feel constrained to keep the talk light. "I don't discuss his girl with Frank or who he's going to marry," says Dean Martin. "All I discuss are movies, TV, golf and drinking." Joey Bishop says "we substitute wit for logic" with Sinatra. Sammy Davis, acknowledging the "aura of mystery about him," sees it as a professional virtue: "Only two guys are left who are not the boy next door—Cary Grant and Frank Sinatra."

There is every reason to think Sinatra was never the boy next door, not even to the other boys next door in the Hoboken of his youth. He was set apart, first by his family's ability to provide well for him in a fairly uncom-

fortable minority neighborhood, and then by his own relentless deter-
mination to make it in the world. ("The set of qualities that seems to
distinguish Italian-Americans," write sociologists Moynihan and Glazer in
Beyond the Melting Pot, "includes individuality, temperament and ambition . . . perhaps the ideal is the entertainer—to give him a name, Frank
Sinatra—who is an international celebrity, but still the big-hearted, generous, unchanged boy from the block.")

ENVIED BY ALL

In present-day Hollywood, where virile, kinetic, magnetic, splenetic stars
like Sinatra are in desperately short supply, this unchanged boy from the
block is feared by many, respected by many and envied by all. "He is what
we would all like to be," says Alfred Hart, president of the City National
Bank and overseer of Sinatra's own banking matters.

Sinatra's current popularity is a worldwide phenomenon. The audience
to which he appeals, from kids of college age to solid citizens in their forties
and fifties, has more money in its pockets than the kids who go squealing
after Animals and Beatles. (One Beatle fan, fourteen, says of Sinatra: "He
was OK then. He was for that generation. The Beatles are for ours."
Another says: "Ich.")

His old records are worth $33 each in the Soviet Union. His new films
sell out theaters in Rio, and his status in Japan is "almost like a god,"
according to a Tokyo editor. Sinatra Center, a two-story building, stands in
the middle of Nazareth, near Mary's Well, and Israeli children, when they
want to tell someone where they are going, say, "I am going to Frank
Sinatra." He is no longer merely a singer, an actor or a cabaret entertainer.
What is he, then?

"I think it's all the same job, it's so correlated," he says. "Everything
depends on the other." Records, picture popularity, personal appearances
all reinforce the other, just as they refused to do between the late 1940s and
1953, when a suddenly successful nightclub engagement at the now-
vanished Riviera in Fort Lee, New Jersey, and the Oscar-winning role of
Maggio in *From Here to Eternity* put a sudden end to his professional decline, or, as his friends style it, recession.

HONOR

Sinatra the actor likes to shoot fast and to try to get it on the first take. Fred
Zinnemann, who directed him in *From Here to Eternity*, admiringly recalls
Sinatra as "a total rebel" who relied "completely on his own spontaneity
rather than careful rehearsing." A clue to Sinatra's view of his own acting
image—and, perhaps, his own real-life image as well—is provided by his
comment on Humphrey Bogart: "There'll never be another performer like
Bogey was." His characters "had a lot of fun in them. They had cynicism,

and they had honesty, and he was a seedy character but he had honor all the time."

Sinatra's one directorial effort, *None but the Brave*, was not a success, but he is eager to tackle directing again. "The toughest thing I had to do on the first day of shooting was to say 'print,'" he recalls. "It took me ten minutes, because I liked the take but I figured the minute I say 'print' I'm on the record . . . the race is off, it's gone, the horses are running around."

Sinatra the singer is as meticulous as a fine watchmaker. "Somewhere in my subconscious there's the constant alarm that rings, telling me what we're putting on that tape might be around for a lotta, lotta years. Maybe long after we're dead and gone somebody'll put a record on and say 'Jeez, he could've done better than that.'" In contrast to films, Sinatra feels, "records are so much more available."

THE ROOTER

When he is not performing, Sinatra sublimates some of his energies into politics, an arena in which most entertainers fear to cavort. "I like rooting for people who run for office," he says. "I make what contributions I can, whether it's financial contributions to the man's campaign fund or if I can sing a song, but I think its important." Most of Sinatra's political activities are in aid of Democratic causes. One room of his Palm Springs house is filled with Kennedy memorabilia, and people who know him say his deep admiration for the late president was not affected by the administration's decision, for reasons of expediency or delicacy, to put an end to publicity linking Sinatra and his friends with the White House. His various defenses of civil-rights causes and his friendship with Davis have hurt him commercially in the South, while his contributions to Israeli charities have gotten him, his records and movies banned in the Arab countries.

THROUGH THE RANKS

Against these good works, there is the old talk of Sinatra's evil companions, notably criminals. Anyone coming up through the ranks of the music and cabaret world would be hard put to avoid criminals, but there is some specific, demonstrable evidence in Sinatra's case, witness the Giancana matter. Of course, no wrongdoing has been proved, even though entertainers of Sinatra's rank, whose every engagement is a benefit for the Bureau of Internal Revenue, are often under government scrutiny. There is some pseudo-psychiatric speculation that Sinatra needs the occasional company of dubious characters because he was never as tough a youth as his press agentry once implied. It may be that he simply enjoys it. His own attitude: "In answering, it looks like a defense. If there were any criminal associations I wouldn't be where I am today."

Where is that? Today people speak of the "new" Sinatra. Sometimes they mean the newly, unprecedentedly popular Sinatra. Sometimes they mean a man who, in some Machiavellian way, has set about to change his "image." Sometimes they mean a man who, in *The September of My Years,* as his latest album title puts it, has shown new signs of growth, has widened his circle of friends to include older and more sophisticated executives of the movie industry, bankers and prominent politicians, the Sinatra who last year switched tailors from the stylish but jazzy Sy Devore to the stylishly sedate Carroll and Co.

GROOMING

Rumor has had it for some time that Sinatra, now Jack Warner's "special assistant," is being groomed to take over the studio. He concedes that he has heard such stories, but says only that the Warner lot, with board of directors and production staff under one roof in Burbank, is the only place he would choose if the time to run a studio should come. For the rest of the movie industry, turbulently split between New York front offices and California studios, Sinatra says: "Most of those men on the boards of directors have as much creative ability to make a movie as I have to build a space capsule."

Where can he go from here? "Where the hell can he go?" asks Joey Bishop. "He knows the production end of the movie buisness and the business end of the record business. I mean, where can he go from here?" Dean Martin thinks Sinatra is tiring of acting in movies and headed toward concentrated production activites. But "he loves singing too much to tire of it. He always sings, he always has, and he always will."

Indeed, it is through his records that the essence of Sinatra's appeal comes clear. His former shrine, the Paramount Theater, is closed now, probably for good. The big bronze doors are tarnished, the glass in them is coated with dust and grease. On one of the side walls is scrawled "The Animals Are Loved Only By Girls Namely Josephine." But the generation that first squealed at The Voice, that necked to the "mmmmmmmm's" of "Paradise," that changed its steel needles after eight plays or sharpened its cactus needles after two, is still around and strongly kicking.

It is the first generation Sinatra sang to, the people from whom he learned that all people, from cradle to grave, love to be sung to. They first heard him when he sang, adenoidally, with Dorsey; when, in the last falsetto note of "The Song Is You," he seemed oddly and engagingly close to internal explosion. Then they heard a new Sinatra, free of the insistent big-band beat, sing simple ballads simply, eloquently.

> The smile of Turner and the scent of roses,
> The waiters whistling as the last bar closes . . .

Now all is changed. The soft uncertainties have left his voice, though sex has not. It has a metallic quality: spring steel. At its best it is commanding, at its worst it is tinny, as if he were wearing a straight mute. He uses short, adroitly clipped phrases now, swinging with the same authority a cop swings his billy. The high notes seem to give him pain, but even that becomes a virtue and sounds like passion. New listeners love it, and the first generation, upon hearing him now, mourns the loss of his innocence and the loss of its own innocence, which it never had any more than Sinatra had. The bedroom voice is now the playroom voice, but that first generation, the one that no longer sips sodas for fear of calories, has plenty of playrooms and still want to play.

"You get the feeling," says William B. Williams, the New York disk jockey (who dubbed Sinatra "chairman of the board") "that he is living life to the hilt, getting all there is to get from every moment. In 'Come Fly with Me' you say 'Boy, here's a guy who's got it made and he knows, as we know, that it's all transitory so he's going to grab it while he can.'"

SWELLING FIDDLES

All Sinatra's authority derives, finally, from music, and it was on abundant display at his latest recording session in Hollywood one night last week. He had learned the tunes, both from the forthcoming Broadway musical *Skyscraper*, only that afternoon, but already he possessed them. The studio, filled with a fifty-piece orchestra and sixty spectators, fell silent when he came in.

"Saxophones in bar nineteen—can you get to the diminuendo a little sooner?" he asked during rehearsal. "Crazy." After one take: "Cool the first part. Letter A should be nice and light. OK, now, once more right away." Then, in his three-walled booth, Sinatra sang, absorbed by the music and himself. The swelling fiddles swung his head up and to the side, the drums turned his torso, the brass went to his shoulders. He and the young conductor, Torrie Zito ("The Italians are taking over the world," Sinatra had said to him earlier), conducted each other with outstretched arms, eyes bolted to eyes. In the control booth, composer Van Heusen was grinning like a little boy. Soon the playback came and the singer, sitting on the podium, listened to himself sing:

"Every . . . body . . . has the right to be wrong . . . at least ONCE!"

Sinatra smiled and the audience applauded. It had to.

Frank Sinatra Has a Cold
Gay Talese ★ 1966

Frank Sinatra, holding a glass of bourbon in one hand and a cigarette in the other, stood in a dark corner of the bar between two attractive but fading blondes who sat waiting for him to say something. But he said nothing; he had been silent during much of the evening, except now in this private club in Beverly Hills he seemed even more distant, staring out through the smoke and semidarkness into a large room beyond the bar where dozens of young couples sat huddled around small tables or twisted in the center of the floor to the clamorous clang of folk-rock music blaring from the stereo. The two blondes knew, as did Sinatra's four male friends who stood nearby, that it was a bad idea to force conversation upon him when he was in this mood of sullen silence, a mood that had hardly been uncommon during this first week of November, a month before his fiftieth birthday.

Sinatra had been working in a film that he now disliked, could not wait to finish; he was tired of all the publicity attached to his dating the twenty-year-old Mia Farrow, who was not in sight tonight; he was angry that a CBS television documentary of his life, to be shown in two weeks, was reportedly prying into his privacy, even speculating on his possible friendship with Mafia leaders; he was worried about his starring role in an hour-long NBC show entitled *Sinatra—A Man and His Music*, which would require that he sing eighteen songs with a voice that at this particular moment, just a few nights before the taping was to begin, was weak and sore and uncertain. Sinatra was ill. He was the victim of an ailment so common that most people would consider it trivial. But when it gets to Sinatra it can plunge him into a state of anguish, deep depression, panic, even rage. Frank Sinatra had a cold.

Sinatra with a cold is Picasso without paint, Ferrari without fuel—only worse. For the common cold robs Sinatra of that uninsurable jewel, his voice, cutting into the core of his confidence, and it affects not only his own psyche but also seems to cause a kind of psychosomatic nasal drip within dozens of people who work for him, drink with him, love him, depend on him for their own welfare and stability. A Sinatra with a cold can, in a small way, send vibrations through the entertainment industry and beyond as surely as a president of the United States, suddenly sick, can shake the national economy.

For Frank Sinatra was now involved with many things involving many people—his own film company, his record company, his private airline, his missile-parts firm, his real-estate holdings across the nation, his personal staff of seventy-five—which are only a portion of the power he is and has come to represent. He seemed now to be also the embodiment of the fully emancipated male, perhaps the only one in America, the man who can do anything he wants, *anything*, can do it because he has the money, the energy, and no apparent guilt. In an age when the very young seem to be taking over, protesting and picketing and demanding change, Frank Sinatra survives as a national phenomenon, one of the few prewar products to withstand the test of time. He is the champ who made the big comeback, the man who had everything, lost it, then got it back, letting nothing stand in his way, doing what few men can do: he uprooted his life, left his family, broke with everything that was familiar, learning in the process that one way to hold a woman is not to hold her. Now he has the affection of Nancy and Ava and Mia, the fine female produce of three generations, and still has the adoration of his children, the freedom of a bachelor, he does not feel old, he makes old men feel young, makes them think that if Frank Sinatra can do it, it can be done; not that *they* could do it, but it is still nice for other men to know, at fifty, that it can be done.

But now, standing at this bar in Beverly Hills, Sinatra had a cold, and he continued to drink quietly and he seemed miles away in his private world, not even reacting when suddenly the stereo in the other room switched to a Sinatra song, "In the Wee Small Hours of the Morning."

It is a lovely ballad that he first recorded ten years ago, and it now inspired many young couples who had been sitting, tired of twisting, to get up and move slowly around the dance floor, holding one another very close. Sinatra's intonation, precisely clipped, yet full and flowing, gave a deeper meaning to the simple lyrics—"In the wee small hours of the morning/while the whole wide world is fast asleep/you lie awake, and think about the girl . . ."*—it was, like so many of his classics, a song that evoked loneliness and sensuality, and when blended with the dim light and the alcohol and nicotine and late-night needs, it became a kind of airy aphrodisiac. Undoubtedly the words from this song, and others like it, had put millions in the mood, it was music to make love by, and doubtless much love had been made by it all over America at night in cars, while the batteries burned down, in cottages by the lake, on beaches during balmy summer evenings, in secluded parks and exclusive penthouses and furnished rooms; in cabin cruisers and cabs and cabanas—in all places where Sinatra's songs could be heard were these words that warmed women, wooed and won them, snipped the final thread of inhibition and gratified the male egos of ungrateful lovers; two generations of men had been the beneficiaries of such ballads, for which they were eternally in his debt, for which they may eternally hate him. Nevertheless here it was, the

* © Redd Evans Music Corp.

man himself, in the early hours of the morning in Beverly Hills, out of range.

The two blondes, who seemed to be in their middle thirties, were preened and polished, their matured bodies softly molded within tight dark suits. They sat, legs crossed, perched on the high bar stools. They listened to the music. Then one of them pulled out a Kent and Sinatra quickly placed his gold lighter under it and she held his hand, looked at his fingers: they were nubby and raw, and the pinkies protruded, being so stiff from arthritis that he could barely bend them. He was, as usual, immaculately dressed. He wore an oxford-grey suit with a vest, a suit conservatively cut on the outside but trimmed with flamboyant silk within; his shoes, British, seemed to be shined even on the bottom of the soles. He also wore, as everybody seemed to know, a remarkably convincing black hairpiece, one of sixty that he owns, most of them under the care of an inconspicuous little grey-haired lady who, holding his hair in a tiny satchel, follows him around whenever he performs. She earns $400 a week. The most distinguishing thing about Sinatra's face are his eyes, clear blue and alert, eyes that within seconds can go cold with anger, or glow with affection, or, as now, reflect a vague detachment that keeps his friends silent and distant.

Leo Durocher, one of Sinatra's closest friends, was now shooting pool in the small room behind the bar. Standing near the door was Jim Mahoney, Sinatra's press agent, a somewhat chunky young man with a square jaw and narrow eyes who would resemble a tough Irish plainclothesman if it were not for the expensive continental suits he wears and his exquisite shoes often adorned with polished buckles. Also nearby was a big, broad-shouldered two-hundred-pound actor named Brad Dexter who seemed always to be thrusting out his chest so that his gut would not show.

Brad Dexter has appeared in several films and television shows, displaying fine talent as a character actor, but in Beverly Hills he is equally known for the role he played in Hawaii two years ago when he swam a few hundred yards and risked his life to save Sinatra from drowning in a riptide. Since then Dexter has been one of Sinatra's constant companions and has been made a producer in Sinatra's film company. He occupies a plush office near Sinatra's executive suite. He is endlessly searching for literary properties that might be converted into new starring roles for Sinatra. Whenever he is among strangers with Sinatra he worries because he knows that Sinatra brings out the best and worst in people—some men will become aggressive, some women will become seductive, others will stand around skeptically appraising him, the scene will be somehow intoxicated by his mere presence, and maybe Sinatra himself, if feeling as badly as he was tonight, might become intolerant or tense, and then:

headlines. So Brad Dexter tries to anticipate danger and warn Sinatra in advance. He confesses to feeling very protective of Sinatra, admitting in a recent moment of self-revelation: "I'd kill for him."

While this statement may seem outlandishly dramatic, particularly when taken out of context, it nonetheless expresses a fierce fidelity that is quite common within Sinatra's special circle. It is a characteristic that Sinatra, without admission, seems to prefer: *All the Way; All or Nothing at All.* This is the Sicilian in Sinatra; he permits his friends, if they wish to remain that, none of the easy Anglo-Saxon outs. But if they remain loyal, then there is nothing Sinatra will not do in turn—fabulous gifts, personal kindnesses, encouragement when they're down, adulation when they're up. They are wise to remember, however, one thing. He is Sinatra. The boss. *Il Padrone.*

I had seen something of this Sicilian side of Sinatra last summer at Jilly's saloon in New York, which was the only other time I'd gotten a close view of him prior to this night in this California club. Jilly's which is on West Fifty-second Street in Manhattan, is where Sinatra drinks whenever he is in New York, and there is a special chair reserved for him in the back room against the wall that nobody else may use. When he is occupying it, seated behind a long table flanked by his closest New York friends—who include the saloonkeeper Jilly Rizzo, and Jilly's azure-haired wife, Honey, who is known as the "Blue Jew"—a rather strange ritualistic scene develops. That night dozens of people, some of them casual friends of Sinatra's, some mere acquaintances, some neither, appeared outside of Jilly's saloon. They approached it like a shrine. They had come to pay respect. They were from New York, Brooklyn, Atlantic City, Hoboken. They were old actors, young actors, former prizefighters, tired trumpet players, politicians, a boy with a cane. There was a fat lady who said she remembered Sinatra when he used to throw the *Jersey Observer* onto her front porch in 1933. There were middle-aged couples who said they had heard Sinatra sing at the Rustic Cabin in 1938 and "We knew then that he really had it!" Or they had heard him when he was with Harry James's band in 1939, or with Tommy Dorsey in 1941 ("Yeah, that's the song, "I'll Never Smile Again"—he sang it one night in this dump near Newark and we danced . . ."); or they remembered that time at the Paramount with the swooners, and him with those bow ties, The Voice; and one woman rememberd that awful boy she knew then—Alexander Dorogokupetz, an eighteen-year-old heckler who had thrown a tomato at Sinatra and the bobby-soxers in the balcony had tried to flail him to death. Whatever became of Alexander Dorogokupetz? The lady did not know.

And they remembered when Sinatra was a failure and sang trash like "Mairzy Doats," and they remembered his comeback and on this night they were all standing outside Jilly's saloon, dozens of them, but they could not get in. So some of them left. But most of them stayed, hoping that soon they might be able to push or wedge their way into Jilly's be-tween the elbows and backsides of the men drinking three-deep at the bar, and they might be able to peek through and *see* him sitting back there. This is all they really wanted; they wanted to see him. And for a few moments they gazed in silence through the smoke and they stared. Then they turned, fought their way out of the bar, went home.

Some of Sinatra's close friends, all of whom are known to the men guarding Jilly's door, do manage to get an escort into the back room. But once they are there, they too must fend for themselves. On this particular evening, Frank Gifford, the former football player, got only seven yards in three tries. Others who had somehow been close enough to shake Sinatra's hand did *not* shake it; instead they just touched him on the shoulder or sleeve, or they merely stood close enough for him to see them and, after he'd given them a wink of recognition or a wave or a nod or called out their names (he has a fantastic memory for first names), they would then turn and leave. They had checked in. They had paid their respects. And as I watched this ritualistic scene, I got the impression that Frank Sinatra was dwelling simultaneously in two worlds that were not contemporary.

On the one hand he is the swinger—as he is when talking and joking with Sammy Davis, Jr., Richard Conte, Liza Minnelli, Bernice Massi, or any of the other show-business people who get to sit at *the* table; on the other, as when he is nodding or waving to his *paisanos* who are close to him (Al Silvani, a boxing manager who works with Sinatra's film company; Dominic Di Bona, his wardrobe man; Ed Pucci, a 300-pound former foot-ball lineman who is his aide-de-camp), Frank Sinatra is *Il Padrone*. Or better still, he is what in traditional Sicily have long been called *uomini rispettati*—men of respect: men who are both majestic and humble, men who are loved by all and are very generous by nature, men whose hands are kissed as they walk from village to village, men who would *personally* go out of their way to redress a wrong.

Frank Sinatra does things *personally*. At Christmas time, he will person-ally pick dozens of presents for his close friends and family, remembering the type of jewelry they like, their favorite colors, the sizes of their shirts and dresses. When a musician friend's house was destroyed and his wife was killed in a Los Angeles mud slide a little more than a year ago, Sinatra personally came to his aid, finding the musician a new home, paying whatever hospital bills were left unpaid by the insurance, then personally supervising the furnishing of the new home down to the replacing of the silverware, the linen, the purchase of new clothing.

The same Sinatra who did this can, within the same hour, explode in a towering rage of intolerance should a small thing be incorrectly done for him by one of his *paisanos*. For example, when one of his men brought him a frankfurter with catsup on it, which Sinatra apparently abhors, he angrily threw the bottle at the man, splattering catsup all over him. Most of the men who work around Sinatra are big. But this never seems to intimidate Sinatra nor curb his impetuous behavior with them when he is mad. They will never take a swing back at him. He is *Il Padrone.*

At other times, aiming to please, his men will overreact to his desires: when he casually observed that his big orange desert jeep in Palm Springs seemed in need of a new painting, the word was swiftly passed down through the channels, becoming ever more urgent as it went, until finally it was a *command* that the jeep be painted *now,* immediately, yesterday. To accomplish this would require the hiring of a special crew of painters to work all night, at overtime rates; which, in turn, meant that the order had to be bucked back up the line for further approval. When it finally got back to Sinatra's desk, he did not know what it was all about; after he had figured it out he confessed, with a tired look on his face, that he did not care when the hell they painted his jeep.

Yet it would have been unwise for anyone to anticipate his reaction, for he is a wholly unpredictable man of many moods and great dimension, a man who responds instantaneously to instinct—suddenly, dramatically, wildly he responds, and nobody can predict what will follow. A young lady named Jane Hoag, a reporter at *Life's* Los Angeles bureau who had attended the same school as Sinatra's daughter, Nancy, had once been invited to a party at Mrs. Sinatra's California home at which Frank Sinatra, who maintains very cordial relations with his former wife, acted as host. Early in the party Miss Hoag, while leaning against a table, accidentally with her elbow knocked over one of a pair of alabaster birds to the floor, smashing it to pieces. Suddenly, Miss Hoag recalled, Sinatra's daughter cried, "Oh, that was one of mother's favorite . . ."—but before she could complete the sentence, Sinatra glared at her, cutting her off, and while forty other guests in the room all stared in silence, Sinatra walked over, quickly with his finger flicked the *other* alabaster bird off the table, smashing it to pieces, and then put an arm gently around Jane Hoag and said, in a way that put her completely at ease, "That's okay, kid."

Now Sinatra said a few words to the blondes. Then he turned from the bar and began to walk toward the poolroom. One of Sinatra's other men friends moved in to keep the girls company. Brad Dexter, who had been standing in the corner talking to some other people, now followed Sinatra.

The room cracked with the clack of billiard balls. There were about a dozen spectators in the room, most of them young men who were watching Leo Durocher shoot against two other aspiring hustlers who were not very good. This private drinking club has among its membership many actors, directors, writers, models, nearly all of them a good deal younger than Sinatra or Durocher and much more casual in the way they dress for the evening. Many of the young women, their long hair flowing loosely below their shoulders, wore tight, fanny-fitting Jax pants and very expensive sweaters; and a few of the young men wore blue or green velour shirts with high collars, and narrow tight pants and Italian loafers.

It was obvious from the way Sinatra looked at these people in the poolroom that they were not his style, but he leaned back against a high stool that was against the wall, holding his drink in his right hand, and said nothing, just watched Durocher slam the billiard balls back and forth. The younger men in the room, accustomed to seeing Sinatra at this club, treated him without deference, although they said nothing offensive. They were a cool young group, very California-cool and casual, and one of the coolest seemed to be a little guy, very quick of movement, who had a sharp profile, pale blue eyes, light brown hair, and squared eyeglasses. He wore a pair of brown corduroy slacks, a green shaggy-dog Shetland sweater, a tan suede jacket, and Game Warden boots, for which he had recently paid $60.

Frank Sinatra, leaning against the stool, sniffling a bit from his cold, could not take his eyes off the Game Warden boots. Once, after gazing at them for a few moments, he turned away; but now he was focused on them again. The owner of the boots, who was just standing in them watching the pool game, was named Harlan Ellison, a writer who had just completed work on a screenplay, *The Oscar*.

Finally Sinatra could not contain himself.

"Hey," he yelled in his slightly harsh voice that still had a soft, sharp edge. "Those Italian boots?"

"No," Ellison said.

"Spanish?"

"No."

"Are they *English* boots?"

"Look, I donno, man," Ellison shot back, frowning at Sinatra, then turning away again.

Now the poolroom was suddenly silent. Leo Durocher, who had been poised behind his cue stick and was bent low, just froze in that position for a second. Nobody moved. Then Sinatra moved away from the stool and walked with that slow, arrogant swagger of his toward Ellison, the hard tap of Sinatra's shoes the only sound in the room. Then, looking down at Ellison with a slightly raised eyebrow and a tricky little smile, Sinatra asked: "You expecting a *storm?*"

Harlan Ellison moved a step to the side. "Look, is there any reason why you're talking to me?"

"I don't like the way you're dressed," Sinatra said.

"Hate to shake you up," Ellison said, "but I dress to suit myself."

Now there was some rumbling in the room, and somebody said,

"Com'on, Harlan, let's get out of here," and Leo Durocher made his pool shot and said, "Yeah, com'on."

But Ellison stood his ground.

Sinatra said, "What do you do?"

"I'm a plumber," Ellison said.

"No, no, he's not," another young man quickly yelled from across the table. "He wrote *The Oscar*."

"Oh, yeah," Sinatra said, "well I've seen it, and it's a piece of crap."

"That's strange," Ellison said, "because they haven't even released it yet."

"Well, I've seen it," Sinatra repeated, "and it's a piece of crap."

Now Brad Dexter, very anxious, very big opposite the small figure of Ellison, said, "Com'on kid, I don't want you in this room."

"Hey," Sinatra interrupted Dexter, "can't you see I'm talking to this guy?"

Dexter was confused. Then his whole attitude changed, and Dexter's voice went soft and he said to Ellison, almost with a plea, *"Why do you persist in tormenting me?"*

The whole scene was becoming ridiculous, and it seemed that Sinatra was only half-serious, perhaps just reacting out of sheer boredom or inner despair; at any rate, after a few more exchanges Harlan Ellison left the room. By this time the word had gotten out to those on the dance floor about the Sinatra–Ellison exchange, and somebody went to look for the manager of the club. But somebody else said that the manager had already heard about it—and had quickly gone out the door, hopped in his car and drove home. So the assistant manager went into the poolroom.

"I don't want anybody in here without coats and ties," Sinatra snapped.

The assistant manager nodded, and walked back to his office.

It was the morning after. It was the beginning of another nervous day for Sinatra's press agent, Jim Mahoney. Mahoney had a headache, and he was worried but not over the Sinatra–Ellison incident of the night before. At the time Mahoney had been with his wife at a table in the other room, and possibly he had not even been aware of the little drama. The whole thing had lasted only about three minutes. And three minutes after it was over, Frank Sinatra had probably forgotten about it for the rest of his life—as Ellison will probably remember it for the rest of *his* life: he had had, as hundreds of others before him, at an unexpected moment between darkness and dawn, a scene with Sinatra.

It was just as well that Mahoney had not been in the poolroom; he had enough on his mind today. He was worried about Sinatra's cold and worried about the controversial CBS documentary that, despite Sinatra's protests and withdrawal of permission, would be shown on television in less than two weeks. The newspapers this morning were full of hints that Sinatra might sue the network, and Mahoney's phones were ringing without pause, and now he was plugged into New York talking to the *Daily News*'s Kay Gardella, saying: ". . . that's right, Kay . . . they made a gentleman's agreement to not ask certain questions about Frank's private life, and then Cronkite went right ahead: 'Frank, tell me about those associations.' *That* question, Kay—*out!* That question should never have been asked. . . ."

As he spoke, Mahoney leaned back in his leather chair, his head shaking slowly. He is a powerfully built man of thirty-seven; he has a round, ruddy face, a heavy jaw, and narrow pale eyes, and he might appear pugnacious if he did not speak with such clear, soft sincerity and if he were not so meticulous about his clothes. His suits and shoes are superbly tailored, which was one of the first things Sinatra noticed about him, and in his spacious office opposite the bar is a red-muff electrical shoe polisher and a pair of brown wooden shoulders on a stand over which Mahoney can drape his jackets. Near the bar is an autographed photograph of President Kennedy and a few pictures of Frank Sinatra, but there are none of Sinatra in any other rooms in Mahoney's public-relations agency; there once was a large photograph of him hanging in the reception room but this apparently bruised the egos of some of Mahoney's other movie-star clients and, since Sinatra never shows up at the agency anyway, the photograph was removed.

Still, Sinatra seems ever present, and if Mahoney did not have legitimate worries about Sinatra, as he did today, he could invent them—and, as worry aids, he surrounds himself with little mementos of moments in the past when he did worry. In his shaving kit there is a two-year-old box of sleeping tablets dispensed by a Reno druggist—the date on the bottle marks the kidnapping of Frank Sinatra, Jr. There is on a table in Mahoney's office a mounted wood reproduction of Frank Sinatra's ransom note written on the aforementioned occasion. One of Mahoney's mannerisms, when he is sitting at his desk worrying, is to tinker with the tiny toy train he keeps in front of him—the train is a souvenir from the Sinatra film *Von Ryan's Express*; it is to men who are close to Sinatra what the PT-109 tie clasps are to men who were close to Kennedy—and Mahoney then proceeds to roll the little train back and forth on the six inches of track; back and forth, back, and forth, click-*clack* click-*clack*. It is his Queegthing.

Now Mahoney quickly put aside the little train. His secretary told him there was a *very* important call on the line. Mahoney picked it up, and his voice was even softer and more sincere than before. "Yes, Frank," he said. "Right . . . right . . . yes, Frank. . . ."

When Mahoney put down the phone, quietly, he announced that

Frank Sinatra had left in his private jet to spend the weekend at his home in Palm Springs, which is a sixteen-minute flight from his home in Los Angeles. Mahoney was now worried again. The Lear jet that Sinatra's pilot would be flying was identical, Mahoney said, to the one that had just crashed in another part of California.

On the following Monday, a cloudy and unseasonably cool California day, more than one hundred people gathered inside a white television studio, an enormous room dominated by a white stage, white walls, and with dozens of lights and lamps dangling: it rather resembled a gigantic operating room. In this room, within an hour or so, NBC was scheduled to begin taping a one-hour show that would be televised in color on the night of November 24 and would highlight, as much as it could in the limited time, the twenty-five-year career of Frank Sinatra as a public entertainer. It would not attempt to probe, as the forthcoming CBS *Sinatra* documentary allegedly would, that area of Sinatra's life that he regards as private. The NBC show would be mainly an hour of Sinatra singing some of the hits that carried him from Hoboken to Hollywood, a show that would be interrupted only now and then by a few film clips and commercials for Budweiser beer. Prior to his cold, Sinatra had been very excited about this show; he saw here an opportunity to appeal not only to those nostalgic, but also to communicate his talent to some rock-and-rollers—in a sense, he was battling The Beatles. The press releases being prepared by Mahoney's agency stressed this, reading: "If you happen to be tired of kid singers wearing mops of hair thick enough to hide a crate of melons . . . it should be refreshing to consider the entertainment value of a video special titled *Sinatra—A Man and His Music*. . . ."

But now in this NBC studio in Los Angeles, there was an atmosphere of anticipation and tension because of the uncertainty of the Sinatra voice. The forty-three musicians in Nelson Riddle's orchestra had already arrived and some were up on the white platform warming up. Dwight Hemion, a youthful sandy-haired director who had won praise for his television special on Barbra Streisand, was seated in the glass-enclosed control booth that overlooked the orchestra and stage. The camera crews, technical teams, security guards, Budweiser ad men were also standing between the floor lamps and cameras, waiting, as were a dozen or so ladies who worked as secretaries in other parts of the building but had sneaked away so they could watch this.

A few minutes before eleven o'clock, word spread quickly through the long corridor into the big studio that Sinatra was spotted walking through the parking lot and was on his way, and was looking fine. There seemed great relief among the group that was gathered; but when the lean, sharply dressed figure of the man got closer, and closer, they saw to their dismay that it was not Frank Sinatra. It was his double. Johnny Delgado.

Delgado walks like Sinatra, has Sinatra's build, and from certain facial angles does resemble Sinatra. But he seems a rather shy individual. Fifteen years ago, early in his career, Delgado applied for a role in *From Here to Eternity*. He was hired, finding out later that he was to be Sinatra's double. In Sinatra's latest film, *Assault on a Queen*, a story in which Sinatra and some fellow conspirators attempt to hijack the *Queen Mary*, Johnny Delgado doubles for Sinatra in some water scenes; and now, in this NBC studio, his job was to stand under the hot television lights marking Sinatra's spots on the stage for the camera crews.

Five minutes later, the real Frank Sinatra walked in. His face was pale, his blue eyes seemed a bit watery. He had been unable to rid himself of the cold, but he was going to try to sing anyway because the schedule was tight and thousands of dollars were involved at this moment in the assembling of the orchestra and crews and the rental of the studio. But when Sinatra, on his way to his small rehearsal room to warm up his voice, looked into the studio and saw that the stage and orchestra's platform were not close together, as he had specifically requested, his lips tightened and he was obviously very upset. A few moments later, from his rehearsal room, could be heard the pounding of his fist against the top of the piano and the voice of his accompanist, Bill Miller, saying, softly, "Try not to upset yourself, Frank."

Later Jim Mahoney and another man walked in, and there was talk of Dorothy Kilgallen's death in New York earlier that morning. She had been an ardent foe of Sinatra for years, and he became equally uncomplimentary about her in his nightclub act, and now, though she was dead, he did not compromise his feelings. "Dorothy Kilgallen's dead," he repeated, walking out of the room toward the studio. "Well, guess I got to change my whole act."

When he strolled into the studio the musicians all picked up their instruments and stiffened in their seats. Sinatra cleared his throat a few times and then, after rehearsing a few ballads with the orchestra, he sang "Don't Worry About Me" to his satisfaction and, being uncertain of how long his voice could last, suddenly became impatient.

"Why don't we tape this mother?" he called out, looking up toward the glass booth where the director, Dwight Hemion, and his staff were sitting. Their heads seemed to be down, focusing on the control board.

"Why don't we tape this mother?" Sinatra repeated.

The production stage manager, who stands near the camera wearing a headset, repeated Sinatra's words exactly into his line to the control room: "Why don't we tape this mother?"

Hemion did not answer. Possibly his switch was off. It was hard to know because of the obscuring reflections the lights made against the glass booth.

"Why don't we put on a coat and tie," said Sinatra, then wearing a high-necked yellow pullover, "and tape this. . . ."

Suddenly Hemion's voice came over the sound amplifier, very calmly: "Okay, Frank, would you mind going back over. . . ."

"Yes I *would* mind going back," Sinatra snapped.

The silence from Hemion's end, which lasted a second or two, was then again interrupted by Sinatra saying, "When we stop doing things around here the way we did them in 1950, maybe we . . ." and Sinatra continued to tear into Hemion, condemning as well the lack of modern techniques in putting such shows together; then, possibly not wanting to use his voice unnecessarily, he stopped. And Dwight Hemion, very patient, so patient and calm that one would assume he had not heard anything that Sinatra had just said, outlined the opening part of the show. And Sinatra a few minutes later was reading his opening remarks, words that would follow "Without a Song," off the large idiot-cards being held near the camera. Then, this done, he prepared to do the same thing on camera.

"Frank Sinatra Show, Act I, Page 10, Take 1," called a man with a clapboard, jumping in front of the camera—*clap*—then jumping away again.

"Did you ever stop to think," Sinatra began, "what the world would be like without a song? . . . It would be a pretty dreary place. . . . Gives you something to think about, doesn't it? . . ."

Sinatra stopped.

"Excuse me," he said, adding, *Boy*, I need a drink."

They tried it again.

"Frank Sinatra Show, Act I, Page 10, Take 2," yelled the jumping guy with the clapboard.

"Did you ever stop to think what the world would be like without a song? . . ." Frank Sinatra read it through this time without stopping. Then he rehearsed a few more songs, once or twice interrupting the orchestra when a certain instrumental sound was not quite what he wanted. It was hard to tell how well his voice was going to hold up, for this was early in the show; up to this point, however, everybody in the room seemed pleased, particularly when he sang an old sentimental favorite written more than twenty years ago by Jimmy Van Heusen and Phil Silvers—"Nancy," inspired by the first of Sinatra's three children when she was just a few years old.

> If I don't see her each day
> I miss her. . . .
> Gee what a thrill
> Each time I kiss her. . . .

As Sinatra sang these words, though he has sung them hundreds and hundreds of times in the past, it was suddenly obvious to everybody in the studio that something quite special must be going on inside the man, because something quite special was coming out. He was singing now, cold or no cold, with power and warmth, he was letting himself go, the public arrogance was gone, the private side was in this song about the girl who, it is said, understands him better than anybody else, and is the only person in front of whom he can be unashamedly himself.

Nancy is twenty-five. She lives alone, her marriage to singer Tommy Sands having ended in divorce. Her home is in a Los Angeles suburb and she is now making her third film and is recording for her father's record company. She sees him every day; or, if not, he telephones, no matter if it be from Europe or Asia. When Sinatra's singing first became popular on radio, stimulating the swooners, Nancy would listen at home and cry. When Sinatra's first marriage broke up in 1951 and he left home, Nancy was the only child old enough to remember him as a father. She also saw him with Ava Gardner, Juliet Prowse, Mia Farrow, many others, has gone on double dates with him. . . .

> She takes the winter
>   And makes it summer. . . .
> Summer could take
>   Some lessons from her. . . .

Nancy now also sees him visiting at home with his first wife, the former Nancy Barbato, a plasterer's daughter from Jersey City whom he married in 1939 when he was earning $25 a week singing at the Rustic Cabin near Hoboken.

The first Mrs. Sinatra, a striking woman who has never remarried ("When you've been married to Frank Sinatra . . ." she once explained to a friend), lives in a magnificent home in Los Angeles with her younger daughter, Tina, who is seventeen. There is no bitterness, only great respect and affection between Sinatra and his first wife, and he has long been welcome in her home and has even been known to wander in at odd hours, stoke the fire, lie on the sofa and fall asleep. Frank Sinatra can fall asleep anywhere, something he learned when he used to ride bumpy roads with band buses; he also learned at that time, when sitting in a tuxedo, how to pinch the trouser creases in the back and tuck the jacket under and out, and fall asleep perfectly pressed. But he does not ride buses any more, and his daughter Nancy, who in her younger days felt rejected when he slept on the sofa instead of giving attention to her, later realized that the sofa was one of the few places left in the world where Frank Sinatra could get any privacy, where his famous face would neither be stared at nor cause an abnormal reaction in others. She realized, too, that things normal have always eluded her father: his childhood was one of loneliness and a drive toward attention, and since attaining it he has never again been certain of solitude. Upon looking out the window of a home he once owned in Hasbrouck Heights, New Jersey, he would occasionally see the faces of teen-agers peeking in; and in 1944, after moving to California and buying a home behind a ten-foot fence on Lake Toluca, he discovered that the only way to escape the telephone and other intrusions was to board his paddle boat with a few friends, a card table and a case of beer, and stay afloat all afternoon. But he has tried, insofar as it has been possible, to be like everyone else, Nancy says. He wept on her wedding day, he is very sentimental and sensitive. . . .

"What the hell are you doing up there, Dwight?"
Silence from the control booth.
"Got a party or something going on up there, *Dwight?*"
Sinatra stood on the stage, arms folded, glaring up across the cameras toward Hemion. Sinatra had sung "Nancy" with probably all he had in his voice on this day. The next few numbers contained raspy notes, and twice his voice completely cracked. But now Hemion was in the control booth out of communication; then he was down in the studio walking over to where Sinatra stood. A few minutes later they both left the studio and were on the way up to the control booth. The tape was replayed for Sinatra. He watched only about five minutes of it before he started to shake his head. Then he said to Hemion: "Forget it, just forget it. You're wasting your time. What you got there," Sinatra said, nodding to the singing image of himself on the television screen, "is a man with a cold." The he left the control booth, ordering that the whole day's performance be scrubbed and future taping postponed until he had recovered.

Soon the word spread like an emotional epidemic down through Sinatra's staff, then fanned out through Hollywood, then was heard across the nation in Jilly's saloon, and also on the other side of the Hudson River in the homes of Frank Sinatra's parents and his other relatives and friends in New Jersey.
When Frank Sinatra spoke with his father on the telephone and said he was felling awful, the elder Sinatra reported that *he* was also feeling awful: that his left arm and fist were so stiff with a circulatory condition he could barely use them, adding that the ailment might be the result of having thrown too many left hooks during his days as a bantamweight almost fifty years ago.
Martin Sinatra, a ruddy and tattooed little blue-eyed Sicilian born in Catania, boxed under the name of "Marty O'Brien." In those days, in those places, with the Irish running the lower reaches of city life, it was not uncommon for Italians to wind up with such names. Most of the Italians

and Sicilians who migrated to America just prior to the 1900s were poor and uneducated, were excluded from the building-trades unions dominated by the Irish, and were somewhat intimidated by the Irish police, Irish priests, Irish politicians.

One notable exception was Frank Sinatra's mother, Dolly, a large and very ambitious woman who was brought to this country at two months of age by her mother and father, a lithographer from Genoa. In later years Dolly Sinatra, possessing a round red face and blue eyes, was often mistaken for being Irish, and surprised many at the speed with which she swung her heavy handbag at anyone uttering "Wop."

By playing skillful politics with North Jersey's Democratic machine, Dolly Sinatra was to become, in her heyday, a kind of Catherine de Medici of Hoboken's third ward. She could always be counted upon to deliver six hundred votes at election time from her Italian neighborhood, and this was her base of power. When she told one of the politicians that she wanted her husband to be appointed to the Hoboken Fire Department, and was told, "But, Dolly, we don't have an opening," she snapped, *"Make* an opening."

They did. Years later she requested that her husband be made a captain, and one day she got a call from one of the political bosses that began, "Dolly, congratulations!"

"For what?"

"Captain Sinatra."

"Oh, you finally made him one—thank you very much."

Then she called the Hoboken Fire Department.

"Let me speak to *Captain* Sinatra," she said. The fireman called Martin Sinatra to the phone, saying, "Marty, I think your wife has gone nuts." When he got on the line, Dolly greeted him:

"Congratulations, *Captain* Sinatra!"

Dolly's only child, christened Francis Albert Sinatra, was born and nearly died on December 12, 1915. It was a difficult birth, and during his first moment on earth he received marks he will carry till death—the scars on the left side of his neck being the result of a doctor's clumsy forceps, and Sinatra has chosen not to obscure them with surgery.

After he was six months old, he was reared mainly by his grandmother. His mother had a full-time job as a chocolate dipper with a large firm and was so proficient at it that the firm once offered to send her to the Paris office to train others. While some people in Hoboken remember Frank Sinatra as a lonely child, one who spent many hours on the porch gazing into space, Sinatra was never a slum kid, never in jail, always well-dressed. He had so many pants that some people in Hoboken called him "Slacksey O'Brien."

Dolly Sinatra was not the sort of Italian Mother who could be appeased

merely by a child's obedience and good appetite. She made many demands on her son, was always very strict. She dreamed of his becoming an
aviation engineer. When she discovered Bing Crosby pictures hanging on
his bedroom walls one evening, and learned that her son wished to become a singer too, she became infuriated and threw a shoe at him. Later,
finding she could not talk him out of it—"he takes after me"—she encouraged his singing.

Many Italo-American boys of his generation were then shooting for the
same star—they were strong with song, weak with words, not a big novelist among them: no O'Hara, no Bellow, no Cheever, nor Shaw; yet they
could communicate *bel canto*. This was more in their tradition, no need for a
diploma; they could, with a song, someday see their names in lights . . .
Perry Como . . . Frankie Laine . . . Tony Bennett . . . Vic Damone . . .
but none could see it better than *Frank Sinatra.*

Though he sang through much of the night at the Rustic Cabin, he was
up the next day singing without a fee on New York radio to get more
attention. Later he got a job singing with Harry James's band, and it was
there in August of 1939 that Sinatra had his first recording hit—"All or
Nothing at All." He became very fond of Harry James and the men in the
band, but when he received an offer from Tommy Dorsey, who in those
days had probably the best band in the country, Sinatra took it; the job paid
$125 a week, and Dorsey knew how to feature a vocalist. Yet Sinatra was
very depressed at leaving James's band, and the final night with them was
so memorable that, twenty years later, Sinatra could recall the details to a
friend: ". . . the bus pulled out with the rest of the boys at about half-past
midnight. I'd said good-bye to them all, and it was snowing, I remember.
There was nobody around and I stood alone with my suitcase in the snow
and watched the taillights disappear. Then the tears started and I tried to
run after the bus. There was such spirit and enthusiasm in that band, I
hated leaving it. . . ."

But he did—as he would leave other warm places, too, in search of
something more, never wasting time, trying to do it all in one generation,
fighting under his *own* name, defending underdogs, terrorizing top dogs.
He threw a punch at a musician who said something anti-Semitic, es-
poused the Negro cause two decades before it became fashionable. He also
threw a tray of glasses at Buddy Rich when he played the drums too loud.

Sinatra gave away $50,000 worth of gold cigarette lighters before he was
thirty, was living an immigrant's wildest dream of America. He arrived
suddenly on the scene when DiMaggio was silent, when *paisanos* were
mournful, were quietly defensive about Hitler in their homeland. Sinatra
became, in time, a kind of one-man Anti-Defamation League for Italians in
America, the sort of organization that would be unlikely for them because,
as the theory goes, they rarely agreed on anything, being extreme indi-

vidualists: fine as soloists, but not so good in a choir; fine as heroes, but not so good in a parade.

When many Italian names were used in describing gangsters on a television show, *The Untouchables*, Sinatra was loud in his disapproval. Sinatra and many thousands of other Italo-Americans were resentful as well when a small-time hoodlum, Joseph Valachi, was brought by Bobby Kennedy into prominence as a Mafia expert, when indeed, from Valachi's testimony on television, he seemed to know less than most waiters on Mulberry Street. Many Italians in Sinatra's circle also regard Bobby Kennedy as something of an Irish cop, more dignified than those in Dolly's day, but no less intimidating. Together with Peter Lawford, Bobby Kennedy is said to have suddenly gotten "cocky" with Sinatra after John Kennedy's election, forgetting the contribution Sinatra had made in both fund-raising and in influencing many anti-Irish Italian votes. Lawford and Bobby Kennedy are both suspected of having influenced the late president's decision to stay as a house guest with Bing Crosby instead of Sinatra, as originally planned, a social setback Sinatra may never forget. Peter Lawford has since been drummed out of Sinatra's "summit" in Las Vegas.

"Yes, my son is like me," Dolly Sinatra says, proudly. "You cross him he never forgets." And while she concedes his power, she quickly points out, "He can't make his mother do anything she doesn't want to do," adding, "Even today, he wears the same brand of underwear I used to buy him."

Today Dolly Sinatra is seventy-one years old, a year or two younger than Martin, and all day long people are knocking on the back door of her large home asking her advice, seeking her influence. When she is not seeing people and not cooking in the kitchen, she is looking after her husband, a silent but stubborn man, and telling him to keep his sore left arm resting on the sponge she has placed on the armrest of a soft chair. "Oh, he went to some terrific fires, this guy did," Dolly said to a visitor, nodding with admiration toward her husband in the chair.

Though Dolly Sinatra has eighty-seven godchildren in Hoboken, and still goes to that city during political campaigns, she now lives with her husband in a beautiful sixteen-room house in Fort Lee, New Jersey. This home was a gift from their son on their fiftieth wedding anniversary three years ago. The home is tastefully furnished and is filled with a remarkable juxtaposition of the pious and the worldly—photographs of Pope John and Ava Gardner, of Pope Paul and Dean Martin; several statues of saints and holy water, a chair autographed by Sammy Davis, Jr., and bottles of bourbon. In Mrs. Sinatra's jewelry box is a magnificent strand of pearls she had just received from Ava Gardner, whom she liked tremendously as a daughter-in-law and still keeps in touch with and talks about; and hung on the wall is a letter addressed to Dolly and Martin: "The sands of time have turned to gold, yet love continues to unfold like the petals of a rose, in God's garden of life . . . may God love you thru all eternity. I thank Him, I thank you for the being of one. Your loving son, Francis. . . ."

Mrs. Sinatra talks to her son on the telephone about once a week, and recently he suggested that, when visiting Manhattan, she make use of his apartment on East Seventy-second Street on the East River. This is an expensive neighborhood of New York even though there is a small factory on the block, but this latter fact was seized upon by Dolly Sinatra as a means of getting back at her son for some unflattering descriptions of his childhood in Hoboken.

"What—you want me to stay in *your* apartment, in *that* dump?" she asked. "You think I'm going to spend the night in *that* awful neighborhood?"

Frank Sinatra got the point, and said, "Excuse *me*, Mrs. Fort Lee."

After spending the week in Palm Springs, his cold much better, Frank Sinatra returned to Los Angeles, a lovely city of sun and sex, a Spanish discovery of Mexican misery, a star land of little men and lithe women sliding in and out of convertibles in tense tight pants.

Sinatra returned in time to see the long-awaited CBS documentary with his family. At about nine P.M. he drove to the home of his former wife, Nancy, and had dinner with her and their two daughters. Their son, whom they rarely see these days, was out of town.

Frank, Jr., who is twenty-two, was touring with a band and moving cross country toward a New York engagement at Basin Street East with The Pied Pipers, with whom Frank Sinatra sang when he was with Dorsey's band in the 1940's. Today Frank Sinatra, Jr., whom his father says he named after Franklin D. Roosevelt, lives mostly in hotels, dines each evening in his nightclub dressing room, and sings until two A.M., accepting graciously, because he has no choice, the inevitable comparisons. His voice is smooth and pleasant, and improving with work, and while he is very respectful of his father, he discusses him with objectivity and in an occasional tone of subdued cockiness.

Concurrent with his father's early fame, Frank, Jr., said, was the creation of a "press-release Sinatra" designed to "set him apart from the common man, separate him from the realities: it was suddenly Sinatra, the electric magnate, Sinatra who is supernormal, not super*human*, but super*normal* And here," Frank, Jr., continued, "is the great fallacy, the great bullshit, for Frank Sinatra *is* normal, *is* the guy whom you'd meet on a street corner. But this other thing, the supernormal guise, has affected Frank Sinatra as much as anybody who watches one of his television shows, or reads a magazine article about him. . . .

"Frank Sinatra's life in the beginning was so normal," he said, "that nobody would have guessed in 1934 that this little Italian kid with the curly hair would become the giant, the monster, the great living legend. . . . He met my mother one summer on the beach. She was Nancy Barbato, daughter of Mike Barbato, a Jersey City plasterer. And she meets the fireman's son, Frank, one summer day on the beach at Long Branch, New Jersey. Both are Italian, both Roman Catholic, both lower-middle-class summer sweethearts—it is like a million bad movies starring Frankie Avalon. . . .

"They have three children. The first child, Nancy, was the most normal of Frank Sinatra's children. Nancy was a cheerleader, went to summer camp, drove a Chevrolet, had the easiest kind of development centered around the home and family. Next is me. My life with the family is very, very normal up until September of 1958 when, in complete contrast to the rearing of both girls, I am put into a college-preparatory school. I am now away from the inner family circle, and my position within has never been remade to this day. . . . The third child, Tina. And to be dead honest, I really couldn't say what her life is like. . . ."

The CBS show, narrated by Walter Cronkite, began at ten P.M. A minute before that, the Sinatra family, having finished dinner, turned their chairs around and faced the screen, united for whatever disaster might follow. Sinatra's men in other parts of town, in other parts of the nation, were doing the same thing. Sinatra's lawyer, Milton A. Rudin, smoking a cigar, was watching with a keen eye, an alert legal mind. Other sets were watched by Brad Dexter, Jim Mahoney, Ed Pucci; Sinatra's makeup man, "Shotgun" Britton; his New York representative, Henri Giné; his haberdasher, Richard Carroll; his insurance broker, John Lillie; his valet, George Jacobs, a handsome Negro who, when entertaining girls in *his* apartment, plays records by Ray Charles.

And like so much of Hollywood's fear, the apprehension about the CBS show all proved to be without foundation. It was a highly flattering hour that did not deeply probe, as rumors suggested it would, into Sinatra's love life, or the Mafia, or other areas of his private province. While the documentary was not authorized, wrote Jack Gould in the next day's *New York Times*, "it could have been."

Immediately after the show, the telephones began to ring throughout the Sinatra system conveying words of joy and relief—and from New York came Jilly's telegram: "WE RULE THE WORLD!"

The next day, standing in the corridor of the NBC building where he was about to resume taping his show, Sinatra was discussing the CBS show with several of his friends, and he said, "Oh, it was a gas."

"Yeah, Frank, a helluva show."

"But I think Jack Gould was right in the *Times* today," Sinatra said. "There should have been more on the *man*, not so much on the music. . . ."

They nodded, nobody mentioning the past hysteria in the Sinatra world when it seemed CBS was zeroing in on the *man;* they just nodded and two of them laughed about Sinatra's apparently having gotten the word "bird" on the show—this being a favorite Sinatra word. He often inquires of his cronies, "How's your bird?"; and when he nearly drowned in Hawaii, he later explained, "Just got a little water on my bird"; and under a large photograph of him holding a whiskey bottle, a photo that hangs in the home of an actor friend named Dick Bakalyan, the inscription reads: "Drink, Dickie! It's good for your bird." In the song, "Come Fly with Me," Sinatra sometimes alters the lyrics—". . . just say the words and we'll take our birds down to Acapulco Bay. . . ."

Ten minutes later Sinatra, following the orchestra, walked into the NBC studio which did not resemble in the slightest the scene here of eight days ago. On this occasion Sinatra was in fine voice, he cracked jokes between numbers, nothing could upset him. Once, while he was singing "How Can I Ignore the Girl Next Door," standing on the stage next to a tree, a television camera mounted on a vehicle came rolling in too close and plowed against the tree.

"Kee-frist!" yelled one of the technical assistants.

But Sinatra seemed hardly to notice it.

"We've had a slight accident," he said, calmly. Then he began the song all over from the beginning.

When the show was over, Sinatra watched the rerun on the monitor in the control room. He was very pleased, shaking hands with Dwight Hemion and his assistants. Then the whiskey bottles were opened in Sinatra's dressing room. Pat Lawford was there, and so were Andy Williams and a dozen others. The telegrams and telephone calls continued to be received from all over the country with praise for the CBS show. There was even a call, Mahoney said, from the CBS producer, Don Hewitt, with whom Sinatra had been so angry a few days before. And Sinatra was *still* angry, feeling that CBS had betrayed him, though the show itself was not objectionable.

"Shall I drop a line to Hewitt?" Mahoney asked.

"Can you send a fist through the mail?" Sinatra asked.

He has everything, he cannot sleep, he gives nice gifts, he is not happy, but he would not trade, even for happiness, what he is. . . .

He is a piece of our past—but only we have aged, he hasn't . . . we are dogged by domesticity, he isn't . . . we have compunctions, he doesn't . . . it is our fault, not his . . .

He controls the menus of every Italian restaurant in Los Angeles; if you want North Italian cooking, fly to Milan. . . .

Men follow him, imitate him, fight to be near him . . . there is something of the locker room, the barracks about him . . . bird . . . bird . . .

He believes you must play it big, wide, expansively—the more open you are, the more you take in, your dimensions deepen, you grow, you become more what you are—bigger, richer. . . .

"He is better than anybody else, or at least they think he is, and he has to live up to it." (Nancy Sinatra, Jr.)

"He is calm on the outside—inwardly a million things are happening to him." (Dick Bakalyan)

"He has an insatiable desire to live every moment to its fullest because, I guess, he feels that right around the corner is extinction." (Brad Dexter)

"All I ever got out of any of my marriages was the two years Artie Shaw financed on an analyst's couch." (Ava Gardner)

"We weren't mother and son—we were buddies." (Dolly Sinatra)

"I'm for anything that gets you through the night, be it prayer, tranquilizers or a bottle of Jack Daniels." (Frank Sinatra)

Frank Sinatra was tired of all the talk, the gossip, the theory—tired of reading quotes about himself, of hearing what people were saying about him all over town. It had been a tedious three weeks, he said, and now he just wanted to get away, go to Las Vegas, let off some steam. So he hopped in his jet, soared over the California hills across the Nevada flats, then over miles and miles of desert to The Sands and the Clay-Patterson fight.

On the eve of the fight he stayed up all night and slept through most of the afternoon, though his recorded voice could be heard singing in the lobby of The Sands, in the gambling casino, even in the toilets, being interrupted every few bars however by the paging public address: ". . . Telephone call for Mr. Ron Fish, Mr. Ron Fish . . . *with a ribbon of gold in her hair. . . .* Telephone call for Mr. Herbert Rothstein, Mr. Herbert Rothstein . . . *memories of a time, so bright, keep me sleepless through dark endless nights. . . .*"

Standing around in the lobby of The Sands and other hotels up and down the strip on this afternoon before the fight were the usual prefight prophets: the gamblers, the old champs, the little cigar butts from Eighth Avenue, the sportwriters who knock the big fights all year but would never miss one, the novelists who seem always to be identifying with one boxer or another, the local prostitutes assisted by some talent in from Los Angeles, and also a young brunette in a wrinkled black cocktail dress who was at the bell captain's desk crying, "But I want to speak to Mr. Sinatra."

"He's not here," the bell captain said.

"Won't you put me through to his room?"

"There are *no* messages going through, Miss," he said, and then she turned, unsteadily, seeming close to tears, and walked through the lobby into the big noisy casino crowded with men interested only in money.

Shortly before seven P.M., Jack Entratter, a big grey-haired man who operates The Sands, walked into the gambling room to tell some men around the blackjack table that Sinatra was getting dressed. He also said that he'd been unable to get front-row seats for everybody, and so some of the men—including Leo Durocher, who had a date, and Joey Bishop, who was accompanied by his wife—would not be able to fit in Frank Sinatra's row but would have to take seats in the third row. When Entratter walked over to tell this to Joey Bishop, Bishop's face fell. He did not seem angry; he merely looked at Entratter with an empty silence, seeming somewhat stunned.

"Joey, I'm *sorry*," Entratter said when the silence persisted, "but we couldn't get more than six together in the front row."

Bishop still said nothing. But when they all appeared at the fight, Joey Bishop was in the front row, his wife in the third.

The fight, called a holy war between Muslims and Christians, was preceded by the introduction of three balding ex-champions, Rocky Marciano, Joe Louis, Sonny Liston—and then there was "The Star-Spangled Banner" sung by another man from out of the past, Eddie Fisher. It had been more than fourteen years ago, but Sinatra could still remember every detail: Eddie Fisher was then the new king of the baritones, with Billy Eckstine and Guy Mitchell right with him, and Sinatra had been long counted out. One day he remembered walking into a broadcasting studio past dozens of Eddie Fisher fans waiting outside the hall, and when they saw Sinatra they began to jeer, "Frankie, Frankie, I'm *swooning*, I'm *swooning*." This was also the time when he was selling only about 30,000 records a year, when he was dreadfully miscast as a funny man on his television show, and when he recorded such disasters as "Mama Will Bark," with Dagmar.

"I growled and barked on the record," Sinatra said, still horrified by the thought. "The only good it did me was with the dogs."

His voice and his artistic judgment were incredibly bad in 1952, but even more responsible for his decline, say his friends, was his pursuit of Ava Gardner. She was the big movie queen then, one of the most beautiful women in the world. Sinatra's daughter Nancy recalls seeing Ava swimming one day in her father's pool, then climbing out of the water with that fabulous body, walking slowly to the fire, leaning over it for a few moments, and then it suddenly seemed that her long dark hair was all dry, miraculously and effortlessly back in place.

With most women Sinatra dates, his friends say, he never knows whether they want him for what he can do for them now—or will do for them later. With Ava Gardner, it was different. He could do nothing for her later. She was on top. If Sinatra learned anything from his experience with her, he possibly learned that when a proud man is down a woman cannot help. Particularly a woman on top.

Nevertheless, despite a tired voice, some deep emotion seeped into his singing during this time. One particular song that is well remembered even now is "I'm a Fool to Want You," and a friend who was in the studio when Sinatra recorded it recalled: "Frank was really worked up that night. He did the song in one take, then turned around and walked out of the studio and that was that. . . ."

Sinatra's manager at that time, a former song plugger named Hank Sanicola, said, "Ava loved Frank, but not the way he loved her. He needs a great deal of love. He wants it twenty-four hours a day, he must have people around—Frank is that kind of guy." Ava Gardner, Sanicola said, "was very insecure. She feared she could not really hold a man . . . twice he went chasing her to Africa, wasting his own career. . . ."

"Ava didn't want Frank's men hanging around all the time," another friend said, "and this got him mad. With Nancy he used to be able to bring the whole band home with him, and Nancy, the good Italian wife, would never complain—she'd just make everybody a plate of spaghetti."

In 1953, after almost two years of marriage, Sinatra and Ava Gardner were divorced. Sinatra's mother reportedly arranged a reconciliation, but if Ava was willing, Frank Sinatra was not. He was seen with other women. The balance had shifted. Somewhere during this period Sinatra seemed to change from the kid singer, the boy actor in the sailor suit, to a man. Even before he had won the Oscar in 1953 for his role in *From Here to Eternity*, some flashes of his old talent were coming through—in his recording of "The Birth of the Blues," in his Riviera-nightclub appearance that jazz critics enthusiastically praised; and there was also a trend now toward L.P.'s and away from the quick three-minute deal, and Sinatra's concert style would have capitalized on this with or without an Oscar.

In 1954, totally committed to his talent once more, Frank Sinatra was selected Metronome's "Singer of the Year," and latter he won the U.P.I. disc-jockey poll, unseating Eddie Fisher—who now, in Las Vegas, having sung "The Star-Spangled Banner," climbed out of the ring, and the fight began.

Floyd Patterson chased Clay around the ring in the first round, but was unable to reach him, and from then on he was Clay's toy, the bout ending in a technical knockout in the twelfth round. A half hour later, nearly everybody had forgotten about the fight and was back at the gambling tables or lining up to buy tickets for the Dean Martin–Sinatra–Bishop night-club routine on the stage of The Sands. This routine, which includes Sammy Davis, Jr. when he is in town, consists of a few songs and much cutting up, all of it very informal, very special, and rather ethnic—Martin, a drink in hand, asking Bishop: "Did you ever see a Jew jitsu?"; and Bishop, playing a Jewish waiter, warning the two Italians to watch out "because I got my own group—the *Matzia*."

Then after the last show at The Sands, the Sinatra crowd, which now numbered about twenty—and included Jilly, who had flown in from New York; Jimmy Cannon, Sinatra's favorite sports columnist; Harold Gibbons, a Teamster official expected to take over if Hoffa goes to jail—all got into a line of cars and headed for another club. It was three o'clock. The night was young.

They stopped at The Sahara, taking a long table near the back and listened to a baldheaded little comedian named Don Rickles, who is probably more caustic than any comic in the country. His humor is so rude, in *such* bad taste, that it offends no one—it is *too* offensive to be offensive. Spotting Eddie Fisher among the audience, Rickles proceeded to ridicule him as a lover, saying it was no wonder that he could not handle Elizabeth Taylor; and when two businessmen in the audience acknowledged that they were Egyptians, Rickles cut into them and their country's policy toward Israel; and he strongly suggested that the woman seated at one table with her husband was actually a hooker.

When the Sinatra crowd walked in, Don Rickles could not be more delighted. Pointing to Jilly, Rickles yelled: "How's it feel to be Frank's tractor? . . . Yeah, Jilly keeps walking in front of Frank clearing the way." Then, nodding to Durocher, Rickles said, "Stand up, Leo, show Frank how you slide." Then he focused on Sinatra, not failing to mention Mia Farrow, nor that he was wearing a toupee, nor to say that Sinatra was washed up as a singer, and when Sinatra laughed, everybody laughed, and Rickles pointed toward Bishop: "Joey Bishop keeps checking with Frank to see what's funny."

Then, after Rickles told some Jewish jokes, Dean Martin stood up and yelled, "Hey, you're always talking about the Jews, never about the Italians," and Rickles cut him off with, "What do we need the Italians for—all they do is keep the flies off our fish."

Sinatra laughed, they all laughed, and Rickles went on this way for nearly an hour until Sinatra, standing up, said, "All right, com'on, get this thing over with. I gotta go."

"Shaddup and sit down!" Rickles snapped. "I've had to listen to you sing. . . ."

"Who do you think you're talking to?" Sinatra yelled back.

"Dick Haymes," Rickles replied, and Sinatra laughed again, and then Dean Martin, pouring a bottle of whiskey over his head, entirely drenching his tuxedo, pounded the table.

"Who would ever believe that staggering would make a star?" Rickles said, but Martin called out, "Hey, I wanna make a speech."

"Shaddup."

"No, Don, I wanna tell ya," Dean Martin persisted, "that I think you're a great performer."

"Well, thank you, Dean," Rickles said, seeming pleased.

"But don't go by me," Martin said, plopping down into his seat, "I'm drunk."

"I'll buy that," Rickles said.

By four A.M. Frank Sinatra led the group out of The Sahara, some of them carrying their glasses of whiskey with them, sipping it along the sidewalk and in the cars; then, returning to The Sands, they walked into the gambling casino. It was still packed with people, the roulette wheels spinning, the crapshooters screaming in the far corner.

Frank Sinatra, holding a shot glass of bourbon in his left hand, walked through the crowd. He, unlike some of his friends, was perfectly pressed, his tuxedo tie precisely pointed, his shoes unsmudged. He never seems to lose his dignity, never lets his guard completely down no matter how much he has drunk, nor how long he has been up. He never sways when he walks, like Dean Martin, nor does he ever dance in the aisles or jump up on tables, like Sammy Davis.

A part of Sinatra, no matter where he is, is never there. There is always a part of him, though sometimes a small part, that remains *Il Padrone*. Even now, resting his shot glass on the blackjack table, facing the dealer, Sinatra stood a bit back from the table, not leaning against it. He reached under his tuxedo jacket into his trouser pocket and came up with a thick but *clean* wad of bills. Gently he peeled off a one-hundred-dollar bill and placed it on the green-felt table. The dealer dealt him two cards. Sinatra called for a third card, overbid, lost the hundred.

Without a change of expression, Sinatra put down a second hundred-dollar bill. He lost that. Then he put down a third, and lost that. Then he placed two one-hundred-dollar bills on the table and lost those. Finally, putting his sixth hundred-dollar bill on the table, and losing it, Sinatra moved away from the table, nodding to the man, and announcing, "Good dealer."

The crowd that had gathered around him now opened up to let him through. But a woman stepped in front of him, handing him a piece of paper to autograph. He signed it and then *he* said, "Thank you."

In the rear of The Sands' large dining room was a long table reserved for Sinatra. The dining room was fairly empty at this hour, with perhaps two dozen other people in the room, including a table of four unescorted young ladies sitting near Sinatra. On the other side of the room, at another long table, sat seven men shoulder-to-shoulder against the wall, two of them wearing dark glasses, all of them eating quietly, speaking hardly a word, just sitting and eating and missing nothing.

The Sinatra party, after getting settled and having a few more drinks, ordered something to eat. The table was about the same size as the one reserved for Sinatra whenever he is at Jilly's in New York; and the people seated around this table in Las Vegas were many of the same people who are often seen with Sinatra at Jilly's or at a restaurant in California, or in Italy, or in New Jersey, or wherever Sinatra happens to be. When Sinatra sits to dine, his trusted friends are close; and no matter where he is, no matter how elegant the place may be, there is something of the neighborhood showing because Sinatra, no matter how far he has come, is still something of the boy from the neighborhood—only now he can take his neighborhood with him.

In some ways, this quasi-family affair at a reserved table in a public place is the closest thing Sinatra now has to home life. Perhaps, having had a home and left it, this approximation is as close as he cares to come; although this does not seem precisely so because he speaks with such warmth about his family, keeps in close touch with his first wife, and insists that she make no decision without first consulting him. He is always eager to place his furniture or other mementos of himself in her home or his daughter Nancy's, and he also is on amiable terms with Ava Gardner. When he was in Italy making *Von Ryan's Express*, they spent some time together, being pursued wherever they went by the *paparazzi*. It was reported then that the *paparazzi* had made Sinatra a collective offer of $16,000 if he would pose with Ava Gardner; Sinatra was said to have made a counter offer of $32,000 if he could break one *paparazzi* arm and leg.

While Sinatra is often delighted that he can be in his home completely without people, enabling him to read and think without interruption, there are occasions when he finds himself alone at night, and *not* by choice. He may have dialed a half-dozen women, and for one reason or another they are all unavailable. So he will call his valet, George Jacobs.

"I'll be coming home for dinner tonight, George."

"How many will there be?"

"Just myself," Sinatra will say. "I want something light, I'm not very hungry."

George Jacobs is a twice-divorced man of thirty-six who resembles Billy Eckstine. He has traveled all over the world with Sinatra and is devoted to him. Jacobs lives in a comfortable bachelor's apartment off Sunset Boulevard around the corner from Whiskey à Go Go, and he is known around town for the assortment of frisky California girls he has as friends—a few of whom, he concedes, were possibly drawn to him initially because of his closeness to Frank Sinatra.'

When Sinatra arrives, Jacobs will serve him dinner in the dining room. Then Sinatra will tell Jacobs that he is free to go home. If Sinatra, on such evenings, should ask Jacobs to stay longer, or to play a few hands of poker, he would be happy to do so. But Sinatra never does.

This was his second night in Las Vegas, and Frank Sinatra sat with friends in The Sands' dining room until nearly eight A.M. He slept through much of the day, then flew back to Los Angeles, and on the following morning he was driving his little golf cart through the Paramount Pictures movie lot. He was scheduled to complete two final scenes with the sultry blonde actress, Virna Lisi, in the film, *Assault on a Queen*. As he maneuvered the little vehicle up the road between the big studio buildings, he spotted Steve Rossi, who, with his comedy partner Marty Allen, was making a film in an adjoining studio with Nancy Sinatra.

"Hey, Dag," he yelled to Rossi, "stop kissing Nancy."

"It's part of the film, Frank," Rossi said, turning as he walked.

"In the garage?"

"It's my Dago blood, Frank."

"Well, cool it," Sinatra said, winking, then cutting his golf cart around a corner and parking it outside a big drab building within which the scenes for *Assault* would be filmed.

"Where's the fat director?" Sinatra called out, striding into the studio that was crowded with dozens of technical assistants and actors all gathered around cameras. The director, Jack Donohue, a large man who has worked with Sinatra through twenty-two years on one production or other, has had headaches with this film. The script had been chopped, the actors seemed restless, and Sinatra had become bored. But now there were only two scenes left—a short one to be filmed in the pool, and a longer and passionate one featuring Sinatra and Virna Lisi to be shot on a simulated beach.

The pool scene, which dramatizes a situation where Sinatra and his hijackers fail in their attempt to sack the *Queen Mary*, went quickly and well. After Sinatra had been kept in the water shoulder-high for a few minutes, he said, "Let's move it, fellows—it's cold in this water, and I've just gotten over one cold."

So the camera crews moved in closer, Virna Lisi splashed next to Sinatra in the water, and Jack Donohue yelled to his assistants operating the fans, "Get the waves going," and another man gave the command, *"Agitate!"* and Sinatra broke out in song. "Agitate in rhythm," then quieted down just before the cameras started to roll.

Frank Sinatra was on the beach in the next situation, supposedly gazing up at the stars, and Virna Lisi was to approach him, toss one of her shoes near him to announce her presence, then sit near him and prepare for a passionate session. Just before beginning, Miss Lisi made a practice toss of her shoe toward the prone figure of Sinatra sprawled on the beach. As she tossed her shoe, Sinatra called out, "Hit me in my bird and I'm going home."

Virna Lisi, who understands little English and certainly none of Sinatra's special vocabulary, looked confused, but everybody behind the camera laughed. She threw the shoe toward him. It twirled in the air, landed on his stomach.

"Well, that's about three inches too high," he announced. She again was puzzled by the laughter behind the camera.

Then Jack Donohue had them rehearse their lines, and Sinatra, still very charged from the Las Vegas trip, and anxious to get the cameras rolling, said, "Let's try one." Donohue, not certain that Sinatra and Lisi knew their lines well enough, nevertheless said okay, and an assistant with a clapboard called, "419, Take 1," and Virna Lisi approached with the shoe, tossed it at Frank lying on the beach. It fell short of his thigh, and Sinatra's right eye raised almost imperceptibly, but the crew got the message, smiled.

"What do the stars tell you tonight?" Miss Lisi said, delivering her first line, and sitting next to Sinatra on the beach.

"The stars tell me tonight I'm an idiot," Sinatra said, "a gold-plated idiot to get mixed up in this thing. . . ."

"Cut," Donohue said. There were some microphone shadows on the sand, and Virna Lisi was not sitting in the proper place near Sinatra.

"419, Take 2," the clapboard man called.

Miss Lisi again approached, threw the shoe at him, this time falling short—Sinatra exhaling only slightly—and she said, "What do the stars tell you tonight?"

"The stars tell me I'm an idiot, a gold-plated idiot to get mixed up in this thing. . . ." Then, according to the script, Sinatra was to continue, ". . . do you know what we're getting into? The minute we step on the deck of the *Queen Mary*, we've just tattooed ourselves," but Sinatra, who often improvises on lines, recited them: ". . . do you know what we're getting into? The minute we step on the deck of that mother's-ass ship. . . ."

"*No*, no," Donohue interrupted, shaking his head, "I don't think that's right."

The cameras stopped, some people laughed, and Sinatra looked up from his position in the sand as if he had been unfairly interrupted.

"I don't see why that can't work . . ." he began, but Richard Conte, standing behind the camera, yelled, "It won't play in London."

Donohue pushed his hand through his thinning grey hair and said, but not really in anger, "You know, that scene was pretty good until somebody blew the line. . . ."

"Yeah," agreed the cameraman, Billy Daniels, his head popping out from around the camera, "it was a pretty good piece. . . ."

"Watch your language," Sinatra cut in. Then Sinatra, who has a genius for figuring out ways of not reshooting scenes, suggested a way in which the film could be used and the "mother" line could be recorded later. This met with approval. Then the cameras were rolling again, Virna Lisi was leaning toward Sinatra in the sand, and then he pulled her down close to him. The camera now moved in for a close-up of their faces, ticking away for a few long seconds, but Sinatra and Lisi did not stop kissing, they just lay together in the sand wrapped in one another's arms, and then Virna Lisi's left leg just slightly began to rise a bit, and everybody in the studio now watched in silence, not saying anything until Donohue finally called out:

"If you ever get through, let me know. I'm running out of film."

Then Miss Lisi got up, straightened out her white dress, brushed back her blonde hair and touched her lipstick, which was smeared. Sinatra got up, a little smile on his lips, and headed for his dressing room.

Passing an older man who stood near a camera, Sinatra asked, "How's your Bell & Howell?"

The older man smiled.

"It's fine, Frank."

"Good."

In his dressing room Sinatra was met by an automobile designer who had the plans for Sinatra's new custom-built model to replace the $25,000 Ghia he has been driving for the last few years. He also was awaited by his secretary, Tom Conroy, who had a bag full of fan mail, including a letter from New York's Mayor John Lindsay; and by Bill Miller, Sinatra's pianist, who would rehearse some of the songs that would be recorded later in the evening for Sinatra's newest album, *Moonlight Sinatra*.

While Sinatra does not mind hamming it up a bit on a movie set, he is extremely serious about his recording sessions; as he explained to a British writer, Robin Douglas-Home: "Once you're on that record singing, it's you and you alone. If it's bad and gets you criticized, it's you who's to blame— no one else. If it's good, it's also you. With a film it's never like that; there are producers and scriptwriters, and hundreds of men in offices and the thing is taken right out of your hands. With a record, you're *it*. . . ."

> But now the days are short
> I'm in the autumn of the year
> And now I think of my life
> As vintage wine
> From fine old kegs. . . .

It no longer matters what song he is singing, or who wrote the words— they are all *his* words, *his* sentiments, they are chapters from the lyrical novel of his life.

> Life is a beautiful thing
> As long as I hold the string. . . .

When Frank Sinatra drives to the studio, he seems to dance out of the car across the sidewalk into the front door; then, snapping his fingers, he is standing in front of the orchestra in an intimate, airtight room, and soon he is dominating every man, every instrument, every sound wave. Some of the musicians have accompanied him for twenty-five years, have gotten old hearing him sing "You Make Me Feel So Young."

When his voice is on, as it was tonight, Sinatra is in ecstasy, the room becomes electric, there is an excitement that spreads through the orchestra and is felt in the control booth where a dozen men, Sinatra's friends, wave at him from behind the glass. One of the men is the Dodgers' pitcher Don Drysdale ("Hey, Big D," Sinatra calls out, *"hey,* baby!"); another is the professional golfer Bo Wininger; there are also numbers of pretty women standing in the booth behind the engineers, women who smile at Sinatra and softly move their bodies to the mellow mood of his music:

> Will this be moon love
> Nothing but moon love
> Will you be gone when the dawn
> Comes stealing through. . . .

After he is finished, the record is played back on tape, and Nancy Sinatra, who has just walked in, joins her father near the front of the orchestra to hear the playback. They listen silently, all eyes on them, the king, the princess; and when the music ends there is applause from the control booth, Nancy smiles, and her father snaps his fingers and says, kicking a foot, *Ooba-deeba-boobe-do!"*

Then Sinatra calls to one of his men. "Hey, Sarge, think I can have a half-a-cup of coffee?"

Sarge Weiss, who had been listening to the music, slowly gets up.

"Didn't mean to wake ya, Sarge," Sinatra says, smiling.

Then Weiss brings the coffee, and Sinatra looks at it, smells it, then announces, "I thought he'd be nice to me, but it's *really* coffee. . . ."

There are more smiles, and then the orchestra prepares for the next number. And one hour later, it is over.

The musicians put their instruments into their cases, grab their coats, and begin to file out, saying good-night to Sinatra. He knows them all by name, knows as much about them personally, from their bachelor days, through their divorces, through their ups and downs, as they know him. When a French-horn player, a short Italian named Vincent DeRosa, who has played with Sinatra since the Lucky Strike *Hit Parade* days on radio, strolled by, Sinatra reached out to hold him for a second.

"Vicenzo," Sinatra said, "how's your little girl?"

"She's fine, Frank."

"Oh, she's not a *little* girl any more," Sinatra corrected himself, "she's a big girl now."

"Yes, she goes to college now. U.S.C."

"That's great."

"She's also got a little talent, I think, Frank, as a singer."

Sinatra was silent for a moment, then said, "Yes, but it's very good for her to get her education first, Vicenzo."

Vincent DeRosa nodded.

"Yes, Frank," he said, and then he said, "Well, good-night Frank."

"Good-night, Vicenzo."

After the musicians had all gone, Sinatra left the recording room and joined his friends in the corridor. He was going to go out and do some drinking with Drysdale, Wininger, and a few other friends, but first he walked to the other end of the corridor to say good-night to Nancy, who was getting her coat and was planning to drive home in her own car.

After Sinatra had kissed her on the cheek, he hurried to join his friends at the door. But before Nancy could leave the studio, one of Sinatra's men, Al Silvani, a former prizefight manager, joined her.

"Are you ready to leave yet, Nancy?"

"Oh, thanks, Al," she said, "but I'll be all right."

"Pope's orders," Silvani said, holding his hands up, palms out.

Only after Nancy had pointed to two of her friends who would escort her home, and only after Silvani recognized them as friends, would he leave.

The rest of the month was bright and balmy. The record session had gone magnificently, the film was finished, the television shows were out of the way, and now Sinatra was in his Ghia driving out to his office to begin coordinating his latest projects. He had an engagement at The Sands, a new spy film called *The Naked Runner* to be shot in England, and a couple more albums to do in the immediate months ahead. And within a week he would be fifty years old. . . .

> Life is a beautiful thing
>   As long as I hold the string
> I'd be a silly so-and-so
>   If I should ever let go. . . .

Frank Sinatra stopped his car. The light was red. Pedestrians passed quickly across his windshield but, as usual, one did not. It was a girl in her twenties. She remained at the curb staring at him. Through the corner of his left eye he could see her, and he knew, because it happens almost every day, that she was thinking, *It looks like him, but is it?*

Just before the light turned green, Sinatra turned toward her, looked directly into her eyes waiting for the reaction he knew would come. It came and he smiled. She smiled and he was gone.

Sinatra Power
Roy Newquist ★ 1968

MIAMI, MARCH 1968

Fifteen hundred people at $60 a head pack La Ronde, the supper club at Miami's fabled Fontainebleau Hotel. Minks defy the March night. The room is close, gray with smoke. Liquor is served only by the bottle. The food is indifferent. Why, then, this mob scene?

Sinatra. The King, still—at fifty-three.

I sit at Sinatra's table, ringside. My date for the evening: Raquel Welch, his costar in *The Lady in Cement,* the movie he is making by day after a few hours of tossing, early-morning sleep following his nightly show at the Fontainebleau.

Sinatra comes on. Striding to center front, whipping the cord of his hand-held mike. Grinning, riding out the applause, sobering as the spot is dimmed to exclude the orchestra, the stage, his body, everything but that thin face.

> That's life,
>   That's what people say,
> You're ridin' high in April,
>   Shot down in May . . .

Sinatra. Belting it out. Handsome, a little heavier. Looking, finally, pretty close to fifty.

> When I was seventeen,
>   It was a very good year,
> It was a very good year
>   For small town girls . . .

There are cracks on the high notes, a reediness in the sustained ones, frequent throat clearings, not a few coughs. But the Sinatra charisma takes over. The room is his, as rooms always are. Filled with women leaning forward to reach him, to move in a little. . . .

> When I was thirty-five,
>   It was a very good year . . .

Let me make it clear; the voice is not "gone." Rebellious vocal cords almost destroyed his career during those few down-and-out years preceding his comeback in *From Here to Eternity.* Perhaps middle age has diminished his vocal thrust. But to say that the voice is gone is like saying Raquel Welch is ugly because she has a mole on her shoulder.

. . . And now I think of my life
As vintage wine
From fine old kegs . . .

The lights go up. Pandemonium. The women cry out, one so loudly that Sinatra laughs and calls to her:

"Where does it hurt you, baby!"

He perches on a stool, center stage, a brandy snifter in hand. "One of these," he lifts the glass in a toast, "and I'll get through the second half of the show. Two of them, and you'll have to sing while I lie down and listen."

Sinatra's talk with the audience is dry, laconic, cool. His stories that night are about Dean Martin, Sammy Davis, Jr., and Bobby Kennedy. The first two men he admires.

"Bobby Kennedy's advisers told him to get new pictures taken so he'd look older for the campaign. Bobby agreed, so they took him to a photographer. The whole business didn't work out, however, because Bobby kept falling off the horse."

He returns to the orchestra and swings into a second full song set: "Just One of Those Things," "The Lady Is a Tramp," the Cole Porter, Rodgers and Hart, Gershwin numbers he has made his own. And, finally, the crowd-blower: a gutsy "Out of My Head," with all stops pulled.

They're standing now. Cheering, yelling, clapping—fifteen hundred of them. It's another $90,000 night at the Fontainebleau. Raquel Welch turns to me: "He's as good as show business gets. He's what it's all about."

Sinatra's night doesn't end after the show. They never do. This night there's a party in his hotel penthouse for intimates, cast members of his movie, and director Elia Kazan. All guests are screened, by Sinatra's watchful staff, before entering.

Sinatra is in a good mood tonight, because the show has gone better. He is a perfectionist, and each crack in his voice moves across his psyche like a dark cloud. His recent bout with pneumonia hasn't helped. "I feel like I'm cheating people when the voice is bad. They don't put out that kind of dough to listen to a bullfrog."

Before Sinatra's arrival, Penthouse A of the Fontainebleau had been completely redone for the King's occupancy: the huge terrace floored with brilliant-red outdoor carpeting, the enormous master bedroom painted shamrock green, three bathrooms fitted with fourteen-karat-gold fixtures. The King-size living room is dominated by a massive grand piano, one entire wall covered by a smoked mirror. The indirect lighting adjusts to eighteen degrees of softness.

Finally the party fades out. Sinatra, still wound up, takes a few pals to his favorite club, Jilly's South, where the go-go girls gyrate on five platforms until morning. "I don't go for topless," Sinatra says. "I've never seen a girl in a topless bathing suit, but I don't have to see one to know I wouldn't like it. I don't go for extreme cleavage, either. I like women to be women."

Had there been no party, no Jilly's, Sinatra still would not have turned in until dawn. As nocturnal as a tomcat, he can never sleep before four or five A.M. When there is no one to drink with or talk to, he reads. Two to five newspapers daily, ten magazines, and five books per week. His interests are wide-ranging, his tastes catholic. He listens a lot, but when he starts to talk, everybody else stops.

"As far as sex is concerned, I don't think the American man gives his woman a fair shake. There's not enough quantity and certainly not enough quality. People talk the game but they don't play it very well."

On race relations:

"We've got a hell of a long way to go in this racial situation. As long as most white men think of a Negro as a Negro first and a man second, we're in trouble. I don't know why we can't grow up. It took us long enough to get past the stage where we were calling all Italians 'wops' and 'dagos,' but if we don't drop this 'nigger' thing, we just won't be around much longer.

"Hell, actors have got to take a stand politically, even if we're afraid we'll get hurt at the box office. We're citizens first. This time out, there'll be more actors in politics and speaking out on issues than ever before."

Politically, Sinatra is a working liberal. Today he is a passionate Humphrey man, giving him the same all-out support that he once accorded John F. Kennedy. On May 22 he invited several thousand California Democrats to a Sinatra "star-studded spectacular" for Humphrey in the Oakland Coliseum Arena.

The causes of the Sinatra break with the Kennedy camp and his decision to support the vice president have been subjects of wide speculation. One party leader attributes it to his old friendship with Humphrey and the fact that "there was never the camaraderie between him and Bobby as there had been between Frank and Jack." Another insider believes the break was due to Sinatra's involvement in Nevada gambling palaces at the time Attorney General Kennedy moved against some of the gamblers.

Either way, the Sinatra spectacular, held just when the Kennedy forces were steppping up their California efforts, was a switch from 1960, when Sinatra led his Rat Pack in total support of John F. Kennedy.

It is likely that Sinatra's political concerns were born early in his life, inspired by his volatile mother, Dolly Sinatra, who ruled as the unofficial queen of a large section of Hoboken, New Jersey, dispensing patronage for family and friends from the Democratic organization. The street-gang atmosphere of that neighborhood fed on words like "wop" and "dago," words that drive Sinatra up the wall.

He heads the league against defamation of Italians, despite the opposition of a few Italians who feel that his adverse publicity and a rumored connection with the Mafia do their cause little good. His films and records are banned in Arab countries because of his contribution to Israel and his support of the Israeli cause. Even before his strong friendship with Sammy Davis, Jr.—whom he catapulted to stardom by getting him a Las Vegas engagement—he fought for the Negro cause. To this day the word "nigger," even in jest, excludes the speaker from Sinatra's company.

HOLLYWOOD, DECEMBER 1967

The Oak Bar of the Beverly Wilshire Hotel. I have tried for a year to see Sinatra, but my efforts kept coinciding with traumatic periods in his life. First the widely publicized slugging in Beverly Hills, then the missing-teeth fracas at Las Vegas. And now the rumored breakup with Mia Farrow. They separate, return, separate. She is in, then out, of his new film, *The Detective*. At the Oak Bar, talk is subdued. Sinatra looks tired, says little as it eddies around him.

His companions during such idle hours vary. His costar in *The Detective*, Lee Remick, spends long hours with him. So do the regular members of his well-publicized entourage, the men who seem to accompany him everywhere, keep him out of the headlines, fill his hours to the point where Mia Farrow once complained, "We are never alone."

They are always at his various homes, in his hotel suites, on his sets, aboard his $200,000 yacht, in the lavish limousines that whisk him about. Sinatra's loyalty to them is so deeply personal, so old-fashioned Italian, that any one of the following men would probably give his life for him:

Dominic DiBona, in charge of the vast Sinatra wardrobe. Since Sinatra is a fastidious dresser, this is no easy assignment.

Blaine "Shotgun" Britton, his makeup man, loud, profane, and very funny. Himself a legend, Shotgun is a burly ex-football player who turned to a vocation normally considered effete.

George Jacobs, valet. Jacobs has now been with Sinatra for so many years he has senior standing in the group.

Mike Romanoff, possibly the most fascinating member of the group. Mike, now in his eighties, once the fabled "Prince" of Hollywood, who befriended Sinatra during his bad days, has been under the singer's wing ever since he lost his restaurant—and most of his "friends"—ten years ago.

These partisans often explain that of the ninety-nine men who admire Sinatra's work, his wealth, and his womanizing, there will always be the hundredth man who wants to take a crack at him. When Sinatra was younger, particularly during his volatile Copacabana engagements in New York, he did provoke assault and battery. Today he is essentially a gentle man who tries to avoid unpleasant encounters. "Life is too short for trouble," he says a little wearily, and Mike Romanoff shakes his head in agreement.

A blonde, probably nineteen, enters the bar, sits down, notices Sinatra. She whispers to her escort, then sends a note to him, asking for his autograph for her birthday present.

Sinatra hops off his bar stool and walks over to her. "So it's your birthday." Grinning, he writes, "With very best wishes, Frank Sinatra." The grin widens. "A birthday deserves a kiss, doesn't it?" He leans down and kisses her, a long, thorough kiss, chats for a few minutes before returning to the bar. The girl, dazed, goes off to the ladies' room. . . .

A few weeks later, I fly to Florida when Sinatra starts filming *The Lady in Cement*. Within days, pneumonia strikes the King. The cast shoots around him until he recovers. From the beginning, the script has posed problems. Raquel Welch, anxious that "people have a chance to see me with clothes on," is especially upset. So the rewrite goes on, day after day, under Sinatra's dogged guidance.

It's not difficult to tell when Sinatra has had a bad night, when the show at La Ronde has not met his standards. He is strained, tense. But on days when the previous night's show has gone well and he hasn't closed down the go-go bars, his mood is so high that everyone on the set is up with him. He jokes, clowns, greets Raquel Welch with a hefty slap on the behind: "Sorry, baby, that's a thing only your husband should do."

He is his most tense waiting it out during days before the decisive weekend when Mia Farrow comes to Miami to see him, a move that caught everyone but Sinatra by surprise. She leaves after one night. The marriage is over. Mia flies to London to finish a picture with Elizabeth Taylor. She seems as unhappy as though her days of meditation in India with the guru Maharishi Mahesh Yogi had never taken place.

Strangely, Sinatra is at his most buoyant when shooting resumes on Monday. But he refuses to talk about Mia—to anyone. The ban is on.

Next to come to the Sinatra Mecca is ex-wife Ava Gardner. Sinatra and this once exquisite, still handsome, good-humored woman are the best of friends. Like Sinatra's first wife, Nancy, Sr., Ava seems to bear him no resentment, no malice. Also like Nancy, Sr., she is emphatic in her respect for him, her loyalty to him. While Ava is in Miami, Sinatra stays in great form.

Then comes word that daughter Nancy, Jr., will fly in for a long weekend. Sinatra is elated. They make it their private weekend, most of their time spent aboard the *Roma*.

Still to come: daughter Tina and son, Frank, Jr. After they've left, Frank says, "All I need now is a visit from Nancy, Senior, and everyone who matters in my life will have made the scene."

During a break on the set, after a stormy love scene with Raquel Welch,

Sinatra talks about his family. I tell him I recently interviewed his daughter Nancy and had come away her fan. I'd also seen Frank, Jr., at a Dallas nightclub. His show was superbly styled and polished.

"They're good kids," Sinatra said, "and they're lucky. An entertainer's kids usually have terrible problems if they try to make it in the same field. They're intimidated by him to begin with, and the public intimidates them more by comparing them to him or by saying they'd never have made it without him.

"Nobody, for example, knows how hard Nancy's worked. She's put everything into her career, and I'm delighted that it's worked. She knows how to live with success, too, and that's important.

"Even though she's my daughter, she did it the hard way, earned it with hard work, and she's so beautifully balanced I think she's going to be able to enjoy it all. Tina's taking a TV job, and I've an idea she's on her way, too.

"Frank has had the roughest time of all of them. That kidnapping was a terrible thing for him. The trauma was bad enough, but after that came the real hell—the press sniping at him, audiences making rude remarks. As though the whole business were a publicity stunt, not the dreadful thing it really was. I can't understand how people can be so unkind, but he took it, right on the chin, and he's bounced back.

"In a funny kind of way, he's an old young man. He's got such a deep knowledge of music—history, harmonics, everything—that he makes me seem absolutely uneducated. I can't read music, and I never had any formal study. But the thing I do have is an ear. If a flute player in the back row hits a bad note, baby, I know it.

"When the chance came for Frank to go on the road, I said, "Why not?" Great training. And he's young, so he can enjoy it. Like the way I could take those one-nighters when I toured with Dorsey.

"Hell, it's fun when you've got youth on your side. And all the audiences he'll hit will teach him a lot, polish him. That bad period he went through is over with, thank God.

"Sure, my kids are lucky—but it's more than that. Their mother, Nancy, has raised them beautifully. She's given them their character, their poise, their ability to adjust. She's been wonderful. Without the background she gave them, the good things might not have happened."

A call comes for Sinatra to return to the set. He slings his jacket over his shoulder. "Stick around. This won't take long."

When he returns, we talk about music. I ask him how, without training, he evolved his own style.

"I used to go to concerts when I was a kid—I don't know how many times I heard Heifetz play the violin. The fantastic things he did with the notes—holding them, sustaining them—impressed me so much I decided to see how close I could come to doing the same thing with my voice. I think that whatever style I might have sort of developed from that."

What is he recording next?

"Hell, I've run out of the Cole Porter and the Rodgers and Hart and Gershwin repertoire—the standards that have always meant the most to me. And I can't go rock. But I'm going to do an album of country-Western that Lee Hazelwood is putting together for me, so I guess the old dog will be learning a few new tricks."

The Lady in Cement, like all Sinatra's films, is so geared to him that even his absence from the set overshadows each move that is made. The picture, whatever its quality, will undoubtedly earn more than Sinatra's off-the-top $1,000,000 guarantee. Considering the fact that it was shot in four weeks, Sinatra's salary could be figured at $250,000 per week, which places him alongside Elizabeth Taylor, Richard Burton, Shirley MacLaine, and Julie Andrews in earning power.

Final verdicts on the advantages and disadvantages of working in a Sinatra film come in from cast and crew members constantly subject to his changing schedule and varying moods.

"He has no consideration for anyone. He's the star, the King, and he knows it. After a few weeks, you just shrug and say, 'That's Sinatra.' You might as well, because that's the way it is, baby."

"If the whole industry worked this way, pictures would cost half as much to produce as they do. He's so frighteningly efficient there's not a wasted motion."

"When this picture started shooting, I thought it was a hopeless project. But I've seen how he's worked that script over and the way he's deepened the characters and the gimmicks he's added to make things work for him or Raquel or whoever. And if it's good, it's all his."

Finally, Raquel Welch's verdict:

"I wouldn't have missed working with Frank for the world. He's an education for any actor—you actually learn how to make everything count. Working with him is exciting. He has a magnetism I've never come across before."

On one of the last nights in Miami—actually it is very early in the morning—Sinatra, whistling, enters his hotel lobby after a night of go-go. The picture has gone well. The months of backing and filling with Mia Farrow are over. He seems at peace with himself.

As Sinatra reaches the elevator, he is blocked by a tall, heavyset man, who has obviously been drinking. "You dago S.O.B.!"

Sinatra punches him three times in rapid succession. The man goes down. Sinatra steps over him and enters the elevator. He is finally ready for a good night's sleep.

☆ ☆ ☆ ☆ ☆ ☆ ☆ ☆ ☆ ☆ ☆ ☆ ☆ ☆ ☆ ☆

The two articles that follow, both of which were published in *High Fidelity*, are by music critic, lyricist, novelist, and publisher of *Jazzletter* Gene Lees, whose songs include "Quiet Nights of Quiet Stars" ("Corcovado"), "Someone to Light Up My Life," and "Yesterday I Heard the Rain." The first article recounts his experience observing a recording session at which Sinatra made a bossa-nova album with Antonio Carlos Jobim. Included on this album is a performance of a Gene Lees lyric. Lees captures well the palpable tension that many have reported feeling at Sinatra's recording sessions and the precision that the singer demands from his co-workers. In the second piece, Lees comments on Sinatra's albums as personal statements. In the one under consideration, *Cycles* (1969), Lees hears a new Sinatra—one who is less bombastic and arrogant than he was earlier and more accepting of his weaknesses and errors now; one who is less divided and contradictory and more prone to confession and forgiveness.

The Performance and the Pain
Gene Lees ★ 1967

He stands by a microphone not far beyond the double-glass window that separates the studio from the control booth. He is tanned. He wears an impeccably tailored black suit and highly shined, well-cut black shoes. His gray tie is pulled loose at the neck, but that is his only departure from sartorial conservatism as he stands, hands in trouser pockets, wearing a look of almost pained concentration, and studies the words-and-music on a tilted drafting table in front of him.

As the orchestra goes through the first arrangement, then repeats parts of it to clean up the details, he seems superfluous to the proceedings. Until the orchestra is ready, a singer at a record date goes ignored, like the bridegroom in the last minutes before a wedding, and this man is no exception. His public relations office can keep the press off his neck (some of the time); his accountants and attorneys can set up record companies for him and dispose of them, buy and sell his airplanes; he can delegate his power as he sees fit. But this part of his job nobody can do for him. Frank Sinatra still has to do his own singing, and at this moment he looks as lonely as any other singer before the first take of the first tune of a record date.

The worried look breaks. He jokes with some of the musicians, lights a cigarette, reaches over to light one for Antonio Carlos Jobim, who is playing guitar in this album. Seven of the tunes are, in fact, by Jobim; three are standards. The album is to be called, with dry humor, *Francis Albert Sinatra/ Antonio Carlos Jobim*.

At last arranger Claus Ogerman, who has been flown to Los Angeles from New York to write and conduct the arrangements, is ready. The Brazilian drummer Dom um Romão, who has been flown out from Chicago to get a better bossa nova feeling than American drummers are capable of, touches his cymbals. They start. The first song is "Once I Loved." They go through it, Sinatra not really getting into it properly. He sings well, but not with his usual depth of understanding. After a while, he consults with Ogerman and says into the microphone to producer Sonny Burke in the booth, "Let's go on. Let's do 'Quiet Nights.'"

I tense up like a watchspring. I wrote this lyric, and no singer has ever sung it absolutely accurately, a problem that has bugged Jobim and me for five years. They start, and I barely breathe. As Jobim had said earlier, "This man is Mount Everest for a songwriter." If he gets it right, we can quit worrying.

He does, and I realize that what I've heard about Sinatra's respect for a songwriter's intentions is quite correct. They do it again to raise the level even further, and at last they're satisfied.

They go on to the next one. They do several takes, one of them almost perfect, except for the release. "I think you've got it on another take," Sinatra says. An intercut will take care of it. "Yes, there was a rough spot in the release," Burke says.

Sinatra laughs. "That was an old cigarette that came up. From about 1947."

As the date progresses, the atmosphere grows looser. By now the control booth is crowded. There is an executive or two from Reprise Records. Singer Keely Smith has dropped by to listen. Nancy Sinatra, much prettier and softer than she seems in photographs, comes in with several friends. She walks into the studio to see her father. He hugs her and grins. He has a warm, rich smile.

They do another tune. After the first run-through, Sinatra says to Burke, "That's very short. I think we're going to have to pull it down a little for time, for length. It's too abrupt. Let's try one, huh?"

They do it slower. At the end of the take, Sinatra says, "We've got a couple little strangers in there. In the strings." He means wrong notes. They check, and he's right. Another thing I'd heard about him is true: this man can *hear*. Then he says, "In the opening—can't we get more feeling in the strings?" He makes the motions of playing violin: he wants the players to lean more into the phrasing. He's right about this too.

They finish a good take on the song, then go into Jobim's "The Girl from Ipanema." Sinatra wants Jobim to sing duet with him. He does a chorus in English, then Jobim does one in Portuguese. Sinatra figures out a routine to trade phrases at the end. It's charming, it works beautifully.

They stop for a minute. Ogerman walks down to the back of the studio to correct something in the strings. Sinatra calls for him: "Claus!" Then he says, affecting a German accent (Ogerman is from Munich), *"Achtung!* Claus, I need you."

And here we note a subtlety. All his jokes, all his small pleasantries, have drawn laughs from the control booth. But gradually I realize that it is more laughter than they deserve, and at this latest remark, everyone cracks up as if this were one of Fred Allen's most pungent witticisms. It's as if they *have* to, all these surrounding people. What's odd about it is that they're separated from him by a double window; he can't hear them, has no way of knowing who laughed hardest at his joke. But they do it anyway. By reflex, I guess.

This is the one hint of the staggering power that inheres in this contradictory man, whose tangled and obviously lonely life is a strange amalgam of elegance and ugliness, of profound failure and dizzying success, of adamant loyalties and equally adamant dislikes, of kindness and courtesies and rudeness.

Yet how can anyone judge him? What would I be like, what sort of things would I do, if I had that much power? What would you be like, with all external limitations removed from your behavior?

Two weeks later, I receive an acetate dub of the album from Reprise. Some things are better than they seemed at the time, some not as good. One of the tracks, however, a Jobim song called "Jinji," sends chills up my arms and back. Sinatra's reading of it is one of the most exquisite things ever to come out of American popular music. It is filled with longing. It aches. Somewhere within him, Frank Sinatra aches. Fine. That's the way it's always been; the audience's pleasure derives from the artist's pain.

Frank Sinatra: Confessions and Contradictions
Gene Lees ★ 1969

We leave our handprints on everything we touch. The clothes we select, the music we like, the way the pitch of the voice rises when we're tense or insecure—these things are confessions. Even in trying to evade confession, we confess: in being phony, we only tell the truth backwards.

The creative artist makes the most obvious confessions. But the interpretative artist makes them too: he confesses in the material he selects and in the way he performs it. Even if he doesn't like the material, he reveals himself in his approach to it. "Strangers in the Night" is dreck. Frank Sinatra recorded it. He stated his contempt for the song in the *dooby-dooby-doo* tag he attached to the end of it. He thereby told us that he's a snob about material. But then he told us something he didn't intend to: that there was a streak of hypocrisy in him. If he didn't respect the song, he shouldn't have recorded it—not even for money, which he hardly needed at that point.

Some years previously, his recording of "Old MacDonald Had a Farm" told us that he was a man of great arrogance. It said: "I'm so big and I'm so great that I can make a hit out of anything, even something as lousy as, say, 'Old MacDonald Had a Farm.'"

Three years ago, Sinatra turned fifty. Evidently it rocked him to his heels. In quick succession, he recorded *A Man and His Music* and *The September of My Years*—the one a retrospective of his career, the other a retrospective of his life. The latter comprised material about growing old. You could sense a qualitative change in the man: a real and heavy despair. It is the darkest album he's ever made, and his eyes during that period, the loneliest eyes I have ever seen, seemed to verify that he meant every word of it.

That was a milestone album. Every once in a while, Sinatra makes such a record, one I think is meant to be a personal statement. And now he's made another—*Cycles*. If you listen to it carefully, you can hear that the man has made some sort of progress, progress in that part of the self we used to call the soul. The despair is gone. Much of the arrogance is gone. He sounds like a man who has come to grips with himself and life. The title track says he keeps discovering that life runs in cycles. Another song, Gayle Caldwell's excellent "Wandering," says that sometimes he thinks he's on the right track, but he keeps coming back to "the same place, the same place where I started." "From Both Sides, Now" says that after looking at them from both sides, he really doesn't know love or life at all.

Two of the songs are dreadful: "Rain in My Heart" and "My Way of Life," both of which are "big" songs, flamboyant and pretentious. "Rain in My Heart" has a particularly bombastic and self-important key change that I find terribly annoying. And "My Way of Life" has a weirdly ghastly lyric. If the words of *People* are neurotic in their belly-crawling dependency, those of "My Way of Life" are almost psychotic in their jealous possessiveness. The character of the "singer" here (and every song is a fictional characterization of sorts) is that kind of man who surreptitiously reads his wife's diary, accuses her unjustly of infidelities, and drives her half crazy with his own madness. Yet we can see why Sinatra did the song: there's a line that says he's tired of the people at the door, the applause from the

Frank Sinatra at age three (1919). *(Frank Driggs Collection)*

Sinatra with his first singing group, the Hoboken Four, performing on *Major Bowes Original Amateur Hour* (1935). *(The Billy Rose Theatre Collection, The New York Public Library for the Performing Arts, Astor, Lenox and Tilden Foundations)*

Bandleader Harry James (playing trumpet) gave Sinatra his first major break as a singer (1939). *(Frank Driggs Collection)*

Bandleader Tommy Dorsey (left) gave the singer national exposure to launch his solo career in 1942. Standing on either side of Sinatra are members of the singing group the Pied Pipers (1940). *(Frank Driggs Collection)*

Sinatra's first stint as a nightclub entertainer (ca. 1943). *(The Bettmann Archive)*

Early "Swoonatra" (1943–1944). *(Frank Driggs Collection)*

The solo sensation on stage at the Paramount, with conductor Raymond Paige behind him and screaming bobby-soxers in front (1944). *(Frank Driggs Collection)*

The scene of mass hysteria, the Paramount Theatre in New York (1944). *(Frank Driggs Collection)*

At the height of his early fame, Sinatra performs at Lewisohn Stadium in a benefit to aid the New York Philharmonic (1943). *(Pictorial, Star File)*

A crowd of frenzied admirers welcomes the new actor to California (1943). *(UPI/Bettmann Newsphotos)*

"The Crooner" (ca. 1944).
(Frank Driggs Collection)

Sinatra talks with Nat King Cole, pianist for the Metronome All Stars
(1946). *(Frank Driggs Collection)*

Sinatra and his most important arranger and conductor, Nelson Riddle, work together on a Capitol album in the 1950s. *(Starchives, Star File)*

With his second wife, actress Ava Gardner, Sinatra attends the Academy Awards ceremony at which he won an Oscar for best supporting actor in *From Here to Eternity* (1954). *(Starchives, Star File)*

Sinatra during one of his conducting gigs, with Nelson Riddle (seated right) at his side (1956). *(UPI/ Bettmann Newsphotos)*

Fellow legend Bing Crosby and Sinatra sing "Well, Did You Evah?" in the film *High Society* (1956). *(Frank Driggs Collection)*

The quintessential 1950s Sinatra, in the film *Pal Joey* (1957). *(The Museum of Modern Art, New York City)*

"The Saloon Singer" appears on *The Dean Martin Show* (1959). *(Frank Driggs Collection)*

Sinatra with 1950s singing phenomenon Elvis Presley following the rock and roll star's discharge from the military (1960). *(Frank Driggs Collection)*

Sinatra with fellow Rat Packers Dean Martin and Sammy Davis, Jr. (1961). *(UPI/Bettmann Newsphotos)*

Practice makes perfect (1961). *(The Billy Rose Theatre Collection, The New York Public Library for the Performing Arts, Astor, Lenox and Tilden Foundations)*

Sinatra with President
John F. Kennedy in
Las Vegas (ca. 1960).
(Pictorial, Star File)

Recording with the Count Basie Orchestra for Sinatra's own label, Reprise
Records, in the early 1960s. *(UPI/Bettmann Newsphotos)*

Sinatra appears as a "love child" in the television special *Francis Albert Sinatra Does His Thing* (1968). *(UPI/Bettmann Newsphotos)*

The Summit: legends Ella Fitzgerald and Count Basie join Sinatra at the Uris Theater in New York (1975). *(Frank Driggs Collection)*

Sinatra with his current wife, Barbara. (Danny Chin, Star File)

Still swingin' after all these years at the Golden Nugget in Atlantic City, New Jersey (1983). *(Mary D'Anella,* Philadelphia *magazine)*

The Elder Statesman of Entertainment at the Meadowlands, New Jersey, in the 1990s. *(Todd Kaplan, Star File)*

floor. Put that together with the last lines of *Cycles,* an interesting lyric on a very ordinary country-and-western melody: "So I'll keep on tryin' to sing, but please don't ask me now."

Traces of Sinatra's old snobbery turn up in two of the songs. In "Moody River," he sings the word "sin" and then, finding that the rhyme word for it is "friend" (country-and-western, rock, and folk writers are notoriously sloppy about rhyming) he sings it with amused contempt as "frind," thereby putting the writer down. But if he didn't dig it (and I don't dig it either) he shouldn't have done it. As a matter of fact, the song is out of style and context with the rest of the album.

He makes lyric changes in John Hartford's "Gentle on My Mind." At the end, he "corrects" Hartford's grammar: he sings "the rivers flowing *gently* on my mind," and it kills the mood. Hartford's use of "gentle" as an adverb is an Americanism, parallel to "Drive Slow," which bothers none of us any more. We are in the process of dropping a lot of adverbial endings on this continent, and the English language in another fifty years is going to be radically different than it is now. As Chaucer used a lot of "low" English only to have it become standard English, Hartford uses the people's English of our time, and Sinatra makes a serious error in tampering with it. As a matter of fact, he doesn't do the song at all well. He tries to make it swing in the manner of jazz, and country-and-western music swings in quite another way. By punching out the time, he kills the swing and diminishes the depth of the song. Finally, he omits the powerful second verse. He almost gets into the mood of the song at the end, when he slows to ballad tempo. Maybe he should have done the whole thing that way, as he does "Little Green Apples."

You haven't heard "Little Green Apples" until you hear Sinatra do it. It's the high point of the album. He slows it up, does the recitativelike section ad lib, then the refrain softly in tempo. And we discover that Bobby Russell's song about the joys of ordinary married life is not merely good, it is exquisite—one of the loveliest songs in years.

We also discover where Frank Sinatra is these days: he is finding out that there is a proletarian poetry going on in our time—not the angry, up-tight, and frequently ugly little songs of purported social significance, but songs that embrace the big little lyrical things of this world. It is in Jim Webb's "By the Time I Get to Phoenix," which Sinatra does here, in Bobby Hebb's "Elusive Butterfly," and in all of Hartford's work. We're witnessing a rediscovery of simple values, and it is coming out in some of our songs. And this is where Sinatra's professional life starts to flow in a common stream with his personal life. He is saying here, "Hey, contrary to what I said in *Life* magazine a few years ago, there's some fine material being written these days," and he's also saying sadly that the life he's lived is not where it's at. For all the fantastic success of his career, he's missed out on much of what makes life good. And don't tell me I'm reading things into this album: the handprint of the man is all over it.

Frank Sinatra has always been a mass of contradictions. I have heard countless stories of his arrogance, hostility, rudeness, and contempt for others—genuinely ugly little bits of behavior. At the same time, I know of many incidents of his incomparable consideration and kindness. Nor have the latter been grandstand displays: the public has never heard of most of them. Indeed, he has as a matter of policy so carefully concealed acts of thoughtfulness that one had to conclude he was afraid people might think him soft.

If this album is a personal statement—and I am convinced it is—it says that the two Frank Sinatras are becoming one, and that this person accepts weakness and error in himself and therefore in others. He is saying, "I have been a fool." And the day you say that, and say it with a sigh of self-forgiveness, you begin to find peace.

The September of My Years had a mood of anguish. *Cycles* has the mood of a sad smile, and it is full of compassion. It sounds as if this remarkable talent may be turning into a remarkable man.

Many articles were written on the occasion of Frank Sinatra's retirement in 1971, but none more immediate, moving, and descriptive than the following piece by the late Thomas Thompson, entertainment editor of *Life* and best-selling author of *Blood and Money, Serpentine,* and *Celebrity.*

Frank Sinatra's Swan Song
Thomas Thompson ★ 1971

The program was running long, as all charity galas do, and there was a restless, unexpected hour to kill before Frank Sinatra could walk onto the Los Angeles stage and sing in public for what he said would be the last time. It was twenty-nine years since those wild nights at the Paramount Theatre in New York. He was nervous. He had carefully orchestrated this finale and, being the most meticulous of men, he wanted it played with style and grace. He took the typewritten lists of the fourteen songs he would sing and he looked at it over and over again. He threw it down on the table and began doodling. His felt pen created a house, then he filled it in with black strokes, covering the windows and doors as if no one lived there any more.

He was making small talk and a frog crept into his voice. Someone noticed it. "You want something to drink, Frank?" There is always someone there to fetch for him. "Yeah . . . thanks . . . I'd like a vodka." The man started out. Frank stopped him. "Either that or a cup of hot tea." The man hurried away. Frank stopped him once more. "Better get booze. Forget the tea."

Al Viola, Frank's longtime guitar player, came in and the two men went to a quiet corner of the dressing room to run through one of the old songs. "This goes back to the beginning," Frank said, closing his eyes and moving deep within himself. He began singing, quietly, "Try a Little Tenderness." The voice was whispery, from far away, but gleaming, burnished like a gold coin kept in a velvet box. He was seated in front of a wall-length mirror with his dinner jacket off and one black-patent boot crossed over his knee. The smoke from his cigarette seemed to hang about him, making clouds of time. In the middle of the song he opened his eyes and looked at his reflection. What looked back was a man of fifty-five, a trim, well-made man with a face so reddened from the desert sun—he had played twelve holes of golf earlier this day before hurrying to L.A.—that there was no need of makeup. There were rumors around that he was really quitting because he was ill, gravely ill. I had the question ready, but it seemed not the time to ask it. I would ask it later, if at all.

When the song was finished, he grinned because the notes were all there. "Can you remember the very first time you sang in public?" I asked.

"Wow," he said, looking up at the ceiling for an answer. He shook his head. "God, I honestly don't remember." He circled the coffee table in meditation for a few moments. "I must have been a hot twelve years old," he finally said. "Probably at some political rally. . . . No, wait, I think it was at some hotel in Elizabeth, New Jersey. Late '20s. I had a hairline down to here." He drew an imaginary line across the middle of his eyes. He was remembering now and his face was lighting up. "I probably sang "Am I Blue?" and I probably got paid a couple of packs of cigarettes and maybe a sandwich. So here I am tonight, forty years later, going out the same way I came in—singing for nothing."

The vodka came and Frank squeezed half a lemon into it and took a long drink. "A fella came up to me the other day with a nice story," he said. "He was in a bar somewhere and it was the quiet time of night. Everybody's staring down at the sauce and one of my saloon songs comes on the jukebox. "One for My Baby," something like that. After a while, a drunk at the end of the bar looks up and says, jerking his thumb toward the jukebox, 'I wonder who *he* listens to? . . .'"

Fair question. Who *does* Sinatra listen to? Is there anybody whose voice does for him what his has done for us, all of us over thirty, all of us who recollect Sinatra drifting over from the phonograph in the corner of the living room, the fire low, the wine spent, Sinatra murmuring reassurances. Sinatra, every man's advocate in seduction, Sinatra, every man's ally in romantic defeat? He has even led that kind of life: one good woman and three children, a second marriage to the most tempting and beautiful woman in the world, a third and saddening one to a girl half his age. He is all of our fantasies.

Cary Grant came into the dressing room, the first of what would be a pageant of Hollywood's celebrated. The evening would raise $800,000 for the Motion Picture and Television Relief Fund, and Gregory Peck, as the man in charge, had persuaded many of the great names in the business to perform: Jack Benny, Bob Hope, Barbra Streisand, Pearl Bailey, Mitzi Gaynor. Grant and Sinatra embraced warmly. They talked quietly of being nervous (Cary Grant *nervous?*), of what they had to do in the show that night. Then their conversation turned to their children. Grant quietly retired from films a few years ago, with no public statement. Frank chose to announce his publicly. Someone in the corridor outside had said earlier, "Frank's shrewd. He's letting people know he's stopping by his own decision. You go a few months in this town without a picture, and people start saying you can't get work. They won't be able to say that about Frank."

Now came the comedians. Don Rickles burst in dragging Sammy Davis, Jr., under his arm in a bear hug. "We warmed 'em up for you, Frank," he said, his voice breaking the quiet room like a trombone full out. "You're gonna be great out there, Frank. People love pity, Frank."

Jack Benny ambled in. He had his violin out and Frank backed off in mock horror. Benny breaks up Sinatra the way George Burns breaks up Benny. "This man," announced Benny, fluttering a hand toward Frank, "this man endorses Ronald Reagan for governor of California. Now *I* would have endorsed Reagan quietly, but Frank did it first. So I come out second with a little endorsement, and what do I get from Frank Sinatra the next day but a one word telegram. It says 'copycat.'" Benny pauses; his timing is always impeccable. Frank is ready to fall off the couch. Benny recommences. "Now *I* would like to retire, only . . . " He starts sputtering, "only, I *can't*." He points at Frank, who is seizing his sides in laughter.

They talk golf. Frank says he is playing three times a week; his score is down to the mid-eighties and as soon as the strength returns to his right hand, he may do better. Last year he underwent painful surgery on this hand. The tissue in the palm had bunched, causing two of his fingers to bend inward like claws. It took six months before he regained the use of his hand. "I've been sitting at the piano playing octaves," he said, showing how he could stretch his hand from his thumb to his little finger.

Now seemed the time for the question. "How is your health, Frank?"

"My health is spectacular," he replied, annoyed that he would have to defend it. "In fact, it's never been better. That's why those goddamn rumors burn me so. It shows the irresponsibility of the American press."

Benny left and the room was briefly quiet. "Are you *really* quitting?" I asked.

There was no hesitation. "I'm absolutely serious about retirement," he answered. "You can't make an idle statement like the one I made. At least *I* can't. I'm not built that way." I have known Sinatra for some time. He is not a devious man.

He drank some more vodka, but it did not seem to be relaxing him. The evening had too many ghosts in it. He was as tense as a fighter waiting for the bell. "I've had enough. Maybe the public's had enough, too."

I shook my head.

"I've got things to do," he went on. "Like the first thing is not to do anything at all for eight months, maybe a year." He would roam around the desert taking pictures of cactus, he said. He would hang them on the brick walls of the hospital wing he has endowed in Palm Springs. He would "read Plato and grow petunias." He would paint a little, maybe try once again with watercolors. "I've never been able to control them," he said.

"Will you write that book?"

He shook his head, doubtfully. "I'm not that much of a talkative guy," he said. "I probably won't do a book." He fell silent. He thought about it for a while. Something came to him. "If I did," he said, "it wouldn't be one of those 'and then I did' kind of books. Maybe it could be short things, little anecdotes, bits and pieces, poignant memories. Take the band days. I wanted very much to go with Glenn Miller—and he said he'd take me—but in those days he didn't *feature* the vocalist. His musical arrangements very much took precedence over the singer. So I went with Dorsey. I've often thought how different things might have been if I'd gone with Miller. Probably wouldn't be here tonight, that's for sure."

Five years ago Frank had told me he would quit when he felt his voice was going, "when the vibrato starts to widen, when the breath starts to give out." When that happens, he would say good-bye. Had that time come? Vigorous denial.

"Physically, the voice is a long way from going. Hell, I just quit, that's all. I don't want to put any more makeup on. I don't want to perform anymore. I'm not going to stop living. Maybe I'm going to start living."

He bounded outside to inspect the stage as any performer likes to do. As he worked his way there, people stopped him, embraced him, congratulated him. Rosalind Russell, who a few minutes later would break down completely as she introduced him, gave him a hug and a wisecrack about retirement. "I can't wait," Frank said. "I couldn't be happier. You'll follow me one of these days, Roz. It comes with age." He seemed anxious to enlist others into inactivity, as a man seeks allies when venturing into the unknown. He spotted Joe Namath. "You're next to get out," he cried to the football player. He saw Bob Hope. They kidded together. "Hey, you really look emotional, Frank."

It was past midnight now. Barbra Streisand was finishing a rocking version of "Oh, Happy Day" and the huge audience was enthusiastic, though nearly surfeited with four hours of entertainment. Frank slipped on his coat and Don Rickles yelled, "Somebody help the old man on with his coat. Make way! Make way for the old-timer. Help him go out in a blaze of glory. Remember, Frank. Pity!"

Roz Russell was onstage, struggling with a voice that kept going out of control. "Our friend has made a decision," she said in fits and starts, "a decision we don't particularly like, but one which we must honor. He's worked long and hard for thirty years with his head and his voice and especially his heart . . . but it's time to put back the Kleenex and stifle the sob, for we still have the man, we still have the blue eyes, those wonderful blue eyes, that smile, for one last time we have the man, the greatest entertainer of the twentieth century. . . ."

The audience stood in ovation when Frank came out, and they stood three or four more times during his thirty minutes out front. Almost cruelly he jarred their memories. He had chosen his songs to represent periods in his life—in all our lives. He sang "All or Nothing at All" and "I've Got You Under My Skin" and "I'll Never Smile Again" and "The Lady Is a Tramp" and "Ol' Man River."

He sang with power, with breath strong enough to hold the notes, keep the notes—strong, full, lush Sinatra notes. There was the old phrasing, the attention to the lyric, the delicate shading, the long melodic line. He sang almost as if throwing out a challenge. Try that! At last he sang "My Way" with its emotional chords and words, and the crowd leaped up, thinking it was over. But Sinatra would fool them. He had another song. He had built his career, he said softly, on saloon songs. He would end quietly on such a song. He slipped from his words into "Angel Eyes," surely a song for the short hours. He ordered the stage dressed in darkness, a pin spot picking out his profile in silhouette. He lit a cigarette in mid-song and its smoke enveloped him. He came to the last line. "Excuse me while I . . . disappear." And he was gone.

A limousine was waiting to whisk him and Roz Russell to her home for a party. Frank said he could stay but a few minutes. "It's late, an old retired man has to get to bed," he said. The Cadillac sped through the quiet streets.

"I'm tired," he said. "It's been a helluva thirty-five years. I always sang a tough book, you know. Not a lot of phony talk. It used to wring me out. I used to do five full shows a night at the Jersey shore. From 8:15 P.M. to 4 A.M. I'd see the sun come out as I'd walk home. And then, at the Paramount in New York, we did ten shows a day—eleven on Saturdays . . . ."

The radio came on, a Spanish-language station sending out a south-of-the-border lament. Frank made up some quick lyrics about a cowboy and his horse. He sang a few bars. He stopped.

"And that, ladies and gentlemen," he said, "is the last time Frank Sinatra will open his mouth." He sank back in the seat and closed his eyes.

All of us laughed, but in our laughter was the unmistakable edge of sadness.

The sadness was to be short-lived, for Sinatra returned in 1973. No one was sure why he had ever left. Some had speculated that it was for health reasons, others cited the effects of the loss of his father, and still others spoke of the singer's disenchantment with the kinds of songs being written—rock songs and other material that did not fit his style. His return stimulated further speculation. Was he bored with his life? Was his financial empire in disarray? Maybe there is a simpler answer. If Beethoven had to compose and Gauguin had to paint, why not assume that Sinatra had to sing?

His return occasioned a television special and an album entitled *Ol' Blue Eyes Is Back*. Although the singer sounded somewhat rusty, the material (for example, "Send in the Clowns" and a specially written song, "Let Me Try Again") let the world know that Sinatra was indeed back. On the eve of the TV special, actress Rosalind Russell, an old friend of Sinatra and the hostess of his last farewell concert, paid tribute to her pal in print.

Sinatra: An American Classic
Rosalind Russell ★ 1973

His face may never be part of the frieze at Mount Rushmore, but this legendary Italian-American from Hoboken, New Jersey, is an appropriate subject for a Norman Rockwell study. Because Frank Sinatra *is* an American classic, a man who has had his ups and his downs but who has never been counted out. The performer of the century, however, did step aside in June 1971, after completing 58 films, 100 record albums, more than 2,000 individual recordings; and I believe that after three decades of concentrated work his decision to retire was a sincere one.

That June night at the Music Center when I introduced him and announced his "final" appearance, many people questioned my emotion. It came from the fact that I felt it was sad indeed that this talent was literally being silenced by Frank himself—whose voice was, by the way, never better. I thought of the night I heard him in Philadelphia, where he held thousands of people spellbound for over two hours; of the charities for which he sang his heart out to help so many. (I asked him once if he could count the benefits he had done, and he just laughed.)

We drove back from the Music Center that night to my home. Was he really happy now that it was over? "Rosie," replied the Chairman of the Board, "you can't imagine the relief I feel. I did not start, as many people think, singing at a well-known nightclub in New Jersey. I started as a teenager singing in joints on the Jersey Shore for cigarettes and my dinner." (Note to Mom Sinatra: true, your Frankie was well-fed at home, but when "The Voice" developed, so did the ambition to entertain.)

There were multiple reasons for Frank's retirement. I believe that his father's passing had shocked and hurt him deeply. Then, too, he wanted to pause to think things over, to be without pressure for the first time in his active life.

Three generations recognize Francis Albert Sinatra as Frank, Frankie, or just Sinatra. I have known him since 1940, when he sang "I'll Never Smile Again" to my husband Freddie and me during our courting days; Frank was singing with the Tommy Dorsey Band then. He sang the song again, among others, at the twenty-fifth wedding anniversary party that he gave for Freddie and me—a three-day festival which no one who attended will ever forget.

To be Frank's friend is like one of his songs: "All or Nothing at All." It is a total, unconditional commitment, a never-fraying security blanket. He has a short fuse when it comes to criticism of friends he holds in high regard, and he is willing to accept the heat and the flak. True, he is sometimes noisy in his reaction to someone else's abuse because his feelings are intense—as is his sense of justice.

He dislikes women who smoke or drink too much or who wear heavy perfume. He dislikes roast lamb, fair-weather friends, green salads, phonies, complainers and welshers. He enters any public place with trepidation. It is almost a ritual that some man will leave his group, walk over to Frank's table, tap him on the shoulder and ask, "Are you really the lover my wife thinks you are?" Take my word for it, Frank remains patient far longer than he is ever given credit for.

When the *Ladies' Home Journal* suggested that I do this article, the editor asked me to describe Sinatra in one word. Without hesitating I responded "compassionate." I have never seen him refuse a child anything. When Claudette Colbert's husband was critically ill in Barbados, a group of us were at Frank's Palm Springs compound, where he spent the entire night arranging for a plane to fly non-stop to Barbados—complete with medical staff and change of crew (required by law) to pick up Claudette and her husband. After Sammy Davis's serious accident, it was Frank who made him dance again. But most of this rarely reaches the press.

There are several Frank Sinatras. Perhaps this is what makes him both fascinating and controversial. He is tempestuous, tender, searching, indefatigable, unexpected. As a father, he is doting, generous, always involved. I overheard him remark to his daughter on the phone one day, "Yes, Nancy, go ahead, cut your hair if you feel you'll like it." He hung up, shaking his head slightly. "You know, Rosie, I never really left home," he said.

The lover? Of course! Marlene Dietrich once called him "the Mercedes-Benz of men."

Then there is Sinatra, the practical-joker. One night at the compound, my husband Freddie asked if he could have some cheese and crackers before retiring. "There'll be no night food," said Frank. "Lights out!" A half-hour later, we heard the wildest racket coming from an ear-shattering bell, and there was Frank pushing a serving cart full of food, beer, an assortment of goodies.

He is, of course, the perfect host—a great Italian cook, a knitter-together of people, a constant plate-filler and glass-replenisher. He himself is what I call a "fake" drinker; more times than not he talks more about drinking than he actually imbibes. He needs very little sleep. He lets people believe he is swinging every night in the week, whereas he is often home reading. He is an Eric Hoffer buff, a best-seller addict, and has an insatiable interest in history. He recently acquired a brace of French Impressionist paintings, but as a guess I would say his taste runs from the humor of Hirshfeld to Andrew Wyeth.

Then there is another Frank Sinatra—one he may not like my discussing: Sinatra the loner, the constant observer, a profoundly sensitive man. "My Way" has not always been his way. There have been troublesome times, painful times, which he has harbored within himself and shared with no one.

Then there is Sinatra the American. Some may mock it, as is the fashion today, but deep down he is the original all-American, Fourth of July boy. Maybe it is because his father was an Italian immigrant—a prizefighter whom Frank watched become a respected fire captain. Maybe it is because Frank always knew that he himself never could have happened in any country but this one.

Though his political affiliations may change, his respect for his country does not. He raises and lowers the American flag in front of his house every day. Recently he was invited and welcomed to the White House. President Nixon himself led the applause for Frank Sinatra's after-dinner singing with the comment, "Once in a while there is a moment when there is magic in this room." Excuse me, Mr. President, there is magic in every room, in every life, that Mr. Sinatra has ever touched.

IV

Legend

★ ★ ★

1 9 7 3 –

FROM THE MOMENT he returned to his performing roles, Sinatra has been in the public eye. Although he has only rarely entered the recording studio—less than a dozen new albums have appeared in more than twenty years—such releases as *The Main Event, Trilogy, L.A. Is My Lady,* and both *Duets* were major events in the world of pop music. Except for a made-for-television movie in 1977, his recent film work comprises only one starring role and one cameo. But neither the dearth of recordings nor a nonexistent film career has diminished his presence. On the contrary, he has become a legendary figure, acclaimed both for his accomplishments and—perhaps more important in shaping the mythos that surrounds him—for his willful individuality. He has been served well by his adoring fans and by his own combativeness with the media and the publicity hounds.

Ongoing feuds with media people around the world have helped maintain his public visibility. Although the Sinatra of the 1990s appears to have mellowed, his contretemps with the press (whether to his career advantage or not is debatable) began after his first marriage dissolved in the early 1950s and have continued on and off ever since. In the period following his comeback, the battles seemed especially virulent and even reached international proportions. On a tour of Australia in July 1974, Sinatra did not appreciate the hot pursuit by that country's journalists. After the singer publicly characterized these journalists as "hookers" and "parasites," Australian trade unions, in sympathy with the journalists' association, refused to service the singer. No food or drink would be brought to him at his hotel, his baggage would not be moved, and his private plane would not be serviced unless he made amends. Essentially stranded in Australia, Sinatra had managed to unite a nation's entire laboring class against him! Only negotiations between union heads and the singer's attorney brought the standoff to an end, with vague and grudging apologies from both sides. Again, Sinatra had made worldwide headlines. Famous to some, notorious to others, the Sinatra persona—forged in large measure by media reports of incidents like this one—has served to magnify his reputation in the postretirement period.

We would do well to keep in mind, moreover, that the "myth" surrounding the Sinatra legend is not something merely manufactured by adoring fans or the media. Sinatra has also contributed, whether deliberately or passively, to the promulgation of iconic beliefs. When he recorded his famous version of "I'm a Fool to Want You" (1951), it was widely assumed that the song was a lament for his tumultuous experience with Ava Gardner. Yet Sinatra has never commented on whether it was or not, just as he has never disclaimed the notion that his songs are autobiographical.

Babe Ruth, that other great American icon, adopted a similar stance and thereby enhanced his legendary status. When Ruth was asked by the press to verify that he had actually called where he would hit a home run in a 1932 World Series game, he refused to clarify the point, merely stating, "Why don't you read it in the papers? It's all right there in the papers." Whether he actually called the hit or not is unimportant. In the popular imagination, as reflected in the film version of Babe Ruth's life, the hero did nothing less than deliver on his audacious boast.

So it has been with Sinatra. He has let the media and his songs shape his popular image. His use of the song "My Way" attests to his canny manipulation of his private/public image. This decidedly mawkish song does not arouse the listener's desire to hear the other versions by Elvis Presley, Paul Anka, and Sid Vicious. It is Frank's song, and despite his manipulative use of the tune, his performance still rings with enough authenticity to suck in the most cynical members of his audience.

Despite the manic profusion of concerts that was to follow, Sinatra's comeback was not an overnight success. In his first concert appearance at Caesar's Palace Las Vegas, in January 1974, two of the shows in the 1,200-seat room drew a crowd of only 400. Perhaps there were suspicions that the singer was a has-been, an old-timer with little left to give. Gradually, however, the irresistible showman reasserted himself, and while doubts about his performance skills have recurred periodically, they've been quieted in much the same ways—with a sizzling television performance or a reassuring album or a sensational concert tour.

Concert appearances have been Sinatra's mainstay. He toured in 1974, topping off his first year back with the well-publicized "Main Event" concert, televised live from Madison Square Garden. The next year found him even more active on concert stages. In less than a month during the spring of 1975, he played San Francisco, Portland, Seattle, Denver, Chicago, St. Louis, Indianapolis, Montreal, Toronto, Providence, and New Haven. In a two-week period, he played Monte Carlo, Paris, Vienna, Munich, Berlin, London, Brussels, and Amsterdam, and later that year, he performed in

Israel. According to Derek Jewell, "Sinatra press ads at the end of 1975, his 60th year, boasted that in 105 days he had given 140 performances to audiences of more than half a million."*

Many of Sinatra's concerts and tours, including "The Main Event" (1974), "The Concert for the Americas" (Dominican Republic, 1982), "The Ultimate Event" (1988), and "The Diamond Jubilee World Tour" (1991), have been promoted as extravaganzas. These extravagant titles, which do not presage the entrance of a humble artist, were well earned by the singer, not only for his superb performances, but also by his sheer drawing power. A single 1980 concert in Brazil attracted an audience of 175,000—a number that, at the time, qualified as a Guiness world record for a solo performer. "The Ultimate Event" was a forty-concert tour of twenty-nine cities in the United States, featuring Sinatra, Dean Martin, and Sammy Davis, Jr. Early on, Martin left the tour and was replaced by Liza Minnelli. Although Sinatra seemed tired during many of the performances, he embarked on yet another world tour three years later. "The Diamond Jubilee World Tour," while still evidencing inconsistencies, offered a number of sizzling performances. On his Philadelphia stop, Sinatra was on fire, demanding far more of himself than did the audience, many of whom would have settled for just about anything from their idol. In this show, as in virtually all the others he has given over the decades, Sinatra appeared to judge himself against his own stringent standards and not merely by audience approval.

Despite inconsistencies in Sinatra's performances, owing in large measure to his advancing age, he succeeded in further developing his electrifying stage presence during the 1970s and beyond. Modern dance choreographer Twyla Tharp introduced her *Sinatra Suite* in the 1980s, but the singer had invented a choreography of his own over the years. As a concert performer, Sinatra is a very *physical* presence. His every move helps to create the mood of the song—his arms wave, his head droops, his finger points, and his foot stomps. All these gestures, whether expressing despondency or bursting with swing, are dictated by the song. Recalling Sinatra's performance of "Angel Eyes," one devoted fan noted that

> his movements under that lonely spotlight were hypnotic. Bent over to the side, he had lighted a cigarette, tortuously. A nimbus of smoke enshrouded him. At times his body would hunch over, or his arm would shoot out at a crazy angle under the spotlight, piercing the smoke and the shadows. He looked like a marionette in agony. . . ."†

*Derek Jewell, *Frank Sinatra: A Celebration* (Boston: Little, Brown, 1985), p. 123.
†Lee Grove, "Last Night When We Were Young," in the cumulative supplement to Albert I. Lonstein and Vito R. Marino, *The Revised Compleat Sinatra*, 3rd ed. (New York: Musicprint, 1981) p. 14.

Anyone who has been to a Sinatra concert over the past three decades will instantly recognize this description.

Since the 1960s, Sinatra has been the biggest game in town for Las Vegas and, more recently, for that other casino mecca, Atlantic City. His appearances have drawn people to both towns, and the singer has even lent his own personal endorsements to television commercials and billboard and print ads for the casino–hotels at which he has played. Sinatra's casino and concert appearances have attracted so many of the faithful that one travel agency sponsored package deals to New York and Atlantic City and to a Sinatra-sponsored golf tournament, including a performance by Sinatra in Las Vegas. (A Sinatra cruise featuring a sound-alike singer and Sinatra videos was also available.) In short, Sinatra has been more than a great concert draw over the past three decades—he's also been a money maker for others.

The impact of Sinatra's persona extends beyond his own concerts, recordings, and casino performances. It extends beyond the army of musicians who have been so lavish in their praise for his musical talents. And it extends beyond the legions of fans who have adored his singing over the decades. For many, Sinatra has assumed the iconic character of an American cultural institution. He serves not only as a reference point for romantic music (and even romance itself), but also as a guide to personal conduct. He is an inspirer of dreams of success, an icon within the Italian-American community, and a strong and ubiquitous cultural presence. Unlike James Dean or Elvis Presley, who achieved their greatest fame after their lifetime, the legendary Sinatra is part of our everyday experience. Despite his declining powers, which would demythologize a lesser hero, he continues to receive our unqualified respect.

Within the pop-culture psyche, Sinatra is more than an aging man or a superstar or a hero. After more than fifty years of media exposure, he is a legend, and, as is the case with all legendary personae, history (fact) is far less important than image. Accordingly, references to and images of him appear frequently in motion pictures, television dramas and comedies, radio and television commercials, local community life, and even commentaries on our manners and morals.

Apart from his own fine acting, Sinatra's motion-picture presence has been varied and interesting. In the 1940s, he was represented in animated cartoons as the ultra-skinny hero of swooning teenagers or as a crooning bird who was the rival of another crooning bird, Bing Crosby. More recently, in *Who Framed Roger Rabbit?* (1988), he was seen as an animated sword (appropriately named Swingin' Sword) whose blade turns into Sinatra's head singing "Witchcraft."

Sinatra's singing has been heard on the soundtracks of many films, usually to underline a thematic point. For example, his "Summer Wind" is a constant in *The Pope of Greenwich Village* (1984), "Fly Me to the Moon" gives voice to the greedy yearnings of the Gordon Gecko character in Oliver Stone's *Wall Street* (1987); and Sinatra's photograph is prominently displayed on the walls of the ill-fated pizzeria in Spike Lee's *Do the Right Thing* (1989). In 1983, John Sayles scripted and directed *Baby, It's You*, a story set in the 1960s about the relationship between two Trenton, New Jersey, teenagers—a middle-class Jewish girl and a working-class Italian-American boy nicknamed the Sheik who aspires to be another Sinatra. Late in the film, in a very poignant scene, we observe him working in a Florida club lip-synching Sinatra recordings.*

Sinatra's presence also extends to television, even though he has made comparatively few appearances over the past thirty years. He has not made the talk-show rounds or been interviewed very often, and the musical specials in which he has appeared are few and far between. The same can be said of his commercial endorsements. He has done some high-profile promos for the Golden Nugget and the Sands in Atlantic City, Chrysler cars, and Michelob beer, along with a handful of public-service announcements, but his appearances in such spots are rare. And yet, his iconic stature in the entertainment industry pervades the TV and radio fare. Sinatra-style singers do voice-overs on commercials, and his name is mentioned frequently in television series. One episode of the police series *Kojak* centered around a sensitive and troubled young woman's fascination with Sinatra's singing. On the NBC weekly series *Saturday Night Live*, comic actor Joe Piscopo built many a skit around his physical and vocal impersonations of Sinatra, and he even recorded a comic album impersonating Sinatra performing rock hits such as the Rolling Stones's "Under My Thumb," Bruce Springsteen's "Born to Run," and Pat Benatar's "Hit Me with Your Best Shot."

In television situation comedies, moreover, getting-too-big-for-their-britches types have been asked, "Who do you think you are, Frank Sinatra?" Meeting Sinatra or attending a concert by Ol' Blue Eyes has been the subject of episodes of *Who's the Boss?* and *The Golden Girls*. A poster of Sinatra hangs in rock musician Jesse's room in *Full House*. Sinatra's "Fly Me to the Moon" is heard during an episode of *The Wonder Years*, a poignant wedding scene which concludes with Frank singing "I—I LOVE—YOU!" And the sitcom *Married with Children* has Sinatra's recording of "Love and Marriage" as its theme song. (In fact, this Van Heusen–Cahn song had its

---

*A real-life variation on this idea was reported in a news feature on an Iranian-born singer known as Farshad who had emigrated to the United States in 1977. After studying opera at a state university, he began a three-year study of Sinatra's style. Farshad stated that nobody "on earth can match his [Sinatra's] interpretation of delivering words and music. Singing is easy—how you deliver it is the key" (quoted in Phyllis Guth, "Iranian-Born Singer Dreams Big: Success on Par with Sinatra," *Philadelphia Inquirer*, 28 November 1991, p. 24B).

origin in a 1955 television production of Thornton Wilder's *Our Town*, in which Sinatra was cast as the Stage Manager.)

Owing to his aggressive "my way" reputation, Sinatra sometimes serves as a role model in commentaries on contemporary manners. In 1991, two writers for different publications playfully considered the question, What would Frank do?* to handle rude or abusive situations and still come out with your pride intact. Of course, their answer—swift and aggressive Sinatra-style retaliation—is based less on knowledge of Sinatra than on public perception.

Sinatra's heroic attributes are most fervently embraced by Italian-Americans. Sinatra became the Phenomenon at a time when Italian-Americans were still subjected to pejorative epithets because of their status as recent additions to the American melting pot. His rise to fame and power, along with his self-confident personality and his long history of fighting ethnic, racial, and religious bigotry (by political means as well as the quick punch-in-the-mouth style of justice), endeared him in a special way to those of Italian heritage. As suggested by Leonard Mustazza in "Sinatra's Enduring Appeal," Sinatra's rise preceded that of the many Italian-Americans who now hold high positions in society—the Iacoccas, Scalias, Rodinos, and Cuomos. Even at the level of local politics, longtime Americans and "respectable" immigrants like the Irish-Catholics predominated; Italian-Americans did not move into positions of power and high visibility until the 1960s (and even then, baseball player Rocky Colavito was denied the right to purchase a home in a "high-class" neighborhood because his complexion was too dark). And yet two decades earlier, Sinatra, this most brilliant and enduring of stars, was proudly Italian, and even his alleged mob associations did not dampen his appeal to a community that felt picked on and excluded.

In Sinatra's hometown of Hoboken, New Jersey, a visitor to Leo's Grandevous Restaurant, located several blocks from Sinatra's birthplace, will find a traditional Italian restaurant and bar with a Wall of Fame displaying close to 100 black-and-white photos of Frank, whose voice is also heard most of the time on the jukebox. Certainly this salute to the singer may be attributed partially to home-boy pride, but that distinction alone does not account for the duplication of this kind of scene wherever there is a Little Italy in the United States. In such places across the country—notably in New York, New Jersey, Pennsylvania, and other older, urban communities—barbershops and restaurants, bakeries and delis are festooned with Sinatra memorabilia.

Sinatra's place in American culture is recognized by admirers of all ages; however, there is a generation gap. For some, Sinatra is an unknown

---

*"What Would Frank Do?" *Esquire*, June 1991, p. 27; Karen Heller, "Before You Grovel, Ask: Would Frank Do It?" *Philadelphia Inquirer*, 29 September 1991, p. 3J.

or, even worse, the remnant of some former and clearly inferior generation. For still others, Sinatra's continuing presence is a form of punish-
ment, a way for those of an earlier generation to express their exasperation
with the current one by bringing musical "enlightenment" to the young.
According to several newspaper and magazine accounts, a high-school
teacher in Riverside, Illinois, a suburb of Chicago, heads the Frank Sinatra
Detention Club, wherein students who misbehave must listen to thirty
minutes of Sinatra tapes. The students apparently see it as the cruelest of
punishments, whereas the teacher hopes to enlighten them about their
musical heritage. If necessary, he's thinking of becoming more severe and
expanding the treatment to include Tony Bennett and Mel Tormé!*

In light of these perceptions of Sinatra within the context of popular
American culture, one is bound to wonder what the "real" Sinatra is like?
Put another way, is it really possible finally to understand the human side
of this mass-culture phenomenon? And isn't such a task rendered more
difficult when that someone has metamorphosed into a myth the size of
Frank Sinatra? Some of the singer's acquaintances have attempted to shed
light on the person; other talented observers have also made the effort.
Perhaps their combined impressions can unlock the mystery behind this
contradictory musical giant—tough/tender, ruffian/gentleman, kind/vi-
cious, private/exhibitionist, unreachable/vulnerable are a few of the pair-
ings that come immediately to mind.

Sinatra's friends offer boundless praise and devotion to the man. Not
only Rosalind Russell, whose assessment appears earlier in this book, but
countless others have attested to the kindness and generosity of their
friend. Among many others, Sammy Davis, Jr., Peggy Lee, Buddy Rich
(with whom the singer engaged in a few altercations in their early days),
Milton Berle (who seems puzzled by the many brawls in which he participated while in Sinatra's company), Richard Burton, Gregory Peck, and
Kirk Douglas have publicly commented in books and other sources on
Sinatra's generosity. (Indeed, there is hardly a biography of any Hollywood figure that does not mention his name, and the comments are usually very favorable.) Praise has come from people whom one would not
automatically think of as Sinatra cronies or associate with his sociopolitical
ilk. In his published diaries, Noel Coward, whose public style was certainly very different from the singer's, had only marvelous things to say
about the man he calls "Frankie." A frequent guest at Sinatra's home, he
describes his host as someone who "contrives, apparently without effort,
to be cheerful and unflagging and, at the same time, sees that everyone has
drinks and is looked after." Coward further describes him as "a remarkable personality—tough, vulnerble and somehow touching. He is also im-

---

*Anita Manning, "Chicago School Starts Spreading the Detention Blues," *USA Today*, 22
September 1992, p. 1A.

measurably kind.''* Even beyond his generosity to friends, there is evidence of a humanitarianism of major-league proportions that crosses international borders.

There are, however, at least two sides to every story—certainly far more than two sides in a story as complex as Sinatra's—and so it is that other show-business figures present a more negative view of their encounters with Sinatra. In his autobiography, Mel Tormé, while acknowledging his worship of Sinatra the singer, laments that he has ''had an unhappy history with him.''† Sinatra's verbal and physical brawls have punctuated his entire career. On many occasions, he has used the concert stage to attack his enemies, often in raw language. These battles have ranged from verbal attacks on the press to at least one admitted rabbit punch that decked a member of the fourth estate. His bad experience in Australia was nearly duplicated in other venues as well. Critic Joseph Sobran writes that Sinatra's ''celebrity is the enemy of his genius'' in that ''he has forced an admiring public to associate him with the Rat Pack, ugly feuds with the press, thuggish bodyguards, a self-advertised appetite for booze and broads'' and the like. While Sobran clearly has disdain for this side of the singer, he concludes that ''the wonder is that this uncouth man once sang the best American popular songs . . . with such uncanny sensitivity and finesse.''‡

In 1965, Gay Talese was sent by *Esquire* magazine to Los Angeles to interview Sinatra. Although the meeting had been arranged with the singer's publicist, Talese wound up spending about five days in L.A. without ever speaking privately with Sinatra. In his article, Talese recounts his interviews with Sinatra's protective retinue and what he was able to observe from a distance. He describes a number of Sinatras. One is a man who seems to be somewhat detached from the scene, wherever he is. Another is a person of enormous kindness and generosity. But ''the same Sinatra . . . can, within the same hour, explode in a towering rage of intolerance should a small thing be incorrectly done for him,'' Talese warns. He views Sinatra as ''a wholly unpredictable man of many moods and great dimension, a man who responds instantaneously to instinct— suddenly, dramatically, wildly he responds, and nobody can predict what will follow.''§

Critic Mikal Gilmore observes that ''for all the grace of his talent, there is also a considerable darkness about Sinatra: a desperate hunger for the

---

The Noel Coward Diaries, ed. Graham Payne and Sheridan Morley (Boston: Little, Brown, 1982), p. 301.

†Mel Tormé, *It Wasn't All Velvet* (New York: Zebra, 1990), pp. 80–83.

‡Joseph Sobran, ''The Man Who Was Sinatra,'' *National Review*, 7 February 1992, p. 54.

§Gay Talese, ''Frank Sinatra Has a Cold,'' in *Fame and Obscurity* (New York: Dell, 1981), pp. 178–79.

validation that comes from love and power, and a ruinous anger toward anything that challenges that validation."* While Sinatra has denied many of the allegations concerning his behavior, he has, in his own way, also acknowledged his darker side. "I don't know what other singers feel when they articulate lyrics," he told a *Playboy* interviewer in 1963, "but being an 18-carat manic-depressive and having lived a life of violent emotional contradiction, I have an over-acute capacity for sadness as well as elation."† Although he is referring here to his art, the "violent emotional contradiction" also defines the manner in which he's lived his life. Indeed, even longtime musical associates have been left in the dark by the enigmatic singer. Nelson Riddle once noted that Sinatra never really praised him directly for his work. Riddle simply assumed that Sinatra was pleased because he kept employing the arranger–conductor.

Composer–lyricist Sammy Cahn was another longtime Sinatra associate. The singer first recorded a Cahn lyric, "I Could Make You Care," with Tommy Dorsey in 1940. The relationship was strengthened by Sinatra's loyal insistence that Cahn's participation in some of his film projects was the price for his own presence. During the 1940s, Cahn teamed up with melodist Jule Styne to create the scores to *Step Lively*, *Anchors Aweigh*, and *It Happened in Brooklyn*. Although they were never extremely close (Cahn seemed keenly aware of the singer's temperament and the price it could exact), their professional friendship endured. Sinatra recorded more than eighty-five Cahn lyrics over the years, significantly more than those of any other lyricist. Cahn also contributed special material, such as the 1960 campaign lyrics for "High Hopes" and the lyrics for "Teach Me Tonight" on Sinatra's *L.A. Is My Lady* album.

During a radio interview in the 1980s, Cahn commented on what he saw as the basic elements of the Sinatra legend: his fame and notoriety, his musicianship, and his mysterious personality. Pointing out that the singer's fame had endured for more than fifty years, he noted that the *New York Times* rarely went for several weeks without at least mentioning the singer's name. Cahn also spoke of his respect for Sinatra's musical ear and his ability with a song. The lyricist recalled an incident that took place while they were recording the title tune for the film *The Tender Trap*. Just as Sinatra approached the last few bars, he suddenly stopped, stormed out of the recording booth, and confronted Cahn. "Did you see how high the note is for the last 'love' in the song?" he shouted. "How can you expect me to hit such a high note?" Cahn calmly responded, "Because you're Frank Sinatra." The singer stormed back to the booth, began the next take, and, when he came to the infamous note, hit it perfectly and with a vengeance while glaring furiously at Cahn. As to Sinatra's personality, Cahn,

---

*Mikal Gilmore, "The Wonder of Sinatra," *Rolling Stone*, 24 January 1991, p. 47.
†"Frank Sinatra" (1963), in *Playboy Interviews* (Chicago: Playboy Press, 1967), p. 7.

like many others, had a difficult time figuring it out. He maintained that there are three questions about Sinatra that no one can ever answer at any given moment: What is he like? Where is he now? Will he show up tonight?

The articles that follow consider Sinatra the recording artist, the concert performer, the casino promoter, the pop-culture icon, and the man behind the myth.

Following his emergence from retirement, inaugurated by the album and television special *Ol' Blue Eyes Is Back*, Sinatra has released only seven albums of freshly recorded material, although compilations and reissues continually appear. And yet, this dearth of recordings has not diminished the Sinatra presence or his stature as the "Legend." In fact, even though the quality of these albums and audience response has varied, these seven albums have contributed, each in its own way, to his reputation, if only to prove that he is indeed a survivor.

Drawing on his audience's relief over his return to show business and his own continual desire to update his material, he released an album in 1974 entitled *Some Nice Things I've Missed*. In the following review of the album, *High Fidelity* music critic Morgan Ames comments on Sinatra's ability to put his imprimatur on every contemporary song he takes on.

He's Still—Well, Sinatra
Morgan Ames ★ 1975

This is in defense of Frank Sinatra, a man who is always in his prime one way or another, by nature. I'm tired of the smirks of people who handle their youth as if it were something earned, like a judgeship.

I like the fact that Sinatra could not stay in retirement. That's my kind of inconsistency. It confesses with a shrug that singing is more fun than not; being an ass with the Australian press is more alive than planting daffodils around your golf course or grave. What other singer of Sinatra's roots has the outrageous ease to take Stevie Wonder's 1974 Grammy winner, "Sunshine of My Life," and translate it into his own terms, with no apologies to anyone? The same goes for Neil Diamond's "Sweet Caroline" and the late Jim Croce's "Bad Bad Leroy Brown" (the last fits the singer by default).

For those of us attuned to today's attitudes and rhythm sections, this album takes a moment's getting used to. But to deny the effort is to be as mean and narrow as the contingent that must shrink all artists into their own cute little skull sizes. The conservativeness of youth is a crashing bore.

Frank Sinatra operates from the same intuitive sense of style as ever. Despite the album title, many of these songs are not his kind of thing, but he spits right in their eye with a respectful challenge, ready to make a performance out of a language barrier.

The ballads of the set are a more likely fit for the singer, since he was father to most of them. On "What Are You Doing the Rest of Your Life?" by Michel Legrand and Alan and Marilyn Bergman, Don Costa reminds us and himself that, when he's feeling inspired and exquisite, he can still outwrite any song arranger in the entire business.

Let us also note that, in a business totally dominated by its rhythm sections, necessitating adjunct horn and/or string sweetening sessions after the fact, Sinatra still works live with an orchestra—the same guys who have shared record dates with him for years. The same producers too.

As for the voice: the less it is perfect, the more it is human. And about time.

Styles change like the laundry: In with one load, and out with another. God help Elton John in a few years when we fall out of love with him, when he must express his strength against our tides instead of with them. Ask Burt Bacharach. But I still find it an operative privilege to work in the same industry with Mr. Frank Sinatra.

In 1974, Sinatra toured the United States in an extravaganza billed as "The Main Event," which climaxed in October with a televised concert from Madison Square Garden. In keeping with its name, the concert was promoted as though it were a major boxing attraction featuring the world champion in the ring. (Indeed, the announcer for the evening was sportscaster Howard Cosell.) The musical backing was provided by Woody Herman's band plus strings conducted by Sinatra's long-time pianist Bill Miller. Sinatra insisted on a live telecast, even though he paid the price in some respects. Burdened by a cold and an occasional "frog" in the throat, he had a difficult time with some of the ballad material. Still, he was happy to be there and most desirous to please the audience. The album that resulted from the event (with some tunes spliced in from prior concerts in the series) is marred by the singer's voice problems, but the excitement running through the crowd is palpable, as is the relationship between the singer and his audience. The actual television production (later released on videotape) permits the viewer to observe and hear Sinatra admonishing the audience to be quiet and snappily demanding the elimination of sound-system feedback. The video also captures the honesty of a Sinatra performance, a quality that does not necessarily appeal to all observers. The following reviews of the concert and television special (one by New York Times television critic John J. O'Connor, the other by Times music critic John Rockwell), while agreeing on some matters, have different emphases and ultimately reach different conclusions regarding the concert's worth.

Expert Pacing and Polish
of the Sinatra Show
John J. O'Connor ★ 1974

As a television "event," the live transmission of "Sinatra—The Main Event" from Madison Square Garden on Sunday evening was accomplished with a maximum of professional polish or, if you prefer, hustle. Once ABC and Roone Arledge, producer, moved into the occasion, the setting, complete with 20,000 enthusiastic spectators, became little more than a gigantic prop for a TV spectacular. Smile and whoop it up, you're on national television.

Saturday's version of the show was used as a rehearsal run-through for the following evening, when ABC made sure there was a liberal sprinkling of celebrities at ringside to lend a touch of pop class to the proceedings. For home consumption, the program opened with splendid shots of Manhattan at sunset, obviously filmed a couple of hours earlier, and the grotesque hyperbole of Howard Cosell.

Mr. Cosell paid tribute to the "great arena" in "the heart of the metropolis" and confided that Frank Sinatra was about to come live "to the Western Hemisphere." Actually, except for the East Coast and central states, the program would be transmitted later on tape in most areas.

There was a brief flurry of celebrity titillation. Spotting Walter Cronkite, Mr. Cosell didn't hesitate to dub the CBS News anchorman "Mr. Believable," immediately making that believability suspect. Then the cameras switched to Mr. Sinatra in a passageway, looking relatively calm in the middle of a nervous entourage. One gentleman couldn't resist planting a kiss on the singer's cheek.

The performance itself displayed most of the assets of any live production on television. The sense of immediacy and spontaneity was maintained superbly. Mr. Sinatra, who years ago was one of the first performers to insist on the safeguard of tape for his TV appearances, was putting himself on the vulnerable line, vocal warts and all.

The voice proved to be in good condition, particularly in the up-tempo numbers. Only once, in the opening of "Autumn in New York," did the very professional machinery come close to failing.

Visually, the TV production was paced expertly, if predictably. Shots of the singer were alternated with shots of the audience (John and Mary Lindsay for "Autumn in New York," Mr. Cronkite and the American flag for the brazenly hokey "House I Live In"). Occasionally the ebullience of the audience threatened to degenerate into outright exhibitionism, with the focus shifting away from the performer, but Mr. Sinatra quickly regained control.

Dealing with a Sinatra performance, however, means being forced to deal with the Sinatra personality, and it is this element that separates the intensely devoted fans from the merely curious or thoroughly uninterested. The devoted, still reeling from his early Paramount Theater days, are overwhelmed by what they see as his boyish cockiness. The others can detect only an aging arrogance.

Mr. Sinatra doesn't leave much room for compromise. If an attempt is made to forget briefly his recent fiasco in Australia, his labeling of women journalists as "hookers," he is quick to insert instant reminders. In the middle of a number, he sticks his tongue out at someone in the audience. His calculated male-chauvinist routine even spills over into his improvised lyrics. Gals and ladies in a Cole Porter song are transformed into chicks and broads.

You either buy it whole or you don't. Obviously, a lot of people still do. But watching the program at home, about midway through the proceedings, I heard a guest announce that she was going home to finish reading a mediocre novel. Given a choice in the matter, I would have gladly settled for a similar alternative.

Sinatra at the Garden Is Superb TV as Well
John Rockwell ★ 1974

Frank Sinatra's hour-long live telecast last night from Madison Square Garden turned out to be quite a show, both for television watchers and for those actually at the Garden. It was certainly a high point in Mr. Sinatra's career, and it came, of all eves, on the eve of Columbus Day.

Mr. Sinatra sang eleven songs in all, ranging from old favorites like "Lady Is a Tramp" and "I've Got You Under My Skin" to recent hits like "Leroy Brown" and "You Are the Sunshine of My Life" to his signature song, "My Way," at the end.

About the only thing overtly wrong from the point of view of the audience at [the] Garden was that Mr. Sinatra's remarks to them during commercial breaks tended to break momentum and be hard to hear. On television, one might have complained occasionally about excessive cutting from camera to camera; in an attempt to avoid being too static, the director sometimes simply got too busy. But for the most part, it was a superb show at the Garden and if anything an even more superb show on television— technically smooth yet full of the feeling of a live event.

The television show was produced by the ABC sports crew, and even had the stentorian services of Howard Cosell (whom the Garden audience could see but not hear) to make the introduction. All told, there were eight stationary cameras and three hand-held models, with Roone Arledge as the over-all producer. Reprise is also recording several of the shows for a tour album, but was an altogether separate technical production.

The show was telecast directly or on a delayed basis throughout the Western Hemisphere, and the promoters grandly claimed a potential audience of 490 million. The 20,000-plus at the Garden missed some of the TV show's closeups of Mr. Sinatra, rapturous fans and celebrities like Robert Redford, Carol Channing, Rex Harrison and John V. Lindsay.

But what the Garden audience did get that home viewers didn't—apart from the dubious virtues of the warmup show—was the immediacy of actually being there. And the exigencies of a live TV show, which normally entails obtrusive cameras and blinding lighting, were remarkably camouflaged: the dappled lighting effect on the crowd that looked so good on television looked even prettier in person.

As he had on Saturday night, Mr. Sinatra worked easily on all four sides of what looked to be a disguised boxing ring in the center of the Garden floor, flanked on one side by Bill Miller leading a forty-piece orchestra.

Both nights, Mr. Sinatra managed to hold his audience securely under his spell. The voice may have its failings—it always did, really. But it has its unique virtues, too, and as a stylist of a certain kind of pop-jazz sensibility, Mr. Sinatra remains the master of his generation.

There were many of that generation at the Garden over the weekend, but Mr. Sinatra's appeal is more to a social strata—the white middle class and lower-middle class—than to a particular age group. For them, he remains a spokesman and even a hero, and all his much-publicized private imbroglios and feuding with the press only add leaves to his laurel.

But his excellence as a singer and as a singing actor are such that his appeal easily transcends such limitations. When Mr. Sinatra is doing his thing, which is singing songs, he exercises his craft so securely that one forgets everything else. The man is one wonderful entertainer, and millions of people had that fact reaffirmed last night.

In 1980, Sinatra released a three-part set entitled *Trilogy*. The parts are named, respectively, "The Past: Collectibles of the Early Years," "The Present: Some Very Good Years," and "The Future: Reflections on the Future in Three Tenses." "The Past," arranged by Billy May, is made up of songs from the pre-rock period, some previously recorded by the singer, most not; "The Present," arranged by Don Costa, includes tunes composed since the onset of rock; and "The Future" is an original suite of related pieces written for the album by Gordon Jenkins. Each part of the trilogy employs orchestra and chorus. The broad range of instrumentalists includes violinist Glenn Dicterow, jazz-trombone pyrotechnician Bill Watrous, longtime Sinatra drummer Irv Cottler, and such greats as saxophonists Al Klink, Walt Levinsky, and Sol Schlinger. The choral performers include Alan Copeland, Loulie Jean Norman, crooner Bernie Knee, and Clark Burroughs (an original member of the Hi-Los). Literally hundreds of instrumentalists and singers perform on the three parts, which were recorded in Los Angeles and New York. Sinatra even duets on a Kris Kristofferson song with opera great turned pop singer Eileen Farrell.

"The Past" has Sinatra coming out blazing—this is obviously the material with which he is most comfortable, and you can tell that he's having a ball! From "The Song Is You" to "They All Laughed," Sinatra sings with confidence, full voice, and great sensitivity. Some of the tunes are old stand-bys, but most are first-time recordings for him, and they are all knockouts. "I Had the Craziest Dream" subtly swings, with the singer almost blending with the chorus in a fashion that can best be called rapturous. "It Had to Be You" is so romantically perfect that nine years after the recording was made, this rendition was used in the romantic film *When Harry Met Sally*. What is striking about its usage is that the film features a soundtrack of Sinatra songs performed by the young singer–pianist Harry Connick, Jr., including Connick's own version of "It Had to Be You"; however, when the song is repeated during the film's climactic scene, it is sung by Sinatra, the romantic legend himself. Its dramatic impact on any romantic soul is undeniable.

"The Present"—with songs composed by Billy Joel, Peter Allen, George Harrison, Jimmy Webb, Neil Diamond, and Elvis Presley—is well sung, but it also presents the listener with a more tentative Sinatra working with contemporary material of uneven quality. One dramatic exception is the singer's performance of the Fred Ebb and John Kander song "New York, New York," the theme from the film of the same name. First performed by Liza Minnelli in the film, the song had gone nowhere—until Sinatra attacked it. The single made the charts, and the song became a Sinatra theme and concert fixture. Its introductory vamp is an audience-pleasing tease on a par with the vamps to Gene Kelly's rendition of "Singin' in the Rain" or "One" from *A Chorus Line*. Sinatra's performance is romping, growling, brash, swaggering, and electric. It has given new life to the city of New York through song, and one can hear it blaring at New York public events such as Mets games.

"The Future" can arguably be called pretentious, innovative, self-revealing, egomaniacal, and bloated. Yet the risk-taking Sinatra, with ego intact, approaches the material with gusto. Employing 154 musicians, this "Reflection on the Future in Three Tenses" has songs about world peace and space travel, along with those that concern Sinatra's own future and past dreams. In content and attitude, this material and its performance definitely constitute a "trip." But, again, this is Sinatra—take it or leave it.

Trilogy attracted much attention, and the criticism, while varied with respect to the material, was nearly unanimous in its praise of Sinatra the musician. Even the rock press, usually cool to the singer, paid attention and began viewing him, in Stephen Holden's words, as a "proto-punk rocker, spitting at the world with pugnacious arrogance."* But what finally counts is that, at age sixty-four, Sinatra shocked us by producing an album that contains some of his best singing ever, as noted in the following review from the *Los Angeles Times* by Leonard Feather, music critic and distinguished author of the classic *Encyclopedia of Jazz* and *Inside Jazz*.

Trilogy—*The Voice in Command*
Leonard Feather ★ 1980

A new Sinatra record of any kind is newsworthy, like a volcanic eruption; you can't tell when its liable to happen, but there can be little doubt it will make the headlines. In the case of *Trilogy*, a better adjective might be historic.

Except for a few minor singles, and a couple of LPs still on the shelf, Sinatra has not recorded an album since 1974 (the live set at Madison Square Garden). His last prior studio-recorded album to reach the stores was made in 1973, shortly after his return from a 1971–1973 retirement.

Trilogy may not be incontestably the greatest period of a recording career that began July 13, 1939, when he cut "From the Bottom of My Heart" with the Harry James orchestra. Still, it ranks very close to the top, and most notably includes as extraordinary a piece of special material as has ever been written for him, Gordon Jenkins's "Reflections on the Future in Three Tenses."

More about Jenkins in a moment; before we get our tenses mixed up, it must be pointed out that the package was predicated on three titles and subtitles: Record One, the Past (Collectibles of the Early Years); Record Two, the Present (Some Very Good Years), and Record Three, the Future, consisting of the Jenkins opus.

If the results had to be judged on the basis of the first two records we might nod wisely, acknowledging that the Voice is in better shape than has

---

*Stephen Holden, "Guide to Middle Age," *Atlantic,* January 1984, p. 84.

been heard on records in quite some years, that the material and arrangements are respectively well chosen and skillfully written. Having said
which, we could congratulate Sinatra & Company and let it go at that. But
that third record makes it necessary to backtrack and assess the whole
undertaking in greater detail.

The ambition and scope of the project is hinted at by the elaborate
production. Each record is in a black sleeve; each sleeve has white-on-black
liner notes (an admirably literate essay by David McClintock) or, in the
case of the third record, the complete libretto. The sleeves in turn are
wrapped in cardboard envelopes; the envelopes come in a box, all with an
overly somber black-and-white theme. An additional loose sheet lists the
personnel, a cast of hundreds that includes, of course, Sinatra's regular
pianist, Vinnie Falcone, and occasional obbligato-suppliers such as trum-
peter Chuck Findley.

Joseph Francis (Sonny) Burke, who conceived the entire triptych, is a
composer and conductor from Scranton, Pa., who in the 1950s became a
successful producer and bandleader at Decca (later MCA) Records. A man
of rare sensitivity and taste (i.e., an atypical producer), Burke has been
associated with more than a dozen Sinatra albums over the past twenty
years, most notably *September of My Years, A Man and His Music* and the
singer's unique, successful collaborations with the Duke Ellington and
Count Basie orchestras and with Antonio Carlos Jobim.

"Frank really trained for this project," said Burke. "He has developed
this gorgeous cello sound; his range now is pure and full; I've never seen or
heard him more deeply involved."

The choice for arranging and conducting showed Sinatra's confidence
in his old allies. Billy May, who handled the "Past" LP, began writing for
Frank in 1954; Don Costa has arranged numerous sessions for him since
1961, and Gordon Jenkins has arranger-conductor-composer credits with
him spanning 1957–1975. Even Nelson Riddle, Sinatra's main arranger
throughout his Capitol Records career from 1953, found time, though busy
with other assignments, to write one chart, "Something," for the center
album.

The "Past" set has its predictably nostalgic aspects: the sometimes
naive, pre-Hays-code-era lyrics, the Tommy Dorseyish trombone of Dick
Nash, and the 1940 vocal group aura in "But Not for Me." The Voice
throughout is assured, and with rare exceptions the notes that need to be
sustained are sustained. In this set, "My Shining Hour" is the consummate
cut, in the view of both Billy May and this reviewer.

Familiar though the songs may sound, only four numbers in the *Trilogy*
have been previously recorded by Sinatra. He clearly finds it hard to stay
away from "The Song Is You." This is his fourth recorded version.

On the second disc, "The Present," the selections may appeal to a younger audience, though most in fact are dated by the standards of these speed-of-sound times: "Love Me Tender" dates back to 1956, "MacArthur Park" to 1968 and "Song Sung Blue" to 1972. "Summer Me, Winter Me," with its constant substitution of nouns and adjectives for verbs, may not be as cold as yesterday's mashed potatoes, but it is hardly the work by which the brilliant team of Alan and Marilyn Bergman deserves to be remembered. It is, however, a typically beautiful Michel Legrand melody.

"For the Good Times" is billed as a duet with Eileen Farrell, though hers is little more than a token appearance. The lyrics of "That's What God Looks Like" sound better suited to, say, Pat Boone than to the world's foremost self-styled saloon singer.

On a scale of one octave, "The Past" rates a major seventh; "The present"—well arranged, well sung and well played though it is—a flatted fifth. But "The Future" is almost beyond rating. Let's give Gordon Jenkins at least a tenth.

Jenkins is three geniuses. One writes engaging, intricate, amusing and poignant lyrics. Many verses here are so perfectly tailored that it is hard to believe, though true, that Sinatra's hand was not guiding Gordon's. A second Jenkins writes exquisite themes, the kind in which you never know what unexpected note or chord will land in which unpredictable place. The third Jenkins, of course, arranges and conducts the products of the other two.

Billed as "A Musical Fantasy in Three Tenses," backed by a huge orchestra and mixed chorus, "Reflections on the Future" is part ghost-written autobiography, part space odyssey, part sentimental speculation. The long first movement, "What Time Does the Next Miracle Leave?" is the intergalactic trip, with Sinatra and the chorus trading lines. The visit to Pluto begins:

> *Sinatra:*
> Pluto is a rotten place
> An evil, misbegotten place,
> It's Hades! It's Hades!
> Filled with graduates of the pen,
> A sordid flock of criminal men
> And ladies. (*Men:* Ladies?) (*Girls:* Ladies, ladies, ladies!)
> It's pure hell when your journey ends there
> But you can bet your ass I'll meet a lot of friends there!
> (*Men:* We did it your way!)

The first side ends in basic blue: Beverly Jenkins, Gordon's wife, lends her pure, sweet alto voice to a traditional twelve-bar blues.

The work calls for a Sinatra in total charge, in confident command, believing in the stories he spins and making us credulous in turn. He pulls it off without a hitch. In the Mercury passage he hits a perfect low E on the last note of the phrase "deep blue sea." Oh, yes, he's still got it.

"Sometimes," said Sonny Burke, "as I play this record back—and you can imagine how many hundreds of times I've heard it—it's as if Frank were talking to me, instead of singing words someone else wrote for him."

The finale is the most affecting blend of material, singer and setting:

Sinatra:
And when the music ends, I'd like it to end this way,
I'll ask Chester to write one more song,
I'll ask Lefty to make me one more chart
And I'll make one more record with the best musicians in the world
And when that cat with the scythe comes tugging at my sleeve
I'll be singing as I leave
(*Chorus:* Sinatra, Sinatra, Sinatra, Sinatra!)

Chester is Sinatra's favorite songwriter friend, Jimmy Van Heusen; Lefty is Gordon Jenkins, the world's most talented southpaw conductor (and that's no left-handed compliment).

If Sinatra and Jenkins left us nothing more than "Reflections in the Future in Three Tenses" to show the twenty-first century what popular music could achieve during the twentieth, their accomplishment could hardly have been more ideally designed.

In 1981, Sinatra released what many assumed would be the sixty-six-year-old singer's last album, a collection of standard Sinatra fare entitled *She Shot Me Down.* Although he is in fairly good voice on the album, the set is unremarkable except for a superb medley of "The Gal That Got Away" and "It Never Entered My Mind." In the final analysis, it would have made a poor showing as his last recording, but then, three years later, there he was, swinging again. *L.A. Is My Lady* (1984) is an interesting piece in a number of ways. The big band, under the direction of Quincy Jones, is made up of well-known jazz players, new and old, including the Brecker brothers, Steve Gadd, George Benson, Ray Brown, and Lionel Hampton. The arrangements are very jazzy, with some good room for soloists. And while Sinatra's voice may be that of an aging singer, in the words of British critic Derek Jewell, "phrasing, adventurousness, and above all, *life* were intact in a record of impressive quality."[*] The singer is at his best in the medium groovy tempos of "If I Should Lose You," "One Hundred Years from Today," and "Until the Real Thing Comes Along." These pieces allow him to bounce off the band, make his entrances and exits in clever ways, and

---

*Jewell, *Frank Sinatra,* p. 142.

employ his innate sense of time toward swinging ends. As critic Peter Reilly described it, "He's in supercharged voice, better than he's been on recordings in years, and in a kind of vigorous, joyful, artistic command that signals he could mow you down with a performance of 'Happy Birthday' if he chose to."* And, in much the same vein, John Rockwell, commenting on the latter-day recordings, noted that

> what makes Sinatra so marvelous this late in life is his unflagging commitment to his craft and art. He never gave up, never (or hardly ever) let even the silliest material overcome his sense of style, never (for long, at least) allowed the routine of performance or the indulgences of vast wealth to dull his desire to do the very best he could.†

At age sixty-nine, Sinatra had done it again—and now *really* for the last time, one would assume.

Then, remarkably, in 1993 and again in 1994, Sinatra answered our doubts with two new recordings featuring duets with some of the major pop stars of today. Released one month before his seventy-eighth birthday and staged to appeal to virtually every radio station's musical format, the first *Duets* went on to become the largest-selling album of his career. Frank topped the charts, along with Pearl Jam and Meatloaf! According to one buyer for a major New York music retailer, "For Sinatra to pull that off is amazing, considering that the CD market is owned by kids."‡ Despite mixed reviews, the making of the album and its reception in the business were its most fascinating aspects.§ The two articles that follow, by well-known columnists Stephen Holden of the *New York Times* and Murray Kempton of *New York Newsday*, provide a sense of the album's conception, invention, and reception.

Pop's Patriarch Makes Music Along with His Heirs
Stephen Holden ★ 1993

The most remarkable moment in *Frank Sinatra Duets*, the new album that returns the seventy-seven-year-old singer to the mainstream of popular music with a startling force and authority, is a rendition of "I've Got You

---

*Peter Reilly, "Supercharged Sinatra," *Stereo Review*, November 1984, p. 92.

†John Rockwell, *Sinatra: An American Classic* (New York: Random House/Rolling Stone, 1985), p. 231.

‡Gersh Kuntzman, "Frank Puts Pearl in Jam," *New York Post*, 10 November 1993, p. 23.

§Examples of some of these reviews are cited in the bibliography. Favorable reviews appeared in the *New York Times* (see Holden's "Pop's Patriarch") and the *Philadelphia Inquirer* (see Moon's "Swinging with the Saloon Singer). Lukewarm or unfavorable notices appeared in *Newsweek* (see Gates's "Too Much Togetherness?"), the *Washington Post* (see Harrington's "Sinatra's 'Duets': Neither Here nor There"), and *USA Today* (see Stearns's "In 'Duets,' Sinatra Clashes with Titans").

Under My Skin" in which the Chairman of the Board is joined by Bono of U2.

After Mr. Sinatra punches out the opening phrases of Cole Porter's standard, Bono slips into the song, crooning the words, "so deep in my heart, you're really a part of me," in a soft, sexy growl. From here, the two singers, who sound as though they are sitting elbow to elbow in a bar comparing notes about love and life, trade the song back and forth, with the thirty-three-year-old Irish rock star occasionally drawing back to interpolate high, plaintive vocal doodles around his companion's gruff assertions.

The song hits a peak of passion when Bono exclaims, "Don't you know, blue eyes, you never can win." In a flash, it conjures up a picture of a young man in the throes of romantic turmoil sharing his exhilaration and confusion with a tough, resilient father who has been through it all.

With its mixture of sagacity and sexiness, "I've Got You Under My Skin" is a stunning intergenerational collaboration that reveals how profoundly Mr. Sinatra has influenced younger singers, even rockets like Bono, who is a longtime Sinatra admirer.

More important, the album marks the triumphant return to recording, a medium Mr. Sinatra seemed to have abandoned nine years ago, by an American icon at an age when most performers have called it quits. What makes this comeback especially nervy is Mr. Sinatra's choosing several of his partners from the generation that had contemptuously turned its back on his kind of music in the late 1960s and 70s. The album, which is likely to become the best-selling recording of his career, can be seen as a symbolic healing of that generational gap in pop taste, as a final, reconciliatory swan song.

The singer's emphatically aggressive vocals on the album are a sharp reminder that fifty years ago Mr. Sinatra was the first white American pop singer to inject quirky personal feelings and a sense of erotic intimacy into a polished but bland pop crooning tradition. In the mid-1950s, a more mature Mr. Sinatra re-invented himself and in the process defined the image of the grown-up pop singer as a hip urban sophisticate with a streak of romanticism under a swinger's facade.

In the 1970s and 80s, as his voice hardened and his interpretations became raw, unvarnished expressions of his moods and attitudes, it became clearer than ever that Mr. Sinatra had paved the way for everyone from Bob Dylan to Willie Nelson to Bono to sing however they pleased. Some critics even discerned a punk-rock attitude in his singing.

Frank Sinatra Duets, especially the Bono duet, makes all those connections explicit. The interplay of the two voices conveys a mythic pop resonance as Mr. Sinatra, the patriarch of naked pop self-expression, shares his feelings with a singer who is the incarnation of fervent rock passion.

They really do sound like father and son. Or even grandfather and grandson.

The duet, which may be turned into a rock video if a deal can be negotiated between Mr. Sinatra's label, Capitol, and Bono's label, Island, should introduce Mr. Sinatra to a younger rock audience that may have heard of him but may be unfamiliar with his music. At the same time, the album's duets with Luther Vandross, Aretha Franklin and Anita Baker should bring his voice to a young adult black audience.

But because of the way most pop records are made nowadays, the vocal intimacy between Mr. Sinatra and his vocal partners on the record is really an illusion. Mr. Sinatra's performance of "I've Got You Under My Skin" was recorded in Capitol Records Studio A in Los Angeles in early July. Bono's vocal was added eight weeks later at a small recording studio in Dublin. Ms. Franklin and Ms. Baker recorded their parts in Detroit. Some other contributors, like Carly Simon (in Boston), Gloria Estefan (in Miami), and Liza Minnelli (in Rio de Janeiro) almost literally phoned in their vocal parts by using the Entertainment Digital Network, a fiber-optic system that links recording studios by telephone.

If the album was compiled like an intercontinental jigsaw puzzle, *Frank Sinatra Duets* still exudes the feeling of a hot all-star recording session. Not since the sessions in 1985 for the U.S.A. for Africa charity single "We Are the World" have so many pop superstars performed on the same record.

The album's thirteen songs are all Sinatra standards, most of them recorded with a fifty-four-piece orchestra using mostly vintage arrangements by Nelson Riddle, Don Costa and other longtime Sinatra collaborators, touched up by Patrick Williams, a Los Angeles–based arranger and composer of television themes.

The numbers include "The Lady Is a Tramp" (with Mr. Vandross), "What Now My Love" (Ms. Franklin), "I've Got a Crush on You" (Barbra Streisand), "Summer Wind" (Julio Iglesias), "Come Rain or Come Shine" (Ms. Estefan), "New York, New York" (Tony Bennett), "They Can't Take That Away from Me" (Natalie Cole), "You Make Me Feel So Young" (Charles Aznavour), a medley of "Guess I'll Hang My Tears Out to Dry" and "In the Wee Small Hours of the Morning" (Ms. Simon), "I've Got the World on a String" (Ms. Minnelli), "Witchcraft" (Ms. Baker), and a medley of "All the Way" and "One for My Baby" (the soprano saxophonist Kenny G).

The illusion of intimacy was cinched by modern performers accustomed to creating illusions by overdubbing. For example, when Ms. Streisand recorded her portion of "I've Got a Crush on You," she coyly inserted the words, "You make me blush, Francis." A couple of weeks later, in a dressing room while on tour, Mr. Sinatra added his response: "I have got a crush, my Barbra, on you."

It is a coup for Capitol Records that all thirteen artists, aware of the historic nature of the recording, agreed to perform for no payment or royalties. According to the deal masterminded by Charles Koppelman, who runs the recording conglomerate that includes Capitol, Liberty, EMI, Chrysalis, SBK and Angel Records, the artists are free to release their contributions on their own solo albums. To have negotiated a royalty with each artist, Mr. Koppelman said would have taken at least three years.

Frank Sinatra Duets, which is being released on Tuesday, is already a pre-sold hit, with 1.3 million advance orders. In record-industry parlance, it is "shipping platinum" (more than 1 million orders), a feat that no previous Sinatra album has come close to matching.

Although Mr. Sinatra has not talked to the press in years, those around him say he is so enthusiastic about the project that a second volume is in the works. In two recording sessions during the second week of October, he recorded "A Foggy Day," "Fly Me to the Moon," "For Once in My Life," "Angel Eyes," "Moonlight in Vermont," "My Funny Valentine," "Where or When" and "Chicago." The Sinatra sessions for round two are scheduled to be finished in December, with the album to be released in the middle of next year.

For the half-dozen executives and producers who conceived and planned *Frank Sinatra Duets,* the making of the album, which cost more than $750,000, involved considerable risk. It had been nine years since Mr. Sinatra had recorded his last album, *L.A. Is My Lady,* a punchy but ragged sounding swing album, for Reprise Records that most people had assumed was his final recorded statement. In the years since, the singer's contract with Reprise, the label he founded in 1960, had expired.

Although Mr. Sinatra has kept a rigorous touring schedule (this year he will give more than seventy concerts), his increasing reliance on stage Teleprompters to remember lyrics has led to rumors of failing mental powers. This is not true, say those close to the singer.

"He enjoys working," says his manager, Eliot Weisman. "Sometimes out on the road he gets a little tired. But after he's been home a couple of weeks, he'll call and say, "What are we doing? Who told you I retired?"

Mr. Sinatra, who has three homes in southern California, remains an inveterate night owl. After the *Duets* sessions, he would adjourn to an Italian restaurant with a group of cronies and be the life of the party, regaling the company with stories about his early days in show business while smoking Camels and sipping Scotch.

The notion of a Sinatra duet album, which the singer and his wife Barbara had suggested some years ago, was revived shortly after Mr. Koppelman, in April, assumed the leadership of Capitol Records, the label for which Mr. Sinatra had recorded many of his greatest records in the middle and late 1950s. It also appealed to the showman's instincts of Mr. Koppelman, who has had spectacular success with duets. He masterminded Ms. Streisand's 5-million-selling 1980 album, *Guilty*, in which she sings with Barry Gibb of the Bee Gees, and teamed Ms. Streisand with Donna Summer for a No. 1 hit in 1979, "No More Tears (Enough is Enough)" and Diana Ross with Lionel Richie for "Endless Love," also No. 1 in 1981.

Mr. Sinatra had qualms. It was agreed that if he felt unhappy with his performances, the record would not be released. Mr. Koppelman assembled a creative team led by the record producer and engineer Phil Ramone that included Mr. Weisman, Mr. Williams, the singer's concert production manager Hank Cattaneo, and Don Rubin, a longtime Koppelman business partner and artists and repertory executive for EMI Records. The story of how the album was made comes from interviews with all six members of the team and several of the artists.

From Mr. Sinatra's current concert repertory of more than fifty songs, twenty were chosen. In consultation with the singer, a wish list of vocal partners was drawn up, the plan being to offer each artist several choices. "The easiest part was getting the artists to say yes," said Mr. Koppelman. "There was no arm twisting."

Not all could participate. The biggest disappointment was the unavailability of Luciano Pavarotti, who, it was hoped, would join Mr. Sinatra on "My Way."

At the first recording session on June 28, the orchestra was assembled and rehearsed in the same cavernous studio where Mr. Sinatra had recorded many of his classic albums. But when the singer arrived, anxiety and a touch of laryngitis made him freeze. At one point, he absentmindedly asked why he was being asked to do material he had recorded twenty or thirty years ago. Mr. Koppelman received a phone call in the middle of the night asking what should be done.

"I told them that maybe he would feel better tomorrow, and that they should have the orchestra ready to go," he said. "And if it didn't work tomorrow to try it again the night after that."

The second night was just as bad. Mr. Sinatra felt so isolated recording in a specially built air-conditioned sound booth, equipped with a Teleprompter, that he gave up and left the studio.

Two nights later, however, things clicked.

"He said he wanted to be inside the band," Mr. Ramone recalled. "We isolated an area in the middle of the orchestra where he could see the rhythm section and the horns and strings and built a small platform and gave him his hand mike which he used on stage."

At ease at last, Mr. Sinatra breezed through nine songs in five hours.

His confidence restored, he became ebullient. For the remaining two sessions, he arrived hours early, dressed as though ready to go on the stage. In the three sessions, he recorded twenty numbers, of which seventeen were deemed usable.

Mr. Vandross, the first singer to record his part, was viewed as a test case. If the duet worked, the project would he home free. The team members held their breath when playing the finished duet for Mr. Sinatra.

"He was very excited," Mr. Rubin recalled. "He just kept shaking his head and saying it was marvelous, it was wonderful, wonderful."

Some duets were more complicated than others. Ms. Streisand insisted that the orchestra be reassembled for her to sing with a live accompaniment and wanted her producer David Foster to be brought in to help create a vocal arrangement.

Ms. Minnelli who had been asked to add her voice to "New York, New York" balked at doing the song that she had already recorded with Mr. Sinatra for a concert videotape. Ms. Simon was originally invited to sing "One for My Baby" but backed down when her husband, James Hart, pointed out that the song is about drinking and driving. Ms. Simon has spoken out against drunk driving.

A cold-eyed view of *Frank Sinatra Duets* might dismiss the project as a sensational technological stunt, a feat of trickery. But that view disregards the album's extraordinary vitality and emotional heat. Throughout the album, Mr. Sinatra stands as a kind of vocal Rock of Gibraltar around whom the singers unfurl their vocal sails. Mr. Vandross hasn't sounded so exuberant in years, or Ms. Franklin so elegantly sassy, or Ms. Streisand so relaxed.

In "Summer Wind," Mr. Iglesias and Mr. Sinatra are two roués waxing nostalgic. In "You Make Me Feel So Young," Mr. Aznavour and Sinatra are two agile geezers celebrating their longevity with style and humor.

As it should be, Mr. Sinatra has the last word on the album, in a version of "One for My Baby" that is almost harrowing in its vulnerability. Sounding like a wounded boxer fighting back tears, he intones the lyric in a husky murmur that trails off on words that evoke the amazing span of his career.

Against the tinkling of a faintly bluesy piano, the singer considers leaving the bar and getting in his car, and driving on "that long, long, long road."

"Man, it's long," he sighs near the end of the song, concluding the album on a note of weary introspection that is the other side of the perennial swinger.

Sinatra: The Lion in Winter
Murray Kempton ★ 1993

Frank Sinatra came home again yesterday to Capitol Records where he spent the glories of his unforgettable autumn twenty-five years ago. *Duets*, his newest album, is second on the Billboard chart this week and has already sold a million copies.

Capitol could thus at once crow over Sinatra's fragile but still profit-making present and celebrate his indestructible past by presenting him to the photographers as the first laureate of its "Tower of Achievement" award.

Sinatra's part in the ceremonies was rationed down to the five minutes he spent docilely lifting and lowering his award as the cameramen bade him. When he was told it was time to leave, he complied with an amiable "OK, you're the general" to his escort. He was being shepherded by strangers, but then too many of his familiar attendants are dead and gone.

The lion tamed by winter is a melancholy sight. We miss even the times when he could be mean because they were so small a price for his tenderness. What remains eternal in Frank Sinatra was simply that tenderness; and he can never bring it back alive because he doesn't have the breath left for the long lingerings that could take a word like "wish" and sustain it through unending wistfulnesses of the heart.

He knows the songs better and is truer to the essentials of their style than most of those juniors who sing with him on *Duets*. But that is not their fault; his generation was both more harshly and more subtly taught than theirs. For all its undeniable pleasures, *Duets* is somehow artificial; Sinatra recorded the songs and then his collaborators did voice-overs at long distance. The moments of spontaneous creativity were reserved then for only one half of the coupling; and, unless each party can feed off the other in intimately direct interchange, we cannot have a real duet and must settle for those lower reaches where novelty records make their way.

The effects are, however, not without their charms. Carly Simon takes over "In the Wee Small Hours"—which Sinatra may have felt beyond his existing resources—and makes out of it a touching testament to all she has learned from him. Natalie Cole brings off a scat passage full of all she learned from her father. To hear these young women draw so richly upon those who came before them is to rejoice for the hope that the Alzheimer's disease afflicting so much of our popular culture is not yet universal.

And Sinatra can still exert sizable charms, although they survive more for swinging than reflecting. He well remembers the bounce of these songs but he has forgotten how they feel. The voice still drives as of old, but it can never again breathe the loneliness of the heart. Sinatra's supreme gift was to make us glad to be unhappy. He can't do that any longer; and, although he may well be happier and nearer peace than ever before, to see him now is just to be unhappy.

But that, we may suppose, is what it means to grow old and be cured at last of achings for what you cannot have. He is free of the illusions of anger and of romance, free of tenderness and meanness. He is no longer lonely because he has come to the place where he has nothing to aspire to. The final sadness is that Frank Sinatra can never fall in love again.

Once the old singers go, the Gershwins and Cole Porter and Rodgers and Hart will in some special way be gone too. Larry Hart's lyrics will have no realized existence except in the old records of the dead and the too-soon-to-be-dying like Sarah Vaughan and Frank Sinatra; they knew what Larry Hart meant.

He will work on and continue to provide reduced but still substantial rewards. *Duets* proves again how much more he knows than those who have come after him. But it is becoming a mechanical knowledge; the bitter wisdom of the heart has faded and mellowed in the encroaching shadows. How lucky we are to have it still there reaching out and almost touching us from his autumnal years at Capitol Records.

Although Sinatra's recordings over the past three decades have not been the best of his illustrious career—particularly by comparison with his Capitol work in the 1950s and the Reprise albums of the 1960s—his mainstay from the beginning to this day has been his concert work. He was the unquestioned king of the concert stage from his first solo work at the Paramount to his retirement in 1971. But since then, mass-media reviews of his concert work have been mixed, ranging from charges that he is over-the-hill to lavish praise for his masterful performances.

The following concert reviews take us from 1977 to 1990. In the first Robert Palmer, *New York Times* pop-music critic and the author of *Deep Blues*, provides us with a view of a Sinatra whose time has passed. Next, noted rock critic Mikal Gilmore reviews a Fourth of July concert that Sinatra gave at the Universal Amphitheatre in 1980. This piece, which appeared in *Rolling Stone* (hardly a place where you'd expect to see a review of a sixty-five-year-old performer), details the ways in which Sinatra makes good on his reputation as "America's preeminent romantic vocalist." The third review, published in 1982, is by Whitney Balliett, music critic and staff writer for the *New Yorker* and author of numerous volumes on American music, including *Super-Drummer: A Profile of Buddy Rich* and *American Singers: Twenty-Seven Portraits in Song*. Balliett compares the live Sinatra performance he witnessed at Carnegie Hall in 1982 with the one heard on a reissue of *The Tommy Dorsey–Frank Sinatra Sessions*, eighty-three vocals originally recorded between February 1940 and July 1942. Finally, three reviews by the distinguished *New York Times* music critic Stephen Holden trace Sinatra's continuing appeal. He appraises Sinatra's performances at three different venues: the Brendan Byrne Arena in 1983, Carnegie Hall in 1987, and Radio City Music Hall in 1990, when he received the sad news of the death of his longtime friend Sammy Davis, Jr.

Sinatra and Martin, Rock Stars
R o b e r t   P a l m e r   ★   1 9 7 7

Frank Sinatra and Dean Martin brought their show to the Westchester Premier Theater on Tuesday for a week-long run. Both men still radiate tremendous presence; the popping of flashbulbs when each came on stage created an almost blinding strobe effect. And both are still masters of the relaxed, improvisational timing that Mr. Sinatra learned from Louis Armstrong, Billie Holiday and Bing Crosby and established as the dominant approach in American popular singing.

One no longer expects musical revelations from Mr. Sinatra. His voice grows somewhat grainy when he strains, which happens more often than formerly, and his sense of swing seems to have atrophied. The latter problem may be due to his insistence on tackling contemporary material.

Songs like "For Once in My Life" and "Everybody Ought to Be in Love" do not offer sufficiently mercurial harmonic changes for him to exercise his gifts as a melodist, but above all they are different rhythmically from the songs of his heyday. If they are to work, they must prance to a deliberately syncopated, two-beat sort of rhythm; they simply do not fit into the mode of evenly flowing swing that is Mr. Sinatra's métier.

More and more, he scores his most conspicuous successes with melodrama and bombast, as in a labored version of "I Write the Songs" that brought his audience to its feet. On the other hand, his slower, more reflective numbers showcased his spectacular articulation and intonation well. This was the sort of singing that has always delighted musicians and jazz fans, although there was little enough of it at the Westchester Premier Theater.

Mr. Martin sticks to familiar favorites and throws away half the lines in many of them. He is a pleasant enough crooner, but his real strength is as an improvising comedian. Using his celebrated fondness for alcohol as a kind of stage prop—he seemed to be in complete control throughout the show—he trips, slurs, jokes, pretends to forget lines and engages in pantomime, all with the split-second timing of a master entertainer. His comedy of errors is much more effective in person than it is on television.

It is amusing to remember Mr. Martin's hostile comments about the Rolling Stones and other rock groups during the 1960s. In point of fact, he does many of the things followers of the older pop have decried when rockers do them. He advertises drugs—alcohol and nicotine—with in-jokes and conspicuous comsumption onstage. He sacrifices musical qualities for theatrical ones and limits himself to a familarly lightweight repertory—his "hits."

Rock and the older mainstream, once mutually hostile and mutually exclusive, seem to be converging slowly but inexorably. Rock is becoming more harmonically, melodically and rhythmically varied and subtle and moving closer to an acceptance of its place in the tradition of show business. Mr. Sinatra is singing to rock rhythms as best he can, and even Mr. Martin seems to be taking advantage of the more relaxed performing postures introduced by rock.

The Majestic Artistry
of Frank Sinatra
Mikal Gilmore ★ 1980

He walked onstage with a brisk, matter-of-fact stride, wearing a crisp black tuxedo and a bright, cocksure expression. The audience reacted with a volley of cheers, whistles and squeals—just like bobby-soxers had done four decades earlier—and even if the acclamation came as no surprise, he appeared grateful for it, in that indomitable way of his. Then a cross-weave of saxophones and violins wafted through the night breeze, and Frank Sinatra swung into Harold Arlen's "I've Got the World on a String," treating it as if it were tailor-written to illuminate his artistry:

> I've got a song that I sing
> *I* can make the rain go
> Anytime I move my finger. . . .

It seemed like a fairly virile statement for a hoary pop singer, but in the next song, Cy Coleman's "The Best Is Yet to Come," Sinatra went one better. Escorted by a walking blues piano line he entered the tune playfully, toying with syllables and phrases like a spry, sportive house cat pawing at a ball. Then, with a squall of horns swelling behind him, he suddenly tensed his voice into a stealthy instrument and pounced on the middle verse with an awesome iambic roar:

> The *best* is *yet* to *come*, and babe won't that be fine.
> You *think* you *seen* the *sun*, but you ain't seen it shine

With those two songs, Frank Sinatra not only made good on his reputation as America's pre-eminent romantic vocalist, but also served notice
that he was making one final, high-reaching bid for artistic apotheosis. In a
way, it was just an extension of the objective already set by his latest
album, *Trilogy:* to make a monument out of one man's renaissance.

But Sinatra came closer to that goal onstage than on record, mainly
because he *sang* better live. Which isn't to say there's anything flaccid
about his singing on *Trilogy;* indeed, it's probably better than he's committed to vinyl in more than fifteen years: deeper and rawer in his bass
register, lighter and more inflective in the baritone range. In concert,
though, the voice sounded impossibly big, animative, cunning, formidable. It was as if the presence of an audience somehow impelled him to
renewed levels of ingenuity and intensity.

In fact, in a knockout tour de force like "I've Got You Under My Skin,"
Sinatra was plain stunning. He slugged out Cole Porter's lyrics with the
wit and wallop of a superfine prize-fighter, weaving rhythmic punches
between the relentless strokes of baritone and alto saxophones, then hitting the last chorus with a blinding series of staccato jabs

> Don't you *know* you *fool,* you ain't *got* no way to win
> Use your *men-tal-i-ty*
> WAKE UP! STEP UP! *to re-al-i-ty*

that cut between the fleet slashes of the cymbals.

Yet despite that display, there was nothing showy about Sinatra's
singing—none of the grandiloquent, instrumental-style "vocalese" that
typifies such oral exhibitionists as Phoebe Snow, Al Jarreau or Rickie Lee
Jones. In fact, just the opposite: Sinatra's delivery sounded guileless and
"easy," even *colloquial*—meaning his phrasing and intonation seemed to
spring as much from the rhythms of speech as from the cadences of melody. As a result, his vocalizing served to heighten the emotional and
thematic intent of a song, and make its lyrics seem like nothing so much as
a word between friends.

That air of intimacy worked to best effect in Sinatra's "saloon" medley:
a thoughtful mating of Arlen and Gershwin's "The Gal That Got Away"
and Rodgers and Hart's "It Never Entered My Mind" (Saloon songs, late-
night, inebriated soliloquies of unrequited love, are a kind of Tin Pan Alley
equivalent of the blues.) This was Sinatra at the full extent of his affecting
interpretive power: prowling the shadowy fringes of the stage with cigarette in hand, letting the signs of age in his voice—the brandy-tone timbre,
the grainy legato—infuse the lyric:

> The night is bitter
> The stars have lost their glitter

>The winds grow colder
>And suddenly you're older
>And all because of a gal that got away.

For just a second there, Sinatra looked and sang like an old man, stripped of all conceits and most hopes. It didn't matter that the portrait was antithetical to everything we presume about the real Sinatra—it just mattered that Sinatra had the sensibility to make us believe it *was* real.

In other words, he sang the song like it was his, and his alone, to sing. I've seen maybe a handful of other singers who could pull off that trick so effectively: Bob Dylan, Van Morrison, Graham Parker, John Lydon—but then their songs, more or less, *were* theirs and theirs alone. What Sinatra did at the Universal was fundamentally different, but equally important: he took the songs of Porter, Gershwin, Arlen and others, and made them seem personal and imperative. It was an eloquent display of his paradoxical brand of artistry: tough yet sensitive, vain yet compassionate, grasping yet generous. And when Sinatra left the stage, we realized we might never witness artistry that big, and that provocative, again.

King Again
Whitney Balliett ★ 1982

It is hard now to understand why the Frank Sinatra who first appeared with Tommy Dorsey over forty years ago had such an electric effect. RCA has reissued, as *The Tommy Dorsey–Frank Sinatra Sessions*, all eighty-three of the vocals that he did with Dorsey between February 1, 1940, and July 2, 1942, and they are, with a few celebrated exceptions, vapid and inert. Sinatra had broken with the bouncy, gingham style of Bing Crosby (although he seems to have listened to sleeker crooners like Eddy Howard), and, by virtue of his simplicity and straightforwardness, he projected a kind of modernity. But his sense of phrasing was unfinished and his diction was unsteady—he tended to let his words drift away open-ended. There was a slight nasal quality to his singing, he was not always in tune, and he had little sense of dynamics. His vibrato sounded skinny. He has said that he modelled his singing on Dorsey's bland, stainless trombone playing, and his early singing does have the same creaminess, the same reluctance to rock the melodic boat. Of course, Dorsey, whose personality was the direct opposite of his playing, didn't make things easy for Sinatra. Fewer than a quarter of the songs Sinatra was asked to record are worth hearing more than once, and this was during the years when numbers such as "It Never Entered My Mind," "I Concentrate on You," "Blues in the

Night," "The Nearness of You," "Bewitched," "How High the Moon," "It's So Peaceful in the Country," and "Soft as Spring" first came out. The tempos Dorsey chose were often so slow that the music sounded as if it might congeal, and the backgrounds, full of muted trumpets, high-pitched reeds, and dull rhythmic patterns, provided little support for the singer. The best things Sinatra recorded with Dorsey were done with the Pied Pipers. Four of these numbers—"I'll Never Smile Again," "Star Dust," "I Guess I'll Have to Dream the Rest," and "The One I Love"—still have a hymning, bas-relief quality.

It is equally difficult to connect the Sinatra of the Dorsey days with the Sinatra of *Trilogy* the surprising album he put out two years ago, and the Sinatra who recently gave ten concerts at Carnegie Hall. The vicissitudes of his career are well known: his being dumped by Columbia Records in the early fifties; his return to fame and fortune through Hollywood and Capitol Records in the fifties and sixties; his gradual vocal deterioration in the late sixties, and his retirement in 1971 (now referred to by Sinatra as a "vacation"); his often shaky comeback, begun in 1973; and the surpassing of his old strengths in *Trilogy*, which contains several classic recordings—"It Had to Be You," "My Shining Hour," "More Than You Know," "Something," and "Love Me Tender." (The album also contains a section called "Reflections on the Future in Three Tenses." It is a fantasy, with words and music by Gordon Jenkins, in which Sinatra, narrating and singing and backed by a huge chorus and orchestra, takes a trip through space and prepares himself for old age and death. It's Sinatra with the sillies.)

Sinatra's new strengths were displayed in almost all the fourteen songs he did at his second Carnegie Hall concert. His voice, close to a tenor in his Dorsey days, has become a true baritone, and it has taken on timbre and resilience. He can growl and sound hoarse. He can shout. His vibrato is tight and controlled. He has a fine sense of dynamics. He has mentioned his admiration for Billie Holiday, and she seems at this late date to have subtly possessed him. He uses her exhilarating rhythmic devices and her sometimes staccato, rocking diction. Occasionally, his voice resembles the heavy, robed one she developed in the forties. Also evident are the definitive phrasing of Mabel Mercer and, in small pinches, the abandon of Ray Charles. The early Sinatra sang with veiled emotion; the present one was clearly moved by much of what he did at Carnegie Hall, and his transports were passed on to the audience. He did a slow, husky "Come Rain or Come Shine," using Billie Holiday's legato pacing, his face brimming with emotion. He did an ad-lib "When Your Lover Has Gone," backed by organ chords, and a rocking "The Lady Is a Tramp." He did another classic "It Had to Be You," a pushing "I Won't Dance," and an easy ad-lib "As Time Goes By." All his showmanship was in place. There were the searchlight blue eyes that give the impression they are looking into every pair of eyes

in the hall; the ineffable cool and skill that make his singing appear effortless; the flashing smiles that dispel the emotion of the last song and prepare the way for the next one; the fluid stage motions, even including the
seemingly ostentatious sipping of a glass of red wine.

Frank Sinatra
Stephen Holden ★ 1983

Frank Sinatra was in an expansive mood when he took the stage at the
Byrne Meadowlands Arena on Thursday night. For one thing, the singer
was on his home turf. "I knew this area better than the guys who built the
building," the singer recalled in between "My Way" and "Here's to the
Band." "It was a great place to play hooky in, and I got a degree in
escapism."

But more important, Mr. Sinatra, just four days away from his sixty-
eighth birthday, was in remarkable vocal condition. Backed by the Buddy
Rich Orchestra, he demonstrated the range and tonal control of a singer
half his age.

Mr. Sinatra has been such a massive influence on the younger generation
of singers who have developed what could be called "the Las Vegas style"
of saloon singing that it is tempting to blame him for the mannerisms and
the cynicism that singers like Wayne Newton, Robert Goulet and others
have brought to that style. But Mr. Sinatra showed repeatedly that there is
a vast, if subtle, difference between the real thing and his many followers
and imitators. That difference has to do with integrity and commitment.
Along with the emphatic aggressiveness that other singers have cari-
catured came an elegance of phrase and an emotional depth that contra-
dicted the stock image of Mr. Sinatra as a punchy swinger.

One of the evening's many happy surprises was Mr. Sinatra's under-
stated, almost ironically humble rendition of "My Way." In "Come Rain or
Come Shine" and "This Is All I Ask," he drew out the phrases with a
controlled legato that was thrilling in its combination of physical discipline
and emotional openness. Even "New York, New York," a song that one
would normally not expect Mr. Sinatra to do anything more with than he's
already done, took on different resonances. Where ordinarily the song
invites an attitude of feisty braggadocio, Mr. Sinatra gradually built it up
into an anthem of joy and gratitude, expressed in suspended high notes
that surged with triumphant optimism.

Mr. Sinatra also punctuated the evening with moments of cutting humor.
The most acute joke was his deliberate mockery of "Strangers in the

Night," a song he said he hadn't performed in twelve years. "If you like that song, you must be crazy about pineapple yogurt," the singer joked.

Frank Sinatra
Begins Carnegie Series
Stephen Holden ★ 1987

Frank Sinatra was in high spirits at Carnegie Hall on Thursday evening.

"I'm healthy, I'm happy, I'm in love, and that's how I feel," he announced, while introducing "I've Got the World on a String," the final song of his concert. The singer then tore into the Ted Koehler–Harold Arlen standard, turning it into an almost savagely gleeful affirmation of what it must feel like to be an aging lion three months shy of seventy-two and in fine fettle.

The most remarkable thing about Mr. Sinatra in the autumn of his years is the emotional volatility he continues to project onto whatever songs he touches. Unlike the vast marjority of seasoned pop singers, Mr. Sinatra doesn't try to hold onto an image of his younger self. He may have performed the same song hundreds of times before, but his current interpretation springs directly out of the moment and situation at hand.

At Thursday's show—the first performance of an eight-night engagement—the emphasis was more on moody, upbeat reflection than on swinging exuberance. After opening with a ruminative, slow-paced "My Heart Stood Still," Mr. Sinatra made a joking remark about his age. Referring to seventy-eight-year-old Lionel Hampton, who performed a short opening set, he said, "Between the two of us, we're older than one of the sphinxes."

Over the course of the evening, the singer worked his way through a selection of well-chosen standards, sprinkled with modern pop ballads by David Gates, Joe Raposo and others. One was repeatedly reminded that the kind of pop music Mr. Sinatra represents is a rapidly vanishing species. Also dead are not only most of the great songwriters, but also the three principal orchestral arrangers of the evening's program, Nelson Riddle, Gordon Jenkins and Don Costa. And William B. Williams, the local disk jockey and friend of the singer whom he remembered in words that brought tears to his eyes as he spoke them, has died as well.

Mr. Sinatra, however, goes on. And in 1987 he is not afraid to let the cracks and crevices in his voice express toughness, fatigue and hesitancy when those feelings and attitudes fit into an interpretive concept.

The singer brought interesting new resonances to much that was very familiar. "Where or When" was light and sexy. "What Now, My Love" and "Lonely Town" became sepulchrally dark meditations on solitude. "My Heart Stood Still" and "I Have Dreamed" were shaped into proud assertions of marital devotion. For "Mack the Knife," the singer became a tough-guy cutup. The little-known Jerry Leiber–Mike Stoller ballad, "The Girls of Summer," was delivered as a wrenching acknowledgment of youthful longings. "The Gal That Got Away" and "It Never Entered My Mind" were skillfully combined in a medley in which they extended and commented on one another. The evening's most amusing moment came with the singer's introduction of "New York, New York" as "the national anthem."

Frank Sinatra
Opens and Then Cancels
Stephen Holden ★ 1990

Frank Sinatra has never been a performer one could describe as mellow, but on Tuesday evening at the opening night of his sold-out shows at Radio City Music Hall he seemed to be in an unusually good mood. Though he said nothing during the concert about the failing health of his friend Sammy Davis, Jr., the remaining four nights of the engagement were canceled after Mr. Davis died yesterday.

Accompanied by a forty-piece orchestra conducted by his son, Frank Sinatra, Jr., the singer held conversation to a minimum. In the evening's longest anecdote, he recalled taking his father and grandfather to the Paramount Theater in Manhattan during the height of his popularity with bobby-soxers. Afterward, he recalled, his father berated him because he was unable to hear his son above the screams of the audience.

He also recalled Paul Anka giving him the song "My Way," and hating it at first because it was "too much on the nose." The song, he said, "has probably done more for my career than any other song." And in his performance, he gave himself to the lyrics perhaps more intensely than to any other song in a concert that maintained a hot emotional pitch.

One thing that makes Mr. Sinatra, at seventy-four years old, a riveting performer is the spontaneity of phrasing and intonation he brings to almost everything he sings no matter how many hundreds of times he has sung the songs. Even while reading lyrics from a prompter at the front of the stage, Mr. Sinatra still seemed compelled to experiment, trying out little tricks of phrasing, indulging in impromptu scoops and dives and lyrical interpolations that worked as emphatic rhythmic punctuation.

He opened his show with "Come Fly with Me," followed by "You Make Me Feel So Young," then hit his stride with a triumphantly punchy "Come Rain or Come Shine." That performance set the tone for a concert in which Mr. Sinatra pushed his voice for the considerable resonance it still has, especially in the lower end of his baritone register. From a purely vocal point of view, his rendition of "Bewitched" was remarkable for its declamatory force. A song about being enslaved by passion became a grand, heroic announcement.

Other high points of the concert included a slyly phrased version of Cy Coleman and Carolyn Leigh's "Best Is Yet to Come," a brooding "Angel Eyes" and most impressive, "It Never Entered My Mind," performed with just a solo piano. In its tenderness and vulnerability it recalled the 1955 version on Mr. Sinatra's album *In the Wee Small Hours*.

Although his most crowd-pleasing performances these days are those in which he plays the defiant freewheeling swinger, his most expressive and musically coherent singing usually comes in his softer moments. Of course, the show had its share of swingers, the most exuberant being rip-roaring versions of "Mack the Knife" and "The Lady Is a Tramp."

The Count Basie Orchestra, which opened the evening, delivered a short vigorous set whose high points were two Neal Hefti compositions, "Li'l Darlin'" and "Whirlybird." The pianist Peter Nero, who immediately preceded Mr. Sinatra, offered ornate arrangements for piano and orchestra that blended pop, jazz and classical styles into flashy kitsch.

The critics' response to Sinatra's concert performances in this last period has not always been favorable. The following review, from *New York Newsday*, is the harshest, we have yet encountered. The concert by the seventy-seven-year-old Sinatra took place in June 1993 at the Westbury Music Fair in Westbury, New York, a small and intimate theater-in-the-round that seats audiences of fewer than 3,000 per show. Merely scanning the review might lead one to conclude that only a cynical or totally unaware singer could get out there and perform so poorly. In fact, the week after this review appeared, the *National Enquirer* printed a trashy article, complete with lurid pictures of a befuddled-looking Sinatra beneath the headline, "Where Am I?" The piece, which quotes liberally from Wayne Robins's review, asserts that Sinatra was completely unaware of his surroundings and remembered none of the words to his own songs, and it concludes that he should take the advice of unnamed friends and family and pack it in. (Is it any wonder that Sinatra hates the press?) Robins comes to much the same conclusion, and yet a close reading of the singer's quoted comments from the stage reveal that he is hardly unaware of his own vocal inconsistencies and lapses. His remarks provide a glimpse of the honesty he has maintained throughout his professional career—even when that honesty hurts a lot.

Twilight Time
Wayne Robins ★ 1993

The breathtaking special effects that open *Cliffhanger* and the romping, chomping, overgrown Barneys from *Jurassic Park* have none of the excitement of watching Frank Sinatra battle the most inexorable of all worldly terrors: age.

Sinatra can still use the brute force of his indomitable personality to compensate for the fickle voice that, Thursday night at Westbury Music Fair, sounded every bit of his seventy-seven years. Sinatra struck a self-deprecating tone, thanking the audience for putting up with "a throat that sounds like I ate a piece of broken glass."

The quality of his instrument was not really an insurmountable foe. After all, it is Sinatra's phrasing—his peerless feel for the nuance of lyrics— that has made him the greatest of all pop singers. After starting with a scratchy "Come Fly with Me," Sinatra's voice opened up for "You Make Me Feel So Young," which reached exceptional poignancy on lines like "When I'm old and gray / I'm gonna feel the way I do here today."

Sinatra had never before appeared at Westbury. The intimate (2,870 seats) theater in the round is an ideal setting for this larger-than-life icon. But it soon became evident that, even surrounded by seven TelePrompTers with very large print, the singer was having trouble reading—much less remembering—words to songs he made famous.

He occasionally made light of it. Visibly disoriented at the beginning of "Where or When," he paused and said, "We've been so many places, I don't know where we are half the time." The irony was as sad as it was unintentional.

It is not unusual for a performer on tour to lose track of the city, state or even country. I've heard jet-lagged rockers shouting things like, "How ya doin', Pittsburgh!" at Nassau Coliseum. But Sinatra seemed confused so often that the theater bristled with dramatic tension at the beginning of each tune, as the audience wondered if he would get it right or not.

The TelePrompTers carried the names of each composer and arranger (which it is Sinatra's lifelong habit to announce) before scrolling the lyrics. But as the band struck up "For Once in My Life," Sinatra muffed the introduction and then lost most of the first verse. He recovered well, belting out the words for dramatic emphasis.

It went that way, on and off: He sang "Witchcraft" without a hitch, but on "The Lady Is a Tramp," a confused Sinatra asked "Where are we? and improvised his way back to the melody and rhythm. On "Strangers in the Night," which he described, accurately, as "one of the worst songs I ever sang in my life," Sinatra got lost again, inventing the line "a lovely pair of pants away" rather than "a warm embracing glance away." The audience got involved in a bit of psychodrama at that point as well, when a disturbed woman stood up and insisted that Sinatra dedicate the song to a firefighter who died in 1991. "Take a Prozac!" someone yelled back.

Songs continued lapsing in and out of Sinatra's focus. "My Way" went smoothly, as strong and proud as ever. But "Mack the Knife" was incoherent, as Sinatra free-associated phrases like "crap grame" and "the cement is for?" and "innocent, maybe not." During "I've Got a Crush on You," Sinatra shouted to his conductor, Frank Sinatra, Jr., "What the hell are the words." To the audience, Sinatra admitted, "Hey, this is tougher tonight than fighting four rounds." At that point, the ref should have stopped the fight. Now Sinatra must think about hanging up the gloves.

☆ ☆ ☆ ☆ ☆ ☆ ☆ ☆ ☆ ☆ ☆ ☆ ☆ ☆ ☆ ☆

Some two months after Robins's review appeared, Sinatra was back in the East, performing in sold-out concerts at the Garden State Arts Center in New Jersey and at the Sands in Atlantic City. Fans were still stinging from the review, and the headlines surrounding it must have caused a good number to wonder whether Sinatra was indeed finished. No doubt, a great collective sigh of relief (not to mention a good amount of resentment toward Robins) went out when the following piece by Ray Kerrison appeared in the *New York Post*. To all appearances, the champ was still punching.

Ol' Blue Eyes Still Has the Magic
Ray Kerrison ★ 1993

Frank Sinatra, the signature voice of the twentieth century, walked onto the stage of the Garden State Arts Center Monday night in black tux and silver hair, clutching a hand mike.

Before you could say, "Dooby-dooby-do," 10,000 people jumped to their feet and set off rounds of cheering that shook the outdoor amphitheater in the Monmouth County meadows. "We have no new songs," Frank told them. "We're staying with the best of the old standards."

With that, he launched into "Come Fly with Me," backed by a fifty-piece band conducted by Frank Sinatra, Jr. The rich baritone voice boomed out with such power and verve that my startled wife turned and said, "This is unbelievable." It sure was. Right there, we knew we were in for a spectacular night. And before it was through, we saw things we would not have dreamed possible. Sinatra literally had 'em dancing in the aisles. Talk about star power.

I had not been to a Sinatra concert in nearly twenty years. The last was at Carnegie Hall, in the early '70s, when Frank's fabled pipes first began showing signs of age, if not wear. He was reaching for some notes, occasionally scratchy on others. It was a good night, but the signs were ominous. This was the beginning of the end. I left Carnegie unhappy. Every generation creates its own music, the sounds by which it will live. I was too young for Crosby, too old for Presley. Sinatra was mine. I have lived my life against the background of his music. It's been some trip.

A couple of months ago, Sinatra turned up at the Westbury Music Fair for a three-night gig. The critics were merciless. They said he flubbed the lyrics of songs he had been singing for thirty years. They said he stumbled around the stage like a man in a fog, unable to read the big video screens. The voice was rusty and creaky. All in all, the performance was so bad that one critic concluded that Frank should bow out before he is humiliated. "It's time for Frank to sing one for my baby, but no more for the road," he said.

Could it be that bad? We drove the sixty miles down the pike and parkway with considerable trepidation. Then we ran into the traffic jam around the concert hall. Cars by the hundreds were stacked up on the highways. The parking lots were filling up so rapidly they had to use fleets of buses to shuttle the customers to the theater. We paid $25 each for lawn space. Nothing else was available. If Frank Sinatra was washed-up, this audience had not heard it.

How lucky they were. Because for the next seventy-five minutes, Ol' Blue Eyes stood on that stage and sang one sweet ballad after another, weaving a magic I had not felt in a theater in thirty years, not since Judy Garland played the old Palace on Broadway.

Sinatra is very spare with his movements. He does not yell or scream, he employs no diverting theatrical gestures, no hype, no baggage. He presents only himself and his music. On this night, the effect was stunning.

Here they come: "You Make Me Feel So Young," "A Foggy Day in London Town," "For Once in My Life," "Come Rain or Come Shine," "The Lady Is a Tramp," "That's America to Me." Maybe once he fumbled the words. Once, he could not remember the composer of one of his songs. So what? It is Sinatra's unique way to credit every writer, lyricist and arranger for every song he sings, a generous recognition of those who have given him the tools with which to carve his incredible career.

He slips into "Fly Me to the Moon," and the audience is transported into a foot-tapping finger-snapping wave. The spectacle is amazing. "I hope you all live to be 750 years," he says, "and the last voice you hear is mine."

He sings "The Best Is Yet to Come," and 10,000 people start clapping in rhythm. He changes gears with "Moonlight in Vermont," an enormously difficult song—and it shows. He hits them with "Mack the Knife," and the whole place explodes. He is presented with bouquets of flowers, and the reward is a subdued but splendid "My Way."

Then it happened. Frank slid into one of the most beautiful pieces of music ever written, "The Summer Wind." In a moment, young men took their girls and wives into their arms and began dancing and swaying gently in the aisles, to the sweet sounds of Sinatra singing outdoors on a beautiful starlit night. Now that is really romantic. And the author of it all is pushing seventy-eight years of age. Amazing.

Frank wrapped it up with "New York, New York," and let me tell you, he took 'em uptown, baby, all the way, rousing them to such a pitch they were on their feet clapping, whistling, cheering, hollering like thunder. Even Frank seemed taken aback. "You're too much," he said. "You're the finest audience I've had in five years. I love you very much." With that, he was gone. It is one thing for Sinatra, at his advanced age to pull 10,000 through the gate, at an average of $50 a ticket, out of nostalgia or curiosity. It is something else to spellbind them and leave them on their feet, clamoring for more.

I don't know what happened at Westbury. All I know is that on Monday, he gave me one of the best entertainment nights of my life.

Tomorrow, he starts a three-night stand at the Sands Hotel in Atlantic City. I checked the bookings. Sold out. All three nights.

For many years now, Sinatra's concert appearances at casinos in Las Vegas, Atlantic City, and other venues have helped to promote these locales. The following articles concern Sinatra as casino showman in the broadest sense. The first, by Mike Mallowe, considers Sinatra as money maker. Published in *Philadelphia* in 1983, when Sinatra was still with the Golden Nugget in Atlantic City, it shows how Sinatra has extended his sphere of influence both on and off stage, and how Atlantic City casinos employ the singer's magnetic drawing power to market their product. The second article, a 1990 review in a small-town publication, describes the singer's performance at his latest Atlantic City "home," The Sands. On November 20, 1993, Sinatra was the inaugural performer at a 1,500-seat theater in the Foxwoods Casino-Resort, a new complex on the Mashantucket Pequot Reservation in Ledyard, Connecticut. In a review of his performance, New York *Daily News* columnist and novelist Pete Hamill considers the aging but active singer's effect on his aging audience and the effects of time on Sinatra's voice.

The Selling of Sinatra
Mike Mallowe ★ 1983

Will he love us? Onstage, the band is in place: then the house-lights are dimmed. The audience is nervous, expectant. No drinks will be served now, no latecomers admitted, no distractions of any kind will be tolerated. The performance they are about to see cost these people fifty bucks a head—the high rollers maybe fifty times that much in wagers lost and inside straights never filled. Yet here they sit, chastised, meek, praying that the man they are paying to see will be in a good mood tonight.

The medium-size room in the Golden Nugget is hot and smoky, smelling of the forced intimacy of strangers. Then, suddenly a spotlight clicks on, and with the light there comes a chill.

It isn't the chill of air-conditioning or of wind, but the fleshy chill of fear, or excruciating, agonizing anticipation.

Will he like us? they are thinking. Will he glance out beyond the footlights in that quick, all-encompassing way of his and approve of what he sees? Will some smile, some frown, some familiar Atlantic City face bring it all rushing back to Frank Sinatra and thereby elevate him to the peak of perfection tonight?

Will he love us?

Slowly, silently, the band begins to play. First, a few notes, a chord here and there, then, the gentle thumping of percussion. Like a tiny child aborning, the band whimpers its way to life.

We stare at the blackness onstage, peer into the ghostly halo of the spotlight, fantasize about the kind of entrance Sinatra will make and pray with the faith of children that the man, that the legend, will be swinging tonight, will be ring-a-dinging, will be inducting each and every one of us into the clan, just for tonight.

Then, abruptly, with almost disappointingly swift dispatch and economy of movement, Frank Sinatra stands before us, rendered other worldly by the hot lights. In his black tie and tux he looks just as sophisticated as we had dared hope: world-weary, weathered, wary of this night and of a thousand other nights before it, and of the hungry, demanding faces barely visible from *his* side of the footlights.

Will he love us?

"Must you dance?" Sinatra asks, articulating the lyrics as if he's hearing them for the first time, savoring each syllable, not just for *our* benefit, but for *his*, as well.

"Must you dance?" he repeats, as the band begins its inevitable follow-through bathing the lyrics that suddenly seem to have mesmerized him with a familiar, bittersweet melody, as Sinatra, the consummate pro, begins not a performance but a clinic on the arcane art of saloon singing.

"Must you dance every dance with the same fortunate man?"

Then, Frank Sinatra is off and running singing, reprising, joking with the band, paying homage to lyricists, arrangers, writers before every song, and kibitizing with the audience, recalling old dreams, old lies, old anecdotes from his own long history of sunny Atlantic City days and sizzling Atlantic City nights.

"Won't you change partners and dance with me?"

And from that moment on, from those first three plaintive, inquiring words, *"Must you dance?"* we believe that for tonight, at least, for this show, for this moment in time, Frank Sinatra *will* change partners and dance. With us, alone. With each one of us. We may never have to change partners again.

He *will* love us.

"There will never be another Sinatra." Roy Gerber says, sliding into a darkened booth in the lounge of the Golden Nugget. "Nor will there ever be another Sinatra story. I don't see any new Sinatras out there, do you?"

Gerber is big, husky and bald. You could mistake him for Yul Brynner or the Jolly Green Giant. And he talks just as tough as Kojak. It's a good thing, too, because Gerber is the outgoing entertainment director of the Golden Nugget, and the crowd that he has had to deal with is tough.

"This is an Eastern crowd. Vegas is a Western crowd. These people are demanding, sharp, ethnic. You go with a good Italian singer and a funny Jewish comic, or vice versa, and you might by okay. But you'd better know your people here, because an Atlantic City audience is different."

Roy Gerber has done it all in show business—in Los Angeles, in Las Vegas, in New York. He and a buddy used to hang out with the Neil Simon crowd, back when Neil Simon was a nobody. Then, Gerber got divorced and invited another lonely bachelor to share his big empty house with him. The two men and their women and their friends and their lifestyles grated on each other's nerves and produced some classically comic confrontations. For a while there Roy Gerber and his housemate, Lester Colodny, were the funniest odd couple in show business. That's right, "odd couple."

"A friend of ours started to write down all these funny things that kept happening to Lester and me," Gerber explained. "And this man's friend just happened to be Neil Simon's brother, so he took this material to Neil's brother, who then passed it on to Neil. And that, believe it or not, is where the inspiration came from for Neil Simon's *Odd Couple*. Later on, you can meet Lester. He's coming in from New York to film a commercial with Sinatra and Steve Wynn."

Steve Wynn, of course, is *the* Steve Wynn who runs the Golden Nugget and who is seen regularly in TV spots, receiving a cluck on the cheek from Frank Sinatra or a tip from Kenny Rogers or . . . whatever else the Golden Nugget's marketing pros want Lester to film Steve Wynn doing. Those commercials are making Steve Wynn almost as recognizable as the high-price talent he hires to shill for his casino. In the commercials, Wynn looks like a young, dynamic Milton Berle, with thick black hair, a fat grin and the kind of smugness that one has to develop to run a casino in Atlantic City. People keep asking the show-biz types, "Who plays Steve Wynn in the TV commercials?" But the truth is that Steve Wynn plays himself. Right up there on the tube with Frank Sinatra or Kenny Rogers, or whoever else.

"Frank Sinatra is a bargain at any price," Gerber says. "The figures that were bandied about when he switched from Resorts to the Golden Nugget last year were $10 million to $12 million. But those figures are meaningless."

Does that mean that Sinatra is beyond money?

"No. Money never stops counting. Never. Money is always a consideration. With Sinatra, however, it is not the only consideration. He left Resorts for the Nugget because he wanted a new home. He was treated very well there. The people he dealt with were very fine people, but he wanted to make a change. They couldn't help that any more than we could have done that much to get him here. *He* made the decision."

Just how valuable an asset is Sinatra to a casino? Listen to Gerber:

"Suppose you're down here with your wife. You are down here to be entertained for one night, and every casino on the boardwalk has a star. So, you turn to your wife and say, 'Who should we go to see tonight? Frank Sinatra or . . .'"

"There is no 'or.' You go to see a legend or you go to see somebody else. You answer that question honestly, my friend, and then, maybe, you know what Sinatra is all about."

"Sinatra is flypaper," Steve Wynn says. "If Sinatra helps us get somebody in the door from Resorts or Caesars, and they get introduced to the Nugget that way, then he's the perfect guy for us. But let me tell you something. Entertainment is just part of the package. *Sinatra* is just part of the package. Great as he is, *he's* not the attraction. The Nugget is. He helps introduce people to a facility, but he can't be the ongoing thing. *Believe me,* if every time you wanted to get good customers, you needed to have Frank Sinatra here, you'd go broke."

Steve Wynn, as they say, is the Golden Nugget. The marriage between Wynn and Sinatra could not have come at a better time for either man. Because of propitious timing—the trademark of every successful enter-tainer—each happens to have what the other needs right now. Listen to Wynn:

"This man has a hunger . . . a need. He didn't even have to express it to me. I could *sense* it. . . . This man, Frank Sinatra, has been a singer all his life. He's been doing club dates since he was eighteen years old. He's been a wise guy since way back when. So *what* if he knows the president of the United States? There's always a desire to be more creative, to be more expressive. Frank Sinatra wants to be more than just the piano man."

Respect. Of all the continuing themes of Frank Sinatra's stoned life none has been more persistent. He craves acceptance, cachet, the pedigree of belonging. Sinatra wants to become "of the establishment" in the worst way, and Steve Wynn just wants to sell the Golden Nugget. Wynn can make the singer a de facto casino executive, with his opinion solicited on planning, marketing and business strategy. Sinatra, on the other hand, can keep Wynn's high rollers—his *players*—serene in their sense of being a part of the singer's inner circle, that mythic magical institution known as the "clan."

"To me, Frank Sinatra is the greatest host there is," Wynn continues. "But nobody ever used him like that. When Resorts had him, they'd pull in people from Caesars or the Nugget for that night to see Sinatra, but then, they'd never go back. Sinatra is the world's greatest host. *Who gives a shit about his singing?* Everybody knows he can sing. Everybody's heard him. But what they're all dying to get in on is that Sinatra charisma.

"That's where I come in, with the Golden Nugget's high-line marketing strategy. I make the commercials with him. I make him available as a host at parties in Hong Kong, Vegas, New York, New Orleans—anyplace I want. Sinatra flies with me to these places, meets the big crapshooters, the players, gets his picture taken with them, schmoozes with them, says, 'Look, the next time you come to Vegas or Atlantic City, let Steve and me take care of you at the Nugget and be sure to look me up,' then we run in another high-line player, and he goes through the act again. Maybe Frank can meet a hundred people a night that way.

"He said to me, 'Steve, this is what I always wanted to do, but nobody ever asked me. All they wanted me to do was sing and then sit in my room all day. At Resorts, I met Crosby, the guy who runs it, once. Had dinner with him one night. He doesn't talk to me. Then, finally, he looks at me and says, "You know, you *are* pretty good." "You should hear Frank tell that story, it's hilarious."

Perhaps better than anyone who has ever attempted the feat, Wynn knows how to package Sinatra. For the most part, this packaging consists of filming commercials, shooting photo spreads, singing to wildly appreciative audiences composed of high rollers and their ladies. It means carefully conforming to Sinatra's mania for security and tightly controlling every situation in which the singer appears. It also includes catering to his whims, listening to his ideas, experimenting with his schemes, indulging his ego, suffering his eccentricities and shielding him from an inquistive press.

In return, Sinatra must simply be himself—the legend, the Nugget's Ambassador of Goodwill. The Wynn–Sinatra relationship is symbiotic. In fact, the casino owner has reduced it to its essence, to a Wharton School management equation.

"The issue, then," Wynn lectures over a bowl of Pritikin diet soup during a late-night supper in one of the Nugget's restaurants, " . . . the issue is the utilization of the entertainer. That is, his attractiveness as a marketing tool. The way you utilize him as a part of the overall package."

Frank Sinatra as a "marketing tool": the premier singer of his generation, the man who has had a greater impact on our popular culture than any of the occupants of the White House during his five-decade career: this man, this *legend,* reduced to the bottom-line jargon of "marketing tool": that's the way it is in the high-stakes economics of the new Atlantic City. Don't blame Steve Wynn. He's only holding up his end of the equation.

"Sinatra's expensive, we all know that," Wynn goes on, "but so are Kenny Rogers and Diana Ross. The Nugget is *about* customers. It's about keeping our players happy. If the Sinatras and the Kenny Rogerses keep them happy, fine. I want them to feel comfortable here and spend a lot of money here. It costs me $620,000 to operate this *mother* every day. After that, I make my profit. But first I gotta make that $620,000. But I'll tell you something—once you get over the hump, the way this business is, you can make $200,000 a day just as easily as $2,000.

"I want this place to combine the glamour and excitement of The Sands, in Vegas, in the early '50s and '60s, with the way that Bill Harrah from the original Harrah's used to treat his customers. I want them to feel at home at the Nugget. Sinatra loved Bill Harrah. He worked for him for many years and did nothing but rave and kiss Bill Harrah's ass and work his butt off for him: and whatever Bill Harrah wanted to pay him was fair. Bill Harrah knew how to handle Frank Sinatra.

"His attorney is Mickey Rudin. He's the only guy who can handle Sinatra now; been doing it perfectly for thirty years. I always wanted to work with Rudin. I knew Sinatra wanted to work with me. When he was still at Resorts I had dinner with Sinatra when he was down here.

"'I was in your hotel,' Sinatra said to me, 'Wow, what a gas! Geez, what a joint! You got the best joint down here. You know, we oughta talk.'

"I said, *Frank, forget it.* You're too expensive.' He was looking for a new home. So, I get together with Rudin and I say, 'Look, I don't have the patience for all this bullshit. I wanta negotiate, but if I put a package on the table, that's it. We don't come back and renegotiate, even if Resorts offers $400 million to keep him.' Rudin said, 'That's the only way we do business. Now, lay it out again, How do you want to use Frank?'"

From 1979 until last year, Frank Sinatra had been the main attraction at Resorts International. He was doing about forty-two shows a year then, at about $50,000 a show. Steve Wynn says Sinatra jumped to the Golden Nugget for the same money. But at Resorts they don't see it that way. "They offered him $10 million," says a spokesman. "That's a very substantial offer. I presume it was for pure financial reasons that he left. He got along very well here. Wynn didn't steal Sinatra. Not at all. We're sorry to see him go. But, Sinatra was just one entertainer out of seventy-five that we use. Besides, he wasn't hired permanently. He's just there on a three-year contract. In this business people move around."

When Frank Sinatra opened at the Golden Nugget last December, he sang and partied with the high rollers for two full days and part of two other days. He opened during a week that has traditionally been the slowest in Atlantic City. He was fighting weather, the Christmas season and the numbingly depressing prospect of losing at the blackjack table while "Jingle Bells" is playing in the background. It was an acid test. Steve Wynn says he wanted to stack the deck against the singer.

"I said to him, 'Frank, this is a bad week. This is a tough week. Let's *see* how good Ol' Blue Eyes really is.'

"He turns around to me and says, 'Geez, Steve, I guess we will find out, won't we?' Well, for the two nights he was here, people gambled $22 million. We found out how good Ol' Blue Eyes is. You bet we did."

In June, the Nugget took in $21.9 million. Resorts was still slightly ahead at $22.2 million. The key to Resorts' success is its sheer volume of gamblers. The Nugget, like Caesars Boardwalk Regency, is geared more toward the traditional high rollers. Atlantic City's other six casinos are still struggling to find their maximum-profit personalities. During the first six months of 1983, their combined gross revenue was $804.2 million. That represented an increase of nearly 21 percent over the same period in 1982. The Golden Nugget alone had three $1 million days in June.

All this is in contrast to the situation in Las Vegas, where the town, and the gambling industry, appears to be dying a slow death of disinterest. Crowds and profits are down—drastically. Some of the big names like

Sinatra still play Vegas, but only some. Others open to half-empty houses and vow never to return. Atlantic City, on the other hand, is managing to make money for practically everyone involved. And casino executives like Steve Wynn realize the best is still to come. Atlantic City is now the No. 1 tourist destination in the United States, with more than 23 million visitors last year. Considering all this, Wynn might be right on target—Sinatra is but one small part of the most ambitious multimedia marketing offensive ever undertaken in this country.

Frank Sinatra hasn't spoken with the media—print or electronic—not substantially anyway, in fifteen years. Maybe longer. Nobody counts anymore. Lee Solters of Solters Roskin Friedman, Inc., in Los Angeles is his PR man, sort of. Since Sinatra doesn't bother with publicity anymore, or even need it. Solters has a hard time filling the hours as a PR mouthpiece for the singer. What he usually does, instead, is act as a bumper for Sinatra against the press. In the past, Sinatra has frequently yelled and screamed at reporters and allegedly even taken punches at a few. Over the years, a handful of reporters including the late Walter Winchell, have been very close to Sinatra. But now, for the most part, they're dead, and the sixty-seven-year-old singer broods in his self-imposed silence, no longer seeking notoriety, jealously guarding what's left of his privacy. Lee Solters is the access man to get to Sinatra, but that access is hard to come by.

"So you're the guy!" Solters barks over the telephone from his office on the West Coast.

"What are *you, crazy?* Nobody gets to Sinatra unless they go through me. You got that straight? Lee Solters handles Sinatra. Nobody else. You've been bothering the people at the Golden Nugget, and they've been bothering me. What are you doing to those people? I must have got seven calls from Atlantic City today. What is this? You want an interview with Sinatra? That's nice. So, why should he talk to you when *60 Minutes*, Dan Rather and the *New York Times* are all in line to talk to him?

"I got no hope of him granting you an interview, but I will do this. I'll make the request. I will approach him. . . . Let me see. What time is it now in A.C.? His show isn't over yet, but I'll ask. Call me this weekend and please, call those people at the Nugget. Get them off my back and tell them that nobody handles Sinatra but Lee Solters. Who knows, kid? You might get lucky, Sinatra loves Atlantic City. And you want photographs, too. You want the whole schmeer. Maybe for nostalgia sake: maybe for old times. Good-bye!"

We're standing outside the star's dressing room. It's been refurbished for Sinatra with new furniture and a general cleaning up; still, without the star, it looks like just another dressing room.

"Security has been beefed up with bodyguards," the Nugget's former entertainment coordinator Mike Kane explains in the crowded backstage area. "He has his and we have ours. Guys like Jilly Rizzo. They travel with him everywhere. You wanted to know if he's a pain in the ass to deal with? I wouldn't say that he is. It's just that he knows what he wants and he wants it. We keep a butler backstage for him. The high rollers get butlers, too. He requested a piano, a nine foot Steinway, in his suite. We complied. We expected a large entourage. His doesn't even come close to the hordes that travel with rock stars. He's punctual. We have no problem with that, *We'd* better be punctual, that's all. For a rehearsal or show, he gets here precisely on time, ready to work."

Steve Wynn, the chairman of the board of GNI—Golden Nugget Incorporated—with casinos in Atlantic City and Las Vegas, did not bring Frank Sinatra back to the seashore. That distinction belongs to William Crosby, the man who runs Resorts International. What Wynn does deserve credit for doing, however, is once again making those weeks when Sinatra is performing at the Golden Nugget *the* most exciting weeks in the normally throbbing, pulsating life of the boardwalk. At forty-one, Wynn is himself a most unlikely casino entrepreneur. Born in New Haven, Connecticut, he studied as a child at Manlius Military Academy in upstate New York, not far from Syracuse. He was a lieutenant in the ROTC there, and he attended classes wearing a khaki uniform. He marched in military parades and learned to shoot a venerable Springfield rifle in the school gym.

From Manlius, Wynn went to the University of Pennsylvania, class of '63, and majored in English. One of his frat brothers at Sigma Alpha Mu says, "Steve Wynn had the ability to think big. He wasn't tied up in minutiae. He looked at the big picture. He didn't talk about pennies and nickels. He talked about quarters and dollars."

When Wynn approached the state of New Jersey about getting a casino license, his background came in for even closer examination. His father had owned a bingo hall in Upper Marlboro, Maryland, from 1960 on, and Wynn worked there throughout college. After his graduation and his father's death, he started managing the place.

From there it was on to Las Vegas and a minor interest in a casino that has since gone out of business. There were land deals then, and another casino venture—almost all of his dealings were controversial.

Wynn told the state of New Jersey that the man who had the biggest impact on his life in Vegas was a banker. E Parry Thomas. "If Howard Hughes was the glamour figure in Las Vegas," Wynn said, "Parry Thomas was the power figure." The two developed a father–son relationship—the banker with even more clout than Howard Hughes and the young bingo-hall operator with more than enough ambition for both of them. Partly through guidance and partly through loans that Thomas secured for him, Steve Wynn was able to go on to acquire, first, a lucrative liquor distributorship in Vegas and, later, a controlling interest in the Golden Nugget.

A decade after establishing himself on the Vegas strip, Wynn approached the Casino Control Commission in Atlantic City. They accepted Nevada's conclusion that the casino operator was clean, and then looked into some allegations of their own involving cocaine use and distribution by Wynn and two of his employees in Las Vegas. That fishing expedition wound up in what amounted to an apology to Steve Wynn by the CCC and a rather enthusiastic endorsement of his licensing. It was a tough time for Wynn, though, and for his family.

"My kids didn't know what to think about New Jersey," he says. "Every time they'd come here, the papers made me out to be either a monster or a hero. Now, it's better, though. This is a *very* tough business. That's why I pay my people a lot of money. You gotta put in eighteen-hour days here. You burn out *real* fast. From a management standpoint, it's an impossible job. That's why I give them cars and stock. I just want them to be happy so they'll keep the players happy. It might be Frank Sinatra who brings people into the Golden Nugget, but it ain't Sinatra who keeps them here. It's the staff."

The summer after the Nugget opened, Wynn presented new cars to 377 employees at a cost of $4 million. Then he opened his own private gas station to make sure they wouldn't get clobbered at the gas pumps. A week's pay in bonus money came next. Then, Wynn gave every employee—all 3,000 of them—four shares of Golden Nugget common stock—shares that recently split five ways, quintupling their original value. Wynn demands a lot—from Sinatra and everyone else. But he's willing to pay for it. Some of the people who work for him act like he's a minor deity.

There were some rumblings in the press that the galloping egos of Wynn and his No. 1 employee, Frank Sinatra, were starting to grate on each other. Sinatra, so the stories went, had become so disillusioned over the fact that he was actually getting second billing to Wynn on the TV commercials that he was on the verge of once again jumping casinos.

Sinatra isn't talking, but he did make a move to bar from his inner circle all reporters who circulated that story. Wynn denies that there is any substance to it. "It's all a lie," he says. "Bullshit. Frank knows it and I know it. I just wish he'd tell you that himself, but he doesn't like the press. He figures you guys will print whatever you want no matter what he says. But I do think in this instance that the reaction was disproportionate to the stimulation. I mean about the *commercials* and about him wanting out. But, hey, I don't talk for Sinatra."

"This is your hotel," Lester Colodny is saying through clenched teeth, annoyed, exasperated and sweaty. It's commercial cutting time, and Colodny is the very personification of the director as genius at work.

"Who is the kid who owns this hotel?" the director goes on. "That's what everybody is asking, *Steve.* That's what you gotta give 'em, baby. You gotta let 'em know this guy on television is *Steve Wynn,* and he owns the Golden Nugget: he *is* the Golden Nugget. What you see is what you get, and what you get is *Steve Wynn.*"

What you get is tall and good-looking, well-dressed today in a gorgeously tailored, dark-green suit. A minimum of makeup has been applied, and one of Wynn's kids is even on the set, cheering her daddy on. Wynn doesn't look like a casino executive at all, he looks like an actor. Unfortunately, however, the filming of the twenty-nine-second commercial is already nearing its twelfth hour and its sixth take. For some reason, Steve Wynn, who is usually very good at these things, is acting not like an actor, but like a casino executive.

Colodny takes a yank at the hair on either side of his head: readjusts the little director's gadget that hangs around his neck and begins stalking the small set like a hairy, hunched orangutan from Hollywood and Vine.

Finally, completely out of patience, he screams. *"Take a break. Clear the set. Steve, I wanta talk to you."*

Wynn and Colodny huddle, with Wynn smiling nervously and Colodny grasping his shoulders in a friendly bear hug.

It's difficult to imagine anything as boring as a twelve-hour shoot for a twenty-nine-second commercial. If this is what Hollywood is really like, then these people really do earn their big money. Repetition follows repetition, interspersed with tedium, the physical pain of rocking from one foot to the other and the almost impossible feat of attempting to take three steps and hitting a mark on the floor without looking down.

This morning the commercial is being shot in the opulent lobby of the Golden Nugget on the boardwalk. Preparations began at 1:30 A.M. with a crew from New York assembling the lighting scaffolds. Then, the trucks came rolling off the expressway, all from New York, naturally, with Colodny's cameras, cables and crew. A quick count reveals close to thirty people on the set, not counting Wynn and Sinatra. Somebody suggests that this is costing the Nugget about $100,000 an hour, and considering the hardware assembled in the casino's lobby, that figure reeks of conservatism.

For the last two hours, the casino crowd has been milling around, attempting to break through the human chain of Nugget security men and women. One entrance to the casino itself has been cordoned off, costing another small fortune in lost foot traffic that would ordinarily be trooping in to the slots. It seems clear that with every passing moment, Steve Wynn is losing money—big money. But he remains serene. He takes direction and seems intent on doing *anything* not to cross Lester Colodny.

The day trippers in the gawking crowd can't see much, but they have a general idea of what's going on.

"That's the guy from *television*," a man says to his wife. "You know, Steve Wynn. The guy who's on with Frank Sinatra."

"I thought *Sinatra* was here, too," his wife replied. "They said Sinatra's the guy in the hat. *That* can't be him. That ain't Frank Sinatra. That's some old guy in a hat."

"*Look* at the color of his jacket," the husband says from his slightly taller vantage point, "*What* do you call that, *faggy* purple. . . . *You* stay here if you want, but what the hell. Bonnie, we came here to *gamble*. Frank Sinatra, *Big deal*. I gotta get some quarters."

"Go . . . go get your quarters. I'll meet you later. If this is Frank Sinatra, I *gotta* see him. I remember him from thirty years ago. Go, Harve, go. I'll be in. . . . Excuse me, can I move up here? Pardon me. That *is* Frank Sinatra, isn't it."

It is Frank Sinatra in the hat, and he does look old. And the wimpy-looking jacket hardly seems appropriate for the country's last, best specimen of Big City Macho. By the time Sinatra finally leaves the set, he is surrounded by a wall of bodyguards, and if he does acknowledge any of his fans in the crowd, it isn't visible to the naked eye.

The Sinatra security creature moves slowly and purposefully, like a human centipede consisting of dark-suited legs, thick forearms and broad shoulders. It's composed of six or eight human beings or maybe more. It's hard to say. It moves like an ancient Roman wall of shields deflecting not just the curious or the obtrusive, but also the merely human. In the center of this human centipede is Sinatra himself; short, glum, swarthy—the quintessential Italian crooner. He may be the loneliest figure in the bustling casino today.

As Sinatra leaves, the crowd begins to disperse and Steve Wynn and Lester Colodny are left to their own devices, meticulously reshooting Wynn's solo scenes as the meter keeps ticking second by second.

Harve, resplendent in a patent-leather full Cleveland (white shoes *and* white belt), snakes his way through the crowd to fetch his Bonnie. He's carrying a big cardboard cup filled with silver. The cup looks heavy, and Harve looks happy.

"So, did you see your dream boat? Did he talk to you? Frank Sinatra, huh!"

Bonnie is short and heavy, with teased hair, and dressed in a pink pantsuit. For a couple of beats, she doesn't seem to hear Harve. She looks at him but doesn't focus on him.

"What? . . . Did I talk? . . . What? . . . *Oh, Harve,* I *didn't* see you there. Yeah, I saw him. Sinatra walked right past here with his body-guards. He seems so *different,* but it was him all right. It *was* him in the hat. . . . Harve," Bonnie says wistfully, "Harvey, I remember him when I was *just* a young girl. I used to go see him in New York."

Harve looks bored. Bonnie looks sad. Then, she brightens and smiles. "Come on, Harve, lend me some of your quarters. We'll go play the slots."

In 1963 Frank Sinatra was talking. He was at the height of his fame then: the undisputed king of popular music and Hollywood. He was also the leader of the pack—the rat pack, the clan.

The clan was really a gang for grown-ups that the late Humphrey Bogart invented one boozy night in 1955. He christened his gathering of renegades The Holmby Hills Rat Pack. Its purpose was drinking, whoring and outraging any and all straight citizens. In real life, Bogart had been eerily similar to the thugs, gangsters, adventurers and private eyes he portrayed on the screen, and he attracted his middle-age gang easily, naturally, and with very little hype. Besides show business personalities, it included respected writers, such as Nathaniel Benchley, and Hollywood rookies like young Frankie Sinatra. In those days, Bogie was the idol and Sinatra the disciple.

After Bogie's death the rat pack dissolved, to be reborn as Sinatra's clan. In the beginning, it was just a gang of hangers-on, exactly like the pack. It included Joey Bishop, the comic from South Philadelphia; Sammy Davis Jr., the black mascot; Dean Martin, an Italian crooner whose gifts at his peak were easily the equal of Sinatra's; Peter Lawford, the brother-in-law of JFK; and later, several other associate and affiliate members, like Milton Berle, Shirley MacLaine and Tony Curtis.

Whatever the clan was, by 1963 it had become the most powerful single syndicate in Hollywood. Agents, producers, directors, writers, actors and actresses and financial investors reacted to the clan's every whim. The performers the clan took under its protective wing prospered; those it dismissed as beneath contempt, as squares, and "clydes," found them-selves effectively shut out of the entertainment mainstream. When the clan was on the road in Vegas, New York, Atlantic City, Chicago, Philadelphia, Baltimore or any of the other whistle-stops in between, the locus of power in Hollywood traveled with it. The clan *made* Joey Bishop. It damn near destroyed Eddie Fisher by showing up at his openings, heckling the per-former good-naturedly and actually taking over the stage. When Sinatra was in a good mood, the clan seemed warm, generous, philanthropic, but when Sinatra's lips narrowed and that charming smile dissolved into a frown, the clan could turn as vicious, vindictive and unforgiving as any other gang.

The year 1963 was a pivotal one for Sinatra and the clan because that's when it all came apart. That's when the dream ended. That's when Camelot receded back into the misty memories of myth.

Jack Kennedy had been an honorary clansman. Sinatra had worked tirelessly for Kennedy's election and so had other clansmen. Sammy Davis, Jr., even postponed his marriage to a white woman for fear that it would reflect badly on JFK. Even the leader of the pack needed a hero, and Frank Sinatra's certainly seemed to be John Fitzgerald Kennedy. Peter Lawford, whose talents didn't begin to compare with those of the other clansmen, had become the group's most valued member, not just because he was loyal to Sinatra, but because he was wed to a Kennedy.

Sinatra practically turned his estate in Palms Springs over to Kennedy, following the Massachusetts senator's election as president. Allegations have been made that Kennedy and Sinatra shared some of the same interests, including women like Marilyn Monroe. A few years ago, Judith Campbell Exner came forth and claimed that she had been the mistress of both men and that she had, in fact, been introduced to the president by the singer. Neither the Kennedys nor Sinatra ever commented on such claims.

After Kennedy spent a night at Sinatra's house, the singer had a plaque mounted on the door of the bedroom that he used, which proclaimed that JOHN FITZGERALD KENNEDY SLEPT HERE.

By 1963, however, as Arnold Shaw, an excellent Sinatra biographer, has suggested, "A cool wind was blowing from the White House." The president's brother Bobby had never stopped nagging JFK about his friendship with Sinatra and the clan. There were also allegations that Bobby Kennedy himself had been romantically involved with Marilyn Monroe. The younger Kennedy had been especially incensed when Jack had permitted Sinatra and the clan to stage the inaugural festivities in 1960 to celebrate his victory and to raise money for the Democratic National Committee's mounting debt.

In those days Bobby Kennedy was at war with the Mafia, with Jimmy Hoffa's Teamsters and with several other organized crime figures, whose names had been linked—correctly or incorrectly—with Sinatra and the clan.

Back when Sinatra had been but a youngster, he'd been criticized for appearing in public in a Havana casino with Lucky Luciano. After that, the attempt of guilt by association never ceased.

There have been other charges, other accusations. Sinatra was investigated in connection with mob participation in the ownership of the Berkshire Downs Race Track, where he was listed as a vice president.

Following the disclosures concerning the Mafia's participation in plots to kill Fidel Castro, and in the assassination of JFK, a Senate committee investigating the Mafia–Kennedy links considered calling Sinatra, but then decided against it.

In 1969, the state commission of investigation in New Jersey raided a yacht where Sinatra was staying and attempted to bring him in for questioning concerning mob influence in Atlantic City. Eventually, he testified privately before a New Jersey judge and a contempt citation against him was removed.

Sinatra has fought savagely against these intrusions. At one point, he told the house committee investigating the Berkshire Downs situation that he was sick and tired of being treated like a second-class citizen, and that he felt the investigators were obligated to publicize the fact that none of the investigations or allegations had ever amounted to anything. He was telling the committee in his own way that he demanded and deserved respectability—acceptance—just as much as any other multimillionaire member of the entertainment establishment.

Years later an entrepreneur, Steve Wynn, would discover this deep-seated need in Sinatra and would then do his best to exploit it—to "utilize" it as a marketing tool.

Despite his need for respectability, Sinatra seems destined to be followed to his grave by allegations of his friendship with racketeers. When he bought the ritzy Cal-Neva Lodge in Lake Tahoe in the early '60s, the organized crime stigma remained. The Nevada Gaming Commission revoked Sinatra's ten-year-old gaming license, following an incident in the summer of 1963 when Sam (Momo) Giancana, the mob boss of Chicago, had been entertained and had occupied a chalet registered to singer Phyllis McGuire of the McGuire sisters. The following October Sinatra decided not to contest the revocation of his license.

With bad publicity mounting, JFK coldly severed his relationship with the clan that year. During a trip to California, Sinatra made one last effort to make peace with the president, inviting Kennedy to stay over at his house in Palm Springs—the house with the plaque on the door. Kennedy went to Palm Springs, all right, but on the advice of Bobby and others, he snubbed Sinatra and stayed instead with Bing Crosby, a longtime Sinatra rival.

After that, the two men never had a chance to reconcile. Sinatra was left with the ashes of his embarrassing, hollow clan when JFK was assassinated in Dallas.

By 1963 it all ended. The clan collapsed under its own weight, and Frank Sinatra began his long journey toward acceptance by the establishment. Polishing his image—honing it, buffing it, cleansing it—obsessed him. In many ways, Sinatra is still slouching toward respectability. Now, on the boardwalk in Atlantic City in 1983, he's getting a big assist from Steve Wynn.

"He's a very formal guy, Sinatra," Wynn explains perceptively. "Did you see his attitude toward me when we were taking the pictures? It's almost deferential. Sinatra gives as much respect as he gets. It isn't money.

I didn't even pay him the first year he worked here. I couldn't until we were straightened out with the Casino Control Commission. And he came here for not one dollar more per show than he was getting at Resorts. Now, I have him signed to a contract for virtually the rest of his performing life. He's sixty-seven years old, remember, and I got him for three more years. I got him for substantially more money, of course, in that deal, plus stock options in the whole bit. But mainly, I got Frank Sinatra out of respect. I respect him and he respects me. I said, 'Frank, you're the world's most expensive host.' That's all he wants to be. He's a lot more than the piano man to me.''

Upstairs, way upstairs, in the padlocked penthouse section of the Golden Nugget, Frank Sinatra and Steve Wynn are being photographed. It's an adventure just to get to the room where the shooting is taking place. The Nugget is as security conscious as Fort Knox.

The casino itself is the only one in Atlantic City with consistent decor from penthouse to outhouse—a decor that calls to mind a multistory dance hall in Denver, Colorado, circa 1880. Even the Nugget's cocktail waitresses spill out of their blouses like Wild West painted ladies. In fact, they put the Playmates up the boardwalk to shame.

Now, imagine this air-conditioned, reinforced concrete Colorado saloon with several stories of hermetically sealed high rollers's suites near the penthouse level, and the ambience of the Nugget can truly be felt.

Alighting from the elevator on one of those top floors, we're immediately struck by outsize urns, gold-flocked wallpaper, gingerbread mill work, a garish color combination of black and gold and a thick glass wall that looks bulletproof. Beyond the wall, there's a security desk, and at the desk sits a big, brawny, young, blond male, dressed in a butler's uniform. He may be the only butler in A. C. who looks as if he could go the distance with Mr. T.

Entrance is electronically controlled and voice activated. If they ever try to rob Steve Wynn's Golden Nugget, they'd better bring a howitzer.

There's another small crowd gathered outside the sitting room where Wynn and Sinatra are being photographed. It's close to show time, and Sinatra is visibly impatient—pleasantly so, but still impatient. He's already dressed in his tux, and he looks, by God twenty years younger. Bonnie from the lobby should be here to see *this*. Performing electrifies him, and even in those hours when he is preparing to perform, the spark rekindles as if on automatic pilot. Start spreadin' the news, Ol' Blue Eyes is back.

He and Wynn have their arms around each other's shoulders, with the ocean and twilight in the background and the singer's nine-foot Steinway in the foreground. The setting looks stagy and dull, but everyone's behaving professionally. It's tough to tell exactly how long they've been at it, but then Sinatra opens his mouth and the photographers know exactly where they stand.

"Okay . . . you got two minutes."

The photographers start to get schizy and begin clicking in a frenzy. Sinatra looks exactly like the cover of an album. He's in total control, in command. He says five words and fifteen people are suddenly afraid. They're not quite sure why, but they know they'd better be on their toes, and they'd better be cleared out in two minutes.

Up at the piano, Wynn says something apparently soothing to Sinatra. The singer responds. "You couldn't ask for anything nicer than this," he says, indicating the Steinway and the ocean view, with a quick arc of his hand. Wynn's lips move, but no words come out.

Then, abruptly, it's over. Sinatra gets up and starts heading for the door. Wynn takes a couple of giant steps to catch up. "Let's go," the singer says. Then, hesitating in the doorway, as he passes a photographer, Sinatra almost smiles and speaks again, "I want you to know," he says, "that these are the most photos I've had taken in the last fifteen years." The photographer looks transfixed.

Back when Sinatra was young and foolish, back before his bobby-soxers woke up one morning to find that they had become grandmothers, he and comedians like his pal Fat Jack Leonard used to play eleven shows a day in Atlantic City on the Steel Pier. Sinatra recalled those hectic days one night during a recent performance at the Golden Nugget in the new Atlantic City.

"Believe it or not," he tells his audience, "I used to drink malts then. Can you believe that?" He grimaces. "That was before I learned about Jack Daniels." Reaching behind him, Sinatra lifts a glass to his lips. "Boy is that better," he says.

"In those days they used to run people in and out so fast that you barely had time to turn around between the shows. . . ." He pirouettes on stage and gestures with his arms to imitate the perpetual-motion treadmill that whisked those audiences in and out.

"Can you imagine that? Eleven shows a day? I remember one day I had just gotten a bottle of soda and a sandwich, and I was still up on the stage: the curtain had just come down. I was hungry. I weighed all of about a hundred pounds back then. You remember that skinny kid from Hoboken?

"So, I'm there, munching on this sandwich, and I turn around to say something to Jack and up goes the curtain. They were so fast that they brought in a whole new audience seated them and everything. The band starts up and I'm standing there, expected to sing with a sandwich in my mouth.

"Well, I finished that sandwich. Believe me, I needed it. It was brutal then. But let me tell you something. I treasure those days. But, we did it—we got the job done."

"Talk about comebacks," Roy Gerber says. "Sinatra was down and out. I mean he was *out* of show business. Just out of the business altogether. He had friends in Atlantic City, though. He could always get work here, I guess. Or maybe he just likes the ocean. I don't know. He loves this town, though. Always went out of his way to come here. One of his best friends is Skinny D'Amato. He had the old 500 Club, and *that*, let me tell you, *was* a nightclub. I only visited there once in my life. I drove down from New York, caught the show and drove back up. But it was quite an experience. Before Sinatra got the part of Maggio in *From Here to Eternity*, that's all it was for him. Places like the 500 Club—*when* he could get work."

"In the summer of 1959," Arnold Shaw has written, "'the voice of America' . . . played the 500 Club in Atlantic City. He had planned to loaf between the shooting of *Never So Few* and *Can-Can*. But word came from Skinny D'Amato, a friend who owned the 500, that the club was in financial difficulties. On July 25, Frank opened an eight-day run so spectacular that the police had to keep excited fans under control both at the club and his hotel. During his stay, more than 200 women required hospital treatment. Reservations were resold at a 1,000 percent profit. One customer offered Frank $50 for a butt he was about to discard. At the height of the engagement, a forty-year-old woman ran in front of his limousine. As the car screeched to a halt, she pleaded hysterically, "Run over me, Frankie! Run over me!"

We're walking along the darkening boardwalk, accompanied, at a respectful distance of course, by one of Wynn's bodyguards. He rarely takes a step outside the casino walls without the armament. Fear and loathing on the boardwalk, it seems, are as palpably tangy as the taste of salt water in the air.

The night air picks up briskly, and the gulls call out. From our vantage point opposite it, the Golden Nugget seems cold and imposing. Wynn has done his best to humanize it, but for all his painstaking efforts, it still looks like a money-coining factory.

"I always thought Sinatra was over-secure," Wynn says, taking his guest by the arm and gently leading him toward one of the ramps that exits onto a small street behind the casino. The bodyguard follows. Just beyond the Golden Nugget's walls, the last show of Sinatra's midsummer stand is drawing to a close. Right about now, the audience, including Diahann Carroll and her entourage, should be hearing the opening strains of "New York, New York," Sinatra's signature song now that he has jettisoned "My Way" as too sentimental. A strange decision for a saloon singer whose stock-in-trade is reverie.

"I tease him about all the bodyguards," Wynn says. "I asked Frank, 'What is it? You have maniacal security. How can you live with it?'

"He says, 'Steve, I know it's a pain in the ass. But I need it because crazy things happen to me all the time and I get nuts when someone does something stupid to me, and the next thing you know it goes out in the papers and I'm a monster.'

"I'll tell you the truth. I half ignored him," Wynn says, as he leans against the metal handrail across the street from the loading dock of the Golden Nugget. "I brought you here for a reason. I want you to see something 'cause I know you wouldn't have believed me if I just told you about it. This Frank, he's some guy. Greatest guy in the world. I love him. Most generous guy I ever knew. But he has his ways. That's what this whole back-entrance schmeer is all about. See that car over there, squeezed in between the trucks?"

Wynn points to an unmarked Golden Nugget security vehicle, positioned near the loading dock, with still another big bruiser sitting behind the wheel.

"I've been with Frank for more than a year now, and I don't think he's a nut-cake anymore about security. Every time we go outside of a controlled circumstance, let me tell you, something else happens. *Forget it!* Something crazy does happen.

"Kenny Rogers is one of my best friends. Willie Nelson got married at my house in Vegas. I go for walks with Diana Ross on the streets of New York. Nobody bothers them like they bother Frank.

"I knew Elvis very well. *That's* what it's like. Crazy. People go berserk. Nice, well-dressed people. They come up, push you out of the way and then grab at him. I'm talking about irrational behavior. Sinatra needs security. It's the sickest thing I ever saw.

"You check your watch," Wynn says looking at his. The bodyguard looks at his, too. About a half a block away, some crazy guy stands staring at the casino; blank eyed, rocking from side to side. He's holding a big radio on his shoulder and wearing a heavy olive-drab army assault jacket. The temperature is still around 90 degrees.

"*That's* a space cadet," Wynn says, pointing. "Outer space baby." Swiftly, efficiently, the bodyguard positions himself midway between the crazy and Wynn. There's an air of tension that could electrify the boardwalk. The more Wynn talks, the more plausible he sounds. *Anything* can happen in Casino City.

"Now, I wanta tell you what's goin' on inside the theater. I have this timed perfectly. Sinatra's bags have been packed and shipped to Pomona. He's already moved out. He's just here for his show. He's done singing now." Wynn glances at his watch again. "The audience is clapping; they're waiting for an encore. They expect to see Sinatra enter stage right. They're wrong. Sinatra and his security people are now walking briskly toward us, and if you count with me, they will appear on that loading dock in precisely ten seconds. Sinatra will wave to me, duck into the car and holler out, 'Let's go. Wheels up in twenty minutes.'

"He's talking about my DC-9, my airplane. That's part of the deal. He gets to use it. He has this mania about a fast getaway. It's my airplane, right? He can leave now or two hours from now or two days from now. The plane don't take off till he does. I said, 'Frank, *why* are you like this? What is this getaway? Get-out-of-town bit?' He said, 'Steve, I don't know myself. I've always been like that.'

"Count with me . . . *one* . . . *two* . . .

"He'll fly directly back to Palm Springs. What for? For nothing. He'll catch the late show on TV. He'll read a book. He'll sit up all night and work out the *New York Times* crossword puzzle. He'll eat a tunafish sandwich. That's what he does. That's the way he lives. He's a very simple man . . . *eight . . . nine . . . here they come. What'd* I tell you?"

At precisely the count of ten, Sinatra, still in his tux, comes bounding down the ramp and hops into the backseat of the car. Just before his head disappears, he looks over toward Steve Wynn, smiles and waves. Then, Sinatra makes a motion with his hand to his ear. He vanishes.

"That means he'll call me in the morning," Wynn says. The car speeds past us, with recessed red lights blinking crazily. Steve Wynn waves back enthusiastically as the car quickly disappears around the corner.

Ol' Blue Eyes is gone.

Singing and Swinging by the Sea
Don Brennan ★ 1990

They say there's something about this town when he's here, and maybe they're right. A giddy anticipation, like butterflies before a Saturday morning neighborhood football game; nostalgia dripping from stories told by old men with young women on their arms; clubs and lounges in the wee small hours of the morning where the Goodfellas in High-Boy collars and leather wing tips light their cigars with rolled $100 bills.

Atlantic City, New Jersey, despite its sins, possesses the spiritual lure of the ocean. There is something indescribable about this magnetism; it possesses the power to grasp, to hold, to keep. It sets to flames the horror stories of syringes and vials of blood washed ashore. No. There is more to the ocean than just water. Even the pretenders at the clubs know the name of that tune.

So, it is here that he brings his immeasurable talents and baggage lumpy with his ego, his commanding, demanding personality; the streets of dreams that race through this golden ghetto of a neon city are alive with the past. And there is good reason for that. He is no longer just an entertainer, or a singer, or even a folk hero. Somehow, he has become much more than that; *he is the event.* Even the darkest corners of this town are illuminated by snapshots from the mind's eye.

WHO IS SITTING IN JUDGEMENT?

He will come and he will sing and he will not disappoint. After all, who is sitting in judgement? The verdict had been reached long before he grasps the microphone tonight. You see, one does not pay $100 for a ticket to see Francis Albert Sinatra and come away with a shrug of the shoulders. Those who have doubts—and the rest who have long buried him—do not come. The faithful remain to witness, pay homage, give testimony. For us, the legend remains in motion.

The Copa Room inside the Sands Hotel and Casino is, perhaps, the single most appropriate stage upon which Frank Sinatra performs. This is a man who sings and swings like no other, yet, too, enjoys the drama of saloon singing. "Angel Eyes" doesn't sound quite the same in an outdoor stadium. Here, the intimacy of the Copa Room rises to the occasion.

He walks on stage two months before his seventy-fifth birthday, taking long slow careful steps, his body bent forward just a bit, his face less puffy than in recent years. Immediately it is evident that he looks and sounds so much better than the recent tours with Liza and Sammy. (His performance during most of the last year's pay-per-view special was embarrassing to even his most adoring fans.)

Appropriately, the thirty-two piece orchestra led by pianist and friend (and butt of Sinatra's jokes) Bill Miller strikes up "You Make Me Feel So Young." Collectively, the audience listens to Old Blue Eyes, seasoned from centuries of this type of work, snap off the lyrics. It is reminiscent of those rowdy nights in the Las Vegas desert twenty-five years ago when Frank Sinatra *owned* the turf he romped on—usually with three hours-sleep. If it was Spencer Tracy who preached to him about the benefits of sleepless nights, and Joe E. Lewis who prescribed Scotch whiskey for his every ailment, who taught Sinatra how to interpret music like this? Tommy Dorsey? Maybe. But this is more than just holding notes. Bing Crosby? Perhaps. Wasn't it Bing who lamented that a voice like Sinatra's comes just once in a lifetime, but why did it have to be in *his* lifetime?

WITH HIP, SWAGGERING BRAVADO

This performance, one of five sold-out shows over the recent Columbus Day weekend, is vintage Sinatra. A greatest-hits set complete with hip, swaggering bravado and the trademark jab at the air to accentuate the notes. Sinatra's renditions of "Where or When," "The Best Is Yet to Come," and "Rain or Shine" are clearly the highlights. The rumors of his demise were premature.

In fact, his *third* version of "Where or When," a cool, punchy, titillating arrangement (this is even better than the one sung with Count Basie twenty years ago) is more than ample proof that Joe E. Lewis and those filterless Camels didn't corrode all of Sinatra's pipes.

Of course, with roses come thorns. The ballads and the monologues that precede them are dated and predictable: if I "assume the position of a bartender" one more time, I'm asking for a paycheck. And why did Sinatra drop the Jobim songs which fit so tenderly into his performances during the early 80s? Given both his narrowing range and the dramatic experiences of his life itself, who better to breathe Jobim's haunting, perplexing lyrics? You might call it Saloon Songs Samba. Accompained by the brilliant guitarist Tony Mottola, they were a wonderful segment. Bring them back, Francis.

But, Sinatra did sing the two crowd favorites, "My Way" and "New York, New York," the latter a triumphant curtainclosing rendition complete with all the glamour and glitter that naturally comes with this song. And, he performed his least favorite hit, "Strangers in the Night" (without the sarcastic "DoBeeDoBeeDo" at the end), and his favorite, "Summer Wind." Here, the Chairman was in board room form.

NOW THE END IS NEAR

When it was over, when the crowds moved in pursuit of their other lives, now out of the long shadow of this man, this event, outside in the theater lobby two large display cases stood filled with Sinatra memorabilia. It was a remarkable sight.

Behind the glass . . . the war years and the music of TD and the Pied Pipers; the bobby soxers at the Paramount Theater, crying and fainting long before anyone heard of a gospel swinger named Elvis Aron Presley; clowning with Harry James after the first, dramatic recording of "All or Nothing at All"; working with arrangers Axel Stordahl, Gordon Jenkins, Nelson Riddle, Billy May, and great Don Costa; the long, long days before *From Here to Eternity,* when Mitch Miller mortally wounded him with "Mama Will Bark," a recording for which Sinatra never forgave; the passion for Ava Gardner.

The classic Capitol years, followed by the Ring-A-Ding-Ding of his own Reprise label; the Rat Pack with Sammy and Dino and Joey and Peter Lawford, whose Kennedy connection made him oh, so valuable; the sixties and Strings and Costa's lush arrangements; love beads, a goatee and a flower child named Mia Farrow; retirement, followed by a comeback and the recording of "Old Blue Eyes Is Back" in Los Angeles on a day when it was 106 degrees outside, and even hotter in the air-conditioned studio; days and nights with pianist Vincent Falcone, casino mogul Steve Wynn, car dealer Lee Iacocca; the shortlived reunion with Sammy and Dino, followed by the faded, jaded tours with Sammy and Liza when the air had long left the balloon; and, now, in the September of his years, there's pasta sauce and performances again worth framing.

This is the real Francis Albert Sinatra, bouncing his way through a chart, changing the lyrics, keeping time better than any vocalist in history. And now that he's reunited with the Sands and singing by the sea, the thundering applause you hear comes not only from the masses but from the roar of the ocean waves.

Frankly Magic, But It's a Quarter to Three
Pete Hamill ★ 1993

There was a slow steady line of blurred tail lights moving through the damp November fog on Route 2, like a retreating army of red-eyed soldiers.

For miles, the passengers could see only the fog and the skeletal remains of lost factory towns, and then suddenly, up ahead to the right, two gigantic searchlights rose from the dark earth, signaling that the Foxwoods casino was open for business and so was Francis Albert Sinatra.

"It took us five hours," said Rose Cipriano, who wore six decades of life proudly on her face, and spoke in the glorious accents of Hudson County. "But ya know, ya never know when it could be the last time ya see him."

That knowledge moved hundreds of them through the night from Jersey and Providence, New York and Boston and places in between. Sinatra was weeks shy of seventy-eight. He had been singing for money since 1935, when he first took a microphone on the stage of the Union Club in Hoboken and took home $40 for a five-night week. He has done thousands of shows in the years since, greeted hundreds of whiskey dawns, smoked millions of cigarettes. Ya never know.

So they moved into the great ratcheting sound of the slots and out past the craps tables and the roulette wheels, past the fake waterfall and the giant translucent statue of an Indian aiming an arrow at the Big Dipper, checking their watches.

Time was short. None of them stopped to look at the shops peddling Native American art; few cared that this vast casino, perhaps the largest in the world, was here because a group of winners had shoved a group of losers into reservations long ago.

For many decades, Sinatra fans had gathered without asking who owned the joint. This was no different.

"Hey, I don't even gamble," said Brendan Malloy, a sixty-six year-old retired shipfitter from New London. "But I love this guy. I want to see him one more time. I don't care what kind of shape he's in. What the hell kind of shape am I in?"

There were thousands who were not there for Sinatra, of course; they were there to ruin a night, parked at the quarter slots or turning cards. They were in search of luck, not magic; a score, a reversal of fortune.

Only a few were in the old style, out of Vegas in the '50s, of the Colonial Inn in Miami Beach before the reformers ruined everything. The concert-going men wore tailored suits, white ties, an odd pinkie ring; the women fought the lumpiness of age with loose dark dresses and Baroque piles of hair. They were heading for the showroom. Magic first, please; luck could wait.

"I saw him first when I was fourteen," said Catherine Pavese, from Providence. "Our graduating class had a trip to New York, a bus ride, and the first morning we went to the Paramount, where Frank's movie *Johnny Concho* was playing, and he was doing shows in between. The movie was a Western and all the kids laughed, it was so stupid. Then Frank came on and everybody shut up. When he started to sing, forget it. He had us for life." She laughed. "I know he had me."

She was, as the Frank Loesser song urges, going to stick with the fella she had come with; she wasn't gonna blow on another guy's dice. She and the others filed into the showroom, where seats were sold at prices up to $150. She sat through a comedian. She listened to an overture. And there, suddenly, was Sinatra.

He is, of course, a ruin now, if measured against what he was. Measured against what Frank Sinatra was, every popular singer is a ruin. The upper register is gone; the lower register, that great dark baritone, is clogged with cigarette phlegm.

On some tunes, this dosen't seem so much about the erosion of his voice as about the erosion of belief; the core of Sinatra's genius was his sincerity. He took the most banal products of Tin Pan Alley and found in them some emotion that moved him, and thus moved the audience.

Now he does "The House I Live In," that creaky anthem of the New Deal, and it sounds like empty Fourth of July oratory. He labors through "Strangers in the Night" as if he's on work release; it's a song he has always hated, but he has been convinced the customers love it. Too often, he's singing for them, not for himself.

But there are always those flashes, particularly on the up-tempo tunes, where the old exuberance—and the Nelson Riddle arrangements—absolutely transform the room. He did it with "I've Got You Under My Skin" and "Summer Wind" and "Mack the Knife" (" . . . MacHeath, that rat bastid, is back in town . . .").

The words didn't matter so much as the feeling, Sinatra's knowledge that at his age, he had a No. 1 album again with *Duets*, that he had come a long long way from Hoboken. Even on a few ballads, he seemed to match his lyrical heart to his craft, taking a stool at center stage, lighting a cigarette, finding a safe place in an imaginary saloon at closing time.

Sinatra taught several generations how to deal with loneliness, expressing the stoic without being mindlessly macho. In this show, he did it with "Embraceable You" and "Angel Eyes." To the audience before him in the dark, it would always be a quarter to three, with no one in the place except you and me.

But for an encore, he was forced into his personal war horses; "My Way" and "New York, New York." Even on these, he blew some lyrics, looked baffled, and even once—in a flash of the eyes—scared. The audience didn't care; they cheered, gave him a standing O, begged for more. He might be a ruin, they seemed to be saying, but so is the Coliseum in Rome, and it's probably more beautiful in its ruin than it was in its youth.

When it was over, I waited a while, staring at the empty stage, and I remembered covering Sugar Ray Robinson's last fight. The place was Pittsburgh and the opponent was Joey Archer, a tough brave fighter who couldn't break a potato chip with a punch. In the first round, Archer knocked down the greatest fighter who ever lived. Robinson got up, labored across the rounds, absorbing pain, unable any longer to do what he once did, but showing us flashes—a left hook in the fifth round, the wicked jab in the late-rounds—that assured us that our belief in him was no mistake.

Robinson lost a decision, and in the dressing room, Miles Davis, the great trumpet player, told him: "That's it, Ray. You're packing it in." And that was it; Robinson never fought again.

That's how I feel about Sinatra. I wish someone like Miles would tell him to pack it in, to retreat to the recording studio, where the erosions of time can be hidden with craft. There seems to be nobody around him now who will say such words. And out in the casino in the Connecticut darkness, the fans drifted to the tables, to pick up dice and cards and whiskey. They had seen him again, as they had seen him during wars and recessions, during good times and bad, and if Frank Sinatra was still there, then by God, so were they.

In this life business, you have to take what you can get when you can get it. Ya never know.

☆ ☆ ☆ ☆ ☆ ☆ ☆ ☆ ☆ ☆ ☆ ☆ ☆ ☆ ☆ ☆

Frank Sinatra once commented that if he really had done all the things that have been attributed to him, he'd be in a jar on the shelf at UCLA Medical Center. He was referring to the myths that have grown up around him, ranging from his mysterious appearance to help a stranger in need to his instantaneous revenge against any and all enemies. As is the case with all myths, there are some truths about this particular man in all the accounts, but none of the stories can be absolutely trusted, so magnified (and hence distorted) is his reputation in the minds of Sinatra fanatics. Even though he avoids the media and public exposure, he has indirectly helped to create the wonderful and mysterious aura he enjoys. Nowhere is this hero worship better observed than in the many Italian-American enclaves that exist in the United States, especially in Chicago, Las Vegas and cities in Florida, California, and the Northeast.

Little Italy in Philadelphia's "South Philly" is an area of town known for its production of singers—Mario Lanza, Al Martino, Bobby Rydell, Eddie Fisher, Frankie Avalon, Fabian, and others—but even here, Sinatra is worshipped as the entertainment and cultural summit. The singer's ties to the city include his famous marriage to Ava Gardner at the home of friend and record producer Manie Sachs, and the work of Philadelphia-based disk jockey and Sinatra promoter Sid Mark, whose *Friday with Frank* and *Sunday with Sinatra* programs have been going strong for more than thirty years and whose syndicated Sinatra show is now broadcast on more than 100 radio stations nationwide. In the following article from the *Philadelphia Inquirer*, Laurie Hollman describes the Sinatra–South Philly love affair.

Displaying Frank Admiration: In South Philadelphia, Sinatra Is Everywhere
Laurie Hollman ★ 1991

Frank Sinatra is the George Washington of our generation.

Only instead of where George slept, in South Philadelphia, it's where Frank ate.

In pictures and photographs, he's everywhere.

Walk into Nick's Roast Beef, and there's Frank next to the bar in a large photograph taken by a friend of the owner's which shows an older, wiser Francis Albert in tuxedo singing—microphone in one hand, knee up. Someone taped a little green shamrock to his breast pocket, a reminder that you don't have to be Italian to like Sinatra.

There he is again near the entrance to the dining room at Frankie's Seafood Italiano. But forget the photograph, Sinatra—the name, not the man—appears on the menu. Veal Sinatra, named in homage to the singer, is veal wrapped in prosciutto, sauteed with garlic and rosemary, served on rice, garnished with spinach.

"When you serve it," says a waitress who identifies herself as Rose, "they always ask you: 'Does it sing?'"

And there he is yet again above a table clad in red-checkered cloth at the restaurant Cent'Anni over a picture of Frank Palumbo, the famed South Philadelphia restaurateur, and Joe DiMaggio, who has his head in a plate of spaghetti—well, almost in a plate. His mouth is full.

In the gold frame, Frank, the young Frank, lanky and sweet, stands at a microphone looking expectantly at the boxer Jersey Joe Walcott with another boxer, Rocky Marciano. at his other side.

Frank also hangs over another table in red-checkered cloth, only this time, he's older and heavier, and is wearing a crew neck sweater. And he's signed the photograph, "For Charlie, Cent Anni—All the best, Frank Sinatra 1977.

Did anyone ever say South Philadelphia has a special love affair with Frank Sinatra? There. It's said.

Other people may have a love affair, too, with the singer, who performed at the Spectrum last night. His photos hang in the Old Original Bookbinder's, a favorite dining spot of his, and also grace the work space of disc jockey Sid Mark of WWDB-FM, one of Sinatra's more ardent fans. Before it disappeared, the Latimer Club in Center City boasted a Sinatrama Room with pictures, photographs and life-sized cut-outs of the singer.

According to Mark, who knows just about everything there is to know about Sinatra, and then some, the club showed fidelity to its star by relegating a picture of a newspaper columnist Sinatra had feuded with to a lowly place—under the hopper.

But somehow in South Philadelphia, this *thing* for Sinatra seems to inspire more passion in more places. And it also seems to have inspired the purchase of more pictures. Maybe the attraction is because Sinatra is a fellow Italian. Or because he's from "just over the bridge." (Yeah, well, Hoboken. That's not so far.) Or because he sings—or used to sing, depending on your point of view—like a dream.

But the big question is, did Sinatra really eat in all those places where his picture hangs?

"Sure, he ate here," says Al Lucchesi, seventy-six, tending bar at Ralph's Italian Restaurant in the 700 block of South Ninth Street. "A long time ago, when Palumbo's was just a plain cabaret. Then they came here to eat. But what the heck. He was a nobody then."

"He used to bring his limousine and get someone to run in for roast beef sandwiches," says John DeSipio of Nick's Roast Beef at Twentieth and Jackson Streets.

He did not eat at Frankie's Seafood Italiano, at Eleventh and Tasker Streets, but give Frankie Chiavaroli time. He is working on that.

"He's the greatest of all time," says the thirty-two-year-old owner.

Sinatra was at Palumbo's cafe-restaurant and the converted funeral home next to it known separately as the Nostalgia Room. But he and the late proprietor, Frank Palumbo, were friends.

Even before other nightclub and cabaret owners caught on, Palumbo was presenting Sinatra. No wonder the place is full of Sinatra pictures— Sinatra warbling with Bing Crosby in *High Society*, Sinatra lounging with other members of the Rat Pack, including Dean Martin and Sammy Davis, Jr., Sinatra getting his hair cut, Sinatra dancing in a sailor's suit with Gene Kelly in *Anchors Aweigh*, Sinatra supping with Palumbo himself.

But the jewel of the exhibit, the absolute cream, is the black velvet portrait of three faces of Frank in the Nostalgia Room. There's another velvet portrait with only one face on the other side of the room. Together they frame the famed Sinatra table, where the great man actually sat.

"The first time," recalls Vanda Palumbo, also known as Kippee, Frank Palumbo's widow, "we roped half the room off."

At Cent'Anni, they claim the restaurant got its name from Sinatra's lips. "He went down to see Charlie, the original owner. And when he was down there, he was constantly saying cent'anni, cent'anni, which means 100 years. You know? It's like a toast," explains the owner, Al Sorgi. "The restaurant had another name then, but they weren't happy with it. So Frank actually says, 'Why don't you give it another name?' And that's how Cent'Anni was born.

"That why the picture on top of the bar shows him and says Cent'Anni," Sorgi adds. There are three pictures of Sinatra in the restaurant, which is more than there are of Mario Lanza, whom Sorgi claims as a first cousin. In fact, he recalls, Mario Lanza's mother, his Aunt Mary, used to cook for Sinatra.

"Frank used to call her Mama Maria. He used to say that next to his mother, she had the best gravy. . . . Frank loved her sauce."

Sorgi's son Ron, thirty-four, also likes Sinatra, but maybe not as much as his dad. And certainly not as much as his father's friend Millie Amicone. Ron Sorgi dials her number from the restaurant phone.

Say Ms. Amicone, is it true what they say about you celebrating Ol' Blue Eyes' birthday with a cake every year?

"We sing happy birthday, blow the candles out and play Sinatra albums," she replies. This year, same thing. She'll buy a cake for December 12, that's his birthday ("But you probably know that," she says) and put seventy-six candles on it. Maybe Sinatra knows. Maybe he doesn't. She once heard him refer to people who celebrate his birthday.

"I love Frank Sinatra," she says. "I really do."

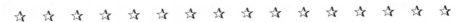

In the folk biographies of legendary figures, one of the mighty powers ascribed to the hero is the ability to heal the physically ill. Anyone who has seen the film version of *The Babe Ruth Story*, starring William Bendix, will be familiar with this trope. In one instance, Ruth inadvertently "heals" a crippled boy who touches him. In another, he points out and hits a home run to the designated place in the stands because he has promised to do so for a mortally ill boy. The boy recovers. While our increasing sophistication—or cyncism—as a culture will no longer allow the creators of fiction to frame such stories for us, we do in our own way cling to our belief in the relationship between fame (art) and recuperation. Sports and show-business stars are often asked to visit children's hospitals to cheer up the kids and make them feel better.

If Sinatra the Legend has any healing powers, they lie decidedly in the inspirational power of his music. In the following articles, a prominent Philadelphia columnist and a three-time Emmy-winning television personality expound on the power of Frank's music to heal and motivate. In the first, Clark DeLeon of the *Philadelphia Inquirer* applies this notion to his own experience, recalling the heartbreak of watching the Phillies lose the first home game of the 1993 World Series after a wonderful championship season. In the second piece, which appears in print for the first time, television host and producer Bill Boggs muses on the intermingling of his own personal history and Sinatra's vocal artistry and how it led to an unusual New Year's resolution.

Please, Mister, Please; Play Fifty-Two-Oh-Nine
Clark DeLeon ★ 1993

Maybe it's a middle-age thing. Otherwise, I can't explain how it could have taken forty-three years and a rain-delayed defeat in the first home game of the World Series for me to finally discover the extraordinary recuperative power of Frank Sinatra's voice upon a soul-sick loser late at night.

Sure, I knew that certain of Sinatra's songs, such as "New York, New York," when played on a jukebox at top volume in a neighborhood tavern, could cause coed softball teams to form high-kicking chorus lines at the sound of the words, "Theeeeese little town blues . . ." But I had never felt the personal impact of a Sinatra song on a heavy hanging heart until the other night when I was sitting on a bar stool at the Pen & Pencil Club staring at a Schmidt's and settling into an inconsolable funk after the Phillies 10–3 doom in Game 3.

Then, in the midst of my hollow-hearted musings, some words floated through the curtain of sadness I had drawn around myself against any conversation expressing hope or offering perspective. It was Frank Sinatra and he was talking to me:

I've been a puppet a pauper a pirate a poet a pawn and a king
I've been up and down and over and out and I know one thing
Each time I find myself falling flat on my face
I just pick myself up and get back in the race.

It was like Popeye finding spinach. By the time Frank hit the title lyric—"That's Life"—I was on my feet, energy renewed, spirit restored and singing along. With one song, Frank Sinatra had drop-kicked my self-indulgent gloom out the window and onto the street. The sound of his voice was a tonic, a wonder drug taken by ear, faster acting than Prozac without the dangerous side effects.

I walked to the jukebox to see what else Frank would have to say on the subject before Games 4, 5, and 6 of the World Series. I played 5207, "The Best Is Yet to Come," and 5214, "All or Nothing at All." And I saved the best for last, "It Was a Very Good Year."

Wasn't it, though?

The Year of Frank: December 1992
Bill Boggs

During the first few minutes after midnight on this past New Year's Eve, I made what seemed to be a whimsical vow to myself. It's taken me most of the year to understand why following through on that resolution has helped as much as it has.

I'd watched the fireworks over Central Park from my apartment, and then turned on the radio. I smiled at the coincidence of hearing Frank Sinatra sing Cole Porter's lyric about champagne as I uncorked a bottle.

I settled into my chair. I watched the bubbles. I listened to Frank. Somewhere between the middle of the glass and the end of the song, I promised myself that this would be the year of Frank. I would go to see him perform as often as I could.

That afternoon at a party, I encountered incredulous faces as I revealed my New Year's resolution. After all, my friends knew that I'd already seen Frank Sinatra perform many times and I'd actually interviewed him on television. I was suddenly telling people I was planning a quest to see more shows, and people were telling me I was nuts.

Why did I need to do this?

It was late in the summer of 1960, and Frank Sinatra was coming to the 500 Club in Atlantic City. I was a teenager working in nearby Ocean City,

New Jersey, and rock and roll was my passion. I'd had the good fortune of having Elvis and my puberty explode at the same time. It was as a joke that someone had given me a Sinatra album, *The Wee Small Hours of the Morning*, for my birthday, July 11.

I started to listen to it late at night when the rooming house wouldn't let me play loud music. At first, it sounded a little bit like an advanced English class. Hound dogs or blue suede shoes were nowhere in sight. These lyrics were expressing intense adult feelings. "Unrequited love's a bore, and I've got it pretty bad," Sinatra sang. Love was locked out. Women were dancing on the ceiling. Ill winds were blowing. The songs seemed to be an insight into the big world I knew I had to enter soon. I better find out what this is all about, I thought.

I couldn't afford the steep cover charge at the 500 Club so I devised a plan to sneak in the back door at midnight, dressed as a busboy. It worked.

I'd never been in a nightclub. Tables seemed to be piled on top of one another. The place was wild, packed with dressed-up adults who were smoking, drinking, and screaming at one another. This is nothing like going to the movies, I thought. I wondered how anyone could get in the mood to listen.

I was standing by a wall next to the stage when Sinatra suddenly appeared from behind a red velvet curtain. Everything changed. I watched him, and I watched what happened to the rowdy crowd.

He sang loud songs that made the people so happy their faces seemed to be floating from their bodies and quiet songs that brought tears to the eyes of men who must have known about the unrequited love.

From my perch, just a few feet away from him, Sinatra appeared to have a source of pure energy. What gives him that? I wondered. He was really experiencing all the emotions that the songs were describing. I could feel it.

That night, without really knowing it, I chose Frank Sinatra to be my hero and his music to help me on my journey down that lonesome road of adulthood.

I bought records. Frank seemed to have a song to describe, define, or reveal any situation. Elements of Frank's life became as inspirational to me as some of the mantras I repeated from his music. Here was a man who set out to be the best there ever was. He'd been a superstar and lost it, yet was able to redefine himself and rise to greater heights.

So much in his music seemed to come true for me. There were nights in the dark when "Only the Lonely" was real. I strolled the Tuilleries Gardens and saw the chestnuts in blossom of "April in Paris." I found myself flat on my face and picked myself up to get back in the race. I'd buoyed myself with the optimism of knowing "The Best Is Yet to Come," yet plenty of times I saw the road get tougher, lonelier, and rougher.

Before the fireworks had exploded over Central Park, I'd been sitting in the quiet of my apartment in the dark. For some reason, during the entire previous year I hadn't been listening to much Sinatra music. It seems strange to realize it now; maybe that was part of what had made it such a rotten year. I'd finally left a boring, desk-bound, noncreative job. On New Year's Eve, I was facing the greatest uncertainty of my life. I was taking a big risk to attempt business for myself. Deals for the television work I wanted were uncertain. I could have the greatest twelve months of my career or experience a colossal financial and emotional disaster.

It was another journey down another potentially lonesome road, and I was afraid. I wanted support from Frank and the music, but I didn't really know what I would find when I leaned against a wall and watched him closely again.

I stuck to my resolution. During the year, I flew to London and saw two shows at Royal Albert Hall. I made two trips to the Sands in Atlantic City. I arranged a business trip to Los Angeles to coincide with a concert there, and I recently went to Radio City Music Hall three times.

Through the years, as I watched Sinatra perform, I'd never been able to pinpoint an exact description of the singular sense of himself that embraces his work with such personal authority. Yet it was, in fact, that magical element that had so welded me to his persona on that long ago night at the 500 Club.

Sinatra is performing now at nearly eighty years of age. He fights the ravages of time and the diminution of capabilities at every show. He is still thrilling audiences. This year, when I observed Frank closely, his face now like luminous granite in the spotlight, I grasped a valuable truth: you are very powerful provided you know how powerful you are. That intrinsic belief was the energy source that had mystified me and seduced me as a teenager.

Each time I saw Frank this year I reconnected with that primal source of energy. I returned from each concert more focused, centered, and grounded in the belief that I could prevail over my objectives.

Men can gain inspiration from many things—the grace of a champion athlete, the actions of a courageous fireman, the vision of a teacher, the touch of a brush to canvas.

My inspiration comes from a man singing on stage. There's a song that describes the past twelve months: "It Was a Very Good Year."

While Sinatra the Legend is readily visible in American culture, Sinatra the man remains fairly elusive. The following articles present observations on the Sinatra persona, emphasizing the lifestyle, the personality, the protected existence, and the "man alone." The first, from *Rolling Stone,* is by Ralph Gleason, West Coast news-paper journalist, jazz critic, and author of *Celebrating the Duke,* who expresses disappointment in what he regards as a kind of broken icon—a musical god ren-dered pedestrian by his politics, appearance, and behavior. Next, novelist, journal-ist, and *New York* magazine contributor Pete Hamill presents an up-close portrait of a Sinatra who, in his isolation, is bewildered by life generally, and the one he leads in particular. In the next piece, from his book *Me and Bogie,* Hollywood producer, Sears, Roebuck heir, and close Sinatra friend Armand Deutsch provides a behind-the-scenes look at a typical Sinatra working evening. Finally, New York radio per-sonality, singer, and longtime Sinatraphile Jonathan Schwartz gives us a glimpse of an isolated and insulated celebrity.

Frank: Then and Now
Ralph J. Gleason ★ 1974

It's hard to put into words now what Frank Sinatra meant to me when I first got hooked on music. I can tell you that when he and Woody Guthrie were both singing in the same city I went to hear Sinatra. I can also tell you that I had three singers I dug then: Louis Armstrong, Billie Holiday and Frankie.

But that's not enough; at best it only lists my personal preference and it doesn't get at all into what it was about Sinatra that turned us all on.

You read today about the Swing era and the bobbysoxers swooning at the Paramount Theater in New York when Frankie sang and all that, but he reached out past bobbysoxers, believe me.

Sinatra had style in a time when style meant not only what passed for sharp clothes, but included manner and, in his case, the sound and use of his voice. He sang the pop songs of that time—those dumb trite ballads that Louis Armstrong treated as vehicles for comedy and Billie Holiday made into tragedies—as though they were real stories. He had the sound and the sliding grace of a good cellist and he phrased like a horn player.

And far beyond the capability he had as a singer, he had a personal sound. You knew it was him when you heard the first notes on the air and on record. And, in another way, he sang as opposed to just mouthing the words or making sound. He gave you the feeling of reaching out to you, either speaking to you or for you, depending on the lyric. Above all, he did it with style.

It is simply weird now to see him all glossed up like a wax dummy, with that rug on his head looking silly and the onstage movement, which used to be panther-tense, now a self-conscious hoodlum hustle. It's even odder to see him with the bodyguards and hear all the gossip about his coterie of friends and their capers in this club or that hotel or that gambling joint.

He used to mean something to my generation and he probably still means something to some. But there are those of us who still dig his voice—that style he set was big enough and broad enough to carry the careers of half a dozen others—but for whom Ol' Blue Eyes is a drag that Frankie never was.

You see, he had the charm. He could turn it on and entertain, let the smile come out of those eyes and the voice out of that mouth and in ten seconds he had you. Sometimes he could do it just walking on the stage. He didn't cheat. He gave a good show every time I ever saw him and you knew *he* knew what he was doing and you knew *he* knew he wouldn't let you down.

Back in the early years he got a lot of hard lines in the press for running with mobsters and visiting Lucky Luciano in Cuba and things like that. It didn't hurt him a bit. His insistence on picking his friends as he wanted to fell short of pure bravado and even had a touch of sincerity.

Today he's swapping Charlie Luckey and the other mobsters for Spiro Agnew and Ronald Reagan and who is to measure the difference? All I know is that what seemed a youthful bravado twenty-five years ago seems like angry perversity now. You used to think of him as a guy who could be Robin Hood, who could help some poor cat who was in real need. Today the guys he helps are millionaires and he behaves, if only half the print is true, like an arrogant despot with a court of sycophants Uncle Tomming their asses off.

You see, somewhere along the line he stopped believing in the art he had. He hit the bottom of public acceptance, people did not come to his shows, his records were stiffs right out of the morgue, and he was broke and had no future. He pulled himself out of that (guts he always had), and made himself into a good actor and then into a singer again and parlayed it all into his own record company and production company and a billion dollars in nickels and dimes.

Now he can't spend his money in one lifetime, even at his pace. His possible appearance on a TV show is the occasion for bodyguards and hush hush phone calls and big security plans and a blanket of secrecy. Why? So the millions of Sinatra fans won't mob him and tear him to bits? So he won't be kidnapped and held for ransom?

You know, I swear to God I don't think anybody but he and those clowns on his payroll really think any of this panoply of power is necessary. For Frank Sinatra, whose voice made him the friend of millions of Americans, whose films made him even greater, to carry on like a Caribbean dictator holding back history with bodyguards and a secret police is simply obscene.

I only met him once. Back in 1941 when he was starting a three-night-a-week CBS radio show which he did for a bit and then went with Harry

James. He was as nice a guy as I ever met, sincere, decent, warm, human. I have dug his singing ever since and I did the liner notes to his first album on his own label.

But I know enough by this time to realize that he doesn't have to be a nice guy to be a great singer. And he *is* a great singer. And he doesn't owe me or you or anybody a damn thing. But by the same token, I can dig his singing and not dig his style anymore, not dig his friends nor his attitudes nor what they imply. I'd still go to hear him instead of Woody Guthrie, but the comparison is a little silly since the content of practically all Sinatra songs has had all the social significance of a good solid burp. Whatever Woody Guthrie may have been, he was no crooner.

Comparisons aside, and even granting his right to be whatever he wants to be, all I can say is that it just ain't the same. Somehow I know in my bones that Frank's not the guy he was that afternoon at 485 Madison Avenue. I'm not the same either but I think he went somewhere I would not go, somewhere that makes him alien now to me in a way he never was before.

The voice is good today. Those warm tones are there and the phrasing. He can really do it like a true professional. But I don't believe, anymore, that he is one of us. He's one of *them* now, singing from the other side of the street and I guess he doesn't even have a whiff of how power-mad and totalitarian it all seems, those bodyguards and the Rat Pack and all that egocentric trivia that has nothing at all to do with music. And he was once a thorough musician, right down to his toes. But then he didn't wear a rug, and I have a feeling he wouldn't have. All that came later when, in truth, he had lost a lot more than his hair.

Sinatra: The Legend Lives
Pete Hamill ★ 1980

One rainy evening in the winter of 1974, I was home alone when the telephone rang. I picked up the receiver, looking out at the wet street, and heard one of the most familiar voices of the century.

It was Frank Sinatra.

"What are you doing?"

"Reading a book," I said.

"Read it tomorrow. We're at Jilly's. Come on over."

He hung up. I put the book down. I didn't know Sinatra well, but despite all the rotten things I'd read about him, I liked him a lot and was sometimes touched by him. We'd met though Shirley MacLaine, who went back a long time with Sinatra. In 1958 Sinatra put her in *Some Came*

Running, expanded her part to fit her talents, and made her a movie star. When they occasionally met, it was clear to me that Sinatra admired her relentless honesty, loved her in some complicated way, and was, like me, a little afraid of her.

I took a cab to Jilly's, a seedy time warp of a saloon at the Eighth Avenue end of Fifty-second Street. The long, dark bar was packed with the junior varsity of the mob; of all the Sinatra groupies, they were the most laughable. They were planted at the bar like blue-haired statues, gulping Jack Daniel's, occasionally glancing into the back room. A maitre d' in a shiny tuxedo stood beside a red velvet rope that separated the back room from the Junior Appalachian conference at the bar.

"Yes, sir?" the maitre d' said.

"Mr Sinatra," I said, "He's expecting me."

He turned nervously, his eyes moving past the empty tables at the booths in the left-hand corner against the wall. Jilly Rizzo looked up from a booth and nodded, and I was let through. "'Ey, Petey babe," Jilly said, coming around a table with his right hand out. Jilly has one glass eye, which gives him a perpetually blurry look. "Hey, Frank," he said, "look who's here."

"Hey, Peter, grab a seat!" Sinatra said brightly, half rising from the booth and shaking hands. He moved clumsily, a newly heavy man who hadn't learned yet to carry the extra weight with grace; he seemed swollen, rather than sleek. But the Sinatra face was—and is—an extraordinary assemblage. He has never been conventionally handsome: There are no clean planes, too many knobs of bone, scars from the forceps delivery he endured at birth. But the smile is open, easy, insouciant, and his blue eyes are the true focal point of the face. In the brief time I'd known him, I'd seen the eyes so disarmingly open that you felt you could peer all the way through them into every secret recess of the man; at other times they were cloudy with indifference, and when chilled by anger or resentment, they could become as opaque as cold-rolled steel.

"You eat yet?" he asked. "Well, then have a drink."

As always, there was a group with him, squashed into the worn leatherette booths or on chairs against tables. They had the back room to themselves and were eating chop suey and watching a Jets game on a TV set. Sinatra introduced Pat Henry, the comic who sometimes opens for him; Roone Arledge of ABC; Don Costa, one of Sinatra's favorite arrangers; a few other men; and some young women. Sinatra was with a thin blonde model in a black dress. He didn't introduce her.

The conversation stopped for the introductions, then started again. Sinatra leaned over, his eyes shifting to the TV screen, where Joe Namath was being shoved around.

"I don't get this team," he said. "They got the best arm in football and they won't give him any protection. Ah *shit!*" Namath was on his back and getting up very slowly. "Oh, man. That ain't *right!*"

They cut to a commercial, and Sinatra lit a Marlboro and sipped a vodka. His eyes drifted to the bar. "Jesus, there's about forty-three indictments right at the bar," he said loudly.

"Present company excluded," Pat Henry said, and everybody laughed.

"It better be," Sinatra said, and they all laughed again. The blonde smiled in a chilly way. The game was back on again, and Sinatra stared at the TV set but wasn't really watching the game. Then the game ended, and Jilly switched off the set. There was more talk and more drinking, and slowly the others began to leave.

"Hell, let's go," Sinatra said. He said something to Jilly, and then he and the blonde and I walked out. A photographer and a middle-aged autograph freak were walking under the tattered awning.

"Do you mind, Mr. Sinatra?" the photographer asked.

"No, go ahead," he said. The flashbulbs popped. The blonde smiled. So did Sinatra. "Thanks for asking."

Then he signed the woman's autograph book. She had skin like grimy ivory, and sad brown eyes. "Thanks, dear," Sinatra said. We all got into the waiting limousine and drove down the rainy street, heading east.

"What do you think they do with those autographs?" he said. "Sell them? To who? Trade them? For *what?* How does it go? Two Elvis Presleys for one Frank Sinatra? Two Frank Sinatras for one Paul McCartney? I don't get it. I never did."

We drove awhile in silence. Then the chauffeur turned right on a street in the Sixties and pulled over to the curb. Sinatra and the blonde got out. He took her into the brightly lit vestibule. He waited for her to find a key, tapped her lightly on the elbow, and came back to the limo.

"You have to go home?"

"No."

He leaned forward to the driver. "Just drive around awhile."

"Yes sir."

And so for more than an hour, on this rainy night in New York, we drove around the empty streets. Sinatra talked about Lennon and McCartney as songwriters ("That 'Yesterday' is the best song written in thirty years") and George Harrison ("His 'Something' is a beauty"), prizefighters ("Sugar Ray was the best I ever saw") and writers ("Murray Kempton is the best, isn't he? And I always loved Jimmy Cannon"). It wasn't an interview; Frank Sinatra just wanted to talk in a city far from the bright scorched exile of Palm Springs.

"It's sure changed, this town," he said. "When I first came across that river, this was the greatest city in the whole goddamned world. It was like a big, beautiful lady. It's like a busted-down hooker now."

"Ah, well," I said. "Babe Ruth doesn't play for the Yankees anymore."

"And the Paramount's an office building," he said. "Stop. I'm gonna cry."

He laughed and settled back. We were crossing Eighty-sixth Street now, heading for the park.

"You think some people are smart, and they turn out dumb," Sinatra said. "You think they're straight, they turn out crooked." This was, of course, the Watergate winter; the year before, Sinatra sat in an honored place at the second inauguration of Richard Nixon. "You like people, and they die on you. I go to too many goddamned funerals these days. And women," he said, exhaling, and chuckling again, "I don't know what the hell to make of them. Do you?"

"Every day I know less," I said.

"Maybe that's what it's all about," he said. "Maybe all that happens is you get older and you know less."

After a while, the limousine pulled up in front of the Waldorf, where Sinatra has an apartment. He told the driver to take me home.

"Stay in touch," he said, and got out, walking fast, his head down, his step jaunty, his hands deep in the pockets of his coat. I remember thinking that it was a desperatly lonely life for a man who was a legend.

At sixty-four, Francis Albert Sinatra is one of that handful of Americans whose deaths would certainly unleash a river of tearful prose and much genuine grief. He has worked at his trade for almost half a century and goes on as if nothing at all had changed. He is currently in New York making his first feature film in ten years, *The First Deadly Sin*. His first new studio album in five years is in the record stores, a three record set called *Trilogy*, and despite one astonishing lapse in taste (a self-aggrandizing "musical fantasy" written by banality master Gordon Jenkins), it reveals that what Sinatra calls "my reed" is in better shape than it has been in since the 1960s. In concert halls and casinos he packs in the fans, and the intensity of their embrace remains scary. But his work and its public acceptance are now almost incidental to his stature. Frank Sinatra, from Hoboken, New Jersey, has forced his presence into American social history; when the story of how Americans in this century played, dreamed, hoped, and loved is told, Frank Sinatra cannot be left out. He is more than a mere singer or actor. He is a legend. And the legend lives.

The legend has its own symmetries. Sinatra can be unbelievably generous and brutally vicious. He can display the grace and manners of a cultured man and turn suddenly into a vulgar two-bit comic. He can offer George Raft a blank check "up to one million dollars" to pay taxes owed to the IRS; he can then rage against one of his most important boosters, WNEW disc jockey Jonathan Schwartz, and help force him off the air. In his time, he has been a loyal Democrat and a shill for Richard Nixon; a defender of underdogs everywhere and then a spokesman for the Establishment; a man who fought racism in the music business and then became capable of tasteless jokes ("The Polacks are deboning the colored people," he said on the stage of Caesars Palace in 1974, "and using them for wet suits"). He has given magical performances and shoddy ones. He has treated women with elegance, sensitivity, and charm, and then, in Lauren Bacall's phrase, "dropped the curtain" on them in the most callous way. He acts like royalty and is frequently treated that way, but he also comes on too often like a cheap hood. He is a good guy–bad guy, tough–tender, Jekyll–Hyde.

"Being an eighteen-karat manic-depressive," Sinatra said once, "I have an over-acute capacity for sadness as well as elation."

Over the years, those wildly fluctuating emotions became a basic component of the Sinatra legend—accepted, even demanded by his audience. That audience is now largely eastern, urban, and aging, with New York at the heart of the myth. The hard-core fans are depression kids who matured in World War II, or part of the fifties generation, who saw him as a role model. In some critical way, Sinatra validates their lives—as *individuals*. He sings *to* them, and *for* them, one at a time. These Americans were transformed by the Depression and the war into unwilling members of groups—"the masses," or "the poor," or "the infantry"—and their popular music was dominated by the big bands. Sinatra was the first star to step out of the tightly controlled ensembles of the white swing bands to work on his own. Yes, he was 4-F (punctured eardrum), but the overwhelming majority of Americans experienced World War II at home, and the 1940s Sinatra was a reminder that Americans were single human beings, not just the masses, the poor, or the infantry. Later, in the 1960s, when crowds once again shoved individuals off the stage of history, he was submerged by musical groups like the Beatles and Rolling Stones and in 1971 even went into a brief retirement. He came back later in the decade, when individual values were again dominant.

"I've seen them come and go, but Frank is still the king," a New Jersey grandmother said at one of Sinatra's weekend performances at Resorts International in Atlantic City. "He just goes on and on, and he's wonderful."

Indeed, Sinatra's endurance has become a rallying point for many people who feel that their sacrifices and hard work are no longer honored, their values demeaned, their musical tastes ignored and sneered at. They don't care that Sinatra got fat; so did they. They don't care that Sinatra moved from the New Deal to Ronald Reagan; many of them did the same thing, for the same basic reason: resentment at being ignored by the Democratic party. They had overcome poverty and survived two wars; they had educated their children and given them better lives; and sometimes even their children didn't care. But it should never be forgotten that Frank Sinatra was the original working-class hero. Mick Jagger's fans bought records with their allowances; Sinatra's people bought them out of wages.

"There's just not enough of Frank's people around anymore to make him a monster record seller," says one Warner Communications executive. "Sinatra is a star. But he's not Fleetwood Mac. He's not Pink Floyd."

Sinatra has never been a big single seller (one gold record—more than a million sales—to twenty for the Beatles), but his albums continue to sell steadily. One reason: Most radio stations don't play Sinatra, so that younger listeners never get to hear him and go on to buy his records. In New York, only WNEW-AM and WYNY-FM play Sinatra with any frequency. As a movie star, he had faded badly before vanishing completely with the lamentable *Dirty Dingus Magee* in 1970. Part of this could be blamed directly on Sinatra, because his insistence on one or two takes had led to careless, even shoddy productions. On his own, he was also not a strong TV performer; he needed Elvis Presley, or Bing Crosby, to get big ratings. Yet Sinatra remains a major star in the minds of most Americans, even those who despise him.

"What Sinatra has is beyond talent," director Billy Wilder once said. "It's some sort of magnetism that goes in higher revolutions than that of anybody else, anybody in the whole of show business. Wherever Frank is, there is a certain electricity permeating the air. It's like Mack the Knife is in town and the action is starting."

That electricity was in the air of Jilly's that night in 1974. But its effect is not restricted to a platoon of gumbahs. The other night, Sinatra came into Elaine's with his wife, Barbara, and another couple. It was after midnight, and Sinatra stayed for a couple of hours, drinking and talking and smoking cigarettes.

I was with some friends at another table. They were people who are good at their jobs and have seen much of the world. But their own natural styles were subtly altered by the addition of Sinatra to the room. They stole glances at him. They were aware that Sinatra's blue eyes were also checking out the room, and unconsciously they began to gesture too much, playing too hard at being casual, or clarifying themselves in a theatrical way. Somewhere underneath all of this, I'm sure, was a desire to want Frank Sinatra to like them.

I knew how that worked, because I'd felt those emotions myself. When I first met Sinatra, I was bumping up against one of the crucial legends of my youth, and sure, I wanted him to like me. Growing up in Brooklyn in the forties and fifties, it was impossible to avoid the figure of Frank Sinatra. He was armored with the tough-guy swagger of the streets, but in the songs he allowed room for tenderness, the sense of loss and abandonment, the acknowledgment of pain. Most of us felt that we had nothing to learn from cowboys or Cary Grant (we were wrong, of course). But thousands of us appropriated the pose of the Tender Tough Guy from Sinatra. We've outgrown a lot of things, but there are elements of that pose in all of us to this day, and when we see Sinatra perform, or listen to the records at night, the pose regains all of its old dangerous glamour.

And make no mistake: Danger is at the heart of the legend. At his best, Sinatra is an immensely gifted musical talent admired by many jazz musicians. He is not a jazz singer, but he comes from the tradition. As a young band vocalist, he learned breath control from trombonist Tommy Dorsey; after work, he studied other singers, among them Louis Armstrong, Lee Wiley, Mabel Mercer, and another performer who became a legend.

"It is Billie Holiday, whom I first heard in Fifty-second Street clubs in the early '30s, who was and still remains the greatest single musical influence on me," he wrote once, later telling *Daily News* columnist Kay Gardella that Lady Day taught him "matters of shading, phrasing, dark tones, light tones and bending notes." And in the saloons of the time, the young Sinatra learned a great secret of the trade: "The microphone is the singer's basic instrument, not the voice. You have to learn to play it like it was a saxophone." As he matured, Sinatra developed a unique white-blues style, supple enough to express the range of his own turbulent emotions. And like the great jazz artists, he took the banal tunes of Tin Pan Alley and transformed them into something personal by the sincerity of his performance; Sinatra actually seemed to *believe* the words he was singing. But Billy Wilder is correct: The Sinatra aura goes beyond talent and craft. He is not simply a fine popular singer. He emanates power and danger. And the reason is simple: you think he is tangled up with the mob.

"Some things I can't ever talk about," he said to me once, when we were discussing the mandatory contents of his book. He laughed and added, "Someone might come knocking' at my f—— door."

Sinatra is now writing that autobiography and preparing a film about his own life. Alas, neither form seems adequate to the full story; autobiographies are by definition only part of the story, the instinct being to prepare a brief for the defense and give youself the best lines. And a two-hour movie can only skim the surface of a life that has gone on for six decades. Faulkner says somewhere that the best stories are the ones we are most thoroughly ashamed of; it could be that the best movies are the ones that can't be photographed. No, Sinatra deserves a novel.

The novelist, some combination of Balzac and Raymond Chandler, would recognize Sinatra as one of those rare public men who actually cast a shadow. The shadow is the mob, and who can tell what came first, the shadow or the act? A conventional autobiography will talk about the wives: Nancy Barbato, Ava Gardner, Mia Farrow, and Barbara Marx, one for each adult decade. It might mention, discreetly, all the other love affairs, passionate or glancing: Lana Turner, Juliet Prowse, Lauren Bacall, Kim Novak, Jill St. John, Lady Adele Beatty, Dorothy Provine, and the anonymous brigade of starlets, secretaries, models, stewardesses, and girls from the old neighborhood.

"I loved them all," Sinatra says now, smiling ruefully, reminding you that he is now a grandfather and all of that was long ago. "I really did."

But the novelist can come closer to the elusive truth than an autobiographer as courtly as Sinatra will ever allow himself to do. Both would deal with the public career, the rise, fall, rise again of Frank Sinatra. We can see the high school dropout watching Bing Crosby sing from the stage of Loew's Journal Square in Jersey City in 1933, vowing to become a singer. We can follow him, one of Balzac's provincial heroes, as he wins an amateur contest and crosses the river to appear for the first time on a New York stage at the Academy of Music (now the Palladium) on Fourteenth Street the following year. The hero then sings with a group called the Hoboken Four on the *Major Bowes Amateur Hour* in 1935, plays local clubs, begs in the hallways of WNEW for the chance to sing for nothing on live remotes. And of course there will be the familiar story of the job at the Rustic Cabin on Route 9W in 1939, and how Harry James heard him late one night and gave him a job in the big time. And then how Sinatra went to work for Tommy Dorsey and played the Paramount and became a star.

And because this is a story with a hero, it must tell the story of The Fall. The hero hurtles into love with Ava Gardner, and his career becomes a shambles: He loses his voice, his wife, his children; he gets into public fights; he wins the love goddess; he loses her; he hits bottom. And then there is The Great Comeback: He pleads for the part of Maggio in *From Here to Eternity*, is paid $8,000, gives a stunning performance, wins the Academy Award, and comes all the way back. He leaves Columbia Records for Capitol, then starts his own company, Reprise, and makes his greatest records. At the same time he consolidates his power in Hollywood, investing his money brilliantly, producing his own films, using power with the instincts of a great politician. These are the years of the private jets, the meetings of the Clan on the stages of Las Vegas, the friendships with Jack Kennedy and other politicians, and the house at the top of Mulholland Drive, where the wounded hero heals his ruined heart with girls and whiskey and friends. It's a good story. A sentimental education or a cautionary tale.

But as autobiography it is not enough. We must have some understanding of the shadows. In *The Godfather* Mario Puzo used some of the elements in the singer he called Johnny Fontane; other novels have used Sinatra-like figures in various ways; yet no fictional account has truly defined the man in all of his complexity. We only know that the mob runs through his story like an underground river. He is the most investigated American performer since John Wilkes Booth, and although he has never been indicted or convicted of any mob-connected crime, the connection is part of the legend. And to some extent, Sinatra exploits it. His opening acts feature comedians who tell jokes about Sinatra's sinister friendships; if you cross Frank, the jokes say, you could end up on a meat hook in a garage. In some circumstances Sinatra laughs at the implications; other times, he explodes into dark furies, accusing his accusers of slander and ethnic racism.

"If my name didn't end with a vowel," he said to me once, "I wouldn't have had all this trouble."

But the facts indicate that he did know some shady people. He was friendly with Jersey hoodlum Willie Moretti until the syphilitic gangster was shot to death. He was friendly with Joseph "Joe Fisher" Fischetti, traveled with him to Havana in 1947, where he spent time with Lucky Luciano. A nineteen-page Justice Department memorandum prepared in 1962 said that its surveillance placed Sinatra in contact with about ten of the country's top hoodlums. Some had Sinatra's unlisted number. He did favors for others.

"I was brought up to shake a man's hand when I am introduced to him, without first investigating his past," Sinatra said huffily during the Luciano uproar. The same could be said about the scandal over the photograph taken a few years ago with mob boss Carlo Gambino, backstage at the Westchester Premier Theater. More serious questions have now been raised about Sinatra and that same theater.

A federal grand jury is investigating whether Sinatra, his lawyer Mickey Rudin, and Jilly Rizzo took $50,000 under the table during a May 1977 gig there. Court papers filed by prosecutor Nathaniel Akerman said that the possible Sinatra connection arose during the trial of one Louis "Lewie Dome" Pacella, supposedly a friend of Sinatra's. The court papers state: "The grand jury's investigation was based in part on evidence introduced at Pacella's trial, which showed that in addition to Pacella, other individuals close to Frank Sinatra had received monies illegally. . . ." Once again, Sinatra is afloat on the dark underground river.

"Did I know those guy?" he said to me once. "Sure, I knew some of those guys. I spent a lot of time working in saloons. And saloons are not run by the Christian Brothers. There were a lot of guys around, and they came out of Prohibition, and they ran pretty good saloons. I was a kid. I worked in the places that were open. They paid you, and the checks didn't bounce. I didn't meet any Nobel Prize winners in saloons. But if Francis of Assisi was a singer and worked in saloons, he would've met the same guys. That doesn't make him part of something. They said hello, you said hello. They came backstage. They thanked you. You offered them a drink. That was it."

He paused. "And it doesn't matter anymore, does it? Most of the guys I knew, or met, are dead."

One of them was Salvatore Giancana, sometimes known as Momo, or Mooney. A graduate of Joliet prison, he ducked World War II by doing a crazy act for the draft board, which labeled him "a constitutional psychopath." He rose through the wartime rackets to the leadership of the Chicago mob in the 1950s. During that period he and Sinatra became friends and were seen in various places together. The star-struck Momo later began a long love affair with singer Phyllis McGuire, and the friendship deepened. In 1962 Sinatra, Dean Martin, and Sammy Davis played a special engagement at a Giancana joint called the Villa Venice, northwest of Chicago. When the FBI questioned the performers, Sinatra said he did it for a boyhood friend named Leo Olsen, who fronted the place for Momo. Sammy Davis was more to the point.

"Baby, let me say this," he told an FBI man. "I got one eye, and that one eye sees a lot of things that my brain tells me I shouldn't talk about. Because my brain says that if I do, my one eye might not be seeing *anything* after a while."

Sinatra's friendship with Sam Giancana was most severely tested in 1963, when the Nevada Gaming Control Board charged that the Chicago hoodlum had been a week-long guest at Sinatra's Cal-Neva Lodge in Lake Tahoe. His mere presence was enough to revoke the casino's gambling license and Sinatra first said he would fight the charge. When Edward A. Olsen, then chairman of the gambling board, said that he didn't want to talk to Sinatra until he subpoenaed him. Olsen claims Sinatra shouted over the phone, "You subpoena me and you're going to get a big, fat, f—— surprise."

But when the crunch came two weeks later, Sinatra chose not to fight the revocation order. Apparently his friendship with Giancana was more important than his investment in Nevada, and he sold his interests for $3.5 million. In 1975 Giancana was shot to death in the basement of his Chicago home. Phyllis McGuire went to the funeral, but Sinatra didn't. Sinatra is again trying to get a gambling license in Nevada.

"It's ridiculous to think Sinatra's in the mob," said one New Yorker who has watched gangsters collect around Sinatra for more than thirty years. "He's too visible. He's too hot. But he likes them. He thinks they're funny. In some way he admires them. For him it's like they were characters in some movie."

That might be the key. Some people who know Sinatra believe that his attraction to gangsters—and their attraction to him—is sheer romanticism. The year that Sinatra was fifteen, Hollywood released W. R. Burnett's *Little Caesar*; more than fifty gangster films followed in the next eighteen months. And their view of gangsters was decidedly romantic: The hoodlums weren't cretins peddling heroin to children; they were Robin Hoods defying the unjust laws of Prohibition. Robert Warshow defined the type in his essay "The Gangster as Tragic Hero":

> The gangster is the man of the city, with the city's language and knowledge, with its queer and dishonest skills and its terrible daring, carrying his life in his hands like a placard, like a club. For everyone else, there is at least the theoretical possibility of another world—in that happier American culture which the gangster denies, the city does not really exist; it is only a more crowded and more brightly lit country—but for the gangster there is only the city; he must inhabit it in order to personify it: not the real city, but that dangerous and sad city of the imagination which is so much more important, which is the modern world.

That is almost a perfect description of Frank Sinatra, who still carries his life in his hands like a placard, or like a club. His novel might be a very simple one indeed: a symmetrical story about life imiating art.

Somewhere deep within Frank Sinatra, there must still exist a scared little boy. He is standing alone on a street in Hoboken. His parents are nowhere to be seen. His father, Anthony Martin, is probably at the bar he runs when he is not working for the fire department; the father is a blue-eyed Sicilian, close-mouthed, passive, and, in his own way, tough. He once boxed as "Marty O'Brien" in the years when the Irish ran northern New Jersey. The boy's mother, Natalie, is not around either. The neighbors call her Dolly, and she sometimes works at the bar, which was bought with a loan from her mother, Rosa Garaventi, who runs a grocery store. Dolly Sinatra is also a Democratic ward leader. She has places to go, duties to perform, favors to deny or dispense. She has little time for traditional maternal duties. And besides, she didn't want a boy anyway.

"I wanted a girl and bought a lot of pink clothes," she once said. "When Frank was born, I didn't care. I dressed him in pink anyway. Later, I got my mother to make him Lord Fauntleroy suits."

Did the other kids laugh at the boy in the Lord Fauntleroy suits? Probably. It was a tough, working-class neighborhood. Working-class. Not poor. His mother, born in Genoa, raised in Hoboken, believed in work and education. When she wasn't around, the boy was taken care of by his grandmother Garaventi, or by Mrs. Goldberg, who lived on the block. "I'll never forget that kid," a neighbor said, "leaning against his grandmother's front door, staring into space. . . ."

Later the press agents would try to pass him off as a slum kid. Perhaps the most important thing to know about him is that he was an only child. Of Italian parents. And they spoiled him. From the beginning, the only child had money. He had a charge account at a local department store and a wardrobe so fancy that his friends called him "Slacksey." He had a secondhand car at fifteen. And in the depths of the Depression, after dropping out of high school, he had the ultimate luxury: a job unloading trucks at the Jersey *Observer*.

Such things were not enough; the boy also had fancy dreams. And the parents didn't approve. When he told his mother that he wanted to be a singer, she threw a shoe at him. "In your teens," he said later, "there's always someone to spit on your dreams." Still, the only child got what he wanted; eventually his mother bought him a $65 portable public-address system, complete with loudspeaker and microphone. She thus gave him his musical instrument and his life.

She also gave him some of her values. At home she dominated his father; in the streets she dominated the neighborhood through the uses of Democratic patronage. From adolescence on, Sinatra understood patronage. He could give his friends clothes, passes to Palisades Park, rides in his car, and they could give him friendship and loyalty. Power was all. And that insight lifted him above so many other talented performers of his generation. Vic Damone might have better pipes, Tony Bennett a more certain musical taste, but Sinatra had power.

Power attracts and repels; it functions as aphrodisiac and blackjack. Men of power recognize it in others; Sinatra has spent time with Franklin Roosevelt, Adlai Stevenson, Jack Kennedy, Richard Nixon, Spiro Agnew, Walter Annenberg, Hugh Carey, Ronald Reagan; all wanted his approval, and he wanted, and obtained, theirs. He could raise millions for them at fund raisers; they would always take his calls. And the politicians had a lot of company. On the stage at Caesars Palace, or at an elegant East Side dinner party, Sinatra emanates power. Certainly the dark side of the legend accounts for some of that effect; the myth of the Mafia, after all, is not a myth of evil, but a myth of power.

But talent is essential, too. During the period of The Fall, when he had lost his voice, he panicked; he could accept anything except impotence. Without power he is returned to Monroe Street in Hoboken, a scared kid. That kid wants to be accepted by powerful men, so he shakes hands with the men of the mob. But the scared kid also understands loneliness, and he uses that knowledge as the engine of his talent. When he sings a ballad—

listen again to "I'm a Fool to Want You," recorded at the depths of his anguish over Ava Gardner—his voice haunts, explores, suffers. Then, in up-tempo songs, it celebrates, it says that the worst can be put behind you, there is always another woman and another bright morning. The scared kid, easy in the world of women and power, also carries the scars of rejection. His mother was too busy. His father sent him away.

"He told me, 'Get out of the house and get a job,'" he said about his father in a rare TV interview with Bill Boggs a few years ago. "I was shocked. I didn't know where the hell to go. I remember the moment. We were having breakfast. . . . This particular morning my father said to me, 'Why don't you get out of the house and go out on your own?' What he really said was 'Get out.' And I think the egg was stuck in there about twenty minutes, and I couldn't swallow it or get rid of it, in any way. My mother, of course, was nearly in tears, but we agreed that it might be a good thing, and then I packed up a small case that I had and came to New York."

He came to New York, all right, and to all the great cities of the world. The scared kid, the only child, invented someone named Frank Sinatra and it was the greatest role he ever played. In some odd way he has become the role. There is a note of farewell in his recent performances. One gets the sense that he is now building his own mausoleum.

"Dyin' is a pain in the ass," he says.

Sinatra could be around for another twenty years, or he could be gone tomorrow, but the jagged symmetries of his legend would remain. For too many years the scared kid lashed out at enemies, real or imagined; he courted his inferiors, intoxicated by their power; he helped people and hurt people; he was willful, self-absorbed, and frivolous. But the talent survived everything, and so did the fear, and when I see him around, I always imagine him as a boy on that Hoboken street in his Fauntleroy suit and remember him wandering the streets of New York a half century later, trying to figure out what all of it meant.

Me and My One-Nighters
with Sinatra
Armand Deutsch ★ 1991

My wife, Harriet, and I enter New York's Waldorf Towers lobby at precisely 6:55 P.M. We are off on another one-nighter with Frank Sinatra.

We greet Frank, Barbara, his retinue, and the other guests who make up our party of twelve. A moment later we are in limousines, airport-bound. A Sinatra one-nighter is timed with the precision of a West Point dress parade. Logistics fascinate him. He would have made a superb travel agent, except that he never could have learned the importance of the cost factor in the travel plans of clients. His preoccupation is to get from here to there and back as quickly as possible.

This specific junket happened to be to Buffalo in 1977. I had long ago learned that the destination is basically immaterial. The one-nighters are as alike as peas in a pod. You land in the dark and you leave in the dark. Unless one knows the name of the city, the locales are totally interchangeable.

A few minutes after takeoff Frank is immersed in his crossword puzzle, which he does rapidly and in ink. As always, he wears slacks, a pullover shirt, a windbreaker or sweater topped with a baseball or golf cap. His headgear collection—gifts from Major League teams, golf clubs, and tournaments—is inexhaustible, but he augments it by buying caps wherever he sees them. It is not that he is partial to caps—he stops just short of being a compulsive buyer. His purchases for himself are, however, overmatched by those he makes for his friends.

As the plane speeds through the night, Harriet and I reflect on the treasure trove in our own home: several clocks affectionately inscribed and signed "Francis Albert," picture frames, a hi-fi system, a windbreaker bearing the slogan "American Olympic Drinking Team," countless tapes and recordings, and draft-beer system together with monthly supplies of the product.

One example of his generosity stands out. Some twenty-five years ago he was having a quiet dinner at out house when our son Stephen, then eleven, told me that he desperately required new sound equipment in his room. It was rather costly and I told him that we might consider it for Christmas. Sinatra said nothing, but the equipment arrived the next day, together with a note from Frank saying that a man would be over to connect it.

The next time we met, I told Frank that I thought that this particular judgment was one I should have made. He was totally unrepentant. "Christmas," he said, "is a ways off. An extra Christmas never hurt anybody." Since he supports this theory by keeping a lighted Christmas tree in front of his Palm Springs home the year round, I saw little to gain from continuing the discussion.

And then, of course, there was Beau Brummel and Quiz. Beau, a yellow Labrador, arrived at our house twenty-three Christmas Eves ago with a red bow around his neck. Ten weeks old, he was a first cousin of Frank's dog, Charlie, whom I not-so-secretly coveted. Everyone in our house loved Beau. When, fifteen years later, he had to be put to sleep, our grief was deep. After several months Frank said, "I'm going to get you another dog. It'll help. It's time, Armando." (Nicknames are a way of life with

Frank. Marvin Davis, the oil and film billionaire, is "Three B"; Bill Miller, his longtime piano player, possessor of an extraordinarily pale complexion, is "Suntan Charlie"; Yul Brynner is "the Chinaman." My all-time favorite remains "the Bookmaker," his affectionate soubriquet for the late Random House publisher, Bennett Cerf.)

I told him sharply not to surprise us, that we didn't want another dog. From time to time he would mention it. Months later, at his Palm Springs home, Frank pointed to Miss Wiggles, Barbara's King Charles spaniel. "A little dog like that, Armando, not like Beau." I said I'd think about it.

A few days later numerous photographs of tiny Kilspindie Quizzical arrived from his breeder in Maine, together with his impeccable pedigree and a long letter extolling his virtues. Quiz himself was not far behind, having made the transcontinental trip in Barbara's lap aboard the Sinatra jet. Frank and Barbara came along a few days later to admire him, signing our guest book "Aunt Barbara and Uncle Frank." Of course, Frank was right. Having another dog helped a lot.

The seat-belt sign flashes, the plane lands, and we glide to a halt. Again the limousines have formed up, and we are quickly on the move. This time a police escort leads us on our way.

As we pull to a stop at the arena's stage door, Frank is out of the car and inside the building in an instant, barely glimpsed by the people behind the barricades.

His dressing room features a lavish hors d'oeuvre table and a fully stocked bar. As Barbara urges us to dig in, Frank is briefed on who is outside. Few will make it into the inner sanctum. More often than not, particularly in a university town, they include children of his friends. Invariably they get in first. This is a high point for Frank, who has usually known them all their lives. His face lights up. "How are you?" "You working hard?" "You got the tickets? Are they okay?" "I had dinner with your mom and dad the other night. They're fine." "Come see me in New York. I'll be around awhile."

Next comes the inevitable celebrity athlete, the mayor, and one or two others. That's it; time has run out.

As Sinatra vanishes to change into his working clothes—dinner jacket, shirt with black tie, and trousers—my mind goes back to a dressing room in Las Vegas many years ago. His piano player, Bill Miller, had recently suffered two broken legs during one of California's dreadful mudslides, an accident that claimed Mrs. Miller's life.

Suddenly realizing that "Suntan" would not be playing with him, I asked Sinatra who would be. He told me that Count Basie was filling in. "A pretty good substitute," I noted. He agreed, but ruefully said that Basie was much tougher than Suntan. The two of them, it seems, had gone out drinking several nights before and stayed out until morning. At six-thirty that evening Sinatra realized that his voice might not be at its best that night. "If I miss a note or two along the way, follow along with me so that it sounds all right," he said to Basie. The Count looked him full in the eye and said, "I play the notes just the way they're written. The rest is up to you." It had made quite an impression on Sinatra. I asked him if he was angry at Basie. "No," he said, "but I'm not going out drinking with him anymore!"

We are barely seated when a ripple of applause starts from the point where we entered. It builds as Frank comes down the aisle, and by the time he enters the prizefight ring that serves as a stage, the audience is on its feet. He holds up his hand and nods several times without smiling. It is clearly a gesture that says, "Let's not get carried away with what's past. We're all here for tonight."

He starts easily. "I've Got the World on a String" is a typical opening. He will perform steadily for about an hour and fifteen minutes. His performance appears effortless, but Sinatra rehearses daily.

He will sing some twenty songs, many of them familiar to the audience. He always, however, includes several new songs, knowing that a few will take hold and finally become favorites.

Invariably someone will call for a favorite that has not yet been heard, and invariably he will respond chattily, "I can't keep singing the same songs. I'd get bored." This casual remark cuts deep with Frank. In 1971 boredom caught up with Sinatra, and he announced his retirement. "I've had it," he told me. "Enough's enough."

Over the next few years he learned what boredom really is, and on September 30, 1973, he came out of retirement at the Dorothy Chandler Pavilion, for the benefit of the Los Angeles Music and Art School. It is no coincidence that both his "final" performance and his comeback were benefits. He plays ten or twelve each year, and they are most meaningful to him. A typical example is the October 30, 1981, benefit he played at the Beverly Hilton Hotel for St. John's Hospital and Health Center in Santa Monica, California. The institution had never raised more than $150,000 for a single event. He met with the committee and told them he wanted the ballroom scaled to net them one million dollars. They were, to put it mildly, apprehensive. He sang, as he always does, without fee (many performers get paid for benefits). He obtained the services of Bob Newhart and the Fifth Dimension, paid for the orchestra and rehearsal time, and arranged for individual gifts from him at each table. He bought the first table, and a few days before the event the room was sold out. St. John's benefited to the tune of $1,300,000.

The audiences' favorites are not always Frank's own. "Strangers in the Night" is an example. Whenever he starts that song, there is applause, and he'll say tolerantly, "You still like it?" shake his head in mild disbelief, and sing on. Privately he'll say that he never liked it, but generally adds that "it has helped keep me in pizza for a long time."

A repertoire favorite is Cole Porter's "I Get a Kick Out of You." When he sings "Mere alcohol doesn't thrill me at all," he often grins or chuckles sardonically. Certainly this particular lyric is not autobiographical.

Since his marriage to Barbara eighteen years ago, he has cut down markedly on his drinking. Her sunny nature and their pleasant life together have also helped him overcome the insomnia that resulted naturally from many years of late nightclub shows and, in the early days, band touring. None of this is to say, however, that he has become the average nine-to-five fellow who has a drink or two before dinner and turns in before eleven.

Literally millions of words have been written about his singing, but the magical quality that has kept him on top for over four decades defies explanation, at least by him. When I asked him about it once, he just said, "I'm damned if I know. If I did, I'd bottle it and sell it. It would be easier than singing."

He pauses only briefly between songs, responding to the applause by saying, "Thank you. Pretty song," and naming the composer, lyricist, and arranger.

After some ten songs, he calls a halt to talk to the audience for about ten minutes. He is a sports buff and whenever possible will discuss the local team. He tells a joke or two and often comments on a national or world event. These references are highly partisan; he makes no secret of his views. In Buffalo that night O. J. Simpson, the great running back, was booed because he had expressed a desire to leave and play for the Los Angles Rams. "You people should understand that," Sinatra said sternly. "He's great. He just wants to finish his career at home. That's not so awful." A nod to the conductor, and the second part of his act gets under way.

Midway through the second half he sits back on a stool, lights a cigarette, and announces that, as the last of the saloon singers, he will sing a song about "a guy whose chick has split and left him in no mood to go out among us." It is my favorite: "One for My Baby (and One More for the Road)." Memories take over. Almost everyone in the house has been consoled somewhere along the line by a Sinatra torch song.

Every singer strives to find a great finishing song. Currently, Frank's finale is "New York, New York," and even as the music starts the audience is applauding.

We do not get to share this moment; ushers tap us on the shoulder and lead us out. As the song concludes and the standing ovation fills the building, we rush into the limousines. Frank, coming down the aisle fast, is not far behind. He jumps into the front car, and the caravan moves out, sirens wailing. We are airborne before the audience has gotten out of the parking lot.

The ride home seems short. We are all naturally exhilarated—all, that is, except Frank. Sipping a drink, still in his dinner jacket, he is simply a man coming home from work. His method of returning from the workplace by jet is, to put it mildly, unusual, but decades of doing it has made it routine to him.

Invariably someone will compliment him on his performance. He looks momentarily blank and then says briefly, "Yeah, Nice audience." The truth is that he has all but forgotten it.

As we get into the cars, he tells us that we will be having dinner at an Italian restaurant. When we arrive at the stroke of midnight, the door is held open for us by the smiling proprietor. Outnumbered by waiters and captains, we head for our special table. Barbara, list in hand, seats us. Drink orders are taken. Bottles of excellent red and white wines appear. Frank, as always, has ordered ahead, and a wide variety of tempting antipasti are soon served, followed by several pastas and a Lucullian veal Milanese sliced very thin. The Sinatras are gracious hosts, and Frank, although a light eater himself, is a lavish provider.

Italian restaurateurs regard a Sinatra visit as a higher award than the Medal of Freedom. In addition to the overwhelming desire to please him, the knowledge that their efforts will not be judged by a novice may act as a spur.

By the time we finish it is almost two-thirty; the evening has clearly drawn to an end. As we stroll out of the darkened restaurant onto the sidewalk, the limousines stand ready to take us home. It is difficult to express one's thanks. Frank recognizes this and takes the initiative. He kisses the wives and hugs the men or shakes their hands. "Good night," he says. "It was fun. Sleep well. We'll talk tomorrow. See you soon."

He has literally been out of the city less than five hours. He has entertained some fifteen thousand people memorably. He has earned a sum well into six figures. Another tiny brushstroke has been added to the vast canvas of his career.

He and Barbara get into their car and are gone.

Sinatra:
In the Wee Small Hours
Jonathan Schwartz ★ 1989

I had a long and gentle telephone talk with Sinatra late last summer. He called me (that very fact is a kind of miracle of validation). We are private acquaintances and are entangled publicly by my interest in his music. He has phoned me before, in varying spirits, but this call, late one Friday afternoon from Rancho Mirage to Palm Springs, was occasioned by some personal matters on both sides, and the tone of the half hour or so was companionable, unpolitical and affectionate.

We haven't spoken since, and may never again. Years can go by, have gone by, between talks with Sinatra. This is true of people who are closer to him than I have ever been, those with the wisdom not to place the call, even if they're just dying, just busting, to tell him something, to ask him something. They'll get more mileage out of *his* call because it's his. Leave the man alone, so the wisdom goes.

Where, then, does the wisdom leave Frank?

Pretty much alone, I would think, though he's got an active social and phone life, and a kind of an existence within correspondence. That is, he shoots off dozens of letters every week, dictated, often on the phone, to his quite extraordinary and ongoing secretary-choreographer, Dorothy Uhlemann, and these letters are received joyously by politicians, other musicians, writers, patients in hospitals, scientists.

And the word spreads quickly in their communities: Holy Jesus! Barnaby's gotten a letter from SINATRA!

Barnaby, taking a letter as a signal of, and invitation to, blood-and-guts friendship with SINATRA, replies at length, crafting his note, articulating his devotion, reading his words to many friends, who agree that they are perfect words, that the letter is perfect. He then frames Sinatra's letter expensively, and sends his own, satisfied.

And that is the end of that.

Sinatra has disappeared behind the shark-infested moat where many of us imagine he lives.

Barnaby will wait up to two, possibly three, years, rationally expecting a response to his carefully crafted, deeply felt, immaculately *enveloped* letter.

Maybe it didn't get through, Barnaby might think along the way.

Through.

Through what?

The sharks in the moat, the dogs at the door, the guards in the hall, the staff in the office, Jilly Rizzo somehow, all of the outer layers of the machine at the center of which resides, usually on the phone, one of the three or four greatest interpretive musicians the world has ever known, a figure of such menace, so desired, so emulated by so many other members of the human species, that he has clearly become loopy.

"If you start with the fact that Frank is crazy, everything else falls into place," says one quite intimate friend.

One wonders about the word "intimate." Frank *knows* a lot of people all over the world. As for intimate friends, well now, that's another story. You've got to take into consideration the simple, amazing truth: This fellow Sinatra has been applauded around-the-clock since he was twenty-five years old. The applause has meant: You are a great man. You are conducting your affairs in ways that are pleasing to us, the populace. You are behaving, for better or worse, with a fascinating bravado and an enviable lurid arrogance. *We would like to be you.* And, most important: The sound you emit when you sing is above and beyond the most spectacular of sounds. You're just too marvelous, too marvelous for words.

All of this does not encourage intimate friendship. There is, for the most part, some kind of spin on the ball, some form of altered behavior when someone is in Sinatra's heady company. People see the music in the face, all of those songs and album covers, and they get, well, scared. Those songs, that sound, stretch too many years, too deeply into people's private injuries, into their heroic families, into their utter aloneness, to be received casually at cocktail.

The eyes are blue and direct, like northern crystals of ice. The speaking voice carries across any room. Raised in anger, it is awful weaponry. The possibility that they may incur such wrath without knowing how not to keeps people sheepishly away, or turns them into cacophonous laughers—whatever comes out of Frank's mouth is Robert Benchley at his best. Or it creates lambs of audiences, semicircled around Frank to hear his stories, his wonderful stories, filled with Harry Cohn and Marlon Brando and Dean Rusk and Dean Acheson or practically anyone in the entire world. The music becomes the menace because it is so *visible*. And so much taller than Sinatra himself—he is actually a short guy; stand next to him and you'll find out.

There are other intimidating considerations.

Sinatra is a movie star. He is being televised most of the time on some channel or another, and being an actor is *not even what he does.*

And there are the women who haunted your fourteen-year-old self. This short guy has actually seen them naked. Eisenhower fourteen-year-olds like myself placed nudity on a pedestal way above what was known as intercourse. Sinatra went beyond intercourse into galactic freedom unavailable to the imagination.

Who among us, then, can say: I am an intimate of Sinatra's?

And without that thread, that binding stuff that keeps people talking to one another and loving one another and holding one another through the storms of passing time and then getting older and older and then getting really sick and then getting slowly better and then getting not so good and then weeping and reaching out and then all at once on a Tuesday dying, where does that leave Frank?

Sadly, it has been widely reported that the Sinatra family is in financial disarray, forcing him to continue out there on the stage with only his knuckleball left; that the annual millions come in and the millions go out.

"I'm a belter now, baby," Sinatra shouted in some massive auditorium not long ago, through the megaphone of his knuckleball. A belter on the run, with his enthusiastic entourage plunging through the nights, looking after him with fastidious attention.

It is 6 A.M. Time to try to go to sleep.

For many years, to get to Sinatra meant pushing through—with the muscle of absolute will, with skin as thick and as coarse as bark, with a heart as cold as death—a sharp cookie named Mickey Rudin. A fat little man with drooping Buddha eyelids and a grim control over whatever you wanted, Rudin represented Sinatra ferociously. He was the Ditka defense in a December coliseum, seldom yielding an inch on a rush. A blocker, too, on offense, he created magical holes for his man with the ball, who waited cozily in the locker room. "Mr. Sinatra, the hole is available now," he would be told by an intermediary. Then and only then would Ol' Blue Eyes rise, make his way out to the field and scamper through to daylight without breaking a sweat.

A Doubleday editor named Sam Vaughan, working on Nancy Sinatra's homage to her father—a coffee-table pictorial with a quirky elegance—found himself tangled up with the Blocker. The Blocker wished the book to go for $50. Vaughan was thinking maybe forty-five.

They met for lunch. Mickey Rudin got down to business.

"I've been selling Frank Sinatra for years," he told Vaughan, the gentlest of gentlemen. "I've always sold him on the basis of what a bottle of Dom Pérignon was going for at the moment. At the moment it's $50. The book will be $50."

The Dom Pérignon business is, in my opinion, properly analogous. Without enological scholarship, I must report that this particular wine has always struck me as head and shoulders above anything else that's come my way. It is a champagne not only symbolically festive but superb to the taste and appropriately coveted all over the world. I can imagine a man whose child has just been born sixty miles south of Oslo making an effort to track down and secure for himself, at practically any price, a bottle of Dom Pérignon champagne.

I myself have set off on lengthy excursions for Sinatra's recordings, driving from Cap Ferrat in the south of France across the French–Italian border into San Remo to secure for myself, at practically any price, an Italian Sinatra album made up of releases I already owned but didn't have handy, packaged in Italy with Italian liner notes.

I have flown from London to the Channel island of Jersey for a tape of an unreleased Sinatra recording of "Roses of Picardy." Just one song.

I have broken into a Capitol Records distributor's office on West sixty-fifth Street in New York City at eleven at night to steal one copy of W803, *A Swingin' Affair!* It had newly arrived on a Friday in May 1957 and had been put out for display in the Capitol window over the weekend. It wasn't possible for me to wait until Monday to try to reason with a clerk for an advance copy. A fire escape, a slightly open window, and I was inside, among boxes of Capitol W803.

Why all of this?

I am the son of a songwriter, the man who wrote the music for "Dancing in the Dark," "That's Entertainment," "By Myself" and other standards. My father was a miniaturist, telling his tale in the short-story form of thirty-two bars of music. It was a language I picked up early in my life, a language that, after all, connected me with him, he who was often somewhere else. The Song was a Morse code to which only the two of us had access. Our secret.

All the while, through the 1940s, a young and tentative Sinatra functioned in my background. His was a pleasant hum, offstage somewhere, the property of bobby-soxer women I saw in newsreels, the whole shebang embroiled in a grotesque romance quite foreign to the ten-year-old that was me.

My arrival at puberty was publicly announced by the release of Sinatra's "Birth of the Blues," a record he made on June 3, 1952. (I have found that this recording had the same effect on dozens of others, both men and women.) It was a shout-out-loud brassy version of a song that didn't mean much to me. The surprise was the singing: surefooted; wildly experimental; openly masculine; entirely musical; and, most important of all, absolutely honest.

Out of the cocoon of innocence there has risen, seemingly overnight, a world-wise honest guy. It was there on that record, with nothing squirreled away in the corner, with no risks not taken, with no unctuous politeness of spirit—manners be damned.

There was to be only one more session at Columbia Records for Sinatra (*Why Try to Change Me Now?*). Nelson Riddle and Capitol were only months away. In the meantime, I began to investigate what had come before "Birth of the Blues," the hum of my early years.

How pretty those records turned out to be, the arranger, Axel Stordahl, working with small groups of violins, helping with the intimate innocence projected on most of them. Even Stordahl had risen to some new plateau with "Birth of the Blues." (I have since discovered what few others know: Stordahl, though credited on the record and through the years since, did not write the arrangement for "Birth of the Blues"; Heinie Beau, a Dorsey reed player, ghosted for Stordahl, and continued as ghost for Billy May and others. Three of the charts on *Come Dance with Me* are his, to give but one example.)

Bing Crosby's greatest piece of luck was, it seems to me, that he came of age with the microphone. Sinatra's good fortune was the advent of the long-playing album, a format that would allow him to string together miniature works to create a specific mood on a broader canvas. It was now possible to include sixteen songs on a phonograph record, with a novelist's scope and vision.

In the Wee Small Hours leaked out of Capitol in two packages of eight songs that were quickly combined to create his first sixteen-song "concept" album. The concept of aloneness, of defeat in romance, on a disc lasting more than forty-five minutes, worried Capitol executives prior to its unveiling. A work so relentlessly dark might be received as oppressive and alienating. But their by now Academy Award–winning singer (for *From Here to Eternity*), who had signed his $200,000 contract in a Hollywood bar called Lucy's in the presence of Alan Livingston, Capitol's chief, and Livingston's new bride, Betty Hutton, had become a hot property. On May 7, 1955, the company released to the world what stands to this day, at least for me, as the greatest album of vocal performance ever realized.

Included is a song written by my father, "I See You Face Before Me." The song was Nelson Riddle's favorite—he told me so in 1984—and for it he wrote his first arrangement ever at Ridgefield High in Ridgefield, New Jersey.

The album enfolded me. It connected me to my father and, as well, to the delicious treacheries of adult romance. It taught me how to sing, if only I could, and what to sing, if I had a choice. It was nakedly honest, unmushy, dignified. It has grown even richer through thirty-four years. On CD it is a miracle. The album has influenced much of the American popular music of the last three decades, including many a contemporary attitude and inflection.

The avalanche of releases that followed *In the Wee Small Hours* was especially astounding to musicians. With disciplined regularity, every few months Capitol issued Sinatra albums of such varying colors and strategies that it became impossible to imagine what might come next. The singing soared, spilling over with impudence and passion. The plate of each work was piled high with feelings, delivered aristocratically by a tough little guy from New Jersey who was informing American life with the flow and content of his personality. The slang of language embraced Sinatra's shorthand. He became grandly metaphoric and accessibly real, all at once. Those who hated him could not, would not, deny the music. What has happened through the years, I believe, is that the dichotomy has widened as the supreme musician has weakened and the actual living being has imploded.

Mickey Rudin one observed that one of his jobs was trying to keep Frank Sinatra even vaguely in touch with the real world. In fact, only a few others have been so cut off from how human beings deal with the day-to-day of it. Presidents and grand officials are kept from the streets of reality for designated periods of time, but the fact is, they sprang out of those avenues and alleys after years and years, bringing to their lofty offices the rich aromas of the daily struggle.

Sinatra, since, let's say, 1942, has been shielded from the way things are. Within the madness of his sanctuary he has *denied by convenience*. Without anyone at all to call his bluff, his real down-there-in-the-dirt bluff, Sinatra has been licensed to lie to himself with absolute conviction, and to raise brutal irresponsibility to an impressive new height.

When Sinatra says that something unseemly did not happen, why, then it didn't happen. There might have been seven or eight guys standing around who saw it happen, but they are the palace guards, they ain't talkin'. The upset within the compound is ignited when someone out there in the world suggests that it did, in fact, occur, that there might even be evidence of its occurring. That's when the missiles of contempt are launched, that's when enemy lists get drawn up. Frank *knows* it didn't happen, how could these cocksuckers be saying what they're saying?

This is not to suggest that people aren't out to get him, trying to demoralize him with falsehoods that are hurtful and ludicrous. At least once a month Sinatra is accused of villainy in Arabia or Bogotá, when all the while he has been giving benefit performances, from his heart, in St. Louis and New Orleans, and has never even thought the word "Bogotá." All of this gets mixed into the stew of outrage and is generously used to justify the denial by convenience.

What stays on the up-and-up is the musician. Sinatra has been, with the exception of two or three little shots at songwriting, an interpretive artist, taking material created by others and running it through the prism of his instinct. Almost invariably there has emerged onto the record or into the concert night something so candid, bruised and nakedly conversational, so gloriously syncopated and sexy, that it is not really possible to consider any other performer of music in the same thought.

I've always imagined that rock and roll was jazz under pressure. In much the same way, Sinatra, beginning in the 1950s, exploded into thousands of pieces of stars and jagged sections of orbiting debris, light-years from the constrictions of popular song. The emotion in his work defied the sedate regulations of his territory; it forced, in effect, the amplification of his instrument, and authorized the implementation of self onto the pages of his book. Thus Sinatra's music became controlled autobiography. Its intensity, in collaboration with the sheer musicality of every note, presented a completely dominating artistic presence.

Much of it survives.

"If I were a pitcher, they'd have taken me out after six and a third innings," Sinatra said to a friend after a shaky Atlantic City performance a couple of years ago.

In 1989, fifty years after starting out, Frank Sinatra is still leaving himself in for the full nine. The tapes I have, taken right from his microphone over the last twenty-four months, reveal the belter that he said he had become. Frank can no longer sustain a line of lyric; he must chop it up and, while doing so, throw in, by repetition of a word or a phrase, or a fallback to his own legendary slang, bits and pieces of deflecting magic. People will look away from the rubble with their ears to enjoy the sideshow the performer has called upon. But going on the basis of the tapes I possess, there is still enough of the real thing to justify the concert, to encourage one last album.

There is a list of songs and some arrangements. Frank Sinatra, Jr., is in charge of that somnolent enterprise. On June 6, 1988, his father went into the Evergreen recording studios in Burbank and tackled "My Foolish Heart" eighteen times (most attempts were incomplete), then took a quick look at the other titles his son had assembled, including "Isn't It Romantic?" "How Long Has This Been Going On?" "Penthouse Serenade," "I'm Old-Fashioned," "When the Sun Comes Out," "Don't Get Around Much Anymore," "Cry Me a River" and "That Face."

He arrived at 7:50 P.M., left at 8:45 and hasn't returned. Sinatra will be seventy-four this December.

For a while, on one of the gates to his home on Frank Sinatra Drive in Rancho Mirage, California, Ol' Blue Eyes had a gold plaque emblazoned with:

NEVER MIND THE DOG,
BEWARE OF THE OWNER

The plaque is gone, the dog is sold or dead, but the owner still rumbles across the land. His face shines down on anyone who enters Penn Station in New York City. He remains a credible salesman to the folks at Michelob and Holiday Inn. He can hold a decent telephone exchange for at least half an hour, and every now and then on the concert circuit he is thrilling. Still thrilling after all these years.

If the owner gathered seven or eight musicians together and spent a few nights making some records, he would allow us all a declarative end to his Proustian sentence, a conclusionary gesture, a closed parenthesis. His life has been, after all, italics sheltered by parentheses, and many of us need some signal of finality from our singular musician. "Maybe" isn't a sufficient farewell. Even if it comes as a whisper, we can bear the burden of such a modest good-bye.

Perhaps an album of silence.

Just his name on the jacket.

Only silence.

Over the years, a variety of musical artists have paid tribute to Sinatra. Pianist Oscar Peterson recorded an album of Sinatra tunes, as did cornetist Ruby Braff. Singers have also acknowledged their mentor. The late Sylvia Syms built her act around Sinatra's famous songs, and Tony Bennett won a Grammy for his 1992 album *Perfectly Frank.* In December 1990, when Sinatra turned seventy-five, *Life* published a piece entitled "Frank and Company," a tribute to American popular singers and an opportunity for these singers to express their thoughts on The Chairman of the Board. "When I worked New York," Ella Fitzgerald stated, "I'd run to the theater and wait among the girls for Tommy Dorsey's band to come on—for him. He's got the heart, the soul, the feeling for a lyric." "I got my education playing hooky and listening to Sinatra at the Paramount," Tony Bennett asserted. "He opened up a whole new bag with the microphone, the artful use of intimate singing to show psychology, real thinking."

As Sinatra approached his seventy-fifth birthday, tributes abounded. Capitol Records and Reprise put out multi-CD sets celebrating the Sinatra years. A two-hour birthday tribute was aired on network television, while public broadcasting stations repeatedly showed a documentary entitled *Sinatra: The Voice of Our Time.* And fans and performers alike expressed their feelings. Included here are three of the many pieces that appeared at the time—one by a famous young performer, the second by a fan who also happens to be the Pulitzer Prize–winning author of *Ironweed,* and the last by *Rolling Stone* rock critic Mikal Gilmore, who reviews the commemorative compilations.

A Perfect Singer,
Ever Since He Began the Beguine
Harry Connick, Jr. ★ 1990

As of today, I've only met Frank Sinatra once. I was about nine years old, and my father took me and my sister to Al Hirt's club in the French Quarter of New Orleans, where Sinatra was performing, so we could meet him.

After my father introduced us, Sinatra patted me on the shoulder and said, "Hello, young man." Then he signed his *All the Way* album for my sister. I had no idea that I had met the man who would shape my whole approach to music.

I believe Sinatra to be the greatest male singer of American popular song. He is accessible to people who know nothing about music.

For one thing, Sinatra is a total master of vocal technique. He was the first to do so many things—hanging over the bar with phrases and holding phrases out for such a long time, sliding from note to note. The way he can get vibrato out on the high notes—it's amazing. Then there is his breath control, the way he can hold phrases for twenty or twenty-five seconds. The best example is on "Old Man River" from the *Concert Sinatra* album. He must have an extra set of lungs; I wish he kept them in my chest.

People always try to analyze his sound. It's got something to do with the way his jaw is shaped, I think. He has very little air in his tone; every note he sings, whether soft or loud, is all sound.

Sinatra is also a musician. He sings every note perfectly. And he does things musicians do. I remember listening to the outtakes on some re-releases and hearing him say things like "On the downbeat I need more viola," or "Give me more of a crescendo."

He surprises me every time he changes melodies, when he sings "no" eleven times on "Mood Indigo," for example, or stretches "e-e-ev-vr-vry" on "I love Paris." He understands everything a musician understands—and he can articulate it because he is dealing with words, not merely sounds. Musically, I trust him implicitly.

When I was about thirteen, Al Hirt told me about Sinatra. "Phrasing, phrasing, phrasing . . ." he said. I didn't know what he meant then, but I do now. Everybody who listens to Sinatra talks about his phrasing, whether or not they know anything about music. Sinatra swings like no one else. He knows where to put the words. He can take liberties; he never gets lost.

There is no way to notate authentic swing; there is no way to teach it, either. But one can develop it if he or she has the potential. Sinatra redefined swing for the American popular singer. Even when he sang "Begin the Beguine" with Tommy Dorsey in the early 40s, his phrasing displayed the purest of swing. On the *Trilogy* album some forty-five years later, "It Had to Be You" swings with an elegance and wisdom that I don't even begin to understand. The way he phrases the first five words— "It . . . had . . . to be you"—perfect triplets. He just knows it. I'm still trying to figure it out.

Frank Sinatra: Pluperfect Music
William Kennedy ★ 1993

So Frank is seventy-five this year, and what does that mean? I remember what it meant when he was sixty-eight in June 1984. He was at Carnegie Hall singing "Pennies from Heaven" and "Fly Me to the Moon" and he was in great voice. When he did "Come Rain or Come Shine," a woman in a box called out to him, "Frank, baby, you're the best."

Frank asked her name and she said it was Angie and he said to her, "You ain't so bad yourself, Angie, you know what I mean?"

"I just wanted to warn you that I love you," Angie said.

"Is that a threat or a request?" Frank inquired.

"I'm leaving my husband for you," she said.

"I think we gotta talk that over a little bit," Frank said.

Angie turned to the audience below to tell us: "I'm gonna wash his underwear, too. I don't care."

"I'm gettin' scared now," Frank said, raising his glass of whiskey. "I'll drink to you."

"You're still twenty-five to me," Angie said.

I'd bumped into Jilly Rizzo, a friend of Frank's, in a New York saloon a few weeks earlier and we talked about the upcoming Carnegie Hall concert, for which tickets were scarce. Jilly said he could get me two, and what's more he'd introduce me to Frank backstage, and would I like that? I said that'd be a little bit of all right, and so there we were (Jilly; my wife, Dana; and me) in Frank's backstage parlor, where half a dozen others were bending his ear.

It was intermission between acts. Buddy Rich and his band, the opening act, had just concluded a hot session and Frank was on next. A roving waiter brought us a drink and I tried to imagine what you could possibly say to Frank. You couldn't gush. You couldn't say you'd been a fan for forty-eight years. Also, you had no friends in common you knew of. Yes, it's true you were in love with Ava thirty-five years ago and once watched her dance barefoot in Puerto Rico, but you couldn't bring that up, and you didn't know his wife or kids.

Jilly broke the ice by telling Frank that I traveled with tapes, meaning, of course, Frank's tapes. So I talked then about my Pluperfect Sinatra tapes, which a friend of mine and I had concocted to take the best of Sinatra from forever forward to right now and tape them, leaving out all songs that do not make you climb the wall.

Frank listened to my Pluperfect story without much surprise, for his record producers had been doing this for him all his life: *Frank Sinatra's Greatest Hits* and *Sinatra's Sinatra*, for example. But I have to say that nobody ever put together seven tapes such as the Pluperfects, in which you climb the wall every time out.

In one sense, the conversation was good practice for writing this memoir on behalf of Frank's seventy-fifth birthday disks, for I climb the wall more often with these Reprise tunes than I ever did before, given this many choices. There are certain exceptions we will not go into, and even if I am tortured I will not mention their titles, for this is not the critic's corner. This is a story of listening to Frank for forty-eight years, maybe forty-nine, and finding out what it means that he is now turning seventy-five.

So I told Frank how I'd planned to be a drummer in 1942, and when I saw Buddy Rich in a movie playing a tom-tom solo called "Not So Quiet Please" I went out and bought the record before I had a phonograph. I would set it on top of my dresser and let my eyes be the needle and I listened to that solo for six months before I came up with enough cash to buy a friend's used phonograph. Frank remembered the solo. It was in a movie called *Ship Ahoy*, with Eleanor Powell and Red Skelton and Tommy Dorsey and guess who else: Frank. You knew that.

I then enhanced the conversation by asking him a historical question: how he decided to record "There's a Flaw in My Flue," one of my favorites among his romantic ballads, whose lyrics, in part, go like this:

> Your lovely face in my fireplace, was all that I saw
> But now it won't draw, 'cause my flue has a flaw.
> From every beautiful ember a memory arose,
> Now I try to remember and smoke gets in my nose. . . .

Frank liked the question and said he'd heard the song on Bing Crosby's Kraft Music Hall radio show, a segment called "The Flop Parade," and he thought it was funny; what's more Bing had never recorded it. So Frank—who felt that the executives at his record company never really listened to his songs—wanted to make that point; and he asked Nelson Riddle to orchestrate "Flue" for an opening slot in an upcoming record.

"When they played it," Frank said, "one of the record company guys says to me, 'What is this?' and I said, 'It's a love song.' I said, 'There's a flaw in my flue, beautiful.'" And so it flawlessly became, and Frank made his point doubly, with a leg pull that stands as a comic gem.

The other significant thing that happened at Carnegie Hall was my wife. She had been a tepid Sinatra fan, growing, if not fond of, then at least used to him as I played his tapes. She knew him as an actor before I came along but not really as a singer and here I was clogging her brain with him on every trip we took. She would sometimes look at me and say, quietly, "Overdose," and I'd then have to put on the Kiri Te Kanawa tape.

But unbeknownst, Frank had been growing on her ever since she'd heard him do "Lonely Town" better than anybody else had ever done it, and then here he was singing "Mack the Knife" and "Luck Be a Lady" and swinging everybody's brain from the highest trapeze and even dancing (which also got to her, for she'd been both a ballerina, and a gypsy on Broadway), and suddenly there she was on her feet like everybody else when he wound up with "New York, New York": Dana, a convert, no longer susceptible to overdose.

That is the remarkable thing about Sinatra recordings: that you can listen to them not only forever, but also at great length without overdosing, once you have been infected. I say this not only on my own behalf but on behalf of the entire set in which I move, and which I have helped infect to the point that Frank is now a common denominator among this group of seriously disparate ages and types. I am the Methuselah of the set and can remember not only Frank's hits with Tommy Dorsey's orchestra when they were new—"I'll Never Smile Again" and "There Are Such Things"— but also tunes that never quite made it—"Everything Happens to Me," for instance, which I knew by heart in 1943 and still remember from that era when listening to records was what you did with your friends when the baseball diamond was a major mud puddle.

In the 1950s, there came *In the Wee Small Hours*, which conditioned your life, especially with a young woman with lush blond hair who used to put the record on and pray to Frank for a lover. All that perfumed hair, and it came undone. That certainly was a good year, but it remained for another album, *Swing Easy*, to teach you how to play a record twelve times in one night, which was merely a warm-up for 1983 when you listened to "New York, New York" for the first time seriously and then played it sixty times until 5:00 A.M., also calling your friends in New York and San Juan and Aspen and permitting them to stop sleeping and get out of bed and listen along.

The true thing about this phenomenon is that you do not have to have Frank on video, or in a movie or TV show, or even invent conversation in person with this fellow who is a stranger. You really don't need those presences. All you need is the music the man has made and that has been with you all your life, and which is even better now because you have all the songs of his maturity (which is why these four disks are so valuable, for they collect tunes he did early on and here does so much better). He was new in the forties and still growing in the fifties into such masterpieces as "Drinking Again" (1967), by Johnny Mercer, the greatest of all torch songs Frank ever sang, and also such breakouts as we have here—"I've Got You Under My Skin" (1966) and "The Lady Is a Tramp" (1974) that put earlier white-bread versions out in the back yard. Of course, these views are open to argument but, even so, I will brook none of it here. This is my memoir.

There is another superb thing Sinatra does, which is Irving Berlin's schmaltziest work—"All Alone" and "What'll I Do?" among others—shameless, cornball, wonderful throwbacks to the Tin Pan Alley time when schmaltz was A-Number One, King of the Hill.

It was the schmaltz and also too many trumpets that turned off my son, Brendan, when I played Frank in the car. (He once listened to a Bing Crosby and the Rhythm Boys tape from 1929, and decided the music was prehistoric.) We would fight over tape time in the car, he opting for the Police, me for guess who? This was 1983 and Bren was thirteen. Now he's in college and last month he told me, "We were at a party and this horrible music was on and this girl and I put on a tape of Frank and danced until somebody shut him off."

Two weeks ago he asked my advice on dance tunes and I recommended *Swing Easy* and the albums with Ellington and Jobim, and so now Brendan also travels with Frank tapes, in case of emergency dancing.

The finale of all this is that Frank turned up in our hometown, Albany, as the opening act for the brand-new Knickerbocker Arena, with seventeen thousand seats. Would Albany turn out for him in any numbers? Word had gone out, as it always does with these mythmaking events, that Frank wasn't well, might not show up, that Liza Minnelli was standing by to go on if he crumpled. What's more, Ava had just died and so maybe this was not one of those very good years.

And yet here he came on January 30, six years older than when I'd last seen him, looking smaller and—how not?—older, his seventy-fifth year just barely under way. He's wearing his single-breasted tux with an orange pocket handkerchief, his hair totally silver, adding to his years. Then he opens his mouth. "Come fly with me," he sings and a cheer goes up from the yes, seventeen thousand who have packed the place to hear and see this legendary character who only *seems* to grow old.

A lifetime of staying young at center stage: how can anybody be so good for so long? You listen and know that this is not Frank in his best voice ever but it doesn't matter. It's *his* sound, *his* cadence, *his* tunes, *him*, and it's as good as it can be and that's still very, very good. He moseys to the improvised bar on stage with the Jack Daniel's and the ice bucket and he sits on the bar stool and says: "I don't drink a lot, but I don't drink a little either." And then he opens his mouth again: "It's quarter to three . . ." and the crowd roars and he calms them with his old torch.

And then, finally, he segues into "New York, New York" and the spotlights circle the crowd, which is stomping, and Frank is making love to all here. He opens his arms, points to everybody. . . . "It's up to you, New York, New York. . . ."

Then it's over and the spots cross on him and the aging bobby-soxers, having come full circle from forty-eight years gone, reach up to shake his hand, and he fades down the stairs and out, and you follow him with your eyes because he is carrying the sound of your youth, the songs of your middle age. And then you think, the song is you, pal, the song is you.

The Wonder of Sinatra
Mikal Gilmore ★ 1991

Frank Sinatra is one of pop music's most abiding prodigies—and also one of its most troubling icons. At the peak of his craft—during the 1950s and 1960s, when he recorded the definitive ballad and swing sessions documented so ambitiously on *Frank Sinatra: The Capitol Years,* and *Frank Sinatra: The Reprise Collection*—Sinatra raised the art of romantic singing to a new height. He treated each song as if it were the inevitable expression of a personal experience, as if there were no separating the singer from the emotion or meaning of the songs he sang, and therefore no separating the listener from the experience of a singular and compelling pop voice. But for all the grace of his talent, there is also a considerable darkness about Sinatra: a desperate hunger for the validation that comes from love and power, and a ruinous anger toward anything that challenges that validation. In many ways, that fierce need for love or vindication is the guiding force behind the best moments of Sinatra's career. Indeed, *The Capitol Years* and *The Reprise Collection* are the life testaments of a man who has learned to cling to one truth above all others: that one can never win love so surely that one can stop imagining the pain of its loss.

It is a lesson that Sinatra learned early, and at great cost. In the 1940s, following his emergence from the Harry James and Tommy Dorsey big bands, Sinatra was pop's biggest star, a romantic balladeer whose sexy, yearning voice made him Columbia Records' biggest-selling recording arist. But then, toward the decade's end. Sinatra fell from grace—fast and hard. In part, his decline simply resulted from shifting musical tastes. In the exuberance of the postwar period, a new audience wanted more effervescence and more soul than Sinatra seemed capable of rendering. In addition, Sinatra shocked many of his remaining supporters by abandoning his wife and family to pursue a steamy public affair with actress Ava Gardner, whom he married in 1951. Within a few years, Sinatra's relationship with both Columbia Records and Gardner turned stormy, and in the seasons that followed, the singer lost everything, including his record and film contracts, his marriage to Gardner and, perhaps most devastating of all, he even lost his voice during a public performance. After that, no record company would take a chance on him, and Sinatra was back on the club circuit, playing to sparse audiences and trying to regain the voice and confidence that had once come so readily.

Finally, in 1953, Capitol Records agreed to risk a one-year contract with Sinatra—if the arist was willing to forfeit his advance and pay all of his own studio costs. It was a humiliating offer, but Sinatra took it and, in the process, turned his life around. With his first few sessions for the label, Sinatra surprised both critics and former fans by flaunting a new voice that seemed to carry more depth, more worldy weight and more rhythmic invention than the half-fragile tone that he had brandished in the 1940s. And then, with his first full-fledged LP—*In the Wee Small Hours,* a deep-blue, after-hours ballad collection conducted by Nat King Cole's up-and-coming arranger Nelson Riddle—Sinatra staked out the vocal sensibility that would become the hallmark of his mature style and that would establish him as the most gifted interpretive vocalist to energe in pop or jazz since Billie Holiday. On the surface, Sinatra's new delivery seemed almost more colloquial than musical. That is, he took supremely mellifluous material like the title track and sang as if it were a hushed yet vital communication: a rueful confession shared with an understanding friend over a late-night shot of whiskey, or, more likely, a painful rumination that the singer needed to proclaim to himself in order to work his way free of a bitter memory. In other words, Sinatra was now singing songs of romantic despair as if he were living inside the experience and as if each tune's lyrics were his and his alone to sing. "It was Ava who did that, who taught him how to sing a torch song," Nelson Riddle later told Sinatra's biographer Kitty Kelley. "That's how he learned. She was the greatest love of his life, and he lost her."

In effect, Sinatra's tenure at Capitol—along with the credibility he gained as an actor from his Oscar-winning performance in *From Here to Eternity*—proved to be the redemption of his career. Over the next ten years, he would record twenty-plus top-selling LPs for the label—alternating between sexy, uptempo, big-band-style dance affairs and brooding reflections on romantic despair and sexual betrayal—and he would also become one of the most consistently popular Top Forty singles artists of the 1950s. It was one of the richest growth periods that any pop artist has ever managed, and *The Capitol Years* aims to pay tribute to it, picking seventy-five of the artist's most sublime musical milestones and cataloging them in rough chronological order. At its best, this box set stands as a definitive summary not only of Sinatra's most revealing vocal performances but also a smart compendium of some of the best songwriting of the prerock era, by enduring songsmiths and lyricists such as Cole Porter, Harold Arlen, Johnny Mercer, Richard Rodgers, Lorenz Hart and George and Ira Gershwin, among others. But by abridging such a broad range of Sinatra's work, *The Capitol Years* also tends to give short shrift to the carefully constructed arcs of mood that made the singer's 1950s albums so innovative—and in Sinatra's art, dwelling on a mood until that mood can give up no other revelations is half the trick.

By contrast, the anthology approach fares better on *The Reprise Collection*, largely because the set makes a surprisingly effective case for a diverse body of work that has often been viewed as fairly negligible. Sinatra started Reprise Records in 1961, and some of his best work for the label— such as his collaborations with the Count Basie orchestra and Quincy Jones, and the *September of My Years* project with composer–arranger Gordon Jenkins—stuck to the mold of the big band and saloon-song theme album that he had popularized at Capitol. But by the mid-1960s, artists like the Beatles and Bob Dylan were transforming the pop mainstream, in effect killing off the generations-old Tin Pan Alley aesthetic that had provided singers like Sinatra with their repertoire. Sinatra had never much liked rock & roll (though he enjoyed a couple of hits in the style during the 1950s, which unfortunately haven't been reissued), but he was shrewd and vain enough to want to match the challenge of the new pop sensibility. Some of his efforts in this regard—like the shamelessly self-mythologizing "My Way" and the wooden, sappy "Something Stupid," a duet with his daughter Nancy—are among his most lamentable recordings. But tracks like the roaring, soulful "That's Life" (with its savvy nod to Ray Charles) and the lilting bossa nova collaborations with Brazilian guitarist–composer Antonio Carlos Jobim are not only fine testaments to Sinatra's self-willed resilience but blissful examples of the undervalued side of 1960s pop.

If *The Reprise Collection* fall short in any way, it is in covering Sinatra's latter-day singing career following his reemergence from a brief retirement in the early 1970s. Granted, this is the singer's most problematic period. After his return in 1973, Sinatra's voice had changed again, settling into a gruffer, brandy-tone inflection and sometimes suffering from a shakiness in pitch and a shortness of breath. Indeed, with the exception of some of his work on *Trilogy*, in 1980, Sinatra never again found a recording voice as virile and affecting as the one that had carried him through the 1950s and 1960s.

And yet, in his live performances over the last ten years or so (a part of his career that has never been documented on record and that is not included in *The Reprise Collection*), Sinatra has often been stunning, putting across big-band standards like "I've Got You Under My Skin," "I've Got the World on a String" and "You Make Me Feel So Young" with a surprising force and agility and rendering his much-loved saloon soliloquies with a matchless sense of depth and grace. In fact, there is something especially poignant in seeing the aging Sinatra perched on a stool center stage, contemplating lost love in Harold Arlen and Ira Gershwin's "The Gal That Got Away" or lost youth in Gordon Jenkins's "This Is All I Ask." In such moments, Sinatra knows enough to surrender to his age, to sing the songs in the voice of an old man stripped of most hopes and all conceits. Then, likely as not, he'll turn around and undercut his own best moments by launching into one of his infamous diatribes against those who don't share his views or passions. All a fan can do at such moments is wince and wait for the singer's next miraculous vocal epiphany—and sooner or later, such patience pays off.

At seventy-five, Frank Sinatra remains indomitable. Night after night, he stands onstage and sings songs about love and longing, hope and despair, and each time he does he communicates the emotional truths of those songs to a mass of strangers as if that mass were a handful of intimates. He is not doing this merely for the money; long ago, Sinatra became rich enough to live in any world he wanted to build for himself. Maybe he does it simply because somehow singing these songs enriches him, helps him realize a depth and compassion that does not come quite so easily in his personal life. Or maybe singing has simply become his most reliable companion—the best way of forestalling the darkness and loneliness that long ago he came to loathe. In any event, it is now 1991, and Sinatra still sings, and will likely continue to do so until he is physically unable to continue.

In an interview from over a quarter century ago, Sinatra uttered what may be his own best defense: "Having lived a life of violent emotional contradictions," he said, "I have an overacute capacity for sadness as well as elation. . . . Whatever else has been said about me is unimportant. When I sing, I believe." When Sinatra stops singing, it is unlikely that we will ever see pop artistry so transcendent, and so sustained, again.

In 1992, the Sinatras presented their own tribute in the form of a five-hour televison biography of the singer produced by Tina Sinatra with the cooperation of her father. When Tina originally announced the project, some interpreted the timing as an attempt to undermine an unauthorized biography that was then being researched. (That bio turned out to be Kitty Kelley's scurrilous book, *His Way*, which, for all its attention to lurid and sensational detail, could almost make one forget that the subject was one of the great artists of the twentieth century.) The TV miniseries, like the book written by daughter Nancy, was far more than mere hagiography. Apparently, the Sinatra sense of honesty extends beyond daddy. What follows is Jonathan Storm's *Philadelphia Inquirer* review of the critically acclaimed program.

Sinatra *Portrays a Singer and a Survivor*
Jonathan Storm ★ 1992

Leaving a wake of busted marriages and battered *paparazzi, Sinatra,* the five-hour life story of the king of the crooners, is surprisingly frank.

You might say the bio of the tempestuous Frank Sinatra, presented tonight and Tuesday on Channel 10 by his daughter Tina, pulls no punches.

But rather than degrading Sinatra, the sum of the scummy details—his mother's nefarious ways, his mobster associates, his string of starlets—becomes a noble portrait of a man whose few admirable excesses, most notably talent and ambition, enabled him to overcome a collection of ignoble ones.

"There's no greater survivor that I've ever known," Tina Sinatra, who executive-produced the show and oversaw every detail, told a group of television critics this summer. "That he survived this life . . . sometimes I find a little bit overwhelming."

Sinatra itself also can be overwhelming—plodding, as so many miniseries do, through uninteresting periods, skipping blithely over others. But though short of a smash, it's a success overall: It informs, entertains much of the time, and presents more than a score of Sinatra standards.

Any show that uses "All the Way," "It Was a Very Good Year" and "My Way" just to unroll the credits already has a lot going for it. Most of the songs are the originals, though some of the older ones are done for TV by Tom Burlinson, an Australian actor, and others are done by Sinatra's son, Frank, Jr. Both are masterly imitators.

Though Philip Casnoff lip-syncs the songs, he makes an exceptional Sinatra. Combining some of the classic Frank mannerisms with his own flourishes, the actor, best known for his work on Broadway, makes it moot that this is not the real Sinatra.

For those unfamiliar with the tale: After a start with radio's *Major Bowes Amateur Hour* in the early '30s, Sinatra becomes vocalist for Harry James, then Tommy Dorsey. Eventually, he's the nation's No. 1 solo songster.

But a lurid personal life and inability to smile sweetly while newspaper columnists call him a commie and ubiquitous photographers pop flash-bulbs in his face cost him his popularity and his movie contract. (It's hard to escape *Sinatra*'s implication that similar behavior today would only enhance his reputation.)

He must begin anew, virtually at the bottom, and thanks partially to the jump-start of an Oscar-winning performance in *From Here to Eternity* (1953), rises once again.

The message is neatly summarized in a bedside scene where Sinatra visits his pal Sammy Davis, Jr., who has just lost an eye in a car crash. "We all hit bottom sometime, Smoky," Sinatra says. "It passes."

Sinatra's story starts in Hoboken, New Jersey, where the little kid sang during Prohibition in his mother's saloon.

The $18.5 million production—lavish, by TV standards—took vintage cars on location. "Hoboken remains locked in time," said Tina Sinatra, "but we did have to be careful about shooting the New York skyline."

In addition to selling liquor illegally, Dolly Sinatra was also an abortionist. If we're to believe *Sinatra* and Olympia Dukakis' shrill portrayal, Dolly was pretty tough on her boy, calling him "a little son of a bitch" all the times she was not calling him "Mr. Smarty Pants" or "Mr. Big Shot." His father, an asthmatic who was clearly not the family's dominant force, most often called the young Frank a quitter.

The child Sinatra knew the value of money.

"Here's a penny," a boozer offers. "Sing with feeling."

"Feeling costs a nickel," Frankie replies. There are surprisingly few such little laughs in such a long program. The best one comes when the aging Sinatra, annoyed at third wife Mia Farrow's musical taste, complains about the demise of lyrics in rock and roll.

"Doo-bee-doo-bee-doo," she responds.

Probably because of obscure music-biz financial limitations, "Strangers in the Night" doesn't make it onto *Sinatra*'s playlist. But Tina Sinatra was able to cut through a pile of contracts with RCA, Columbia, Capitol and Reprise to assemble the music that does. (A two-disc soundtrack has been released, and that's a TV first.)

Sinatra himself wasn't too bad at cutting through contracts, either, the mini-series details. The rumor always had been that the Mafia helped him break his lifetime deal with Dorsey in the early '40s. Tonight we see that it was a different mob—Hollywood lawyers, and music and movie moguls—who helped engineer the extrication.

Sinatra brings home the power of those guys in the '40s and '50s, as touchy executives clamped down on the personal lives of their contract slaves. Louis B. Mayer put a block on Ava Gardner's telephone, for example, to try to keep Sinatra, married and out of favor, from continuing their adulterous relationship.

Eventually Nancy Barbato Sinatra, mother of Frank's three children, agreed to a divorce, and Gardner became Sinatra's second wife.

The Frank-and-Ava relationship is the fulcrum of this biography, partially by script design and partially because Marcia Gay Harden, a New York stage journeyman, is such a commanding presence as Gardner, the legendary movie beauty with a mind of her own. Casnoff sings from all sorts of stages to Harden, as Ava makes grand appearance after grand appearance. Her magnificent entrance at a Houston hotel nightclub, in an awesome black gown, puts new meaning into "Old Black Magic," Sinatra's song of the moment.

"Every cat in here wants to be me," Frank tells her, "and every chick wants to be you."

She was forever walking out on him. "It's torture when we're together and worse when we're not," she explains, after he's flown to Spain from Florida. He was supposed to be recuperating, from a throat hemorrhage, but he saw a newpaper picture of her smooching a matador with whom she was making a movie.

"Hit the bricks, Zorro," he tells the guy, after first calling him "a greaseball." But at least Sinatra doesn't deck this particular señor.

Incidents such as this fill the mini-series, which also looks at Sinatra's dalliance with the Kennedys, portaying them as disloyal connivers, and his time as leader of the Rat Pack, with people who seem more like impersonators than actors portraying Dean Martin, Peter Lawford and Sammy Davis, Jr., one of Sinatra's best friends.

Their renditions make Casnoff's work seem all the more impressive.

Sinatra follows its subject to age fifty-nine, when we leave Frank on top again at Madison Square Garden. Though it's filled with song, there is little examination, after the early years, of how the music came about. That's surprising: Frank Sinatra's musical stature is at least as great as his stature as a star. But this is the story of neither the star nor the music. It's intended to be the story of the man.

"My father had everything to do with the development of the screenplay," Tina Sinatra said, in describing the project that has been eight years aborning. Though some details were modified because Sinatra's recollections could not be verified, "he was the main source of the story," Tina said.

"It will be how I feel about my life," she said Sinatra told a press conference in 1984. "And Frank Sinatra is not ashamed of his life."

The following article represents, we believe, a most fitting conclusion to this collection, since it was written for the occasion of a most fitting tribute to Ol' Blue Eyes. In July 1995, a three-night, all-star tribute was held at Carnegie Hall to commemorate Sinatra's upcoming eightieth birthday, and this piece by Sinatra biographer Will Friedwald appeared in the show's program. Among the nation's most distinguished music critics, Friedwald is the author of *Jazz Singing* and *Sinatra! The Song Is You*. His work has also appeared in the *New York Times*, *New York* magazine, and the *Village Voice*.

Carnegie Tribute
Will Friedwald ★ 1995

> Me and Sinatra, we got our own sound.
> Miles Davis

James Cagney once defined the art of acting as being able to "stand on the balls of your feet and tell the truth." Jazzman Wingy Manone used to hang a sign in front of the clubs where he played with the invitation, "Come in and hear the truth."

Frank Sinatra is, beyond argument, the greatest of all pop singers. In addition, the claim could be made that he's also the single most significant figure in all popular culture. Many attempts have been made to explain precisely how Sinatra gets under our collective skin, but ultimately it may be that listeners have declared him the central voice of the American experience for fifty-six years because everything he tells us is the truth.

In the words of Rosemary Clooney, "I think that he's been true to himself, no matter if that's good, bad or indifferent. What you get is whatever his history is at that moment." Sinatra might be animating what he calls a "saloon song" so vividly that we can't help but visualize a bartender with bent ears wiping clean his shot glasses. Or he could be reinventing some old showtune as a rhythmic bauble in which he bounces the text like a toy balloon. In either case, we accept what he's telling us as the truth.

"Being an eighteen-carat manic depressive," Sinatra has supposedly said, "I have an acute capacity for both sadness and elation." Sinatra carries his depictions of both of these emotions to the furthest imaginable extremes. His swingers, particularly "I've Got You Under My Skin" with Nelson Riddle and any of dozens of cuts with Billy May or Count Basie, are so irresistibly "up" that they invigorate the human soul into uncontrollable levels of giddy euphoria. And his downer discs, particularly *Only the Lonely* with Riddle and *No One Cares* with Gordon Jenkins, don't contain mere saloon-ey tunes, but are instead comprosed of what fans describe as "suicide songs."

Sinatra's combination of rhythm, dynamics, and diction—which we can sum up with the term "phrasing"—was once discussed by the singer's favorite lyricist, Sammy Cahn. Sinatra makes any word sound more like what it is, the late songwriter observed: "When he sings 'lovely,' he makes it sound 'lo-ovely' as in 'weather-wise it's such a lo-ovely day' [in Cahn's 'Come Fly with Me']," Cahn demonstrated, caressing and extending the long soft vowel sound at the center, "it's 'lo-o-vely.' Likewise, when he sings 'lonely' (in 'Only the Lonely') he makes it into such a lonely word."

So much of our lives have been lived to the soundtrack of Sinatra's music, and in a way that runs much deeper than, say, growing up with the Brooklyn Dodgers or Ozzie and Harriet. It's ultimately impossible to tell where our actual experiences end and those we've felt vicariously through Sinatra lyrics begin. Once we reach our thirties, we've long since lost the ability to distinguish whether something really happened to us or if we just felt it through the way Sinatra sings, for instance, "It Was a Very Good Year." The Sinatra-inspired "memories" amount to a collective stock-footage library of shared experiences—most of us can feel the small-town episode of "Very Good Year" amazingly vividly even if we've never been west of Tenth Avenue.

The late orchestrator Gordon Jenkins once illustrated: "Frank does one word in 'Send in the Clowns' and it's the damndest thing I've ever heard. He just sings the word 'farce,' and your whole life comes up in front of you. He puts so much in that phrase that it just takes a hold of you." Where other singers, at best, work with lyrics and melodies, Sinatra deals in mental images and pure feelings that he seems to summon up almost without the intervention of composers, arrangers, and musicians, as vital as their contributions are.

Unlike other cultural figures who managed to stick around for a couple of decades (such as Bing Crosby, whom he called "the father of my career"), Sinatra has remained too enigmatic and uncategorizable to ever be considered part of any kind of social "establishment." And while never advocating rebellion for its own sake, Sinatra completely revolutionized all of popular music on at least four levels before he had turned thirty in 1945.

The first was his singing itself, which began with a masterful synthesis of his earliest influences—the lyric-driven naturalistic approach of Crosby and the idiosyncratic vulnerability (and super-slow tempos) of Billie Holiday, as expressed through the ultra-legato timing of mentor Tommy Dorsey. But there was something more that Sinatra brought to this mix. As colleague Tony Bennett puts it,

Frank took it a whole step further in a way that no one could have imagined. What Sinatra did was psychologically communicate precisely what he was thinking at any moment. After Sinatra, there was no longer any wall between performer and audience—he invited listeners under his skin and into his heart. He perfected the art of intimacy, and that was a big contribution to popular music.

As Mel Tormé has pointed out, "Frank's rise to fame ushered in a new era in popular music—a vocalist's era." When Sinatra left Tommy Dorsey's orchestra and played that remarkable first solo engagement at the Paramount at the dawn of 1943, he changed musical history with a single appearance. Big bands had ruled the roost for over a decade before that engagement, and "singers were strictly secondary." As Ted Nash, Sinatra's favorite tenor saxophone soloist, explains, "Then, when Frank hit that screaming bunch of kids, the bands just went right into the background. From then on, [the idea] was just to feature the singer completely, and then everyone else jumped into it." Sinatra released the pivotal stone that caused the avalanche of solo singers that dominated pop music in the 1940s and 1950s. He then gradually transcended the era he had done so much to inspire by constantly forging ahead into new areas in the 1960s, 1970s, 1980s and 1990s.

"The Voice," as he was known in the 1940s, not only provided the social and economic imperative for a generation of post-Sinatra singers, and changed the nature of how they sang, but also changed what they sang. Up until Sinatra, one magazine noted in 1949, singers "rarely made use of melodies penned prior to six months ago. Sinatra perfected the concept of a repertory of standard songs—going beyond current hits to excavate the great Broadway scores for worthwhile numbers that would stand the test of time. Frank Military, formerly Sinatra's right-hand man (and currently head of Warner-Chappell Music New York), points out, "If you look at songs like 'Glad to Be Unhappy,' and even songs out of flop shows, like 'Guess I'll Hang My Tears out to Dry,' he made them into important standards."

From perfecting the concept of the Great American Songbook, Sinatra then took it a step further and created new forums for jazz and pop musicians of every stripe to perform this material: In an age when movie theaters and nightclubs were the norm, Sinatra was the first pop singer to "concertize" in the classical sense of the term, with a series of amphitheater engagements (culminating at the Hollywood Bowl) in the summer of 1943.

Two years later, Sinatra shifted his focus in recording from simple singles to more in-depth formats with the invention of what came to be known as the concept album. Years before the invention of the long-playing record, Sinatra showed how individual songs could flow into a cohesive whole with *The Voice*, a package that led not only to Sinatra's hundred or so subsequent concept albums—the latest is 1994's *Frank Sinatra Duets II*—but to the greatest works of Miles Davis and the Beatles. "He sat down and carefully planned his albums, and lyrically they had to make sense." Adds Military, "They had to tell a story. He'd spend days and weeks just preparing this album. Each song would be hand-picked, it had a reason for being in the album." "He would pick the tunes," longtime accompanist Bill Miller concurs, "and he would even position them on the album."

Carnegie Hall's current tribute to this most venerable of twentieth-century icons, the premiere of their American Popular Song series, is actually the climax in the long relationship of our culture's greatest singer with the most esteemed venue in music. Sinatra first played here on a two-night benefit in tandem with Lena Horne in October 1963. (Nelson Riddle and Bill Miller were in their place at the podium and the piano.) The event raised over $100,000 in preinflation money for the Gandhi Society for Human Rights and Foundation for International Child Health. When Sinatra came out of retirement in 1974, he chose Carnegie as the site of his first important "comeback" concert (an event recorded but not released by Sinatra's label, Reprise Records), the proceeds of which also went to charity.

James Goldman observed in his play *The Lion in Winter* that "nothing in this world has any business being perfect." The music of Frank Sinatra contradicts that theorem. His artistic canon, as Gordon Jenkins described it, is "as close to perfect as any of us are able to deliver." And that's the truth.

CONCLUSION

H E'S BEEN up and down and over and out, and he seems to know one thing: as long as he has breath and as long as the audiences come back for more, Frank Sinatra will be there to present the best of Tin Pan Alley. Remarkably, as he prepared to enter his eighties, he was still the subject of controversy—musical and extramusical. The inconsistencies of his performances continued to haunt him. His reviews depended on the reviewer and, of course, the particular performance. Some called for him to retire, while others professed amazement at how much this hard-living, seemingly tireless singer had left at this advanced age.

At the beginning of 1994, a competition developed over the location of a Sinatra museum to house his vast collection of memorabilia. The mayor of Hoboken, New Jersey, envisioned his town as the proper location for a museum and library.* New York and the District of Columbia's Smithsonian Institution were also rumored as sites. On March 1, 1994, Sinatra was presented with the Grammy Legends Award for his lifetime achievements and contributions to the profession. During the live broadcast of the ceremonies, Sinatra's rambling acceptance speech was cut short for the television viewing audience, provoking charges, that profit-seeking advertisers were responsible for this "blasphemy." Later, a Sinatra spokesperson reported that she and the network had made the decision to cut him off. Regardless of the cause, however, this Sinatra "event" occupied center stage in the following day's news coverage of the Grammy awards. As if this weren't enough, a few days later, Sinatra again made headlines when, toward the finish of an apparently sensational performance in Richmond, Virginia, he collapsed while singing "My Way." Waving to his distraught audience, he was wheeled off the stage, but the very next day the singer announced that the on-stage heat had been too much for him and he was otherwise fine and would resume his touring within a few weeks.

And so, some eight decades since his birth in Hoboken, we still find the

---

* Paula Span, "Swooning for Sinatra," *Philadelphia Inquirer*, 3 January 1994, pp. E5, E7.

performer donning his tuxedo and walking out onto concert stages night after night. The excitement and tumult of his anticipated arrival on stage still fills each room in which he sings, even though inconsistencies of performance loom larger than ever. Sometimes he's on fire—jousting with the lyric and the audience to give both the best he has to offer. His musical knowledge of how to sing a song can cover deficiencies in almost miraculous fashion, and he remains, as Gary Giddins calls him, the "shaman" of song. There are other times when he clearly is struggling with time itself, an agon that all people—even Francis Albert Sinatra—must eventually endure. His eyesight is no longer sharp; he struggles to remember lyrics and requires visible TelePrompTers to get through performances; his fabulous musical ear now requires a hearing device. And yet, there he stands, an American institution, a life in music.

And so the legendary days march on and dwindle down to a precious few, foreshadowing the inevitable next stage of the legendary performer's life. But for now, we still have him, arguably the greatest popular entertainer who has ever lived. Sinatra—the puncher, the man of comebacks, the risk-taker—goes on. In the words of his own oft-repeated toast, may the last voice any of us hears be his.

DISCOGRAPHY

On the television special *Sinatra: The Best Is Yet to Come,* a celebration of the singer's seventy-fifth birthday, it was estimated that Sinatra has made over 1,800 recordings. These include many unreleased records and Victory Discs made during World War II that belong to the U.S. government. Compounding the problem of trying to assemble anything like a comprehensive discography is the fact that many of Sinatra's early recordings for RCA and Columbia Records were singles, and while many of these single sides were subsequently compiled into albums and packages, they were not conceived as such. There are also many off-labels producing Sinatra recordings here and abroad, much of this material pirated or unauthorized. By the time Sinatra signed with Capitol Records, the LP was fast becoming the most important recording medium, and the singer was among the first artists to use its popularity to put together albums in the fullest sense of the world—material thematically tied together. The following discography includes Sinatra's albums only from the time he joined Capitol Records in 1953 through the present, as well as some later compilations. For a complete list of Sinatra's recordings for all the labels on which he worked through 1992, the reader should consult Albert I. Lonstein and Vito R. Marino, *The Revised Compleat Sinatra,* 3rd ed. (New York: Musicprint, 1981), and Ed O'Brien and Scott P. Sayers, *Sinatra: The Man and His Music: The Recording Artistry of Francis Albert Sinatra, 1939–1992* (Austin: TSD Press, 1992).

1953	*Swing Easy* (Capitol)
1954	*Songs for Young Lovers* (Capitol)
1955	*In the Wee Small Hours* (Capitol)
1956	*Songs for Swingin' Lovers* (Capitol)
	High Society [soundtrack] (Capitol)
1957	*Tone Poems of Color* [Sinatra conducts] (Capitol)
	This Is Sinatra (Capitol)
	Close to You (Capitol)
	A Swingin' Affair (Capitol)
	A Jolly Christmas from Frank Sinatra (Capitol)
	Pal Joey [soundtrack] (Capitol)
	Where Are You? (Capitol)
1958	*Come Fly with Me* (Capitol)
	This Is Sinatra, Vol. 2 (Capitol)
	(Sinatra Sings for) Only the Lonely (Capitol)

1959	*Come Dance with Me* (Capitol)
	[Grammys for Album of the Year and Best Solo Vocal]
	Look to Your Heart (Capitol)
	No One Cares (Capitol)
1960	*Can-Can* [soundtrack] (Capitol)
	Nice 'n Easy (Capitol)
	Sinatra's Swingin' Session (Capitol)
	All the Way (Capitol)
1961	*Come Swing with Me* (Capitol)
	Ring-a-Ding-Ding (Reprise)
	Sinatra Swings (Reprise)
	I Remember Tommy (Reprise)
1962	*Point of No Return* (Capitol)
	Sinatra Sings of Love and Things (Capitol)
	Sinatra and Strings (Reprise)
	Sinatra and Swingin' Brass (Reprise)

271

Sinatra Sings Great Songs from Great Britain (Reprise)
Frank Sinatra Conducts Music from Pictures and Plays (Reprise)
All Alone (Reprise)

1963   *Sinatra–Basie* (Reprise)
The Concert Sinatra (Reprise)
Musical Repertory Theatre [four albums conceived and produced by Sinatra] (Reprise)
Sinatra's Sinatra (Reprise)

1964   *Frank Sinatra Sings Days of Wine and Roses, Moon River, and Other Academy Award Winners* (Reprise)
America, I Hear You Singing [with Bing Crosby, Fred Waring, and the Pennsylvanians] (Reprise)
Sinatra–Basie: It Might as Well Be Swing (Reprise)
Robin and the Seven Hoods [soundtrack] (Reprise)
Softly as I Leave You (Reprise)
Twelve Songs of Christmas [with Bing Crosby, Fred Waring, and the Pennsylvanians] (Reprise)

1965   *September of My Years* (Reprise) [Grammys for Album of the Year and Best Solo Vocal for "It Was a Very Good Year"]
Sinatra '65 (Reprise)
My Kind of Broadway (Reprise)
A Man and His Music (Reprise) [1966 Grammy for Album of the Year and 1965 Emmy and Peabody Awards for television special by this title]

1966   *Strangers in the Night* (Reprise) [Grammy for Song of the Year]
Moonlight Sinatra (Reprise)
Sinatra at the Sands (Reprise)

That's Life (Reprise)

1967   *Francis Albert Sinatra & Antonio Carlos Jobim* (Reprise)
Frank & Nancy (Reprise)

1968   *Francis A. & Edward K.* (Reprise)
Frank Sinatra's Greatest Hits (Reprise)
The Sinatra Family Wish You a Merry Christmas (Reprise)
Cycles (Reprise)

1969   *My Way* (Reprise)
A Man Alone (Reprise)
Watertown (Reprise)

1970   *Sinatra and Company* (Reprise)

1971   *Frank Sinatra's Greatest Hits, Vol. II* (Reprise)

1973   *Ol' Blue Eyes Is Back* (Reprise)

1974   *Some Nice Things I've Missed* (Reprise)
The Main Event (Reprise)

1980   *Trilogy* (Reprise)

1981   *She Shot Me Down* (Reprise)

1983   *Syms by Sinatra* (Reprise)

1984   *L.A. Is My Lady* (Qwest)

1986   *The Voice: The Columbia Years, 1943–1952* [four-disk compilation]

1990   *The Reprise Collection* [four-disk compilation]
The Capitol Years [three-disk compilation]

1992   *Sinatra* [soundtrack from television biography] (Reprise)

1993   *Frank Sinatra Duets* (Capitol)
Frank Sinatra: The Columbia Years, 1943–1952, The Complete Recordings [twelve-disk compilation]

1994   *Sinatra and Sextet: Live in Paris* [first release of a 1962 concert recording] (Reprise)
Frank Sinatra Duets II (Capitol)

FILMOGRAPHY

Although famous primarily for his singing, Frank Sinatra has a list of movie credits that would make many professional actors envious. Also enviable are the accolades he has won from the international film community for his work on the big screen, including a special Oscar in 1946 for *The House I Live In,* an Oscar for best supporting actor in *From Here to Eternity* in 1954, his 1956 best-actor nomination for *The Man with the Golden Arm,* and, for the same film, the Special Award by the British Cinematography Council. The following listing includes the production company and, if different from the corporate producer, the distributor.

1941 *Las Vegas Nights* (RKO)	United Artists)
1942 *Ship Ahoy* (MGM)	*High Society* (MGM)
1943 *Reveille with Beverly* (Columbia)	*Around the World in 80 Days* (Michael
Higher and Higher (RKO)	Todd Production, United Artists)
1944 *Step Lively* (RKO)	1957 *The Pride and the Passion* (Stanley
1945 *Anchors Aweigh* (MGM)	Kramer Production, United Artists)
The House I Live In (RKO)	*The Joker Is Wild* (AMBL Production,
1946 *Till the Clouds Roll By* (MGM)	Paramount)
1947 *It Happened in Brooklyn* (MGM)	*Pal Joey* (Essex–George Sidney Pro-
1948 *The Miracle of the Bells* (RKO)	duction, Columbia)
The Kissing Bandit (MGM)	1958 *Kings Go Forth* (Frank Ross–Eton
1949 *Take Me Out to the Ballgame* (MGM)	Production, United Artists)
On the Town (MGM)	*Some Came Running* (MGM)
1951 *Double Dynamite* (RKO)	1959 *A Hole in the Head* (Sincap Produc-
Meet Danny Wilson (Universal Inter-	tion, United Artists)
national)	*Never So Few* (Canterbury Produc-
1953 *From Here to Eternity* (Columbia)	tion, MGM)
1954 *Suddenly* (Libra Production, United	1960 *Can-Can* (Suffolk–Cummings Pro-
Artists)	duction, Twentieth Century–Fox)
1955 *Young at Heart* (Arwin Production,	*Ocean's Eleven* (Dorchester Produc-
Warner Bros.)	tion, Warner Bros.)
Not as a Stranger (Stanley Kramer	*Pepe* (GS–Posa Films International
Production, United Artists)	Production, Columbia)
The Tender Trap (MGM)	1961 *The Devil at 4 O'Clock* (Columbia)
Guys and Dolls (Samuel Goldwyn	1962 *Sergeants 3* (Essex–Claude Produc-
Production, MGM)	tion, United Artists)
The Man with the Golden Arm (Carlyle	*The Road to Hong Kong* (Melnor Films
Production, United Artists)	Production, United Artists)
1956 *Meet Me in Las Vegas* (MGM)	*The Manchurian Candidate* (MC Pro-
Johnny Concho (Kent Production,	duction, United Artists)

1963 *Come Blow Your Horn* (Essex–Tandem Production, Paramount)

The List of Adrian Messenger (Joel Production, Universal)

1964 *4 for Texas* (Sam Production, Warner Bros.)

Robin and the Seven Hoods (P-C Production, Warner Bros.)

1965 *None but the Brave* (Artanis Production, Warner Bros.)

Von Ryan's Express (P-R Production, Twentieth Century–Fox)

Marriage on the Rocks (A-C Production, Warner Bros.)

1966 *Cast a Giant Shadow* (Mirisch–Llenroc–Batjack Production, United Artists)

The Oscar (Greene–Rouse Production, Embassy)

Assault on a Queen (Sinatra Enterprises–Seven Arts Production, Paramount)

1967 *The Naked Runner* (Sinatra Enterprises Production, Warner Bros.)

Tony Rome (Arcola–Millfield Production, Twentieth Century–Fox)

1968 *The Detective* (Arcola–Millfield Production, Twentieth Century–Fox)

Lady in Cement (Arcola–Millfield Production, Twentieth Century–Fox)

1970 *Dirty Dingus Magee* (MGM)

1974 *That's Entertainment* (MGM)

1976 *That's Entertainment, Part II* (MGM)

1977 *Contract on Cherry Street* [television movie] (Artanis Production, Columbia)

1980 *The First Deadly Sin* (Artanis–Cinema VII Production, Filmways)

1984 *Cannonball Run II* (Golden Harvest Production, Warner Bros.)

SELECTED BIBLIOGRAPHY

In her book *Frank Sinatra: My Father*, Nancy Sinatra asserts that after considerable research, "I came to the conclusion that Frank Sinatra has to be the most documented entertainer in history." Nothing could be more true, and therein lies the problem with any attempt to construct a *comprehensive* bibliography of the man and his long and remarkable career—there is simply too much to include. Without even trying to be comprehensive, we offer the following citations so that the curious reader might easily locate some of the better and more accessible pieces done on Sinatra's career.

Ackelson, Richard W. *Frank Sinatra: A Complete Recording History of Techniques, Songs, Composers, Lyricists, Arrangers, Sessions, and First-Issue Albums 1939–1984*. Jefferson N.C. McFarland 1992.
Altobell, Don. "Have You Heard Sinatra?" *Audio*, December 1970, pp. 40–42.
Ames, Morgan. "He's Still—Well, Sinatra." *High Fidelity*, February 1975, p. 114.
"Back on Top." *Time*, 10 May 1954, pp. 72–74.
Balliett, Whitney. "King Again." *New Yorker*, 4 October 1982, pp. 142–43.
Baumgold, Julie. "Frank and the Fox Pack." *Esquire*, March 1994, pp. 89–96.
Bliven, Bruce. "The Voice and the Kids." *New Republic*, 6 November 1944, pp. 592–93.
Bogdanovich, Peter. "Sinatra and Company." *Esquire*, February 1978, pp. 120–23.
Bornfeld, Steve. "Sinatra Fans Boo." *New York Post*, 3 March 1994, p. 65.
Brennan, Don. "Singing and Swinging by the Sea: Welcome Home, Francis Albert Sinatra." *News Gleaner Magazine*, 17 October 1990, pp. 3–4.
Brown, P. B. "His Way." *Forbes*, 8 October 1984, p. 238.
Browne, David. "Frank 'n' Style." *Entertainment Weekly*, 18–25 February 1994, pp. 36–44.
Bryson, J. "Sinatra at Fifty." *Look*, 14 December 1965, pp. 61–66+.
Burgess, Anthony. *This Man and Music*. New York: Avon, 1985.
"Chairman of the Board." *Newsweek*, 28 October 1963, p. 60.
"Chairman of the Board." *Time*, 16 July 1965, p. 62.
"The Chairman Emeritus." *Time*, 5 April 1971, p. 58.
"The Chairman Is a Punk." *Time*, 13 September 1993, p. 85.
Clines, Francis X. "As Pizza Maker Knows, Sinatra Still Delivers." *New York Times*, 10 October 1993, sec. 1, p. 33.

Connick, Harry, Jr. "A Perfect Singer, Ever Since He Began the Beguine." *New York Times*, 9 December 1990, p. 26-H.

Coward, Noel. *The Noel Coward Diaries*. Ed. Graham Payne and Sheridan Morley. Boston: Little, Brown, 1982.

Davidson, B. "The Life Story of Frank Sinatra." *Look*, 14 May 1957, pp. 36–42 + ; 28 May 1957, pp. 123–24 + ; 11 June 1957, p. 84 +

DeCurtis, Anthony. "Their Way." *Rolling Stone*, 19 May 1994, pp. 97–98 + .

DeLeon, Clark. "Please, Mister, Please; Play Fifty-Two-Oh-Nine." *Philadelphia Inquirer*, 24 October 1993, p. B2.

Deutsch, Armand S. "A Night Out with Sinatra." *McCall's*, August 1983, p. 35 + . Reprinted as "Me and My One-Nighters with Sinatra." In Deutsch, *Me and Bogie*, pp. 231–39. New York: Putnam, 1991.

Douglas-Home, Robin. *Sinatra*. New York: Grosset and Dunlap, 1962.

Evelyn, Maude. "Idol Remembered." *Esquire*, July 1965, pp. 84–85.

Feather, Leonard. "*Trilogy*—The Voice in Command." *Los Angeles Times*, 20 April 1980, Calendar sec., p. 3.

Ferrer, J. M. "Sinatra Special That's Very: Sinatra's Spectacular Revisited." *Life*, 9 December 1966, p. 24.

Fotheringham, Allan. "In Which the Scribe Huddles on the Floor, Watches a Master and Thinks of a Mister." *Maclean's*, 29 October 1979, p. 64.

Frank, Alan. *Sinatra*. New York: Hamlyn, 1978.

"Frank and Company." *Life*, December 1990, pp. 117–20 + .

"Frankie in Madison." *Time*, 25 August 1958, p. 64.

"Frankie's Robert Soxers." *Newsweek*, 23 December 1946, p. 61.

"Frank Sinatra" [interview, 1963]. In *Playboy Interviews*, pp. 2–13. Chicago: Playboy Press, 1967.

The Frank Sinatra Songbook. Secaucus, N.J.: Warner Brothers, 1989.

Frazier, George. "Frank Sinatra." *Life*, 3 May 1943, pp. 54–62.

Friedwald, Will. *Jazz Singing: America's Great Voices from Bessie Smith to Bebop and Beyond*. New York: Collier, 1992.

———. *Sinatra! The Song Is You: A Singer's Art*. New York: Scribner, 1995.

Fulford, R. "Sinatra with Sweetening." *New Republic*, 18 November 1957, p. 22.

Gates, David. "Too Much Togetherness?" *Newsweek*, 8 November 1993, p. 79.

Gehman, Richard. *Sinatra and His Rat Pack*. New York: Belmont, 1963.

Giddins, Gary. "The One and Only Frank Sinatra." *Stereo Review*, February 1984, pp. 53–58. A revised version appears as "Frank Sinatra: An Appreciation." In Giddins, *Rhythm-a-Ning*, pp. 225–35. New York: Oxford University Press, 1987.

Gilmore, Mikal. "The Majestic Artistry of Frank Sinatra." *Rolling Stone*, 18 September 1980, p. 60.

———. "The Wonder of Sinatra." *Rolling Stone*, 24 January 1991, pp. 47–48.

Gleason, Ralph J. "Frank: Then and Now." *Rolling Stone*, 6 June 1974, p. 11.

Goddard, Peter. *Frank Sinatra: The Man, the Myth and the Music*. Don Mills: Greywood, 1973.

Goldstein, Norm. *Frank Sinatra: Ol' Blue Eyes*. New York: Holt, Rinehart and Winston, 1982.

Gould, Glenn. "The Search for Petula Clark." In *The Glenn Gould Reader*, ed. Tim Page, pp. 300–308. New York: Knopf, 1985.

Guth, Phyllis. "Iranian-Born Singer Dreams Big: Success on Par with Sinatra." *Philadelphia Inquirer*, 28 November 1991, p. 24B.

Haber, Joyce. "Frank Sinatra's Swan Song—His Way." *Los Angeles Times*, 15 June 1971, View section, pt. 4, pp. 1, 16.

Hajdu, David, and Roy Hemming. *Discovering Great Singers of Classic Pop*. New York: Newmarket Press, 1991.

Hamill, Pete. "An American Legend: Sinatra at 69." *50 Plus*, April 1985, pp. 26–29+.

———. "Frankly Magic, but It's a Quarter to Three." *Daily News*, 21 November 1993, pp. 3, 21.

———. "Sinatra: The Legend Lives." *New York*, 28 April 1980, pp. 30–35.

Hamm, Charles. *Yesterdays: Popular Song in America*. New York: Norton, 1979.

Harrington, Richard. "Sinatra's 'Duets': Neither Here nor There." *Washington Post*, 7 November 1993, p. G1.

"He Can't Read a Note but He's Dethroning Bing, and Frank Sinatra Is 'Wunnerful' to the Gals." *Newsweek*, 22 March 1943, p. 62.

Heller, Karen. "Before You Grovel, Ask: Would Frank Do It?" *Philadelphia Inquirer*, 29 September 1991, p. 3J.

Henderson, Harry, and Sam Shaw. "Gift to the Girls." *Collier's*, 17 April 1943, p. 69.

Hentoff, Nat. "Can Sinatra Still Be Romantic?" *Progressive*, November 1984, p. 40.

Hewitt, Bill. "Frank Takes a Fall." *People*, 21 March 1994, pp. 46–47.

"His Stuff." *New Yorker*, 2 July 1990, p. 25.

"His Way." *People*, 17 December 1990, pp. 165–66.

Holden, Stephen. "Frank Sinatra." *New York Times*, 11 December 1983, p. 116A.

———. "Frank Sinatra Begins Carnegie Series." *New York Times*, 12 September 1987, sec. I, p. 15.

———. "Frank Sinatra Opens and Then Cancels." *New York Times*, 17 May 1990, p. C21.

———. "Guide to Middle Age." *Atlantic*, January 1984, pp. 84–87.

———. "Pop's Patriarch Makes Music Along with His Heirs." *New York Times*, 31 October 1993, sec. 2, pp. 1, 34.

Hollman, Laurie. "Displaying Frank Admiration: In South Philadelphia, Sinatra Is Everywhere." *Philadelphia Inquirer*, 10 November 1991, pp. 1B–2B.

Howlett, John. *Frank Sinatra*. New York: Simon and Schuster/Wallaby, 1979.

Hunt, George W. "Of Many Things." *America*, 24 November 1990, p. 386.

Jeske, L. "Caught." *Down Beat*, October 1980, pp. 52–53.

Jewell, Derek. *Frank Sinatra: A Celebration*. Boston: Little, Brown, 1985.

Joel, Billy. "Frank Sinatra." *Esquire*, June 1986, p. 300.

Kahn, E. J. "The Voice with the Gold Accessories." *New Yorker*, 26 October 1946, pp. 36–40+.

———. "The Fave, the Fans, and the Fiends." *New Yorker*, 2 November 1946, pp. 37–40+.

———. "Just a Kid from Hoboken." *New Yorker*, 9 November 1946, pp. 36–40+.

———. *The Voice: The Story of an American Phenomenon*. New York: Harper & Brothers, 1947.

Kaltenbach, David. "The Song Is You." *Daytripper*, November 1992, p. 11.

Kelley, Kitty. *His Way: The Unauthorized Biography of Frank Sinatra*. New York: Bantam, 1986.

Kempton, Murray. "Sinatra: The Lion in Winter." *New York Newsday*, 17 November 1993, pp. 7, 112.

Kennedy, William. "Under My Skin." *New York Times*, 7 October 1990, pp. 40–41 + . Reprinted as "Frank Sinatra: Pluperfect Music." In Kennedy, *Riding the Yellow Trolley Car*, pp. 333–38. New York: Viking, 1993.

Kerrison, Ray. "Ol' Blue Eyes Still Has the Magic." *New York Post*, 25 August 1993, p. 14.

Knight, A. "Star Time." *Saturday Review*, 21 November 1970, p. 56.

Korall, Burt. "A Measure of Sinatra." *Saturday Review*, 15 October 1966, pp. 58–59.

Kuntzman, Gersh. "Frank Puts Pearl in a Jam." *New York Post*, 10 November 1993, p. 29.

Kunz, Anita. "What Would Frank Do?" *Esquire*, June 1991, p. 27.

"La Voce and the USO." *Newsweek*, 23 July 1945, p. 90.

Lear, Martha Weinman. "The Bobby Sox Have Wilted, but the Memory Remains Fresh." *New York Times*, 13 October 1974, sec. 2, pp. 1, 12.

Leerhsen, C. "Still Good and Saucy at 75." *Newsweek*, 17 December 1990, pp. 66–67.

Lees, Gene. "Frank Sinatra: Confessions and Contradictions." *High Fidelity*, March 1969, p. 120.

———. "The Performance and the Pain." *High Fidelity*, May 1967, p. 95.

———. "Sinatra—That Certain Style." *Saturday Review*, 28 August 1971, pp. 45 + .

———. "The Sinatra Effect." In Lees, *Singers and the Song*, pp. 101–15. New York: Oxford University Press, 1987.

———. "The Sinatra Phenomenon." *High Fidelity*, October 1977, pp. 22–28.

Levinson, Aaron. "South Philly Sinatra." *Daytripper*, November 1992, p. 7.

Littwin, Susan. "The Man and the Myth." *TV Guide*, 7 November 1992, pp. 11–14.

Long, Jack. "Sweet Dreams and Dynamite." *American Magazine*, Spring 1943, pp. 41 + .

Lonstein, Albert I. *Sinatra: An Exhaustive Treatise*. New York: Musicprint, 1983.

Lonstein, Albert I., and Vito R. Marino. *The Revised Compleat Sinatra*. New York: Musicprint, 1970, 1979, 1981.

Lowthar, W. "Frank Sinatra's Right to Life." *Maclean's*, 5 December 1983, p. 68.

Lupica, Mike. "Sinatra Belts Out a Home Run." *Daily News*, 21 November 1993, pp. 20–21.

Mallowe, Mike. "The Selling of Sinatra." *Philadelphia*, September 1983, pp. 114–18 + .

Manning, Anita. "Chicago School Starts Spreading the Detention Blues." *USA Today*, 22 September 1992, p. 1A.

Marty, Martin E. "Sentenced to Sinatra." *Christian Century*, 11 November 1992, p. 1047.

Marymont, Mark. "They Did It His Way." *Philadelphia Inquirer*, 2 November 1993, pp. E1, E6.

McCaffrey, Neil. "I Remember Frankeee." *National Review*, 26 September 1975, pp. 1060–61.

McClintock, David. "Sinatra's Double Play." *Vanity Fair*, December 1993, pp. 50–52, 62–70.

Moon, Tom. "Swinging with the 'Saloon Singer.'" *Philadelphia Inquirer*, 2 November 1993, pp. E1, E5.

Newquist, Roy. "Sinatra Power." *McCall's*, July 1968, pp. 79 + .

Novak, Ralph. "Looking Back on 50 Years of Popular Music, a Critic Has Two Words for Sinatra: 'The Best'" [interview with John Rockwell]. *People*, 28 January 1985, pp. 80–82.

O'Brien, Ed, and Scott, P. Sayers. *Sinatra: The Man and His Music: The Recording Aritistry of Francis Albert Sinatra, 1939–1992.* Austin: TSD Press, 1992.

O'Connor, John. "Expert Pacing and Polish of the Sinatra Show." *New York Times,* 15 October 1974, p. 79.

Page, Andrew. "A Sunday with Sinatra." *Daytripper,* November 1992, pp. 6–11.

Palmer, Robert. "Sinatra and Martin, Rock Stars." *New York Times,* 19 May 1977, pt. 3, p. 22.

"Paramount Piper." *New Yorker,* 25 August 1956, pp. 23–24.

Peters, Richard. *The Frank Sinatra Scrapbook.* New York: St. Martin's Press, 1982.

Plagens, Peter. "Stranger in the Night." *Newsweek,* 21 March 1994, p. 75.

Pleasants, Henry. "Appoggiatura, Tempo Rubato, Portamento—He Uses 'Em All." *New York Times,* 13 October 1974. sec. 2, pp. 1, 21.

———. *The Great American Popular Singers.* New York: Simon and Schuster, 1974.

———. "Some Singer." *Stereo Review,* March 1982, p. 104.

"Pops Tops." *Time,* 27 December 1954, p. 40.

Pryor, Thomas M. "The Rise, Fall, and Rise of Sinatra." *New York Times Magazine,* 10 February 1957, pp. 17+.

Rayman, Graham. "Sinatra Still Packs House." *New York Newsday,* 18 November, 1993, p. 13.

Reilly, Peter. "Supercharged Sinatra." *Stereo Review,* November 1984, p. 92.

Ressner, Jeffrey. "And Again, One More for the Road." *Time,* 21 March 1994, p. 72.

Ringgold, Gene, and Clifford McCarthy. *The Films of Frank Sinatra.* Secaucus, N.J.: Citadel, 1971.

Robins, Wayne. "Twilight Time." *New York Newsday,* 12 June 1993, pt. 2, p. 21.

Rockwell, John. *Sinatra: An American Classic.* New York: Random House/Rolling Stone, 1985.

———. "Sinatra at the Garden Is Superb TV as Well." *New York Times,* 14 October 1974, p. 42.

Russell, Rosalind. "Sinatra: An American Classic." *Ladies' Home Journal,* November 1973, pp. 26–27.

Scaduto, Anthony. *Frank Sinatra.* London: Michael Joseph, 1976.

Schulberg, Budd. "Secrets of Sinatra: Inside Tales of His Life and Career." *New Choices,* December 1993–January 1994, pp. 58–63.

Schwartz, Jonathan. "One More for the Road." *GQ,* December 1993, pp. 114+.

———. "Sinatra: In the Wee Small Hours." *GQ,* June 1989, pp. 228–31+.

Sciacca, Tony. *Sinatra.* New York: Pinnacle, 1976.

Shaw, Arnold. "Puppet, Pirate, Poet, Pawn, and King: A Sinatra Retrospective." *High Fidelity,* August 1971, pp. 65–68.

———. *Sinatra: The Entertainer.* New York: Delilah, 1982.

———. *Sinatra: Twentieth-Century Romantic.* New York: Holt, Rinehart and Winston, 1968.

Shepard, Richard V. "Sinatra Fans on L.I. Relive Winter of '42." *New York Times,* 10 April 1974, p. 30.

"Show Biz Legends Reunite on U.S. Concert Tour." *Jet,* 7 March 1988, pp. 56–59.

Shuster, Alvin. "Sinatra Enthralls 3,000 at a Concert in London." *New York Times,* 9 May 1970, p. 3.

Simonds, C. H. "For Now." *National Review,* 18 May 1971, p. 532.

Sinatra, Frank. "Foreword." In *The Big Bands,* by George T. Simon. 4th ed. New York: Schirmer, 1981.

———. "Me and My Music." *Life,* 23 April 1965, pp. 86–96+.

———. *Tips on Popular Singing.* New York: Embassy Music, 1941.

Sinatra, Nancy. *Frank Sinatra: An American Legend.* Santa Monica, Calif.: General Publishing, 1995.

———. *Frank Sinatra: My Father.* 1985. Reprint. New York: Pocket Books, 1986.

"Sinatra: Where the Action Is." *Newsweek,* 6 September 1965, pp. 39–42.

"Sinatra Fans Pose Two Police Problems and Not the Less Serious Involves Truancy." *New York Times,* 13 October 1944, p. 211.

Sobran, Joseph. "The Man Who Was Sinatra." *National Review,* 7 February 1992, pp. 54–55.

"Solid-Gold Sinatra." *Newsweek,* 21 October 1957, p. 70.

Span, Paula. "Swooning for Sinatra." *Philadelphia Inquirer,* 3 January 1994, pp. E5, E7.

Stearns, David Patrick. "In 'Duets,' Sinatra Clashes with Titans." *USA Today,* 2 November 1993, p. 8D.

Storm, Jonathan. "*Sinatra* Portrays a Singer and a Survivor." *Philadelphia Inquirer,* 8 November 1992, pp. N1, N10.

"Swooner-Crooner." *Life,* 23 August 1943, pp. 127–28.

"Swoon Song." *Newsweek,* 16 August 1943, p. 80.

Talese, Gay. "Frank Sinatra Has a Cold." *Esquire,* April 1966, pp. 89–98 +. Reprinted in Talese, *Fame and Obscurity,* pp. 173–208. New York: Dell, 1981.

———. "When Frank Sinatra Had a Cold: A Reflection on the Cause of Today's Common Journalism." *Esquire,* November 1987, pp. 161–66.

"Talk with a Star." *Newsweek,* 6 July 1959, p. 84.

Teachout, Terry. "Frank Sinatra." *High Fidelity,* April 1987, pp. 75–76.

"That Old Sweet Song." *Time,* 5 July 1943, p. 76.

Thompson, Thomas. "Frank Sinatra's Swan Song." *Life,* 25 June 1971, pp. 70A–74.

Tormé, Mel. *It Wasn't All Velvet.* New York: Zebra, 1990.

"The Voice." *Newsweek,* 20 December 1943, pp. 94–96.

Werner, Aaron. "Sinatra: An Appreciation." *Daytripper,* November 1992, p. 8.

Wilder, Alec. *American Popular Song: The Great Innovators, 1900–1950.* New York: Oxford University Press, 1972.

Wilson, Earl. *Sinatra: An Unauthorized Biography.* New York: Macmillan, 1976.

Wright, Christian Logan. "Sinatra 101." *Mademoiselle,* April 1991, p. 136.

INDEX

281